APPRAISING
THE
HUMAN
DEVELOPMENTAL
SCIENCES

APPRAISING THE HUMAN DEVELOPMENTAL SCIENCES

Essays in Honor of
Merrill-Palmer Quarterly

Edited by Gary W. Ladd

WAYNE STATE UNIVERSITY PRESS   DETROIT

11 10 09 08 07   5 4 3 2 1

Library of Congress Cataloging-in-Publication Data

Appraising the human developmental sciences :
essays in honor of Merrill-Palmer quarterly / edited by Gary W. Ladd.
p. cm.
ISBN-13: 978-0-8143-3342-6 (pbk. : alk. paper)
ISBN-10: 0-8143-3342-7 (pbk. : alk. paper)
1. Developmental psychology. 2. Child development. 3. Child psychology.
I. Ladd, Gary W., 1950– II. Merrill-Palmer quarterly
(Wayne State University Press)
BF713.5.A67 2007
155—dc22
2006030894

Contents

Contents

Introduction

Merrill-Palmer Quarterly at Age 50, An Occasion for Appraising the Past, Present, and Future of the Human Developmental Sciences

Gary W. Ladd

In 2004 *Merrill-Palmer Quarterly: A Journal of Developmental Psychology* marked its 50th anniversary, which provided an occasion to celebrate the journal's heritage, its long history of scholarly contributions to the human developmental sciences, and its current and future mission as a purveyor of scientific discoveries. This juncture provided a vantage point from which to appraise the scientific endeavors that generated the contents of *MPQ* and its sister publications during the latter half of the 20th century and the first few years of the 21st century.

This Book's Purposes

One can argue that the best way to gauge the progress and prospects of a scientific discipline is to examine it from three perspectives, all of which have the potential to be instructive for current and future investigators. Hindsight offers a view of the past, a viewpoint from which assays can be made of the scientific yield from pursuing various theories and and empirical investments. Coincident, or sidelong, glances permit assessments of the current state of the science, including recent trends, innovations, and discoveries that have emerged within specific subdisciplines or areas of inquiry. Finally, foresight lends itself to the process of projecting the future of existing lines of investigation, anticipating impediments to progress (and devising strategies to circumvent these obstacles), and identifying promising new frameworks and innovative objectives.

This Book's Contributors

To capitalize on this opportunity to assess the state of developmental psychology, the editors of *Merrill-Palmer Quarterly* invited senior investigators whose research programs and accomplishments span many of the last 50 years to write the chapters that appear within this volume. Earlier versions appeared as invited commentaries within special anniversary issues of *Merrill-Palmer Quarterly* during the 2004 calendar year (volume 50, numbers 1, 3, and 4). All the contributors have at least two things in common: each has made a contribution to *Merrill-Palmer Quarterly* at some point in her or his career (e.g., as an author, reviewer, board member, former editor or associate editor, etc.), and all are leaders within their respective disciplines and the larger domain of the human developmental sciences.

An Overview of This Book's Organization and Content

The chapters are remarkably diverse, both individually and as a collection. Each author provides an integrated analysis of one or more interconnected research domains, and in this context they critically review past research accomplishments (e.g., a historical perspective on critical concepts and findings), current progress (e.g., the contemporary status of pertinent theories and findings), and future directions (e.g., a vision of the future; prospects for new lines of investigation). As a whole the anthology speaks to most of the subdisciplines that comprise the human developmental sciences, and, consistent with its purpose, the book reflects the scope and complexity of the research findings that *MPQ* has published during its 50 years of existence.

The first chapter provides a historical overview of the confluence of events, people, institutional forces, and publication trends that brought *Merrill-Palmer Quarterly* into existence and contributed to its longevity (Ladd, 2004). The remaining 22 chapters contain treatises on the scientific enterprise and the utility of specific research agendas that have evolved within the human developmental sciences. Although these chapters need not be read consecutively, the volume is organized to promote an analysis of agendas, accomplishments, and innovations that is relevant not only within major substantive domains but also across subdisciplinary boundaries.

Toward this end, the chapters are organized around ten conceptual themes. The first, methodological and interpretive considerations, contains a single chapter titled "The Limitations of Concepts in Developmental Psychology." The author of this chapter, Jerome

Kagan, considers how past scientific research traditions and agendas have shaped the way that modern investigators conceptualize the phenomena they investigate, how these conceptual commitments may hinder the work of modern developmental scientists, and, ultimately, how they may restrict the progress of the entire discipline. Chief among the concerns that Kagan raises is the theoretical short-sightedness that has accrued from the way investigators have construed and defined developmental phenomena. Kagan argues that developmentalists have too often created concepts to represent aspects of development that have been modeled after approaches used in other branches of science (e.g., physics) and that a consequence of this practice is that these concepts tend to be too rigid and abstract to fully capture developmental phenomena and the full range of properties or dynamics that define these phenomena. Related concerns are definitions of developmental concepts that do not reflect the contexts in which they were discovered or the milieu in which they operate, and that this theoretical imprecision encourages investigators to overestimate the meaning, properties, and applicability of developmental concepts. Kagan also offers guidance as to how contemporary investigators might address these concerns and problems. He explores several potential solutions, including both methodological and substantive avenues, and illustrates them with relevant scientific examples.

The second theme of this book is cognitive development and learning. Three prominent investigators provide appraisals of this domain—or, to be precise, specific areas of investigation that fall within this domain. In Chapter 3, "Theory-of-Mind Development: Retrospect and Prospect," John H. Flavell appraises a long-established research tradition of probing children's understanding of their mental life and development, including their knowledge about mental states, capacities, operations, changes over time, and so on. Flavell surveys several decades of research and in the process provides important insights into this endeavor's theoretical origins, past and recent empirical accomplishments, and future prospects. In Chapter 4, "Cognitive Development Includes Global and Domain-Specific Processes," Robert V. Kail notes that the major explanatory frames that have guided research on children's cognitive development have tended to perpetuate a dichotomy in which cognitive growth is seen as resulting from either global processes (i.e., stage-like shifts that transform thinking across many types of cognitive tasks) or domain-specific processes (i.e., modular growth patterns; transformations in thinking that are specific to particular cognitive realms or types of tasks). Rather than perpetuate this dichotomy, Kail critically analyzes evidence that illustrates how global and domain-specific processes might be linked, and he considers the merits of models that allow for an integration of these metatheories. In the final chapter in this section, "Learning About Learning," Robert S. Siegler chronicles the vicissitudes of research on children's learning during the second half of the 20th century and explicates the forces that have rekindled researchers' interest in this area today. Among the developments that Siegler profiles is the emergence of a new discipline that is predicated on a desire to understand how specific learning processes emerge and are used and managed (selected, applied, and refined or abandoned) by the developing child. He also considers the theoretical insights into childhood learning and learning processes that have been gained from the growing body of evidence in these areas.

The third theme of the book is temperament and emotional development. In Chapter 6, "Temperament and the Pursuit of an Integrated Developmental Psychology," Mary K. Rothbart defines the construct of childhood temperament and traces its origins within psychological theory. She also describes empirical breakthroughs in the study of temperament and illustrates how these discoveries have enhanced the relevance of this construct for researchers working in diverse areas of the human developmental sciences. Rothbart evaluates contemporary accomplishments and future directions for research on temperament, and she shows how progress in other scientific subdisciplines, such as neuroscience and human genetics, have the potential to inform research on temperament and generate broader scientific advances—that is, discoveries that transcend typical disciplinary boundaries. In Chapter 7, "Emotion-Related Regulation: An Emerging Construct," Nancy Eisenberg, Claire Champion, and Yue Ma demonstrate that, although the topic of emotion regulation in children and adolescents is a new area of investigation within the human developmental sciences, it has already captured the interest of a growing cadre of investigators and been credited with a number of important empirical discoveries. Eisenberg and colleagues present several working definitions of emotion regulation, locate this construct in relation to other research endeavors, including the study of temperament, and identify a set of subordinate constructs that have become central to this area of investigation (e.g., effortful control, attentional control, inhibitory control). Other chapter highlights include a review of evidence linking emotion regulation with aspects of children's development and adjustment, and an analysis of future research agendas.

The fourth theme is children's social development and peer relations. This section contains three chapters, the first of which, Chapter 8, is titled "The Role of Mental Representation in Social Development." Here Carol S. Dweck and Bonita E. London consider evidence that reflects on the proposition that children not only create mental representations of their social experience but they also preserve elements of these representations as they mature and subsequently use them in ways that shape their future development and adjustment. Dweck and London identify the types of mental representations that have been investigated in recent years (e.g., beliefs, concepts, attributions) and examine how these representations are linked to different types of referents or targets (e.g., representations of the self versus representations of peers, etc.). Next, the authors weigh evidence that reflects on the potential determinants and consequences of particular mental representations, and they consider how these findings might lead to new research on the socialization of children (e.g., parenting practices) and to the invention of effective technologies for changing children's thinking and behavior (e.g., intervention and prevention programs). In Chapter 9, "Children's Friendships: Shifts Over a Half-Century in Perspectives on their Development and Their Effects," Thomas J. Berndt analyzes what developmental psychology has learned from several decades of research on the origins, formation, and features of children's friendships and the role these relationships play in human development. In particular, Berndt examines the extent to which research has substantiated early theoretical premises about friendship (e.g., those rooted in Sullivan's theory) and illustrates how new discoveries have led to the revamping of these premises and spurred the development of new scientific agendas. Chief among the issues that Berndt examines are the social dynamics of friendships (e.g., positive and negative features of friendships), age changes in friendships, the effects of friendship on children's development, and new directions for research on children's friendships. Kenneth H. Rubin and Robert J. Coplan contributed Chapter 10, "Paying Attention to and Not Neglecting Social Withdrawal and Social Isolation." These investigators point out that, although psychologists have long recognized that some children refrain from interacting with their peers, withdraw from social situations, or avoid their peers altogether, knowledge about these children and their development has been slow to accumulate. Rubin and Coplan trace the history of research on socially withdrawn and isolated children and identify the myriad factors that have slowed investigative progress. More important, however, they help to fill the void by parsing the multiple constructs that earlier investigators coined, by considering the theoretical underpinnings of these constructs, and by analyzing the extent to which these constructs have been empirically substantiated. Rubin and Coplan also review what is known about the correlates and consequences of social isolation and withdrawal during early and middle childhood, and they consider the implications of these findings for future research. In Chapter 11, the last in this section, "The Next 50 Years: Considering Gender as a Context for Understanding Young Children's Peer Relationships," Richard A. Fabes, Carol Lynn Martin, and Laura D. Hanish call attention to to a relatively understudied aspect of children's peer relationships: gender. These investigators focus on the role of children's sex-segregated peer interactions during the early childhood years and the potential effect of these relations on their early and later social development. The authors also provide a critical analysis of why this topic is important for researchers to consider.

Commentaries on two prominent research traditions within the area of family relations make up the volume's fifth theme. In Chapter 12, "Understanding Children's Family Worlds: Family Transitions and Children's Outcomes," Judy Dunn critically analyzes several streams of research designed to clarify how children respond to family transitions and how such changes might affect children's development. She examines several variants in family transitions, including divorce, cohabitation, single parenting, and repartnering. Moreover, Dunn considers how some processes that tend to be inherent within these reconfigurations (e.g., conflict between family members; shifts in parent-child relationships; changing social and economic circumstances) are associated with immediate and long-term consequences for children. Another focus is research that explores differences within a family, or evidence that children in the same family may experience family transitions differently and may be affected by family alterations in different ways. Chapter 13 addresses another aspect of family relations—fathers and their role in children's development. In "Fathers, Families, and the Future: A Plethora of Plausible Predictions," Ross D. Parke examines a broad range of existing and new research findings. It is difficult to underestimate the significance of this research vein and its discoveries because, historically, much more has been learned about mothering and the role of mothers in children's development. Parke shows the importance of fathers and fathering to several aspects of children's development. He also shows how past findings propelled today's investigations and how modern-day discoveries have set the stage for future innovations. Parke shows how recent theoretical, methodological, and analytic advances have expanded the questions that investigators seek to answer and have yielded answers that will shape the next generation of research on fathering. As Parke sees it, we can expect a spate of new discoveries and a raft of new insights that will expand and deepen what we know about fathers and their role in children's development.

Moral development is the volume's sixth theme, and Chapters 14 and 15 profile advances in our knowledge of this domain. In Chapter 14, "Progress and Prospects in the Psychology of Moral Development," Lawrence J. Walker notes that research on moral development informs society and contributes to the socialization of its citizens, including children. He provides a critical analysis of the theoretical models that have guided research on children's moral reasoning and development in the past, and he surveys the empirical advances and limitations that these models have propagated. Walker also discusses the lessons learned from many years of research on the development of moral reasoning in children and adolescents and provides a prescriptive agenda for contemporary and future proponents of moral psychology. In Chapter 15, "Conscience in Childhood: Past, Present, and Future," Grazyna Kochanska and Nazan Aksan reassess the concept of conscience and its theoretical roots and consider factors that have brought about a resurgence of interest in the components and organization of conscience in young children. Their commentary emphasizes the roles of child and family factors, such as temperament, parenting, and parent-child relationships, in the development of conscience. Kochanska and Aksan also examine future directions for research on conscience.

Chapters 16 and 17 address the seventh theme, the nature-nurture debate and behavioral genetics. In Chapter 16, "Genetics and Developmental Psychology," Robert Plomin illustrates how behavior geneticists have gone beyond the original efforts to define and isolate genetic influences on human development and have begun to study the pathways through which genes influence children's behavior. He also makes a case that the future of genetic research in human development will largely be guided by the discoveries that emerge from studies of DNA and the human genome. In "The Nature-Nurture Debate and Public Policy," Chapter 17, Kenneth A.

Dodge contends that recent empirical discoveries indicate that the effects of neither nature nor nurture alone account sufficiently for human development and argues that genes and environments transact in ways that establish joint parameters for child growth and development. As Dodge sees it, environments influence gene expressions, but genes structure the contributions of socialization and other environmental factors. He also considers the practical applications of this perspective, suggesting that the best way to proceed is by socializing children in ways that are sensitive to both forces— that is, by devising approaches to schooling, parenting, and remediative interventions that maximize "gene-environment fit."

The next two chapters explore the domain of cultural psychology. Chapter 18,"Why We Need to Explore Development in Its Cultural Context," by Robert J. Sternberg and Elena L. Grigorenko, argues that investigators should incorporate cultural context into their research, especially when the objective is to understand how children behave in their everyday lives. Too often, the authors say, developmentalists have studied children in sterile laboratory settings without considering the ecological validity of their findings and the generalizability of their conclusions. Recognizing that human development never occurs in a vacuum, Sternberg and Grigorenko illustrate how evidence obtained in monocultural contexts can result in erroneous generalizations, and they identify research objectives and methods that can help researchers avoid these pitfalls. Chapter 19, "Historical Lessons: The Value of Pluralism in Psychological Research," also considers this theme. Here Elliot Turiel examines the conceptual context of scientific research and demonstrates how, throughout the 20th century, investigators' reliance on diverse theoretical perspectives and investigative paradigms enriched the science of human development and the knowledge acquired from it. He traces the temporal succession of dominant and recessive theoretical perspectives, delineating factors associated with the emergence and initial impact of these viewpoints and evaluating the survival and long-term contributions of perspectives once heralded as replacements for existing and competing perspectives. He also considers the dangers of overstating the value or probable contributions of a perspective or paradigm before its merits—or "usefulness" as a heuristic or explanatory tool—have been firmly established.

Chapter 20, "Early Child Care: The Known and the Unknown," by Deborah Lowe Vandell is the first of three chapters about early child care, school readiness, and contextual factors in at-risk populations. Vandell surveys progress in child care research since the mid-

1980s and details what developmentalists have learned about the effects of child care arrangements and programs (e.g., centers, child care homes, and relative care) on children's development. She also considers how children are affected by such factors as child care quality, and the amount and timing of children's participation in child care. In addition to summarizing evidence pertinent to these questions, Vandell outlines potential directions for future child care research. In Chapter 21, "Early Learning and School Readiness: Can Early Intervention Make a Difference?" Craig T. Ramey and Sharon L. Ramey present evidence that children's prekindergarten experiences are related to their school readiness and that certain demographic factors (e.g., economic disadvantage, less educated parents) increase children's risk for underachievement. Ramey and Ramey also present findings from randomized controlled trials that show that developmental deficits in high-risk two-year-olds can be substantially reduced through high-quality preschool programming and that many of these children continue to show improvements in reading and mathematics during elementary and secondary school. The authors also evaluate the implications of these findings for public policy and future research. In Chapter 22, "Contextual Factors in Risk and Prevention Research," John E. Lochman reviews how contextual factors, such as families, schools, and neighborhoods, can affect children's development, including their underlying temperament and associated behaviors and emotions. Recognizing that these findings have important implications for prevention research, Lochman also considers how contextual factors are linked with children's responsivity to prevention programs and how contextual factors shape the effectiveness of interventions that are introduced in natural settings such as homes, communities, and schools.

The book's final theme, evidence-based programming and public policy, is addressed in a single chapter, "Integrating Developmental Scholarship and Society: From Dissemination and Accountability to Evidence-Based Programming and Policies," Chapter 23. The authors, Robert B. McCall, Christina J. Groark, and Robert P. Nelkin, observe that practitioners, policy makers, and funding agencies today increasingly require research evidence as a basis for endorsing and funding social programs and policies. Policy makers, for example, have stressed accountability and are now emphasizing evidence-based practices. McCall and colleagues also note that this trend, although desireable and consistent with the goals of science, creates new demands for researchers, including the need to examine the assumptions of evidence-based programming and to refine the processes by which evidence is brought to bear on policy and funding decisions. Toward this end, the authors suggest that scholars confer with practitioners, policy makers, and funding agency personnel to devise, evaluate, and disseminate evidence-based policies.

Appraising the Purview of this Book

Although the scope of this book is expansive, it is not exhaustive. No anthology can represent all the agendas and subdomains that have been or now are being investigated within a science, and this collection is no exception. It may be instructive to consider two ways in which its scientific purview is limited.

First, readers should recognize that each chapter is, at most, an exemplar of the many interrelated research domains that tend to coexist within a single subdiscipline or set of closely allied subdisciplines within the human developmental sciences. In a sense, each essay is a sample of the population of investigative agendas that exist within a subdiscipline. To illustrate, consider Thomas J. Berndt's essay on children's friendships. His focus is on the theoretical and empirical findings from research on only one form of peer relationship—children's friendships. Yet a survey of the peer relations literature reveals that researchers have defined and investigated many other forms of peer relationships since the early 1900s (e.g., peer group status, cliques, crowds, enemies, bully-victim relations, romantic relationships, etc.; see Ladd, 2005). None receives as much attention as friendship in this book. The same can be said about other closely related research agendas, such as the study of how children form and maintain peer relationships and how they acquire the social competencies to succeed at these interpersonal tasks. Thus one of this book's limitations is that it provides only partial coverage of the multiple research programs and paradigms that coexist within distinct subdisciplines.

A second limitation is that the chapters do not fully represent all the subdisciplines that could be considered divisions of the human developmental sciences. Therefore, it may be useful to describe briefly some additional investigative agendas that are prominent in the human developmental sciences. Readers should be forewarned, however, that the purpose of this supplement is not to survey all possible research agendas but to direct attention to a few prominent investigative endeavors that were omitted for various reasons (e.g., criteria used to solicit contributors; space limitations). I am describing these additional agendas here because doing so expands this book's purview and makes its coverage more representative of the many research domains that comprise the human developmental sciences. Because readers may wish to locate and learn more about these and other relevant research agendas, I have included additional sources of information (e.g., critical reviews published in other books and journals).

One such area of investigation is the study of the human brain and factors that affect neural growth and development. This subdiscipline has a long and distinguished history, and studies conducted in recent years (i.e., the decade of the brain; 1990–2000) have produced many remarkable discoveries (see Nelson, 2005; Shonkoff & Phillips, 2000). Included among these advances are findings that further illuminate the physiological processes that are involved in brain development, the experiential factors that enhance and retard neural growth, and the brain's ability to compensate for injuries and malfunctions.

Equally neglected are advances in theory and research on human language acquisition and development. New theories have been proposed to account for human language development, including the processes through which language is acquired and elaborated. For example, rather than construe language acquisition largely from a "main effects" perspective (e.g., naturist versus nurturist positions), some researchers have begun to think in terms of "transactional" influences, or exchanges between biological and environmental forces that motivate and support language learning (Bohannon & Bonvillian, 2001). Empirically, important strides have been made in understanding many aspects of language learning, including children's phonological, semantic, and grammatical development (see Bloom, 1998; Maratsos, 1998; Menn & Stoel-Gammon, 2001). In addition, knowledge of the processes of language development, and the universality of such processes, has been advanced by studying how language structures emerge and develop across languages. To illustrate, results from a growing number of comparative studies suggest that across-language differences exist in how children acquire and use some language structures, such as nouns versus verbs, and in how they make certain morphological contrasts (Bates, Devescovi, & Wulfeck, 2001).

Another important but underrepresented line of research is the study of ethnicity, ethnic identity, and the role of ethnicity in human development. The population of the United States, like that of many other nations in today's world, is becoming more diverse as a result of immigration, differential growth rates within subcultures, and other complex social dynamics. As a result society has a growing need to understand how children from different ethnic backgrounds are socialized, how they develop within their own and other cultural contexts, and how they cope with dominant and changing societal norms and practices (e.g., peer relations, schooling, employment). For example, researchers have found that, among minority youth, the development of a secure sense of ethnic/racial identity (i.e., a sense of belonging and commitment to their group; Arce, 1981; Cross, 1991) operates as a protective factor against low self-esteem and psychological dysfunction (Helms, 1990; Phinney, 1993). Although somewhat neglected in the past, these topics have become prominent in recent years and have yielded important new findings (see McAdoo & Martin, 2005).

It is unfortunate that research on motivation, schooling, and children's scholastic development receives limited coverage in this book because education is a fundamental impetus for human development. Concerns about lagging educational attainment in America's schools have fueled research that is designed to elucidate the types of schools and schooling that motivate learning, the kinds of educational practices and standards that promote achievement, and the types of laws and policies that provide children with equal access to quality schools (see Blanck, Shah, Johnson, Blackwell, & Ganley, 2005; Eccles & Wigfield, 2002; Wentzel, 2004). Understanding how children adapt psychologically and scholastically to school has been an important objective for researchers interested in promoting competence and preventing educational and psychological problems (see Ladd, 2003; Ladd, Herald, & Kochel, 2006; Perry & Weinstein, 1998). Schools are contexts that present children with a complex array of challenges—demands that are both scholastic and interpersonal—all of which require some degree of adaptation. These diverse challenges create demands that—depending on the child and the resources or constraints that are operating in the child's environment—may affect children on many different levels and may have important implications for their future development.

Some paradigmatic shifts in theory and research also are not chronicled here. For example, since the early 1990s we have seen a movement toward understanding the determinants of psychological health and resilience. This trend, which many see as a move away from a long-dominant emphasis on the causes and consequences of "illness," often is called "positive psychology" (see Diener, Shigehiro, & Lucas, 2003; Masten, 2001; Seligman, 1998). Broadly construed, the driving forces behind this tradition are a desire to understand the origins of human strengths and a commitment to elucidate how health rather than pathology develops during childhood, adolescence, and adulthood. The predictors that are being investigated include human personality, culture, life circumstances, and rearing conditions, and the criteria include indicators of both physical and mental health (e.g., competence, optimism, subjective well-being).

Finally, this book could have profited from greater coverage of the strategies and tools that researchers use to study human development and of the advances in developmental research methodologies. Nearly all aspects of the investigative process have been transformed in recent years, including the methods, measures, designs, and analytic techniques that are used to study human development (see Bollen, 2002; Curran, Bauer, & Willoughby, 2004; MacCallum & Austin, 2000). For example, researchers have become accustomed to conducting longitudinal rather than cross-sectional studies, and gathering data from multiple rather than single informants. Analytic tools, such as structural equations modeling (SEM) and growth curve analyses have been adopted because these methods are more compatible with multisource data and longitudinal designs and offer new ways of overcoming past methodological and interpretive problems. In particular, SEM strategies have allowed developmentalists to study not only larger interrelated sets of variables but also more complex patterns of association among such variables over time. Growth curve analyses have offered researchers more sophisticated ways to map changes in individuals or groups of children over time (e.g., developmental trajectories).

These limitations aside, it seems fair to say that this book's scope is as extensive as many anthologies about the human developmental sciences written since the mid-1990s. Moreover, its goals and content are both timely and novel. As editor of this book, I sincerely hope that this collection offers a fitting tribute to *Merrill-Palmer Quarterly*'s 50th anniversary and becomes a source of inspiration for all those who do research or plan to establish a career in the human developmental sciences.

References

Arce, C. (1981). A reconsideration of Chicano culture and identity. *Daedalus,* 110(2), 177–192.

Bates, E., Devescovi, A., & Wulfeck, B. (2001). Psycholinguistics: A cross-language perspective. *Annual Review of Psychology, 52,* 369–396.

Blanck, M. J., Shah, B., Johnson, S., Blackwell, W., & Ganley, M. (2005). *Reforming education: Developing 21st century schools.* In R. M. Lerner, F. Jacobs, & D. Wertlieb (Eds.), *Applied developmental science* (pp. 227–246). Thousand Oaks, CA: Sage.

Bloom, L. (1998). Language acquisition in its developmental context. In D. Kuhn & R. S. Siegler (Eds.), *Handbook of child psychology: Vol. 2. Cognition, perception, and language* (5th ed., pp. 309–370). New York: Wiley.

Bohannon, J. N., & Bonvillian, J. D. (2001). Theoretical approaches to language acquisition. In J. Berko Gleason (Ed.), *The development of language* (5th ed., pp. 254–314). Boston: Allyn & Bacon.

Bollen, K. A. (2002). Latent variables in psychology and the social sciences. *Annual Review of Psychology, 53,* 605–634.

Cross, W. (1991). *Shades of black: Diverstity in African-American identity.* Philadelphia: Temple University Press.

Curran, P. J., Bauer, D. J., & Willoughby, M. T. (2004). Testing main effects and interactions in latent curve analysis. *Psychological Methods, 9,* 220–237.

Diener, E., Shigehiro, O., & Lucas, R. E. (2003). Personality, culture, and subjective well-being: Emotional and cognitive evaluations of life. *Annual Review of Psychology, 54,* 403–425.

Eccles, J. S., & Wigfield, A. (2002). Motivational beliefs, values, and goals. *Annual Review of Psychology, 53,* 109–132.

Helms, J. (1990). *Black and white racial identity: Theory, research, and practice.* New York: Greenwood.

Ladd, G. W. (2003). Probing the adaptive significance of children's behavior and relationships in the school context: A child by environment perspective. In R. Kail (Ed.), *Advances in Child Behavior and Development* (Vol. 31, pp. 43–104). New York: Wiley.

Ladd, G. W. (2004). Celebrating the 50th anniversary of the *Merrill-Palmer Quarterly, Merrill-Palmer Quarterly, 50,* 1–16.

Ladd, G. W. (2005). *Children's peer relationships and social competence: A century of progress.* New Haven, CT: Yale University Press.

Ladd, G. W., Herald, S. L., & Kochel, K. P. (2006). School readiness: Are there social prerequisites? *Early Education and Development, 17,* 115–150.

MacCallum, R. C., & Austin, J. T. (2000). Applications of structural equation modeling in psychological research. *Annual Review of Psychology, 51,* 201–226.

Maratsos, M. (1998). The acquisition of grammar. In D. Kuhn & R. S. Siegler (Eds.), *Handbook of child psychology: Vol. 2. Cognition, perception, and language* (5th ed., pp. 421–466). New York: Wiley.

Masten, A. S. (2001). Ordinary magic: Resilience processes in development. *American Psychologist, 56,* 227–238.

McAdoo, H. P., & Martin, A. (2005). Families and ethnicity. In R. M. Lerner, F. Jacobs, & D. Wertlieb (Eds.), *Applied developmental science* (pp. 141–154). Thousand Oaks, CA: Sage.

Menn, L., & Stoel-Gammon, C. (2001). Phonological development: Learning sounds and sound patterns. In J. Berko Gleason (Ed.), *The development of language* (5th ed., pp. 70–124). Boston: Allyn & Bacon.

Nelson, C. A. (2005). Neural development and lifelong plasticity. In R. M. Lerner, F. Jacobs, & D. Wertlieb (Eds.), *Applied developmental science* (pp. 31–60). Thousand Oaks, CA: Sage.

Perry, K. E., & Weinstein, R. S. (1998). The social context of early schooling and children's school adjustment. *Educational Psychologist, 33*, 177–194.

Phinney, J. (1993). A three-stage model of ethnic identity development. In M. E. Bernal & G. P. Knight (Eds.), *Ethnic identity: Formation and transmission among Hispanics and other minorities* (pp. 61–79). Albany: State University of New York Press.

Seligman, M. E. P. (1998). Positive social science. *APA Monitor, 29*, 4.

Shonkoff, J. P., & Phillips, D. A. (Eds.), & Committee on Integrating the Science of Early Childhood Development. (2000). *From neurons to neighborhoods: The science of early childhood development.* Washington, DC: National Academy Press.

Wentzel, K. R. (2004). Understanding classroom competence: The role of social motivational and self-processes. In R. Kail (Ed.), *Advances in Child Behavior and Development* (Vol. 32, pp. 213–241). New York: Wiley.

1

Celebrating the 50th Anniversary of *Merrill-Palmer Quarterly*

Gary W. Ladd

Merrill-Palmer Quarterly has not always looked the way it does today, nor has it always enjoyed its current reputation as a scholarly scientific journal. In fact, *MPQ*, which is older than many of its contemporaries, has been through many transformations. Indeed, the journal's purpose, style, and content have changed quite radically in the past 50 years. Accordingly, my purpose here is to review some of the journal's history, including the confluence of events, people, and institutional forces that brought about its creation and contributed to its longevity, and to commemorate some of *Quarterly*'s accomplishments from a historical and contemporary perspective.

The Era Preceding the Inception of *Merrill-Palmer Quarterly*

Much of what is known about the period preceding the establishment of *Merrill-Palmer Quarterly* was reported by Irving Sigel in a *Quarterly* article in 1988. I have based portions of this chapter on his account.

The origins of *Merrill-Palmer Quarterly* can be traced to the social and cultural forces that brought about the child-study movement of the early years of the 20th century and inspired the establishment of child welfare stations and institutes (see Sears, 1975). As Sigel describes it, the events that led to the creation of *Merrill-Palmer Quarterly* were closely intertwined with the founding and mission of the Merrill-Palmer School for Motherhood and Home Training. From its inception, the central mission of the Merrill-Palmer School was to improve the lives of families and children. The origins of the school can be traced to one or more wealthy benefactors, as is documented by the following entry from the Reuther Library's online description of the Merrill-Palmer Corporation's papers: "Established by the Wayne County Circuit Court on June 26, 1918, the Merrill-

Palmer Corporation was formally approved and recorded by the county clerk's office on July 18, 1918. The Corporation was formed by the court to carry out the will of Lizzie (Pitts) Merrill Palmer who left three million dollars to establish a school for motherhood training." Sigel (1988) mentions that initial financial backers of the school were enamored of the notion that parent education, particularly the promotion of effective mothering and child rearing, could substantially improve the lives of children and families. Although it was initially envisioned that this objective could be accomplished by "teaching young girls to be 'good' mothers" (Sigel, 1988, p. 343), one of the school's first directors recast this agenda so that the mission became one of educating professionals for careers as parent educators. During this phase of the school's operation, both undergraduate and graduate students were encouraged to travel to Detroit to receive mentoring in parent education and to study children and families in both home and school settings. For many graduate students these experiences were a prelude to careers in early childhood education, child development, family relations, and family counseling. Moreover, the school's interdisciplinary staff was composed of professionals whose background and training represented many different scientific traditions, including child development, family studies, early childhood education, social work, clinical psychology, family counseling, and social anthropology.

The Establishment of the Merrill-Palmer Institute
and Founding of *Merrill-Palmer Quarterly*

In 1951 Dr. Pauline Park Wilson Knapp became the third director of the Merrill-Palmer School. During her tenure she retained the school's applied and educational focus while moving it toward a developmental and interdisciplinary approach. She also transformed some of the school's objectives and sponsored new initiatives. The school's former emphasis on parent education was broadened to incorporate research on human development in family contexts. To emphasize this scholarly activity, Knapp changed the school's name to the Merrill-Palmer Institute—and encouraged its staff to engage in, along with teaching and training, research on applied child and family issues. Another important initiative was to publicize the products of the institute's service- and scholarly oriented activities, giving rise to the concept of *Merrill-Palmer Quarterly*.

However, at its inception *MPQ*'s format and content bore little or no resemblance to its modern-day counterpart. Sigel (1988), for example, likened the first incarnation of *MPQ* to contemporary magazines such as *Psychology Today*. This was, in part, the result of the institute's then-valued objective of "educating the lay public about human development and family life" (Sigel, 1988, p. 345) as opposed to sharing advances in theory and research within the scientific community. Sigel's analysis of these years suggests that *MPQ*'s success as a popular publication was limited at best and that new proposals for the journal's mission and audience began to surface within the institute. One proposal, ultimately embraced, was to change *MPQ* to a journal that published scientific research. A compelling component of this argument was that *MPQ* would debut at a time when only two journals—*Child Development* and the *Journal of Genetic Psychology*—were publishing original research on child development and family socialization.

Merrill-Palmer Quarterly Becomes a Repository for Scientific Research: The 1950s to the 1990s

Although the process of converting *MPQ* to a research journal did not proceed rapidly, nor was it accomplished without ideological, administrative, and editorial debates and setbacks (see Hoffman, 1988; Sigel, 1988), it eventually achieved this status as a result of the foresight and able leadership of Dr. Martin L. Hoffman. As Sigel recollects, Hoffman had a vision for how *MPQ* could be transformed: it would be a journal devoted to original research on human development that had an international readership and a national board of editors. In his own recollections Hoffman wrote that he "welcomed the chance to have an impact on the field by creating a journal that would not just add to the few existing ones, but provide something different" (1988, p. 349).

THE 1960s

When the redesigned *Quarterly* was launched in the early 1960s, Hoffman was listed as editor on the journal's masthead (see Table 1). He remembers asking Jerome Kagan to be one of his first board members. To attract submissions Hoffman spent many hours calling colleagues and wrote thousands of letters to members of professional research associations and societies. One enticement he used was to tell potential contributors that their articles, once accepted, could be published immediately (no publication lag). Apparently, this approach was successful because by the early 1960s *Quarterly* was publishing only about 20% of the articles submitted.

Table 1

Merrill-Palmer Quarterly's History as a Research Journal: Editors and Associate Editors, 1960–2003

Term	Editor	Associate Editor(s)
1950s		
1960–1980	Martin Hoffman	
1981	Grover Whitehurst	
1981–1982	Eli Saltz	
1982	Carolyn Shantz	Eli Saltz
1986		Eli Saltz; Keith Stanovich
1986		Keith Stanovich
1990		Hilary Ratner; Keith Stanovich
1991		Nancy Eisenberg; Keith Stanovich
1996		Shelley Hymel; Keith Stanovich
1998		Shelley Hymel; Charlotte Patterson; Keith Stanovich
1999		Nicki Crick; Charlotte Patterson; Keith Stanovich
2001	Gary Ladd	Richard Fabes; Mary Gauvain; Lawrence Walker
2003		Mary Gauvain; Marion Underwood; Lawrence Walker

Hoffman's 1988 article for *MPQ* includes an autobiographical account of his aspirations for the journal during this period and his plans for making *MPQ* "something different" from its competitors. Rather than repeat these details, I will simply highlight two policies that were particularly innovative, especially for that period. During a fundamentally positivist era in which editors tended to stress the importance of an investigator's methods and results, Hoffman encouraged authors to better articulate the relation between theory and data. He placed greater emphasis on middle-range theories than on grand theories, both as a guide for investigation and as a context for the interpretation of empirical findings. Hoffman also encouraged the submission of both empirical and theoretical articles. His rationale was as follows: "Theoretical journals rarely published a theory before the confirming research was done. One solution would be to publish all theoretical contributions—some would inspire research and some would not—but this would create new [scientific] problems. The trick, it seemed to me, was, and still is, to predict in advance which theoretical formulations were more likely than others to inspire research and move the field" (1988, p. 349).

Hoffman's editorship lasted more than 20 years, during which *MPQ* grew in reputation and provided readers with theoretical articles and research reports that spanned many different domains within the human developmental sciences. Throughout the 1960s research on infancy was well represented in *MPQ*, owing in part to the Merrill-Palmer Institute's commitment to infant development and to a decadelong conference series (i.e., the Merrill-Palmer Infancy Conferences) that was funded by the National Institutes of Mental Health and organized by Sigel from 1960 to 1970 (see Sigel, 1988, and Table 2).

THE 1970S

In the articles published during the 1970s, infancy remained a prominent topic for *MPQ*. Consistent with the institute's agendas, articles continued to appear on child rearing and parents' child-rearing attitudes, child compliance, parent-child interaction, and marriage and family life. Related but newly emerging topics, such as maternal employment, fatherhood, siblings, child care, and parent-child attachment, began to appear during the later years of this decade.

Spurred by world events (e.g., Sputnik) and the dominant theoretical paradigms of the times, numerous articles appeared on topics related to children's cognitive development, intelligence, and ability to profit from education. Exemplars included papers on Piagetian theory; the mental capacities and processing abilities of infants, children, and adolescents; children's performance on conservation tasks; and so on. Also prevalent were articles that addressed closely related domains, such as early stimulation and infant mental development; age differences in children's reasoning, problem solving, role taking, and egocentrism; and progressions in moral reasoning, language development, and communication skills.

In response to shifts in cultural priorities and government funding, articles began to appear on poverty and the development of children from low-income, disadvantaged backgrounds. During 1973 *MPQ* devoted an entire issue to a symposium titled *New Research Perspectives on the Young Disadvantaged Child* (see Table 2).

Studies of children's social behavior and development were not especially common during this period in the journal's history. Exceptions included a 1976 special issue that offered a series of studies of

Table 2

Special Sections, Special Issues, and Invitational (Guest Edited) Issues of *Merrill-Palmer Quarterly*

Date	Editor	Subject/Title
1970		Papers from the 1970 Merrill-Palmer Conference on research and teaching of infant development
1971		Papers from the 1971 Merrill-Palmer Conference on research and teaching of infant development
1972		Symposium on the meaning of smiling and vocalizing in infancy
1972		Papers from the 1972 Merrill-Palmer Conference on research and teaching of infant development
1973		New research perspectives on the young disadvantaged child
1974		Papers from the 1973 Merrill-Palmer Conference on research and teaching of infant development
1975		Papers from the 1974 Merrill-Palmer Conference on research and teaching of infant development
1976		The impact of social cues on children's behavior
1976		Papers from the 1975 Merrill-Palmer Conference on research and teaching of infant development
1983	Carolyn Shantz	*Popular, rejected, and neglected children: Their social behavior and social reasoning*
1984	Eli Saltz	*Advances in temperament research: Studies of methods, predictions, and adjustment*
1985	Eli Saltz	*Gesture, sign, and word: The beginnings of language development*
1987	Keith Stanovich	*Children's reading and the development of phonological awareness*
1989	Keith Stanovich; Carolyn Shantz	*Children's cognitive and social-cognitive development: Domain specificity and generality*

Table 2 (*continued*)

Special Sections, Special Issues, and Invitational (Guest Edited) Issues of *Merrill-Palmer Quarterly*

Date	Editor	Subject/Title
1990	Frances Degen Horowitz; John Colombo	*Infancy research: A summative evaluation and a look to the future*
1991	Hilary Ratner	*The socialization of children's cognition and emotion: Toward an integrative view*
1992	Catherine Garvey	*Talk in the study of socialization and development*
1993	Keith Stanovich	*The development of rationality and critical thinking*
1994	Nancy Eisenberg	*Children's emotions and social competence*
1996	Carolyn Shantz	*Conflict in families and between children: Advances in theory and research*
1997	Deborah Lowe Vandell	*Child-care research in the 1990s: Child care as context and in context*
1999	Kathryn Urberg	*Peer influences in childhood and adolescence*
1999	Shelley Hymel; Marlene Moretti	*The development of the self: New directions in theory and research*
2003		*Aggressive and adaptive functioning: The bright side to bad behavior*

the influence of social cues on children's behavior. Contributors explored how instructional or evaluative cues, when presented in social contexts, affected children's goal-directed behavior. Around this same time research on the construct of child competence began to appear in the journal. However, only late in the decade did articles on gender, peer relations, aggressive behavior, cooperative learning environments, and other such topics begin to appear in *MPQ* with greater regularity.

THE 1980S

During the early years of the 1980s several changes occurred in *MPQ*'s editorship. Martin Hoffman's tenure ended in 1980, and he was succeeded by Eli Saltz, who assumed the editorship in 1981 after a brief term by Grover Whitehurst, who edited the January and April 1980 issues. In April 1982 Carolyn U. Shantz succeeded Saltz. According to Hoffman (1988), the future of the Merrill-Palmer Institute was uncertain during the early 1980s, leading to uncertainty about *MPQ*'s existence because the two were so closely intertwined. "The Institute was saved when Wayne State University took it over, and the *Quarterly*'s future was assured when it was put into the capable editorial hands of Carolyn Shantz" (Hoffman, 1988, p. 351).

Saltz had given *MPQ* a new look, and it was substantially redesigned again shortly before Shantz took over. During the 1980s *MPQ* added pages and expanded its contents dramatically, publishing more articles in a broader range of content areas. The journal's editorial staff also grew during this period. Hoffman and Saltz had been the only editors during their terms. However, when Shantz took over, Saltz remained with *MPQ* as associate editor, and incoming manuscripts were divided between the two of them. This configuration of editors remained in place throughout this decade and well into the 1990s.

Although infant development continued to be a mainstay, it was somewhat less dominant in *MPQ*'s pages. The journal's expanding range also made it appear that *MPQ* was deemphasizing early childhood development. However, it continued to publish research on parent-child relationships, child rearing, and family relations, as well as evidence that extended or elaborated upon these themes.

The journal also continued to publish numerous articles about children's cognitive development, but the constructs and topics addressed in these papers were less aligned with Piagetian theory. Instead, the ascendant topics were children's learning and memory, judgment and reasoning, attention and attentional processes, social cognition, and cognitive monitoring, or metacognition. In particular, research on children's memory and memory-related processes appeared in *MPQ* with increasing frequency, as did work on children's moral thinking and reasoning.

Articles devoted to children's social development, especially those focused on children's friendships and peer relations, posted a moderate gain during this era. This rapidly advancing area of investigation was uniquely situated for integrating research on social behavior and social cognition. Recognizing this trend, Shantz created an invitational issue of *MPQ* in 1983 titled *Popular, Rejected, and Neglected Children: Their Social Behavior and Social Reasoning*. She also acquired many articles about children's altruism and gender differences, reflecting the growth in research in this area. Studies of children's antisocial behavior (e.g., aggression) and mental health began to proliferate in *MPQ*'s pages as well.

MPQ published other specical issues during this period (see Table 2), focusing on, among other topics, theory and research on children's temperament (1984), language and communication (1985), reading and phonological awareness (1987), and cognitive and social-cognitive development (1989).

Near the end of this era new or oft-neglected areas of investigation, some of which would become prominent decades later, began to emerge in the pages of *MPQ*: children's achievement motivation, affect and emotional development, theories or beliefs about the mind and mental operations, as well as research on adolescents and adolescent development.

THE 1990S

The rapid expansion of *MPQ* that began in the 1980s continued to gather momentum in the 1990s. Whereas *MPQ* averaged 120 pages per issue from 1980 to 1989, its average issue was a fat 156 pages from 1990 to 1999. Articles were both longer and more numerous; the journal averaged eight articles per issue in the 1980s and nine during the 1990s.

Gains in manuscript submissions during this period required an expansion of *MPQ*'s editorial staff. In 1991 a second associate editor joined the staff, followed by a third in 1998 (see Table 1).

As *MPQ* expanded in the 1990s, so did its scholarly purview. Shantz, who continued to lead the staff, augmented its tradition of publishing research on early development—particularly studies of infants, toddlers, and young children—by including articles on prenatal development, pre- and postnatal risk factors, pregnancy, child-birth, and so on. The decade's first issue contained an invited symposium on infancy that was edited by Frances Degen Horowitz and John Colombo. Thereafter, *MPQ* published numerous papers on such topics as infants' and toddlers' cognitive and visual-spatial abilities, temperament and activity levels, and gestures and language development.

Nor did *MPQ* neglect other age groups. Research on children and preadolescents proliferated, and emerging topics included sibling interactions, attachments to caregivers, play and pretend play, peer relations and friendships (real and imagined), and moral development. Studies conducted with adolescent samples now appeared regularly rather than sporadically. Also well represented in the journal during this era were articles on children's cognitive development, language development and socialization, moral reasoning and judgment, and social development. For example, in 1992 *MPQ* published an invitational issue about socialization and development that was edited by Catherine Garvey.

The journal was also breaking new ground in this period by publishing investigations that transcended traditional disciplinary boundaries. Increasingly, researchers were writing about their efforts to examine the interface of two or more aspects of development (e.g., constructs, processes, contexts) within the same rather than separate investigations. For example, research began to focus on links between family relations or processes, such as attachment, child-rearing styles, and marital conflict, and children's social interaction and peer relationships. For example, in 1996 Shantz published a special issue titled "Conflict in Families and Between Children: Advances in Theory and Research." She also published studies of the relation between parents' communication styles and children's academic achievement, children's peer relations and the transition to school, fathering and children's sex role development, parenting style and children's deductive reasoning, children's gender and moral reasoning, family sociodemographic backgrounds and child temperament, and the role of child care in children's development. It is important to note, however, that this trend was not specific to *MPQ* but reflected the broader agenda that pervaded many branches of the human developmental sciences and associated publications.

The emergence of new research priorities during the 1990s also diversified *MPQ*'s contents. More of its pages were devoted to such topics as emotional development, critical thinking, child care, peer influences, and self-understanding. Indeed, each of these areas of investigation was featured in a special issue of *MPQ* (see Table 2).

MPQ also was publishing more articles that examined ethnicity and culture as correlates or antecedents of children's and adolescent's development. These included the examination of ethnic identity, ethnic preferences, and racial prejudice as well as the study of ethnic differences in children's self-perceptions, and in parent's child rearing, disciplinary practices, and communications about children's emotions. Also evident was a trend toward investigating specific aspects of children's development and socialization within and across cultural contexts. *MPQ* published reports on cultural variations in children's expression of emotion, opportunities to engage in social or pretend play, gender role stability, and interaction patterns with family members, and so on.

Finally, the journal's table of contents also began to reflect the growing influence of behavioral neuroscience and psychophysiological assessment on developmental research. Treatises on longitudinal research methods and data analyses became more prevalent as well. For example, it was not unusual to encounter articles in *MPQ* in which researchers assessed adrenocortical arousal (via cortisol assays) or obtained indicators of other physiological or hormonal processes (e.g., galvanic skin response, heart rate, vagal tone, markers of pubertal development) as a means of explicating links among human physiology, endocrinology, and development.

The Postmillennium *Merrill-Palmer Quarterly*

The next major stage in *MPQ*'s development began in June 2000 when Shantz retired and I succeeded her. Shantz's editorship, like Hoffman's, had endured for nearly 20 years. She guided the journal through several transitions and was responsible for numerous innovations that enhanced the journal's growth, scope, and visibility among scholars within the human developmental sciences. Under Shantz's leadership *Merrill-Palmer Quarterly* became one of the most respected journals in the human developmental sciences (see Rushton & Roediger, 1978; Feingold, 1989; Howard & Day, 1995).

As I began my term, the manuscript submission rate remained high. Fortunately, three prominent scholars, Richard Fabes, Mary Gauvain, and Lawrence Walker, agreed to join *MPQ* as associate editors, and the four of us divided the duties of reading new submissions.

Another important development was that Wayne State University Press, in collaboration with the new editors, redesigned *MPQ* from top to bottom, giving the journal a new and contemporary appearance. In addition, Wayne State established a Web site for *MPQ* (http://www.asu.edu/mpq) that provides authors and readers with information about the journal's mission, policies, and substantive focus. This site also contains instructions for manuscript submissions, an archive of recently published articles, and subscription rates and forms for *MPQ*.

In 2001 issues of *MPQ* became available online through Project Muse, an electronic resource that was jointly developed by the Johns Hopkins University Press and the Milton S. Eisenhower Library. Through institutional subscriptions Project Muse provides worldwide access to the full text of *MPQ* and nearly 200 other scholarly journals. These online journals contain the same contents as their print counterparts and are augmented with electronic tools such as advanced search functions, hypertextual linking, and enhanced graphics. (For more information about Project Muse, see http://muse.jhu.edu.)

SETTING A COURSE FOR THE FUTURE: GOALS FOR *MERRILL-PALMER QUARTERLY*

A principal objective for *MPQ* in this new century is to maintain its standards of excellence and continue to advance the scope and quality of scholarship that appears in the journal. This attention to quality is the key to its success. Another objective is to expand its content to embrace diverse academic disciplines, research contexts and paradigms, and geopolitical perspectives while also publishing authors who initiate important new areas of inquiry, transcend traditional disciplinary boundaries, and introduce conceptual, methodological, and analytic innovations. Toward this end, the editors are seeking submissions that reflect diversity in not only the scientific disciplines represented but also in the professional status (junior versus senior investigators), ethnicity and culture, and geopolitical contexts or locations of its contributors. In short, *MPQ* wants to publish contributions from a global community of scholars, especially from investigators outside North America.

MERRILL-PALMER QUARTERLY'S SUBSTANTIVE FOCUS

MPQ's mission is to serve as a primary source of new research studies, theoretical papers, critical reviews of literature, and scholarly commentaries in human development. The purview of *Merrill-*

Palmer Quarterly encompasses theory and research on all areas of child and adolescent development and incorporates the journal's historical commitment to the study of development in context (e.g., sociocultural variations, families, schools, neighborhoods, peers, media, etc.). The majority of papers considered for *Merrill-Palmer Quarterly* are original reports of empirical research that extend knowledge about child and adolescent development. The editors are primarily interested in submissions that advance developmental theory and generate novel findings from sound developmental methods and designs. We are especially eager to publish empirical investigations that contain provocative aims, multiple studies, and innovative methods. Articles that focus on technical issues (e.g., creation and evaluation of measures, methods, statistical analyses, etc.) are of lesser interest unless they also contain an original substantive (developmental) component or contribution. Similarly, we are unlikely to accept articles about undergraduates, adults, or parents/parenting unless they also contain data on infants, children, or adolescents and have an original bent.

These new directions are evident in the pages of *MPQ*. A growing number of articles address questions related to the antecedents and consequences of children's health and illness. Examples include studies of the socialization of preventive health behavior and of processes that may prevent versus exacerbate developmental and behavioral dysfunctions (e.g., sources of vulnerability, risk and protective factors, and resilience).

CELEBRATING THE 50TH ANNIVERSARY OF *MERRILL-PALMER QUARTERLY*

Part of the plan to celebrate *MPQ*'s 50th anniversary was to publish a series of invited commentaries by senior investigators. The scholars who accepted this invitation were asked to analyze and reflect on some of the discipline's most important theoretical and empirical accomplishments and to identify remaining research challenges that are pivotal to the discipline's future. These commentaries initially appeared in *MPQ* in 2004. The purpose of this book is to preserve these contributions within a single venue, and make them available to a broader readership, including professionals who work with infants, children, adolescents, and families.

References

Feingold, A. (1989). Assessment of journals in social science and psychology.

American Psychologist, 44, 963–964.

Hoffman, M. (1988). Launching a journal. *Merrill-Palmer Quarterly, 34,* 349–351.

Howard, G. S., & Day, J. D. (1995). Individual productivity and impact in developmental psychology. *Developmental Review, 15,* 136–149.

Rushton, J. P., & Roediger, H. L. (1978). *American Psychologist, 33,* 520–523.

Sears, R. R. (1975). Your ancients revisited. In E. M. Hetherington (Ed.), *Review of child development research: Vol. 5.* (pp. 1–74). Chicago: University of Chicago Press.

Sigel, I. (1988). Reminiscences of the origins of a journal. *Merrill-Palmer Quarterly, 34,* 349–351.

2

The Limitations of Concepts
in Developmental Psychology

Jerome Kagan

Developmental psychology, like other domains in the social sciences, is being restrained by its history. One limitation is a derivative of its philosophical parents, for the first psychologists tried to gather laboratory evidence that would prove the validity of the abstract concepts of consciousness, perception, morality, and memory. The second pull to the past comes from an awe of physics, because in psychology's early years biology had not yet attained its currently high status.

Unfortunately, both philosophers and physicists like abstract concepts that invite a commitment to Platonic essences. Philosophers, for example, continue to write about consciousness or morality as if these words named unitary natural phenomena. Physicists describe an atom of oxygen as if its features were identical in all instantiations, even though its features in air are not identical to its features when it is part of a molecule of sulfuric acid. Psychology must free itself from both traditions and recognize, as biologists do, that the functions of every hypothetical structure vary with the agent and the context of measurement. The message in this brief essay is that each experimental procedure or method of analysis influences the conceptualization of the phenomena each produces.

Most scientists belong to one of two distinct groups. One cohort begins its empirical work by assuming the validity—some may prefer the word *reality*—of a particular concept, be it fear, intelligence, or depression, and tries to find a procedure that will index the event or processes that the concept implies. For example, neuroscientists and psychologists who are convinced that the term *fear* names a natural phenomenon use conditioned freezing, potentiated startle, increased salivary cortisol, or, in humans, self-reports of fear as valid reflections of the same state. The commitment to the unitary concept is so strong that advocates resist rejecting its utility, despite inconsistent evidence, and instead look for new methods to reaffirm their faith in the idea.

The second group, more loyal to Ernst Mach and Niels Bohr than to Albert Einstein and Werner Heisenberg, reject all concepts that assume Platonic essences. These scholars believe that all nature ever reveals are robust relations between observed phenomena and that we invent words, understood to be conventions, to explain the covariation. When these scientists acknowledge the reliable relation in animals between the presence of a tone that signals electric shock and the display of body immobility (freezing), they attempt to explain the reasons for the relation. Because freezing can be induced without conditioning, and is muted if the electric shock used in conditioning is very intense, they resist ascribing a unitary state of fear to any animal.

Scientific domains cycle over time in their friendliness to one or the other of these attitudes toward the relation between words and events. Because 19th-century scientists had become addicted to a priori concepts like *élan vital*, will, vis nervosa, and the ether, early 20th-century scholars, recognizing that the academy had filled with verbal rubbish, tried to cleanse the halls with the rules that became known as logical positivism. Percy Bridgman, Ludwig Wittgenstein, Rudolph Carnap, and Morris Schlitz led the housecleaning. But because the austerity of the positivistic rules shackled the creative intuitions that are necessary for theoretical advance, these imperatives lost their hold on the next generation, and by the 1960s words naming essences once again began to accumulate in technical journals. It is time for another housecleaning.

Contemporary psychologists are addicted to assigning abstract psychological properties to animals and humans that fail to specify the agent and the context in which the properties are actualized. Obvious examples are concepts like extroversion, fear, intelligence, or secure attachment, for which the situations in which the trait is displayed are unspecified. Fewer biologists are guilty of this error because they understand that every life process is linked to a particular class of organism and actualized under particular conditions. Each person possesses representations of the events encountered most frequently in a particular context, whether forest, office, airport, stadium, television screen, or laboratory scanner. Men holding machine guns are discrepant in most settings but not on television screens. Because humans evaluate every event with respect to the situation in which it normally occurs, every event must be conceptualized as an "event in a context." The context, like a channel setting on a television set, primes the brain to expect a particular set of most probable experiences. This process can be observed in rats, for injecting cocaine into the brain has one consequence if the rat is in a familiar home cage and quite another if the animal is in an unfamiliar place. A 1-year-old is more likely to cry at an approaching stranger if the child is in an unfamiliar room than at home (Kagan, 1984), and adults show greater cardiovascular reactivity to a stressor if they are with their favorite pet than if they are alone or with a spouse (Blascovich & Mendes, 2002).

The influence of the testing context is sometimes surprising. An examiner tells a 4-year-old that if she points to the location where a piece of candy is hidden, a stranger, and not she, will get the sweet. However, if she points to another location, she will get the candy. If the examiner tells the child to use her finger to point, she is honest and informs the stranger of the candy's correct location. However, if she is given a rod as the indicator, she points to the other location and takes the candy for herself (Hala & Russell, 2001). This result affirms the significance of the details of the testing context on the evidence used for inference.

The reluctance to restrict a psychological property to a class of situations is obvious in essays on morality. Western psychologists and philosophers continue to debate whether fairness, justice, honesty, kindness, and restraint on harming another are a priori moral imperatives. Much of the disagreement melts away if we insist that the actions be contextualized. It is easy to argue that killing another without provocation is morally wrong. However, administering a requested lethal dose of morphine to an elderly cancer patient in pain becomes ethically defensible once the context of a moral action is specified. The practice of specifying the context makes it easier to sort behaviors and intentions into moral and amoral categories.

Because every class of experimental procedure is a special context, the meaning and validity of every conclusion must be evaluated in light of the method that produced the evidence. Each procedure produces information representing only a part of the whole that scientists wish to comprehend. Two measures designed to evaluate an infant's ability to recognize a novel event, for example, can be unrelated (Rose, Feldman, & Jankowski, 2003). Simultaneous recordings of psychological and biological measures often lead to different inferences. Most 10-year-olds shown pictures of children they had played with in preschool four to five years earlier, along with pictures of unfamiliar children, had poor recognition memory for the former playmates when they were asked to say whether they had ever seen the child in the photo. However, many children who did not recognize a former playmate produced a galvanic skin response to photos of children they had played with earlier but not to the strangers (Newcombe & Fox, 1994).

The method selected for data analysis influences inferences. When investigators use a heritability equation in a study of intelligence in twin pairs, they are forced to assume that genetic and environmental contributions are additive. When psychologists use analysis of covariance to control for social class influences on the relation between children's vocabulary and adult vocational choice, they are forced to assume that the magnitude of the effect of social class is similar at all levels of vocabulary knowledge. Both assumptions are subject to critique.

Developmental psychologists rely primarily on three different sources of evidence: questionnaires and interviews, behavioral observations (either naturalistic or in a laboratory), and biological measurements. Each procedure provides a specific class of evidence, and the constructs invented to explain the results are limited to the source of evidence. There are usually low correlations among self-report, behavioral, and biological indexes of the same construct, whether fear, attachment, or intelligence. Self-report data, which involve semantic representations, are the least constrained; behavioral observations and biology are more seriously restricted by the context of observation.

The current belief that a particular behavior or biological reaction maintains the same meaning across different incentives and contexts is retarding progress. Consider, again, the popular assumption that the duration of bodily immobility, or the magnitude of potentiated startle, in response to a conditioned stimulus that signals electric shock means that the animal is in a state of fear mediated by the amygdala. Although a rat with a lesioned amygdala shows minimal freezing, implying the absence of a state of fear, the same animal will defecate in the place where it was shocked. This implies that the animal is in a fear state (Antoniadis & McDonald, 2000). Thus the meaning of body immobility depends on the specific context, and a "response in a context" should be the proper construct.

Too many psychological concepts are indifferent to the species, response, and particular situation in which the behavior occurs. As a result words like *fear* and *aggression* are used to describe an animal's state. Nelson and Chiavegatto (2001) assumed that a mouse biting an intruder belongs to the same psychological category as an adolescent who bullies a peer. However, an intention to harm another, which is absent in mice, is an essential feature of all human acts called aggressive.

The problem lies with the borrowing of predicates that are intended to apply to human behavior or states and attributing the same meaning to these words when they are applied to animals. This practice occurs because the number of distinct verbs for living forms is smaller than the number of distinct nouns. The psychological meaning of *bit* in the sentence "The boy bit his brother" is not the same as its meaning in "The mouse bit the intruder." Unfortunately, English does not have a word other than *bit* to describe the animal's behavior. Thus the behavioral biologist selects this word but assumes, incorrectly, that the act is aggressive in intent, whether it occurs in humans or animals. Because the meaning of a predicate often varies with the agent—that is why ancient Romans used different words for the act of kissing when the actor was a mother, spouse, or lover—neurobiologists should be careful when they apply to animals predicates that are intended to describe human behavior. In general, biological measurements require a very different vocabulary than the one used for either self-reports or behavioral observations. A change in cortisol, heart rate, skin conductance, cerebral blood flow, or an event-related potential is a function of a biological system, not a psychological structure. That is why it is important to combine varied sources of evidence.

Many phenomena are events that do not require a special technology in order to be observed, but the layers of disguised mediating processes require special methods that are presumed to represent the conditions necessary, but not sufficient, for display of the public events. It is almost always the case that the easily observed layer can be the product of different underlying processes. Therefore the observed phenomena are usually ambiguous in theoretical significance, and inferences based on them are necessarily uncertain.

Headaches provide an example. The report of chronic headache could be the result of different etiological conditions, for example, constriction of the blood vessels of the head, a tumor, or an infection. Therefore the physician needs additional information from other procedures, including analyses of urine and blood as well as X-rays to diagnose the cause more accurately.

A behavior, test performance, or verbal report, like a headache, represents an easily observed phenomenon that can be produced by different conditions. An infant's display of increased behavioral orientation to an event could be the result of the surprise caused by a violation of an expectation, a change in motion or contour density, or a history of affective experiences with the event (Montague & Walker-Andrews, 2001). A report on a questionnaire of fear of snakes, public speaking, or strangers could be given by individuals who experience physiological arousal when they encounter the feared target, as well as by those who do not have any biological reaction. The self-report of fear has different meanings for these two groups. An IQ score of 75 could be attained by a 6-year-old child who had been isolated from stimulation since infancy, a child with Down or Asperger's syndrome, or one with compromised hearing. One-year-olds who remained playing calmly when their mother left them alone in the laboratory room and did not approach her when she returned might have a parent who is neglectful or might possess a temperamental bias that mutes states of distress to unexpected events. Unless investigators eliminate all the factors that could mediate a particular behavior or self-report, except the one of interest (which rarely happens), the inference drawn from the evidence is vulnerable to critique.

One constructive solution is to quantify several relevant measures rather than one. For example, Sorenson, Mcmanis, and Kagan (2002) discovered that college students showed equivalent magnitudes of potentiated startle to acoustic probes presented when they were looking at aversive pictures or solving arithmetic problems. But the pictures, and not the cognitive problems, also elicited cardiac deceleration and corrugator muscle activity. The arithmetic problems elicited heart rate acceleration and no corrugator activity. Thus the two conditions produced different states, but that inference required the simultaneous measurement of more than one variable. Both adult humans and rats produce a P300 in the event-related potential to a discrepant tone presented in an odd-ball paradigm. But the rats and humans were not in the same psychological state, for only the humans showed a minimal P300 in the parietal area when they did not have to make a response to the discrepant target. The rats showed a large P300 whether they were required to make an instrumental response or not (Sambeth et al., 2003). The suggestion to code multiple variables is essentially similar to arguments for multiple methods in personality assessment. A single behavior, verbal report, or biological reaction can be the product of distinctly different conditions, and quantification of multiple measurements is more likely to separate the varied causes.

Chemists gained major insights when they added information from the spectra produced by a heated element. Neuroscientists attained a deeper understanding of brain anatomy when they exploited electron microscopes. It is now time for developmental psychologists to enjoy a period of progress. But to attain that victory, they should add behavioral and perhaps physiological data to semantic self-reports and add biological evidence to behavioral variables. The measures can be quantitative or qualitative; that distinction is less important than sampling different classes of evidence represented by verbal statements, molar behaviors or test scores, and biology. If psychologists insist on using a concept based on only one of these sources of information, they must accept the restricted meaning that this strategy requires. If "self-esteem" is inferred only from an adolescent's answers to a questionnaire, the theoretical meaning of self-esteem is severely constrained. The same conclusion holds for attributions of social anxiety based only on behavioral observations or ascriptions of fear based only on measurements of the brain. No source of evidence is "better" than another, but each has a particular meaning and validity. Therefore scientists must be careful when they use the same concept to name different classes of evidence.

The indifference to context is stronger in Western than in Asian cultures. One reason for this difference may be that the primary social entity in European American society is the individual. Each person must attain salvation, wealth, status, or happiness on her own, and praise for success or blame for failure is placed on the person rather than on others. By contrast, the imperative for Asian youth is to seek harmony with, and become part of, a group, first family and, later, peers and community. Each person's pride or shame rests on the success or failure of the groups of which the self is a member and not only on the self's talent and perseverance.

The next cohort of developmental psychologists must append a description of the class of agent and the context of observation to every predicate for a psychological process. The meaning and theoretical utility of constructs like "the concept of number" differ if the subject is an infant discriminating two dots from six dots or an adult dividing 162 by 13. Similarly, the meaning of secure attachment will depend on whether the investigator records the infant's behavior to the mother's return in the Strange Situation or an adult's recall of her childhood relationship with her mother. We need to use full sentences to gather more varied sources of evidence!

References

Antoniadis, E. A., & McDonald, R. J. (2000). Amygdala, hippocampus, and discriminative conditioning to context. *Behavioral Brain Research, 108,* 1–9.

Blascovich, A. K., & Mendes, W. B. (2002). Cardiovascular reactivity and the presence of rats, friends, and spouses. *Pychosomatic Medicine, 64,* 727–735.

Hala, S., & Russell, J. (2001). Executive control within strategic deception. *Journal of Experimental Child Psychology, 80,* 112–141.

Kagan, J. (1984). *The nature of the child.* New York: Basic Books.

Montague, D. P. F., & Walker-Andrews, A. S. (2001). Peek-a-boo: A new look at infants' perception of emotion expression. *Developmental Psychology, 37,* 826–838.

Nelson, R. J., & Chiavegatto, S. (2001). Molecular basis of aggression. *Trends in Neuroscience, 24,* 713–718.

Newcombe, N., & Fox, N .A. (1994). Infantile amnesia. *Child Development, 65,* 31–40.

Rose, S. A., Feldman, J. F., & Jankowski, J. J. (2003). Infant visual recognition memory. *Developmental Psychology, 39,* 563–571.

Sambeth, A., Maes, J. H. R., Van Luijtelaar, G., Molenkamp, I. S., Jongsman, M. L. A., & Van Rijn, C. M. (2003). Auditory event-related potentials in humans and rats. *Psychophysiology, 40,* 6068.

Sorenson, D., McManis, M., & Kagan, J. (2002). A study of startle. Unpublished raw data.

3

Theory-of-Mind Development
Retrospect and Prospect

John H. Flavell

Theory-of-mind development investigates the nature and development of our understanding of the mental world—the inner world inhabited by beliefs, desires, emotions, thoughts, perceptions, intentions, and other mental states. Since its beginnings in the mid-1980s, this area has grown to be one of the largest and liveliest in developmental psychology.

One indication of this area's size is that as long ago as 1998 Wellman, Cross, and Watson (2001) were able to identify 178 studies in just the subarea of children's false-belief understanding. Another indication is that a recent computer search turned up 399 publications containing the phrase "theory of mind." Research on theory of mind has proved to be of interest not only to developmental psychologists but also to researchers and practitioners in such fields as philosophy, psychiatry, neuropsychology, social psychology, clinical psychology, comparative psychology, cultural psychology, cognitive psychology, and education. Reviews of theory-of-mind development research include Baron-Cohen, Tager-Flusberg, and Cohen (2000), Bartsch and Wellman (1995), Flavell (2000), Flavell and Miller (1998), Mitchell (1997), Repacholi and Slaughter (2003), and Wellman and Gelman (1998).

In the interest of brevity and flow and because this area has been thoroughly reviewed previously, I will be fairly sparing of references. Thus this chapter is more a high-altitude survey of the area than a thoroughly detailed review of it.

Retrospect

As is true of so many areas of cognitive development, the history of this one mainly begins with Piaget (Flavell, 2000; Flavell & Miller, 1998; Shantz, 1983). A central Piagetian claim is that children begin development by being cognitively egocentric. Piaget and his colleagues used egocentrism and other concepts to interpret their developmental studies of a wide variety of social-cognitive topics: perceptual perspective taking; egocentric communication; the misattribution of mental characteristics to physical objects (animism) and physical characteristics to mental events (realism); and understanding of thoughts, dreams, intentions, and morality. Research on some of these topics continues although usually not from a Piagetian theoretical perspective (e.g., Flavell, Green, & Flavell, 1995b; Woolley & Boerger, 2002).

A second wave of theory and research in this general area was the extensive work on metacognitive development that began in the early 1970s. Surveys of this large literature include Brown, Bransford, Ferrara, and Campione (1983), Flavell, Miller, and Miller (2002), Kuhn (1999), Moshman (1998), and Schneider and Bjorklund (1998). Metacognition (cognition about cognition—hence the *meta*) has been defined as any knowledge or cognitive activity that takes as its object, or regulates, any aspect of any cognitive activity (Flavell, Miller, & Miller, 2002).

The majority of developmental studies classified as metacognitive have investigated children's metamemory—that is, their knowledge of variables affecting memory performance and, especially, their knowledge and use of memory strategies. However, the term has also been applied to numerous studies of children's cognition concerning comprehension, communication, language, perception, attention, and problem solving. Research in the metacognitive development tradition is still being done, although it is not the hot topic it used to be. On the other hand, metacognition in adults appears to be a thriving field (Jost, Kruglanski, & Nelson, 1998; Yzerbyt, Lories, & Dardenne, 1998). Before about 1983 most investigators of children's knowledge about the mind would probably have classified their work as either metacognitive or in the general Piagetian tradition. Today most would say they are doing one or another kind of theory-of-mind research. What happened to bring about this change?

In a 1978 issue of *Behavioral and Brain Sciences*, Premack and Woodruff reported some research to test whether chimpanzees had what they called a "theory of mind." In their commentaries on this article three philosophers (Bennett, 1978; Dennett, 1978; Harman, 1978) independently suggested that one might be able to find out whether an animal possessed the concept of belief in something by proceeding something like this: Researchers watch as the subject animal sees another individual put an object in container A and then leave the scene. The subject then sees someone else transfer the object from container A into container B while the first individual is still absent. The subject animal should then be credited with some understanding of belief if it acts as if it expects that the returning individual will search for the object in A rather than B.

Two Austrian psychologists, Josef Perner and Heinz Wimmer, gave these ideas research expression in the early 1980s. In a pioneering and highly influential series of studies, they used the "unexpected transfer" method proposed by the philosophers to test young children's understanding of false belief (Wimmer & Perner, 1983). Other false-belief tasks of the following type were also developed: After children discover that a cookie box actually contains pencils instead of cookies, they are asked what another child who has not looked inside will think the box contains. Younger preschoolers say pencils; older ones, with a better understanding of belief, say cookies. Around the same time Wellman and his coworkers had independently begun to conceptualize children's developing metacognitive knowledge and understanding of mental terms as the development of a theory of mind (e.g., Wellman, 1985). In addition, other researchers who had not yet begun to conceptualize children's development in quite this way had been doing research that subsequently became part of the theory-of-mind movement. An example would be the work on children's knowledge about perception and about the appearance-reality distinction by Flavell and colleagues (e.g., Flavell, Flavell, Green, & Wilcox, 1980; Flavell, Flavell, & Green, 1983; see Astington, Harris, & Olsen, 1988, for other such projects).

Two conferences held in the spring of 1986 gave the movement added identity and coherence. The presentations at these two conferences later were published in a book titled *Developing Theories of Mind* (Astington, Harris, & Olson, 1988), and the movement was officially launched.

Figure 1 illustrates the main directions that theory-of-mind development research has taken since it began in the early 1980s. Much of the earliest work focused on documenting a striking improvement between 3 and 5 years of age in children's performance on various false-belief (FB), appearance-reality (AR), and Level 2 visual perspective-taking (PT) tasks. Thus, for example, older but not younger preschoolers were usually found to show an understanding that a naive other child would falsely believe that the cookie box contains cookies (false belief), that a fake rock looks like a rock but is really a sponge (appearance-reality), and that a picture book that

Theories: domain-specific theory development, innate or early-maturing modules, simulation, information-processing, etc.

Earlier developments

Later developments

Consequents

Tasks: FB, AR, PT
Ages: 3–5 years

Antecedents

Intracultural

Differences — Intercultural

Interspecies

Other mental states: desires, intentions, emotions, percepts, fictional representations, attention, thinking, consciousness, etc.

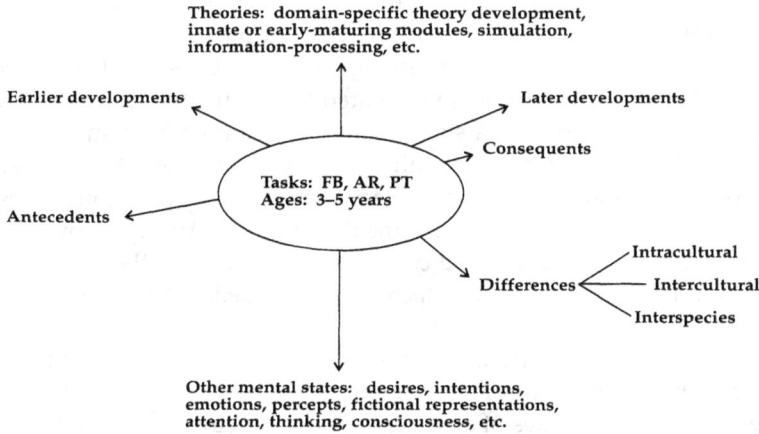

Figure 1. Overview of Research Directions in the Area of Theory-of-Mind Development.
Source: From "Development of Children's Knowledge About the Mental World," by J. H. Flavell, 2000, *International Journal of Behavioral Development, 24,* p. 18. Reprinted with permission.

is oriented correctly for them on the table will look upside down to a person seated opposite (Level 2 visual PT).

From those beginnings work has progressed more or less concurrently in a variety of directions, as shown by the arrows in Figure 1. For more complete discussions of these topics, see the substantive reviews I cited earlier.

THEORIES AND ANTECEDENTS

Several types of theories have been offered as explanations for the development of children's mentalistic understanding. One is the so-called theory theory (Gopnik & Meltzoff, 1997; Gopnik & Wellman, 1994; Perner, 1991; Wellman & Gelman, 1998). Theory theorists argue that our knowledge of the mind comprises an informal, everyday framework or foundational theory, not a formal scientific theory. Researchers have described a number of steps in children's progression toward the adult theory of mind. For instance, Bartsch and Wellman (1995) have argued that children begin with a desire psychology, then progress to a desire-belief psychology, and finally attain our adult belief-desire psychology, in which one recognizes that what people believe, as well as what they desire, crucially affects how they behave. Theory theorists argue that experience plays a major formative role in children's theory-of-mind development.

In contrast, modularity theorists (Baron-Cohen, 1995; Leslie, 1994; Scholl & Leslie, 1999) postulated the acquisition through neurological maturation of a succession of domain-specific and modular mechanisms for dealing with agents versus nonagent objects. Although experience may be necessary to trigger the operation of these mechanisms, it does not determine their nature. Although obviously focused on basic hard-wired competence in this area, these theorists do not neglect performance factors that influence the expression of that competence.

Harris (1992) and others have proposed yet a third approach. According to their simulation theory, children become able to compute the mental states of other people through a kind of role-taking, or simulation, process. What develops is the ability to make increasingly accurate simulations of this kind. Like theory theorists, simulation theorists assume that experience plays a crucial formative role, in that it is through practice in role taking that children improve their simulation abilities.

A number of developmentalists believe that young children's failures on false-belief and other theory-of-mind tasks may be caused by limitations in executive functioning (e.g., Carlson, Moses, & Hix, 1998; Hughes, 1998). For example, an inability to inhibit a dominant, ready-to-go response could cause the child subject to blurt out the cognitively salient real contents of the cookie box when asked what the naive other child thought it contained. According to this view, improvement in children's executive functioning with age helps make possible the acquisition of key theory-of-mind competencies.

Another important antecedent is language development. It is particularly easy to imagine how language competencies might play a variety of roles in assisting theory-of-mind development. People convey information about their own, the child's, or other people's mental states through conversations and stories, verbally make salient different people's perspectives, and help the child see how mental states are caused and changed by verbal and other inputs. Language also provides vehicles for thinking about mental states: a vocabulary of mental terms, a complementation sentence structure for expressing propositional attitudes (e.g., "She thinks that he is nice"), and a way of abstracting and reflecting on mental states and behaviors. And, in fact, the research evidence provides good support for these conjectures about the formative influence of language and interpersonal communication (Astington & Baird, 2005).

CONSEQUENTS

A number of studies have shown that children's theory-of-mind development has consequences for their social behavior; for recent reviews see Repacholi and Slaughter (2003). Most research evidence suggests that children with more advanced understanding (especially of false belief) tend to have more successful social relationships than their less advanced peers. For example, their teachers rated them as having better social skills (Watson, Nixon, Wilson, & Capage, 1999). However, there is also evidence that theory-of-mind competencies can be used for antisocial as well as presocial purposes. For example, some child bullies and adult sociopaths consistently use their mind-reading skills to serve antisocial ends (Repacholi & Slaughter, 2003). Finally, the causal relations between theory of mind and social behavior are complex and bidirectional, with social behavior providing a context for theory-of-mind acquisitions as well as the converse (Astington, 2003). Thus the two could be viewed as both antecedents and consequents of each other.

DEVELOPMENTS DURING INFANCY

Babies are born with or acquire early a number of abilities and propensities that will help them learn about people. They find human faces, voices, and movements especially interesting. They seem impelled to attend to and interact with other people, and they certainly impel other people to attend to and interact with them. Infants respond differently to people than they do to objects and seem to expect people to behave differently than objects do (Poulin-Dubois, 1999). They appear to construe people as agents that are self-propelled, goal directed, and influenceable at a distance by communicative signals. All these seem like the right design features for a creature destined for theory-of-mind development.

Late in the first year, perhaps earlier, infants begin to learn that people's behavior possesses intentionality, or "aboutness" (see Tomasello & Haberl, 2003, for a good, up-to-date review of this general topic). An individual's behavior is about an object in this sense if the individual perceptually attends to it, labels it, thinks about it, wants it, fears it, intends or tries to get it, or relates to it in any other psychological way. Infants do a variety of things that reflect a beginning awareness of intentionality. They try to engender new aboutnesses in others through various communicative gestures, such as pointing to or vocalizing about an object and checking to see whether the other person attends to it. They also develop skill at reading the aboutnesses that the other person is already displaying, as when babies follow another person's gaze. Carpenter, Nagell, and Tomasello (1998) documented a three-step developmental sequence in which infants progress from sharing to following to directing others' attention and behavior. Meltzoff (1995) has demonstrated that 18-month-olds can infer what action another person is trying to perform (e.g., attempting to pull one object away from another object to which it is attached), even though the person is unsuccessful in the attempt (does not succeed in pulling it away) and therefore never actually demonstrates the intended outcome. This and other findings suggest that infants of this age have some sense that people's actions are intentional and goal directed. By age 18 months infants also understand that they should give an experimenter a food that she reacts to with pleasure rather than one toward which she acts disgusted, even when the babies themselves prefer the latter food (Repacholi & Gopnik, 1997); this suggests at least some limited ability to reason nonegocentrically about people's desires.

Infants also recognize that the adult's intentional focus rather than their own is what gives clues to the adult's referential intent when the adult labels an object (Woodward & Markman, 1998). That is, babies recognize that the word refers to the object that the adult is looking at, not the one the babies themselves happened to be looking at when the word was spoken. In this way early theory-of-mind development provides a scaffold for early language development. Similarly, babies develop the ability to learn what an object is like by reading the adult's attentional focus when the adult is expressing a positive or negative emotional reaction to it (a process called social referencing). For instance, babies may selectively avoid an object toward which their parent shows negative affect. Thus by 12 months or so they can recognize that the adult's emotional display refers to, or is about, a particular object, much as they can recognize that the adult's spoken label refers to, or is about, a particular object (Moses, Baldwin, Rosicky, & Tidball, 2001). By the end of infancy children may also do other things suggestive of a beginning understanding of human psychology, such as trying to comfort people in distress and correctly using mental state terms such as *want* and *see* (Flavell & Miller, 1998).

LATER DEVELOPMENTS

A large literature has accrued since the early 1980s on theory-of-mind acquisitions that occur subsequent to the infancy period. What follows is a brief summary of some major findings, organized by type of mental state.

Visual perception

During the early preschool period children already realize that a person will see an object if and only if the person's eyes are aimed in the general direction of the object, and if there are no vision-blocking obstacles interposed between the person and the object (Flavell, 1992, 2004). With this understanding babies are able to do simple, nonegocentric visual perspective taking; for example, they can infer that you may see something that they do not and vice versa (referred to as Level 1 knowledge about visual perception). Later in the preschool period they go on to recognize that the same thing may present different visual appearances to two people if they view it from different positions (called Level 2 knowledge).

Attention

As I have already mentioned, even infants pay attention to other people's attending and seem to have some understanding of its implications (Tomasello & Haberl, 2003). As they grow older, babies come to appreciate that attention is selective and limited and that different people may mentally represent the same attended-to input differently (Fabricius & Schwanenflugel, 1994; Flavell, Green, & Flavell, 1995a; Pillow, 1995).

Desires

By the age of 3 children are not only using some desire terms correctly, they also seem to grasp simple causal relations among desires, outcomes, emotions, and actions—suggestive evidence that they are developing something like an implicit theory. For example, they understand that people will feel good if they get what they want and feel bad if they do not (Bartsch & Wellman, 1995).

Emotions

Although we do not know yet whether infants actually attribute inner feelings to people who display emotions, it seems certain that young preschoolers do (Wellman, Harris, Banerjee, & Sinclair, 1995). In later years children learn more advanced truths about emotions—

for example, that people do not always really feel what they appear to feel and that people's emotional reactions to an event may be influenced by earlier emotional experiences with similar events or by their current mood (Flavell & Miller, 1998).

Beliefs and related mental representations

Many studies have examined children's developing understanding of so-called serious mental representations—that is, nonpretense mental states, such as beliefs that are meant to represent reality accurately (Flavell & Miller, 1998). The majority of these studies have dealt with children's comprehension of representations that differ from person to person or differ from reality: the appearance-reality distinction, Level 2 knowledge of visual perception, interpretation and constructive processing, deception, and—most studied of all—false belief. How well standard false-belief and appearance-reality tasks actually measure these concepts is controversial, however (e.g., Bloom & German, 2000; Hansen & Markman, 2005). Children's knowledge of mental representations continues to increase after the preschool period. In particular, not until middle childhood and later do children appear to gain any substantial understanding of the mind as an active, interpretive, constructive processor (e.g., Barquero, Robinson, & Thomas, 2003; Carpendale & Chandler, 1996). For instance, understanding that people's interpretation of an ambiguous event may be influenced by their preexisting biases or expectations seems to be a largely middle-childhood insight (Pillow & Henrichon, 1996).

Knowledge

Young preschoolers appear to be unclear about just what it means for someone to know something and about how knowledge is acquired (Flavell & Miller, 1998). Even older preschoolers may claim that they have always known information that they have just learned during the experimental session (Taylor, Esbensen, & Bennett, 1994). An important early middle-childhood discovery is that perceptual information has to be adequate as well as merely present to engender knowledge. For example, children come to realize that a person often cannot be certain of an object's identity when only a little bit of it is visible; this realization is another example of their burgeoning conception of the mind as an interpretive device.

Pretense

Leslie (1987, 1994) has argued that the ability to understand pretense and the ability to understand false belief and other mental states are mediated by a common, early-maturing theory-of-mind module. This argument has some plausibility: "Pretending that" and "believing that" are both propositional attitudes. Moreover, adults regard both as mental representations or construals of something as being a certain way—either for real (belief) or just temporarily, for play purposes (pretense). Nevertheless, Leslie's claim is controversial (Harris, 2000; Lillard, 1998a). The related topic of children's understanding of imagination is also being studied (Harris, 2000; Woolley, 1995).

Thinking

Children achieve some important elementary knowledge and skills concerning thinking during the early preschool years (Flavell, Green, & Flavell, 1995b; Wellman, Hollander, & Schult, 1996). For example, they come to construe thinking as an internal human activity that refers to or represents real or imaginary things. However, there are also important knowledge and skills concerning thinking that preschoolers clearly lack (Flavell, 2003; Flavell, Green, & Flavell, 1995b; Flavell & O'Donnell, 1999). They are not aware that people are continually experiencing mental content spontaneously in an ever-flowing stream of consciousness. For example, unlike older children, preschoolers do not consistently attribute any mental activity at all to a person who just sits quietly "waiting."

DIFFERENCES IN DEVELOPMENT

Intracultural differences

Investigators have examined three kinds of differences in development: intracultural, intercultural, and interspecies (Flavell & Miller, 1998). Regarding intracultural differences, in the section on theories and antecedents I mentioned the importance of social-communicative experiences as mediators of within-culture differences in theory-of-mind development (Astington & Baird, 2005; Repacholi & Slaughter, 2003). The most striking intracultural differences, however, are seen in the pronounced deficits in theory-of-mind development in autistic individuals.

Significant intracultural variation that does not necessarily imply deficits or incomplete development also exists. Dweck, Chiu, and Hong (1995) have documented important individual differences in people's implicit theories about intelligence and other human attributes. Textbooks in the fields of personality, social psychology, and social cognition also describe many other ways that normal adults differ from one another in their naive theories and knowledge regarding themselves and other people; great works of literature are an even richer source. And of course psychologists and other scientists have espoused widely different conceptions of human cognition and personality over the years: think, for example, of the differences between B. F. Skinner's and Sigmund Freud's views of the mind.

Intercultural differences

Researchers have also begun to ask questions about the extent to which theory-of-mind development is similar across cultures. It seems likely that at least the fundamental mentalistic understanding observed in infants and very young children would be found universally (Wellman, 1998). There is even evidence that some developmental sequences may be cross-culturally invariant: in a careful study Tardif and Wellman (2000) showed that both Chinese and American children acquire basic desire and belief concepts and also that both acquire them in that order. Some cross-cultural variation obtains in later development, however (Greenfield, Keller, Fuligni, & Maynard, 2003; Lillard, 1998b; Vinden & Astington, 2000). For example, some languages encode mental states more richly than others do, and some cultures (and subcultures) encourage mentalistic thought and talk more than others do.

Interspecies differences

A lively controversy in recent comparative psychology literature involves whether other primates—especially chimpanzees—should be credited with any genuinely mentalistic knowledge. Povinelli and Vonk (2003) believe that other primates are largely lacking in such knowledge. For example, these researchers have offered evidence suggesting that chimps possess a behavioristic rather than a mentalistic conception of seeing. In contrast, Tomasello, Call, and Hare (2003a, 2003b) argue that chimps do understand some psychological states and that "the question is only which ones and to what extent" (2003a, p. 156). Although these researchers have done clever experiments to address the question, exactly what nonhuman primates do and do not understand in the mental domain remains unclear. That the question is an important one, however, is underscored by this comment from Tomasello, Call, and Hare: "At issue is no less than the nature of human cognitive uniqueness" (2003a, p. 156).

Prospect

Researchers have learned a great deal about theory-of-mind development since the mid-1980s. It has proved to be an immensely fruitful area of developmental psychological study. Will it continue to be so in the next few decades? It is hard to see why it would not. Research will continue to address a number of outstanding questions (Flavell, 2000). Here is one example: What factors, processes, or mechanisms (e.g., language, executive functions) contribute to children's theory-of-mind development and exactly what is the nature of their contributions? Another is how much and what kinds of intracultural, intercultural, and interspecies similarities and differences exist among adults in this area?

One exciting future prospect is the possibility of telling longer and richer developmental stories in key sectors of theory-of-mind development (Flavell, 2000). Take, for example, the sector of belief and knowledge development. There is more to the developmental story here than that 4-year-olds tend to pass standard false-belief and knowledge tasks and that 3-year-olds tend to fail them. Many older children and adults will progress to other discoveries, for example, that the mind is an interpretive and constructive device (Carpendale & Chandler, 1996), that there can be higher-order as well as first-order beliefs (e.g., "He thinks that she thinks"), and that scientific and other advanced forms of reasoning and knowledge acquisition have special rules (Kitchener, 2002; Kuhn, 2000; Moshman, 1998). Research on individual differences in adulthood might even include the study of virtuosos in this area—writers, therapists, or others who have acquired exceptional perspective-taking or introspective skills (Gardner, 1983).

As to earlier competencies in this same sector, exciting research is being done on what may be some implicit understanding of belief and knowledge in infants and very young children. Several studies indicate that 3-year-olds who respond incorrectly to standard false-belief task questions nonetheless show by their eye movements that they may have some implicit understanding of false beliefs (Clements & Perner, 1994; Garnham & Ruffman, 2001). Even more surprising, Onishi and Baillargeon (2002) have claimed evidence for such understanding in 15-month-olds. For comparable findings regarding the possibility of an implicit grasp of the concept of knowledge, see O'Neill (1996) and Tomasello and Haberl (2003). Knowledge about vision (Flavell, 2004) and about intentions (Schult, 2003; Tomasello & Haberl, 2003) also show extended developmental itineraries.

Finally, consideration of extended developmental itineraries raises deep questions about developmental diagnosis (Flavell, Miller, & Miller, 2002). How should we conceptualize the various items of mentalistic knowledge that individuals acquire in the course of ontogenesis? Is a given item best conceptualized as implicit, explicit, or some mix of the two? And if explicit, how often is the individual consciously aware of it and how able and disposed to reflect on it? What is the individual capable of using the knowledge for, and how often does the individual actually put it to that use in everyday life? In short, rather like the developing child, we need to learn the different things that it can mean for a creature to "know" something.

References

Astington, J. W. (2003). Sometimes necessary, never sufficient: False-belief understanding and social competence. In B. Repacholi & V. Slaughter (Eds.), *Individual differences in theory of mind* (pp. 13–38). New York: Psychology Press.

Astington, J. W., & Baird, J. (2005). *Why language matters for theory of mind.* New York: Oxford University Press.

Astington, J. W., Harris, P. L., & Olson, D. (Eds.). (1988). *Developing theories of mind.* Cambridge, England: Cambridge University Press.

Baron-Cohen, S. (1995). *Mindblindness: An essay on autism and theory of mind.* Cambridge, MA: MIT Press.

Baron-Cohen, S., Tager-Flusberg, H., & Cohen, D. J. (Eds.). (2000). *Understanding other minds: Perspectives from autism* (2nd ed.). Oxford, England: Oxford University Press.

Barquero, B., Robinson, E. J., & Thomas, G. V. (2003). Children's ability to attribute different interpretations of ambiguous drawings to a naive vs. a biased observer. *International Journal of Behavioral Development, 27,* 445–456.

Bartsch, K., & Wellman, H. M. (1995). *Children talk about the mind.* New York: Oxford University Press.

Bennett, J. (1978). Some remarks about concepts. *Behavioral and Brain Sciences, 1,* 557–560.

Bloom, P., & German, T. P. (2000). Two reasons to abandon the false belief task as a test of theory of mind. *Cognition, 77,* B25–B31.

Brown, A. L., Bransford, J. D., Ferrara, R. A., & Campione, J. C. (1983). Learning, remembering, and understanding. In P. H. Mussen (Series Ed.), J. H. Flavell & E. M. Markman (Vol. Eds.), *Handbook of child psychology: Vol. 3. Cognitive development* (4th ed., pp. 77–166). New York: Wiley.

Carlson, S. M., Moses, L. J., & Hix, H. R. (1998). The role of inhibitory processes in young children's difficulties with deception and false belief. *Child Development, 69,* 672–691.

Carpendale, J. I., & Chandler, M. J., (1996). On the distinction between false belief understanding and subscribing to an interpretive theory of mind. *Child Development, 67,* 1686–1706.

Carpenter, M., Nagell, K., & Tomasello, M. (1998). Social cognition, joint attention, and communicative competence from 9–15 months of age. *Monographs of the Society for Research in Child Development, 63* (4, Serial No. 255).

Clements, W. A., & Perner, J. (1994). Implicit understanding of belief. *Cognitive Development, 9,* 377–395.

Dennett, D. C. (1978). Beliefs about beliefs. *Behavioral and Brain Sciences, 1,* 568–570.

Dweck, C. S., Chiu, C. Y., & Hong, Y. Y. (1995). Implicit theories and their role in judgments and reactions: A world from two perspectives. *Psychological Inquiry, 6,* 267–285.

Fabricius, W. V., & Schwanenflugel, P. J. (1994). The older child's theory of mind. In A. Demetriou & A. Efklides (Eds.), *Intelligence, mind, and reasoning: Structure and development* (pp. 111–132). Amsterdam: Elsevier.

Flavell, J. H. (1992). Perspectives on perspective taking. In H. Beilin & P. Pufall (Eds.), *Piaget's theory: Prospects and possibilities* (pp. 107–139). Hillsdale, NJ: Erlbaum.

Flavell, J. H. (2000). Development of children's knowledge about the mental world. *International Journal of Behavioral Development, 24,* 15–23.

Flavell, J. H. (2003). *Development of children's knowledge about the mind.* 2003 Heinz Werner Lecture Series: Vol. 25. Worcester, MA: Clark University Press.

Flavell, J. H. (2004) Development of knowledge about vision. In D. T. Levin (Ed.), *Thinking and seeing: Visual metacognition in adults and children.* Cambridge, MA: MIT Press.

Flavell, J. H., Flavell, E. R., & Green, F. L. (1983). Development of the appearance-reality distinction. *Cognitive Psychology, 15,* 95–120.

Flavell, J. H., Flavell, E. R, Green, F. L., & Wilcox, S. A. (1980). Young children's knowledge about visual perception: Effect of observer's distance from target on perceptual clarity of target. *Developmental Psychology, 16,* 10–12.

Flavell, J. H., Green, F. L., & Flavell, E. R. (1995a). The development of children's knowledge about attentional focus. *Developmental Psychology, 31,* 706–712.

Flavell, J. H., Green, F. L., & Flavell, E. R. (1995b). Young children's knowledge about thinking. *Monographs of the Society for Research in Child Development, 60* (1, Serial No. 243).

Flavell, J. H., & Miller, P. H. (1998). Social cognition. In W. Damon (Series Ed.), D. Kuhn & R. S. Siegler (Vol. Eds.), *Handbook of child psychology: Vol. 2. Cognition, perception, and language* (5th ed., pp. 851–898). New York: Wiley.

Flavell, J. H., Miller, P. H., & Miller, S. A. (2002). *Cognitive development* (4th ed.). Upper Saddle River, NJ: Prentice-Hall.

Flavell, J. H., & O'Donnell, A. K. (1999). Le développement de savoirs intuitifs à propos des expériences mentales. *Enfance, 51,* 267–276.

Gardner, H. (1983). *Multiple intelligences: The theory in practice.* New York: Basic Books.

Garnham, W. A., & Ruffman, T. (2001). Doesn't see, doesn't know: Is anticipatory looking really related to understanding of belief? *Developmental Science, 4,* 94–100.

Gopnik, A., & Meltzoff, A. N. (1997). *Words, thoughts, and theories.* Cambridge, MA: MIT Press.

Gopnik, A., & Wellman, H. M. (1994). The "theory" theory. In L. A. Hirschfeld & S. A. Gelman (Eds.), *Mapping the mind: Domain specificity in cognition and culture* (pp. 257–293). Cambridge, England: Cambridge University Press.

Greenfield, P. M., Keller, H., Fuligni, A., & Maynard, A. (2003). Cultural pathways through universal development. *Annual Review of Psychology, 54,* 461–490.

Hansen, M. B., & Markman, E. M. (2005). Appearance questions can be misleading: A discourse-based account of the appearance-reality problem. *Cognitive Psychology, 50,* 233–263.

Harman, G. (1978). Studying the chimpanzee's theory of mind. *Behavioral and Brain Sciences, 1,* 576–577.

Harris, P. L. (1992). From simulation to folk psychology: The case for development. *Mind and Language, 7,* 120–144.

Harris, P. L . (2000). *The work of the imagination.* Oxford, England: Blackwell.

Hughes, C. (1998). Finding your marbles: Does preschoolers' strategic behavior predict later understanding of mind? *Developmental Psychology, 34,* 1326–1339.

Jost, J. T., Kruglanski, A. W., & Nelson, T. O. (1998). Social metacognition: An expansionist review. *Personality and Social Psychology Review, 2,* 137–154.

Kitchener, R. F. (2002). Folk epistemology: An introduction. *New Ideas in Psychology, 20,* 89–105.

Kuhn, D. (1999). Metacognitive development. In L. Balter and C. S. Tamis-LeMonda (Eds.), *Child psychology: A handbook of contemporary issues.* Philadelphia: Psychology Press.

Kuhn, D. (2000). Metacognitive development. *Current Directions in Psychological Science, 9,* 178–181.

Leslie, A. M. (1987). Pretense and representation: The origins of "theory of mind." *Psychological Review, 94,* 412–426.

Leslie, A. M. (1994). ToMM, ToBy, and agency: Core architecture and domain specificity. In L. A. Hirschfeld & S. A. Gelman (Eds.), *Mapping the mind: Domain specificity in cognition and culture* (pp. 119–148). Cambridge, England: Cambridge University Press.

Lillard, A. S. (1998a). Wanting to be it: Children's understanding of intentions underlying pretense. *Child Development, 69,* 979–991.

Lillard, A. S. (1998b). Ethnopsychologies: Cultural variations in theories of mind. *Psycholgical Bulletin, 123,* 3–33.

Meltzoff, A. N. (1995). Understanding the intentions of others: Re-enact-ment of intended acts by 18-month-old children. *Developmental Psychology, 31,* 838–850.

Mitchell, P. (1997). *Introduction to theory of mind: Children, autism and apes.* London: Arnold.

Moses, L. J., Baldwin, D. A., Rosicky, J. G., & Tidball, G. (2001). Evidence for referential understanding in the emotions domain at twelve and eighteen months. *Child Development, 72,* 718–735.

Moshman, D. (1998). Cognitive development beyond childhood. In W. Damon (Series Ed.), D. Kuhn & R. S. Siegler (Vol. Eds.), *Handbook of child psychology: Vol. 2. Cognition, perception, and language* (5th ed., pp. 947–978). New York: Wiley.

O'Neill, D. K. (1996). Two-year-olds' sensitivity to a parent's knowledge state when making requests. *Child Development, 67,* 659–677.

Onishi, K. H., & Baillargeon, R. (2002, April). *Fifteen-month-old infants' understanding of false belief.* Paper presented at the biennial meeting of the International Conference on Infant Studies, Toronto.

Perner, J. (1991). *Understanding the representational mind.* Cambridge, MA: MIT Press.

Pillow, B. H. (1995). Two trends in the development of conceptual perspective-taking: An elaboration of the passive-active hypothesis. *International Journal of Behavioral Development, 18,* 649–676.

Pillow, B. H., & Henrichon, A. J. (1996). There's more to the picture than meets the eye: Young children's difficulty understanding biased interpretation. *Child Development, 67,* 803–819.

Poulin-Dubois, D. (1999). Infants' distinction between animate and inanimate objects: The origins of naive psychology. In P. Rochat (Ed.), *Early social cognition* (pp. 257–280). Mahwah, NJ: Erlbaum.

Povinelli, D. J., & Vonk, J. (2003). Chimpanzee minds: Suspiciously human? *Trends in Cognitive Sciences, 7,* 157–160.

Premack, D., & Woodruff, G. (1978). Does the chimpanzee have a theory of mind? *Behavioral and Brain Sciences, 1,* 515–526.

Repacholi, B. M., & Gopnik, A. (1997). Early reasoning about desires: Evidence from 14- and 18-month-olds. *Developmental Psychology, 33,* 12–21.

Repacholi, B. M., & Slaughter, V. (Eds.). (2003). *Individual differences in the theory of mind.* New York: Psychology Press.

Schneider, W., & Bjorklund, D. F. (1998). Memory. In W. Damon (Series Ed.), D. Kuhn & R. S. Siegler (Vol. Eds.), *Handbook of child psychology: Vol. 2. Cognition, perception, and language* (5th ed., pp. 467–521). New York: Wiley.

Scholl, B. J., & Leslie, A. M. (1999). Modularity, development, and "theory of mind." *Mind and Language, 14,* 131–153.

Schult, C. A. (2003). *Wanting this but planning that: Children's understanding of intentions and desires.* Unpublished manuscript, Indiana University, South Bend.

Shantz, C. U. (1983). Social cognition. In P. H. Mussen (Series Ed.), J. H. Flavell & E. M. Markman (Vol. Eds.), *Handbook of child psychology: Vol. 3.*

Cognitive development (4th ed., pp. 495–555). New York: Wiley.

Tardif, T., & Wellman, H. M. (2000). Acquisition of mental state language in Mandarin- and Cantonese-speaking children. *Developmental Psychology, 36*, 25–43.

Taylor, M., Esbensen, B. M., & Bennett, R. T. (1994). Children's understanding of knowledge acquisition: The tendency for children to report they have always known what they have just learned. *Child Development, 65*, 1581–1604.

Tomasello, M., Call, J., & Hare, B. (2003a). Chimpanzees understand psychological states—the question is which ones and to what extent. *Trends in Cognitive Sciences, 7*, 153–156.

Tomasello, M., Call, J., & Hare, B. (2003b). Chimpanzees versus humans: It's not that simple. *Trends in Cognitive Sciences, 7*, 239–240.

Tomasello, M., & Haberl, K. (2003). Understanding attention: 12- and 18-month-olds know what is new for other persons. *Developmental Psychology, 39*, 906–912.

Vinden, P. G., & Astington, J. W. (2000). Culture and understanding other minds. In S. Baron-Cohen, H. Tager-Flusberg, & D. J. Cohen (Eds.), *Understanding other minds: Perspectives from developmental cognitive neuroscience* (2nd ed., pp. 503–519). Oxford, England: Oxford University Press.

Watson, A. C., Nixon, C. L., Wilson, A., & Capage, L. (1999). Social interaction skills and theory of mind in young children. *Developmental Psychology, 35*, 386–391.

Wellman, H. M. (1985). The child's theory of mind: The development of conceptions of cognition. In S. R. Yussen (Ed.), *The growth of reflection in children* (pp. 169–206). San Diego: Academic Press.

Wellman, H. M. (1998). Culture, variation, and levels of analysis in our folk psychologies. *Psychological Bulletin, 123*, 33–36.

Wellman, H. M., Cross, D., & Watson, J. (2001). Meta-analysis of theory-of-mind development: The truth about false belief. *Child Development, 72*, 655–684.

Wellman, H. M., & Gelman, S. A. (1998). Knowledge acquisition in functional domains. In W. Damon (Series Ed.), D. Kuhn & R. S. Siegler (Vol. Eds.), *Handbook of Child Psychology: Vol. 2. Cognition, perception, and language* (5th ed., pp. 523–573). New York: Wiley.

Wellman, H. M., Harris, P. L., Banerjee, M., & Sinclair, A. (1995). Early understandings of emotion: Evidence from natural language. *Cognition and Emotion, 9*, 117–149.

Wellman, H. M., Hollander, M., & Schult, C. (1996). Young children's understanding of thought-bubbles and of thoughts. *Child Development, 67*, 768–788.

Wimmer, H., & Perner, J. (1983). Beliefs about beliefs: Representation and constraining function of wrong beliefs in young children's understanding of deception. *Cognition, 13*, 103–128.

Woodward, A. L., & Markman, E. M. (1998). Early word learning. In W.

Damon (Series Ed.), D. Kuhn & R. S. Siegler (Vol. Eds.), *Handbook of child psychology: Vol. 2. Cognition, perception, and language* (5th ed., pp. 371–420). New York: Wiley.

Woolley, J. D. (1995). The fictional mind: Young children's understanding of imagination, pretense, and dreams. *Developmental Review, 15,* 172–211.

Woolley, J. D., & Boerger, E. A. (2002). Development of beliefs about the origins and controllability of dreams. *Developmental Psychology, 38,* 24–41.

Yzerbyt, V. Y., Lories, G., & Dardenne, B. (Eds.). (1998). *Metacognition: Cognitive and social dimensions.* London: Sage.

4

Cognitive Development Includes Global and Domain-Specific Processes

Robert V. Kail

Many foundational issues in child development research were traditionally framed in "either-or" terms. Development was thought to reflect the impact of either nature or nurture; developmental change was said to be either continuous or discontinuous; and children were said to be either active explorers of their environment or passive recipients of the experiences associated with those environments. However, by the end of the 20th century each of these issues had been recast: no longer considered in terms of one position over another, they were discussed in terms of frameworks that included both influences (e.g., nature and nurture interactively influence development).

The field of cognitive development traditionally has had similar tension. Classic developmental theories tended to depict cognitive development in terms of transitions between stable, pervasive stages. Piaget's theory is illustrative: The four stages in his theory are stable in the sense that they characterize cognition over long periods of time. They are pervasive in describing cognition as it is manifested in a wide variety of tasks. Concrete operations, for example, were thought to span years and characterize children's performance on a wide range of cognitive tasks.

In contrast to the classic theories, modern theories have emphasized domain-specific or modular accounts of cognitive development. Language is the prototypic cognitive module. That children acquire language rapidly, easily, and with relatively little environmental support long ago suggested to theorists (e.g., Chomsky, 1957, 1988) that language is a modular cognitive system. That is, they said that language acquisition (particularly syntax) operates according to a unique set of principles not shared with other realms of cognitive development.

Theorists subsequently proposed a number of other perceptually and cognitively based modules, including, for example, modules for visual analysis of objects and space, for theory of mind, and for perception of faces (e.g., Kanwisher, 2000; Wellman & Gelman, 1998). They still much debate the exact properties that characterize these and other hypothesized modules, but a generic view would be that modules (1) represent well-canalized biological systems and, as such, require only modest amounts of experience for normal development; (2) have evolved over time to meet major challenges of early humans (e.g., to recognize conspecifics, to understand their intentions, and to communicate with them); and (3) are sensitive to very restricted categories of input and, consequently, respond to those inputs rapidly and automatically (without effort or intent).

These properties lead to several criteria that are used to identify modular or domain-specific development. Specifically, domain-specific development should follow a distinct developmental timetable that is reasonably stable across normally developing individuals and that ends in a relatively high level of skill in most individuals (to an extent that the absence of skill is considered a symptom of atypical development). Furthermore, localized brain damage is associated with selective loss of skill in mature individuals and selective impairment of skill acquisition in developing individuals. To illustrate, theory of mind develops rapidly in the preschool years (and impaired development is thought to be a symptom of autism; see, e.g., Baron-Cohen, 1995), and damage to the right medial prefrontal cortex is associated with impaired performance on theory-of-mind tasks (Shallice, 2001). In a similar manner evidence for a face perception module includes rapid development of face perception in infancy (Johnson, 2000) and selective loss of face recognition following damage to the fusiform gyrus (Kanwisher, 2000).

Devotees of domain-specific theories claim that this approach can account for many (if not all) key elements of cognitive development. Within this view pressing debates concern the number and nature of specific domains of cognitive development. However, an alternate view (Case & Okamato, 1996; Demetriou, Christou, Spanoudis, & Plasidou, 2002; Kail, 2003) holds that these domain-specific changes, although critical, are insufficient; instead, domain-specific elements and global elements (i.e., those that transcend individual tasks and domains) are necessary for a full account of cognitive development. That is, the domain-specific approaches that displaced broad structural theories of cognitive development are now being complemented by accounts that emphasize both global and domain-specific contributions to cognitive development.

In the remainder of this chapter I describe the factors leading to a renewed interest in global elements of cognitive development and briefly mention some specific theories that incorporate global and domain-specific elements.

Global Cognitive Processes in Cognitive Development

Global processes are those that contribute to cognitive development in several domains. The global processes that figure prominently in contemporary research include the speed with which children can execute basic cognitive processes (hereafter, processing speed); working memory; and executive functioning, which refers broadly to planning and goal-oriented behavior, self-regulation (including inhibitory processes), and cognitive flexibility.

Each of these constructs is thought to be a key component of the basic architecture of the developing cognitive system. Processing speed, for example, is analogous to the clock speed of a computer's central processing unit, which denotes the number of instructions that the processor can execute per second. Across a wide variety of perceptual and cognitive tasks that require a speeded response, processing speed increases systematically during childhood and adolescence, at a rate well described by an exponential function (Kail, 1991). Working memory is analogous to a computer's random-access memory, which stores data and instructions for use by the central processor. Working memory is typically measured by complex span tasks in which individuals remember information (e.g., words, digits) while they perform other cognitive tasks (e.g., reading text); like processing speed, working memory increases systematically during childhood and adolescence (Kail & Hall, 2001). The key elements in most accounts of executive functioning (Roberts & Pennington, 1996) are planning and inhibition; the analogy with computer architecture is less compelling in this instance, but the planning component of executive functioning is loosely analogous to the computer's operating system, which allocates resources (e.g., random-access memory, accessing the hard drive) during computer operation; similarly, executive functioning provides an organizational framework for cognitive task performance.

Thus processing speed, working memory, and executive functioning are considered crucial elements in the architecture of the developing mind. As such, they should contribute to performance on most behavioral and cognitive tasks, often in conjunction with domain-specific knowledge. In fact, a growing body of research documents the joint contributions of global and domain-specific processes to cognitive development.

One illustrative line of research concerns the factors that contribute to accuracy on arithmetic word problems. With age, children solve such problems more accurately, and this age-related improvement has frequently been attributed to acquisition of skills and knowledge that are specific to mathematics, including greater knowledge of the underlying arithmetic operations (Zentall, 1990) and greater skill in distinguishing the different types of word problems on the basis of the elements and operations that are associated with each (Morales, Shute, & Pellegrino, 1985). However, Kail and Hall (1999) argued that global skills may also contribute to the accuracy with which children solve such problems. Increased processing speed, for example, might allow more rapid retrieval of schemata for different types of problems. In addition, increased working memory might facilitate understanding of the problem (i.e., facilitating reading comprehension) and facilitate storage of problem facts during problem solving.

To evaluate global and domain-specific contributions to age-related change in word-problem performance, Kail and Hall (1999, Study 2) had 8- to 12-year-olds attempt to solve arithmetic word problems like the following: "Pete had 7 marbles. Then Sam gave him 5 more. How many marbles does Pete have now?" In addition, Kail and Hall measured children's knowledge of addition and subtraction, as well as processing speed and working memory. All measures were related positively to performance on word problems. More important, the critical multiple regression analyses showed (1) that arithmetic knowledge accounted for additional variance in word-problem performance beyond that associated with global cognitive skills (i.e., processing speed, working memory), and (2) that, in complementary fashion, global cognitive skills accounted for additional variance in word-problem performance beyond that associated with arithmetic knowledge. Similarly, Hecht, Close, and Santisi (2003) reported that both working memory (global) and children's conceptual understanding of fractions (domain-specific knowledge) accounted for unique variance in the accuracy with which fifth-grade students set up word problems that involved fractions. Thus both studies provide evidence that global cognitive processes and domain-specific knowledge contribute uniquely to the accuracy with which children solve arithmetic word problems.

This general pattern—with global and domain-specific measures accounting for unique variance in cognitive-developmental outcomes—is not restricted to arithmetic word problems. A sampling of findings testifies to the regularity of this result.

- Allen and Ondracek (1995) found that processing speed and children's skill in selecting good landmarks (i.e., locations that would help prevent them from getting lost) predicted the accuracy with which 5- to 9-year-olds ordered scenes from a walk through an unfamiliar neighborhood.

- Shatil and Share (2003) reported that reading-specific skills (e.g., visual-orthographic processing, phonological awareness) and global cognitive constructs (e.g., reasoning skill) predicted reading comprehension by first graders learning to read Hebrew.

- Carlson and Moses (2001) observed that 3- and 4-year-olds' scores on a battery of theory-of-mind tasks were predicted by both domain-specific knowledge (e.g., their understanding of the difference between appearance and reality) and their ability to inhibit irrelevant responses.

Collectively, then, these findings constitute "proof of concept": global and domain-specific components will figure prominently in any complete account of cognitive development. In the next section, I sketch some accounts that accommodate both components.

Linking Global and Domain-Specific Processes

A cognitive architecture specifies the elements of the cognitive system and the operating rules that govern those elements. Such an architecture is linked with domain-specific knowledge to create precise models of task performance. Several architectures have been proposed to explain adults' performance on a range of perceptual, cognitive, and memory tasks; Anderson's ACT-R (1993; Anderson & Lebiere, 1998) and Newell's SOAR (1990) are among the best known. However, these architectures have rarely been used by developmental psychologists (but see Jones, Ritter, & Wood, 2000, for a provocative exception). Instead, developmental psychologists have occasionally relied upon what could be called proto-architectures: a subset of components is specified, along with some minimal operating rules, typically in the context of trying to understand performance on a particular class of problems. Such proto-architectures suggest ways in which global and domain-specific processes could be integrated on a much broader scale; here I describe two such approaches.

NEO-PIAGETIAN THEORIES

Neo-Piagetian theories, which would include those proposed by Case (1992), Demetriou (e.g., Demetriou et al., 2002), Fischer (Fischer & Biddell, 1998), Halford (1993), and Pascual-Leone (1970), typically share Piaget's commitment to comprehensive theorizing that emphasizes qualitative change. But these theories differ from Piaget's original theory in providing a much more heterogeneous view of the mind, one in which knowledge is organized in distinct, broad conceptual structures, and in providing different mechanisms for growth.

Both features are evident in Case's theory (1992; Case & Okamoto, 1996), which has been one of the most influential of the neo-Piagetian theories. Regarding the heterogeneity of mind, Case identified three different conceptual domains—number, social cognition, and spatial relations—and suggested several other possibilities (e.g., self-understanding). Regarding mechanisms of growth, Case suggested that developmental change is driven by experiences that promote growth in the conceptual systems and by more efficient use of working memory as a result of automatic processing and brain maturation.

Case and Okamoto (1996) proposed that working memory establishes an upper limit on the complexity of cognitive processing at a given age. That is, they argued that the capacity of working memory increases in childhood and that elaboration of conceptual structures through childhood follows these increases in working memory. Numerical understanding, for example, is said to progress through four levels, beginning (at about age 4 years) with a state in which children do not quantify precisely and ending (at about age 10) in a state in which children can quantify along two dimensions simultaneously and relate those two domains precisely. With adequate experience (e.g., instruction in school) the modal outcome is for children at ages 4, 6, 8, and 10 to be functioning at levels 1, 2, 3, and 4, respectively. Insufficient experience might yield number knowledge that is less than expected at a given age, but enrichment is not expected to yield advanced knowledge because that is limited by the capacity of working memory.

Case's work (1992; Case & Okamoto, 1996) is invaluable in providing a general framework that both allows for the greater heterogeneity of mind that led developmental theorists to emphasize domain-specific change and encompasses the coordinated growth across domains that is often ignored in domain-specific accounts. But the theory has been criticized for its lack of explicit rules for assigning tasks to different levels and, in the process, establishing the working memory capacity required for successful performance (Siegler, 1996). Phrased differently, the usual method is to simply assert that a task reflects a certain level without testing that assertion formally. A related criticism is that the theory does not address the manner in which working memory contributes to performance in real time. Having asserted, for example, that a particular task requires two units of working memory, the theory does not specify how those units are used while solving the task.

This inability to link global and domain-specific processing in real time is a serious shortcoming of Case's work (1992; Case & Okamoto, 1996)—and of other neo-Piagetian theories as well (e.g., Demetriou et al., 2002). Consequently, the next framework illustrates such a linkage (although not one that involves working memory).

DISTRIBUTION OF ASSOCIATIONS MODEL

Siegler and Shrager (1984) originally proposed the distribution-of-associations model to address children's use of different strategies to solve simple arithmetic problems. To illustrate, when asked to add two numbers, children may simply retrieve the sum from long-term memory, count on their fingers, or use paper and pencil to compute a solution. Children's use of strategies on these problems does not progress in a stagelike manner in which children at a given age typically use one strategy exclusively or even primarily; an individual child is likely to draw on many of these strategies, sometimes solving the same problem with different strategies on successive presentations.

To account for this variability in children's choice of strategies, Siegler and Shrager (1984) proposed a distribution-of-associations model, in which children's arithmetic knowledge is represented as a network consisting of individual problems (e.g., 2 + 5) that are linked, with varying degrees of strength, to candidate answers. When children face an addition problem, they search the network; if the answer that the child retrieves is stronger than a previously established criterion, the child uses that answer; if not, the child resorts to other strategies to solve the problem. Thus this proto-architecture includes a long-term memory network that represents children's knowledge, along with procedures for accessing that knowledge, for evaluating the plausibility of retrieved answers and for determining alternative courses of action in the face of uncertainty.

This approach has been applied to different arithmetic operations and, more important, to a diverse set of domains that includes telling time, spelling, and memory (McGilly & Siegler, 1990; Rittle-Johnson & Siegler, 1999; Siegler & McGilly, 1989). And subsequent versions of the model—notably, the Adaptive Strategy Choice Model (Siegler & Shipley, 1995) and Strategy Choice and Discovery Simulation (Shrager & Siegler, 1998)—include methods for devising new strategies. (I emphasize the distribution-of-associations model here solely for its relative simplicity.) But the important point is that the model integrates global and domain-specific processes in real time. Being presented with a problem leads to a search of domain-relevant knowledge for a strategy (e.g., retrieval) that will generate an answer quickly and effortlessly; if that search fails, children turn to other strategies that generate answers more slowly and with greater effort.

Thus far this approach lacks the breadth of neo-Piagetian theories, which is to be expected inasmuch as it was originally envisioned to account solely for children's solution of simple arithmetic problems. But it has been expanded successfully to a range of different domains and in the process has shown one manner in which global processes (e.g., those dealing with retrieval of knowledge, evaluation of retrieved knowledge) interact with domain-specific knowledge. And it is easy to envision further elaboration of the model to include additional domains and additional global processes.

The 50 years of *Merrill-Palmer Quarterly* have seen the "either-or" characterization of cognitive development shift from Piaget's global characterization to the domain-specific characterizations that began to emerge in the 1980s. In this chapter I have presented evidence that emphasizes the need to consider the contribution of both global and domain-specific processes, and I have described models that show how these processes may be linked. These models are primarily illustrative; they need much elaboration to account for major features of cognitive development. But the critical step may be the growing realization that just as "nature versus nurture" and "active child versus passive child" have been abandoned by developmental theorists as simplistic and artificial dichotomies, so too are cognitive-developmental theorists abandoning global versus domain-specific views of cognitive development in favor of views that are both global and domain specific.

References

Allen, G. L., & Ondracek, P. J. (1995). Age-sensitive cognitive abilities related to children's acquisition of spatial knowledge. *Developmental Psychology, 31*, 934–945.

Anderson, J. R. (1993). *Rules of the mind.* Hillsdale, NJ: Erlbaum.

Anderson, J. R., & Lebiere, C. (1998). *The atomic components of thought.* Mahwah, NJ: Erlbaum.

Baron-Cohen, S. (1995). *Mindblindness: An essay on autism and theory of mind.* Cambridge, MA: MIT Press.

Carlson, S. M., & Moses, L. J. (2001). Individual differences in inhibitory control and children's theory of mind. *Child Development, 72*, 1032–1053.

Case, R. (1992). *The mind's staircase: Exploring the conceptual underpinnings of children's thought and knowledge.* Hillsdale, NJ: Erlbaum.

Case, R., & Okamoto, Y. (1996). The role of conceptual structures in the development of children's thought. *Monographs of the Society for Research in Child Development, 61* (Serial No. 246).

Chomsky, N. (1957). *Syntactic structures.* The Hague: Mouton.

Chomsky, N. (1988). *Language and problems of knowledge.* Cambridge, MA: MIT Press.

Demetriou, A., Christou, C., Spanoudis, G., & Platsidou, M. (2002). The development of mental processing: Efficiency, working memory, and thinking. *Monographs of the Society for Research in Child Development, 67* (Serial No. 268).

Fischer, K. W., & Biddell, T. R. (1998). Dynamic development of psychological structures in action and thought. In W. Damon (Series Ed.) & R. Lerner (Vol. Ed.), *Handbook of child psychology: Vol. 1. Theoretical models of human development* (5th ed., pp. 467–562). New York: Wiley.

Halford, G. S. (1993). *Children's understanding: The development of mental models.* Hillsdale, NJ: Erlbaum.

Hecht, S. A., Close, L., & Santisi, M. (2003). Sources of individual differences in fraction skills. *Journal of Experimental Child Psychology, 86*, 277–302.

Johnson, M. H. (2000). Cortical specialization in infants: Beyond the maturational model. *Brain and Cognition, 42*, 124–127.

Jones, G., Ritter, F. E., & Wood, D. J. (2000). Using a cognitive architecture to examine what develops. *Psychological Science, 11*, 93–100.

Kail, R. (1991). Developmental change in speed of processing during childhood and adolescence. *Psychological Bulletin, 109*, 490–501.

Kail, R. (2003). Information processing and memory. In M. H. Bornstein, L. Davidson, C. L. M. Keyes, K. A. Moore, & the Center for Child Well-

Being (Eds.), *Well-being: Positive development across the life course* (pp. 269–279). Mahwah, NJ: Erlbaum.

Kail, R., & Hall, L. K. (1999). Sources of developmental change in children's word problem performance. *Journal of Educational Psychology, 91,* 660–668.

Kail, R., & Hall, L. K. (2001). Distinguishing short-term memory from working memory. *Memory & Cognition, 29,* 1–9.

Kanwisher, N. (2000). Domain specificity in face perception. *Nature Neuroscience, 3,* 759–763.

McGilly, K., & Siegler, R. S. (1990). The influence of encoding and strategic knowledge on children's choice among serial recall strategies. *Developmental Psychology, 26,* 931–941.

Morales, R. V., Shute, V. J., & Pellegrino, J. W. (1985). Developmental differences in understanding and solving simple mathematics word problems. *Cognition and Instruction, 2,* 41–57.

Newell, A. (1990). *Unified theories of cognition.* Cambridge, MA: Harvard University Press.

Pascual-Leone, J. (1970). A mathematical model for the transition rule in Piaget's developmental stages. *Acta Psychologica, 32,* 301–345.

Rittle-Johnson, B., & Siegler, R. S. (1999). Learning to spell: Variability, choice, and change in children's strategy use. *Child Development, 70,* 332–348.

Roberts, R. J., & Pennington, B. F. (1996). An interactive framework for examining prefrontal cognitive processes. *Developmental Neuropsychology, 12,* 105–126.

Shallice, T. (2001). "Theory of mind" and the prefrontal cortex. *Brain, 124,* 247–248.

Shatil, E., & Share, D. L. (2003). Cognitive antecedents of early reading ability: A test of the modularity hypothesis. *Journal of Experimental Child Psychology, 86,* 1–31.

Shrager, J., & Siegler, R. S. (1998). SCADS: A model of children's strategy choices and strategy discoveries. *Psychological Science, 9,* 405–410.

Siegler, R. S. (1996). A grand theory of development. *Monographs of the Society for Research in Child Development, 61* (Serial No. 246), 266–275.

Siegler, R. S., & McGilly, K. (1989). Strategy choices in children's time-telling. In I. Levin & D. Zakay (Eds.), *Time and human cognition: A life-span perspective* (pp. 185–218). Amsterdam: Elsevier.

Siegler, R. S., & Shipley, C. (1995). Variation, selection, and cognitive change. In G. S. Halford & T. Simon (Eds.), *Developing cognitive competence: New approaches to process modeling* (pp. 31–76). Hillsdale, NJ: Erlbaum.

Siegler, R. S., & Shrager, J. (1984). Strategy choices in addition and subtraction: How do children know what to do? In C. Sophian (Ed.), *Origins of cognitive skills* (pp. 229–293). Hillsdale, NJ: Erlbaum.

Wellman, H. M., & Gelman, S. A. (1998). Knowledge acquisition in foundational domains. In W. Damon (Series Ed.) & R. Lerner (Vol. Ed.), *Hand-*

book of child psychology: Vol. 2. Cognition, perception, and language (5th ed., pp. 523–573). New York: Wiley.

Zentall, S. S. (1990). Fact-retrieval automatization and problem solving by learning disabled, attention-disordered, and normal adolescents. *Journal of Educational Psychology, 82,* 856–865.

5

Learning About Learning

Robert S. Siegler

The prominence of the area of learning within developmental psychology varied widely during the *Merrill-Palmer Quarterly*'s first 50 years. In the journal's first decades, the 1950s and 1960s, the area of children's learning occupied a central place within the field of child development. Consider the following observation from the chapter on children's learning in *Carmichael's Manual of Child Psychology* that covered the period 1954–1970: "The number and quality of studies on children's learning published each year have continued to increase. . . . By now there have been so many studies of children's learning that it is impossible to review them adequately in one chapter. . . . Because of the vast number of publications, no attempt is made to include all possibly relevant studies" (Stevenson, 1970, pp. 849, 851, 852).

Soon after Stevenson's observation, however, the study of children's learning drastically declined. When Stevenson reviewed developments in the field of children's learning between 1970 and 1983 in the next edition of the *Manual* (now called *The Handbook of Child Psychology*), his observation could hardly have been more different: "By the mid-1970s, articles on children's learning dwindled to a fraction of the number that had been published in the previous decade, and by 1980, it was necessary to search with diligence to uncover any articles at all" (1983, p. 213).

The reasons for this decline in the study of children's learning are well known and have been discussed elsewhere (e.g., Brown, Bransford, Ferrara, & Campione, 1983; Siegler, 2000). Simply put, the decline of the field, along with the learning theory approach on which it was based, reflected both the limitations of the approach and the emergence of attractive alternatives. The tasks emphasized by learning theory, often derived from tasks used with nonhuman animals, generally bore only an abstract resemblance to the types of tasks that children learn in their daily lives. The learning theory assumption that acquisition processes were basically the same, regardless of species, age, or knowledge, precluded from consideration issues near and dear to the hearts of many developmentalists, such as developmental, individual, and species differences in learning. The depiction of children as passive organisms, dependent on the environment to stamp in connections, also was unappealing to a wide range of developmentalists.

Thus, when the alternative of Piagetian theory was presented in a clear, appealing form in John Flavell's influential 1963 book, *The Developmental Psychology of Jean Piaget,* the ideas found a ready audience. Although Piagetian theory had been evolving since the 1920s, the lack of translation of many works; the absence of clear, brief, integrative summaries of the central tenets of the theory; the difficult and unfamiliar vocabulary; and the idiosyncratic methodology that Piaget adopted to study children limited its appeal. However, Flavell's compelling summary of the theory made clear its many intriguing aspects, as well as the many controversial claims that would stimulate a new generation of research.

The rise of Piaget's theory contributed to the temporary demise of the study of children's learning not only because it led cognitive developmentalists to focus on other problems but also because Piaget drew a strict distinction between development and learning that dignified the one and devalued the other. This is evident in Piaget's essay on the relation between learning and development: "The development of knowledge is a spontaneous process, tied to the whole process of embryogenesis. Learning presents the opposite case. In general, learning is provoked by situations—provoked by a psychological experimenter; or by a teacher, with respect to some didactic point; or by an external situation. It is provoked, in general, as opposed to spontaneous. In addition, it is a limited process—limited to a single problem, or to a single structure" (1964, p. 7).

A second major influence on the field of cognitive development in the 1970s and 1980s, information processing theories, also contributed to the shift away from the study of learning, albeit for a different reason. Information processing theory always has viewed learning as central to development, but the strategy adopted by information processing researchers was first to describe in detail the beginning and end states of development and only then to focus on how children progress from the one to the other (Klahr & Wallace, 1976). Not until relatively recently have significant numbers of re-

searchers who take an information processing approach to development begun to focus on learning (e.g., Munakata & McClelland,
2003).

Today the field of children's learning is undergoing a revival,
driven not only by information processing researchers but also by
those who take sociocultural (e.g., Gauvain, 2001), theory theory
(e.g., Amsterlaw & Wellman, 2006), dynamic systems (e.g., Smith,
Thelen, Titzer, & McLin, 1999), and neural approaches (e.g., Johnson,
1998). The eventual resurgence of the field was inevitable; learning
is such a central part of children's lives that minimizing attention to
it can lead only to an imbalanced perspective on development. Although the degree of focus on any given fundamental issue in a scientific area waxes and wanes, those fundamental issues that have
fallen into eclipse always return to prominence. The emergence of a
new field of children's learning is one such case.

The New Field of Children's Learning

The resurgence of the field of children's learning reflects both theoretical and methodological innovations. As has often been noted,
these two types of innovations generally have a mutually facilitative
influence. For example, the advent of dynamic systems theories as
an approach to motor development was in part prompted by the advent of increasingly sophisticated technologies for tracing the dynamics of physical movement (e.g., Zernicke & Schneider, 1993). The
precise data yielded by these methods has stimulated, in turn, further theoretical development in the area (cf. Bertenthal & Clifton,
1998).

Another example of this mutually facilitative relation between
theoretical and methodological progress, the one that I will emphasize throughout this chapter, is that between overlapping waves theory and microgenetic methods. Trial-by-trial assessments of children's problem-solving strategies, which themselves were made
possible by video recording technology, revealed far greater strategic variability than envisioned by Piagetian, information processing,
or other theories (e.g., Siegler, 1987). Overlapping waves theory is an
attempt to describe this strategic variability and to explain how and
why the mix of strategies changes with age and experience. The theory is based on the assumption that the evolution of children's
strategies, like the evolution of species, is based on processes of variability, choice, and change. In particular:

1. Assumptions regarding variability

    a. Children of a given age typically know and use a variety of strategies and conceptions, rather than just a single one, for solving a class of problems.

    b. Assumption (a) is true for individual children as well as for groups of children.

    c. Even on a single problem presented on several occasions close in time, an individual child often will use multiple strategies.

    d. The diverse strategies and conceptions coexist for prolonged periods, rather than the variability's being limited to special transition periods.

2. Assumptions regarding choice

    a. Children generally adjust their choices of strategies to problem characteristics, most often choosing the fastest strategy from among those they know are likely to yield accurate performance on the particular problem.

    b. Strategy choices are often quite adaptive from early in learning, but they tend to become more adaptive with experience.

3. Assumptions regarding change

    a. Learning occurs through at least four processes: acquisition of new strategies; increasing reliance on the most effective approaches within the set of strategies that are already known; superior choices among strategies; and increasingly fast, accurate, and effortless execution of strategies.

    b. Strategic change is usually a gradual process; discovery of a superior new strategy is often only the first step toward consistent use of the new approach.

In the sections that follow, I briefly examine evidence relevant to these assumptions regarding variability, choice, and change.

Variability

A major innovation of the new field of children's learning in general, and overlapping waves theory in particular, is their emphasis on cognitive variability. Assessing strategy use on a trial-by-trial basis has revealed use of multiple strategies on a wide range of tasks, including arithmetic (Geary & Brown, 1991), selective attention (Miller & Aloise-Young, 1996), language production (Marcus et al., 1992), serial recall (Coyle & Bjorklund, 1997), scientific experimentation (Schauble, 1996), and biological reasoning (Opfer & Siegler, 2004). On most of these tasks individual children have been found to use three or more approaches on different problems. This already is very different from the depiction within traditional theories, but the reality is even more different. The same child, presented with the same problem on two occasions close in time, often will use different strategies. In both preschoolers' addition (Siegler & Shrager, 1984) and elementary school children's time telling (Siegler & McGilly, 1989), one-third of children used a different strategy on the second presentation of a problem, within a week of the original presentation. The strategy changes were not in general attributable to learning; roughly 55% of shifts were from less advanced to more advanced strategies, but 45% were in the opposite direction.

Strategic variability is not unique to children. For example, Dowker, Flood, Griffiths, Harriss, and Hook (1996) examined estimation strategies on multidigit multiplication and division problems of four groups of adults: mathematicians, accountants, psychology students, and English students. The adults' strategies were remarkably diverse: for example, the 176 participants used 27 different strategies for solving the single problem, $4,645 \div 418$. Across the problem set, individuals in each of the four disciplines averaged more than five strategies apiece. In line with one of the most distinctive predictions of overlapping waves theory, strategic variability was evident within individual and problem. Thus, when the same problems were presented to participants a second time, mathematicians used a different strategy on 46% of items and psychology students on 37%.

As suggested by the findings of Dowker, Flood, Griffiths, Harriss, and Hook (1996), strategic variability is characteristic of cognition throughout life, rather than being restricted to special transition phases. Evidence for this statement has emerged from some surprising places. For example, despite single-digit arithmetic's being an extremely overlearned task, substantial strategic variability is present among 4- and 5-year-olds (e.g., Geary & Burlingham-Dubree, 1989), 9- and 10-year-olds (Goldman, Mertz, & Pellegrino, 1989), and 18- to 23-year-olds (LeFevre, Sadesky, & Bisanz, 1996). Senior citizens (65- to 85-year-olds) show similar strategic variability in multidigit arithmetic (Siegler & Lemaire, 1997). Most participants in these studies, regardless of age, used at least three strategies.

Recognizing the pervasiveness of such variability is important for understanding learning. At the level of individual differences, the amount of initial strategic variability tends to be predictive of subsequent learning. Subsequent learning has been found to corre-late with several measures of initial (pretest) variability: greater number of strategies, multiple strategies on a single problem, ges-ture-speech mismatches, and frequent self-corrections and deletions in self-reports of strategy use (e.g., Alibali & Goldin-Meadow, 1993; Perry & Lewis, 1999; Siegler, 1995).

Variable strategy use also plays an important role within the detailed theoretical accounts of learning provided by computer sim-ulations. For example, within Shrager and Siegler's 1998 SCADS (Strategy Choice and Discovery Simulation) model of addition, gen-eration of new strategies was heavily dependent on combining rel-evant parts of existing strategies. A similar logic generated new pro-ductions within Holland's 1986 genetic algorithm model. In such models the greater the variety of existing strategies, the greater the potential for combining relevant pieces into new, superior ap-proaches.

Not all kinds of variability are positively related to learning. For example, variability of strategy use between successive trials tends to be negatively related to correct recall (Coyle & Bjorklund, 1997). The likely reason is that learners apply the win-stay lose-shift heuristic; children change strategies more often following unsuc-cessful performance (McGilly & Siegler, 1989), which can lead to negative correlations between trial-to-trial strategy shifts and accu-racy. Similarly, strategies that are so flawed that they place the learner in a position that is not useful for exploring the task environ-ment seem unlikely to promote learning. Extremely variable golf swings, for example, may lead to less learning than moderately vari-able swings, because the extreme variability precludes interpretable feedback regarding effective procedures. Determining which types of variability are positively related to learning and which are not seems likely to result in improved understanding of how learning occurs.

Choice

Throughout life people choose strategies in adaptive ways. Such adaptive strategy choices both produce and are produced by learn-ing. The pattern is already evident in infancy. Adolph (1997) created a situation in which mothers of infants beckoned their baby to de-scend ramps of varying steepness to where their mother awaited them. A microgenetic design was used, in which babies returned to the laboratory and were presented with the slopes every three weeks. This allowed examination of the babies' descent strategies at a given age, after a given amount of experience with the mode of locomotion, and after a given number of sessions practicing the descent task.

Most babies altered their descent strategies to the slope of the ramp in highly adaptive ways. When the angle was reasonably shallow, they used their usual mode of locomotion (crawling or walking) to descend; as the slope became steeper, they became increasingly likely to adopt safer strategies, such as sliding down on their belly or behind. These choices allowed quick and safe descent when the infants' usual mode of locomotion would allow such an outcome, and slower but safe descent when it would not.

The adaptiveness of the babies' strategy choices increased with experience with the particular mode of locomotion. Thus, during the period in which crawling predominated, infants became ever more sensitive to which slopes they could descend safely and which required them to lower their center of gravity. However, when the infants began to walk, their choices became less adaptive than they had been when the infants were crawling; some infants became more cautious than necessary, whereas others took risks that would have been dangerous if adults had not been present to catch them. Experience with walking soon brought a return to highly adaptive strategy choices. Thus strategy choices became steadily more adaptive within a given mode of locomotion, but the process had to start anew when the infants switched their predominant locomotor modality.

Adolph's 1997 data illustrated how adaptive strategy choice both facilitates learning and reflects it. The infants' choices of locomotor strategies were fairly adaptive from the beginning; infants usually did not try to crawl or walk down the steepest slopes, and they consistently used their predominant mode of locomotion on flat surfaces and shallow slopes. However, as they gained experience using their predominant mode of locomotion, the babies' strategy choices became more precisely calibrated to the angles that they could traverse without falling. The relevant type of experience turned out not to be experience with the slopes themselves but rather general experience with crawling or walking. Evidence for this conclusion was provided by an age-matched control group that was presented with the descent task only three times: at the outset of the study, ten weeks after that, and when their parents reported that they had started walking. At all points their performance was comparable to that of control-group babies who received experience descending the slopes every three weeks. Moreover, changes in the adaptiveness of strategy choices were positively correlated with the duration of infants' everyday experience with crawling and walking.

Change

The overlapping waves model suggests at least four sources of strategic change: acquisition of new strategies, increasing use of relatively advanced strategies within the set that children use at any given time, increasingly adaptive choices among strategies, and increasingly effective execution of whichever strategies are used (Lemaire & Siegler, 1995).

First consider acquisition of new strategies. Even after children use strategies that yield consistently correct performance, they continue to invent new approaches. Children who can already solve addition problems by counting up from the number one discover that they can also solve the problems by counting up from the larger addend (Siegler & Jenkins, 1989); children who solve number conservation problems by counting discover that they can solve the same problems through logical reasoning (Siegler, 1981); adults who know numerous estimation procedures devise yet others (Dowker et al., 1996) and so on. Sometimes but not always, these new approaches allow more efficient solutions. In other cases people devise specialized strategies that are limited in their applicability across problems but yield fast and accurate performance on the subset of problems where they are applicable (e.g., appending two zeros to the other multiplicand when multiplying by 100). In yet other cases a new strategy can be either superior or inferior to existing ones, depending on when it is used; subtracting by counting up rather than counting down is one such case. Thus learning frequently reflects acquisition of new strategies.

Another source of cognitive change is increasing reliance on the more sophisticated strategies from among those that children already use. Even after children discover new strategies and can explain why the new strategies are superior to their previous ones, they still often use the older, inferior approaches. For example, even after toddlers learned which type of tool would be most effective for pulling in a desirable toy, they still often reverted to less effective approaches, such as reaching or using ineffective tools (Chen & Siegler, 2000). Similarly, although 6-year-olds recognize the superiority of systematic experimentation strategies to unsystematic ones (Sodian, Zaitchik, & Carey, 1991), and although 10-year-olds sometimes generate systematic experiments, even adults often generate unsystematic ones (Schauble, 1996). Much learning involves not replacement of inferior approaches by superior ones but, instead, slowly increasing reliance on the superior approaches.

A third source of cognitive change is increasingly adaptive choices among strategies. Even if the frequency of use of each strategy remains constant, learning can occur in the precision with which strategies are fitted to problem characteristics. For example, a study involving French second graders who were learning single-digit multiplication indicated that their strategy choices were fairly adaptive within 10 days of their initial instruction in the skill. However, subsequent examination of the same children indicated that the precision of their strategy choices was greater 2 months later and that it was still greater 2 months after that (Lemaire & Siegler, 1995). To be specific, problem difficulty (defined in terms of mean solution time for the problem) became increasingly correlated with how often children used strategies other than retrieval on the problem, such as adding one of the multiplicands the number of times indicated by the other. The correlation increased from $r = .50$ to $r = .75$ to $r = .80$ over the three occasions.

The fourth source of cognitive change is the efficiency with which strategies are executed. Even if children continue to use identical strategies on identical problems, learning can still occur in the speed and accuracy with which they execute the strategies. This is another omnipresent source of learning. For example, Chen and Siegler (2000) found that, in attempting to solve two tool-use problems, 18- to 26-month-olds increased their success rate from 57% to 76% in one condition and 75% to 91% in the other by choosing the optimal tool for pulling in a toy. Similarly, the speed with which the toddlers obtained the toy increased both on successive trials within the same problem and across different problems. Newell and Rosenbloom's 1981 review of the literature on the practice law of learning documents the pervasiveness of such improvements in efficiency of strategy execution.

Learning and Development

Unlike learning theory approaches, the overlapping waves model and other approaches to the new field of children's learning have highlighted questions of traditional concern to developmentalists—

for example, developmental differences in learning. One approach to this issue has been to compare microgenetic and age-related change. There is widespread agreement that there is some resemblance between the relatively rapid changes that emerge in microgenetic studies and the more slowly emerging changes that are documented in cross-sectional and longitudinal designs (e.g., Fischer & Biddell, 1998; Granott, 1998; Miller & Coyle, 1999). However, the degree of the resemblance remains a matter of dispute. This issue led Miller and Coyle to conclude, "Although the microgenetic method reveals how behavior *can* change, it is less clear whether behavior typically *does* change in this way in the natural environment" (p. 212; italics in original).

To address this issue Siegler and Svetina (2002) combined microgenetic and cross-sectional components within the same design in a study of matrix completion. They chose this task because it is prominent within Piagetian, information processing, and psychometric traditions alike and because it assesses inductive reasoning capabilities relatively directly. At the outset of the study Slovenian 6-, 7-, and 8-year-olds were presented with the standard matrix completion task to provide a cross-sectional perspective on development. Then, half the 6-year-olds (those in the experimental group) participated in five more sessions, with 22 matrix-completion problems per session, within a 3-week period. On each problem the children in this group received feedback about whether their choice, from among six alternative answers, was correct; then the children were told the correct answer and were asked to explain why that answer was correct. Seven weeks later the 6-year-olds in this experimental group and their age peers in the control group, who had not participated since the first session, were presented with matrix-completion problems in a final session without feedback.

Children in the experimental group improved their percentage of correct answers from pretest to posttest significantly greater than did their peers in the control group. The overall amount of change from the first through the seventh session in the experimental condition was virtually identical to the amount of change between ages 6 and 7 years in the cross-sectional part of the study. Therefore the detailed patterning of microgenetic change was compared with the patterning of cross-sectional change over this one-year period.

The patterning of changes—and nonchanges—proved to be closely comparable. The two groups matched on 10 of the 11 indexes of change that the researchers examined; significant change occurred over both the seven sessions and the one-year period on five indexes of change, and no significant change occurred over sessions on five other indexes. The specificity of the matches was often quite impressive. For example, significant changes over both sessions and years were present in the number of answers that were correct on the size dimension, but no changes occurred over sessions or years in number of explanations that mentioned size. Similarly, the predominant type of error was the same in the experimental group in all seven sessions and in the cross-sectional part of the study at both ages 6 and 7 years.

The microgenetic portion of the study also yielded data that could not have been obtained within any traditional cross-sectional or longitudinal design. For example, results from the experimental condition indicated that rejecting existing approaches and generating superior new approaches were separate processes. Children in the experimental condition shifted away from their predominant error on about a dozen trials before they discovered how to solve the problems correctly. In the interim they generated a variety of incorrect approaches as well as occasional correct answers (as they had previously).

Similar temporal separations between rejecting previous predominant approaches and inventing superior alternatives have emerged in other microgenetic studies of learning, including studies of learning about balance scales, number conservation, and mathematical equivalence (Alibali, 1999; Siegler, 1995; Siegler & Chen, 1998). Whether a similar separation between rejecting predominant earlier approaches and generating superior new approaches also is present when development occurs under more typical conditions remains an open question. However, as the example illustrates, the new field of children's learning is raising crucial issues, and producing relevant data, concerning how children learn.

Predictions

The resurgence of the field of children's learning is likely to continue; in fact, the prominence of the area seems likely to increase further. The inherent importance of learning within children's lives, the development of methodological tools such as microgenetic methods for capturing both quantitative and qualitative aspects of learning, and the advent of theories that emphasize learning all militate in this direction.

One direction that this expansion may take is increasing integration of microgenetic and computer simulation approaches to learning. The two methods have a natural fit. Computer simulations of learning often generate highly specific predictions that can be tested only through the type of high-density observations of learning that microgenetic studies yield. Conversely, microgenetic data are especially helpful for shaping and refining computer simulations of learning, because they provide detailed constraints on the output that such models must produce.

A good example of both advantages is provided by the interplay of computer simulations and microgenetic research regarding preschoolers' discovery of the counting-on strategy in basic addition. The counting-on strategy involves starting at the larger addend and counting upward the number of times indicated by the smaller addend; thus on both 2 + 5 and 5 + 2, a child who used the counting-on strategy would say, "Five, six, seven" or "Six, seven." Cross-sectional studies (e.g., Groen & Parkman, 1972) had shown that in the early elementary school years, children often use the counting-on strategy, although younger children often count from one and older children often retrieve answers to such problems. Based on such findings, Neches (1987) built a computer simulation model of the discovery of the counting-on strategy. The model started by counting from one, then discovered the strategy of counting from the first addend, and then discovered the counting-on approach. This model was consistent with the limited data on learning that the cross-sectional studies had yielded.

However, a microgenetic study that examined preschoolers' addition on a trial-by-trial basis (Siegler & Jenkins, 1989) demonstrated that the Neches 1987 model needed to be reformulated. One reason was that not one child in the study counted from the first addend before using the counting-on strategy, and few children ever used the approach on trials where the first addend was smaller than the second (the only trials that discriminate between the two approaches). Thus counting from the first addend was not transitional to the counting-on strategy. On the other hand, the microgenetic data did indicate that children used a transitional strategy between counting from one and counting-on, but the transitional approach involved a shortcut version of counting from one (the shortcut sum strategy; see Siegler and Jenkins, 1989, for details).

This and other aspects of the microgenetic data from Siegler and Jenkins (1989) provided a large number of useful constraints for generating a new computer simulation model of acquisition of the counting-on strategy. The new model (Shrager & Siegler, 1998) discovered the transitional strategy that children in the microgenetic study used; took about the same number of trials as children did to discover the transitional and counting-on strategies; generalized use of the counting-on strategy to new problems at a slow rate similar to children's; responded to challenging problems in the same way as children (by increasing use of the new strategy); and showed solution time, accuracy, and error pattern data much like those of children in the microgenetic study as well.

The multiple aspects of learning revealed by the microgenetic method provided useful guidance for constructing the simulation model, because it greatly reduced the range of models that could meet all the behavioral constraints. At the same time the simulation model yielded further predictions for empirical testing. This symbiotic relation between microgenetic and computer simulation methods seems likely to promote increased joint use of the two approaches in the future.

References

Adolph, K. E. (1997). Learning in the development of infant locomotion. *Monographs of the Society for Research in Child Development, 62* (3, Serial No. 251).

Alibali, M. W. (1999). How children change their minds: Strategy change can be gradual or abrupt. *Developmental Psychology, 35,* 127–145.

Alibali, M. W., & Goldin-Meadow, S. (1993). Gesture-speech mismatch and mechanisms of learning: What the hands reveal about a child's state of mind. *Cognitive Psychology, 25,* 468–523.

Amsterlaw, J., & Wellman, H. M. (2006). Theories of mind in transition: A microgenetic study of the development of false belief understanding. *Journal of Cognition and Development, 7,* 139–172.

Bertenthal, B. I., & Clifton, R. K. (1998). Perception and action. In W. Damon (Series Ed.), D. Kuhn & R. S. Siegler (Vol. Eds.), *Handbook of child psychology: Vol. 2. Cognition, perception, and language* (5th ed., pp. 51–102). New York: Wiley.

Brown, A. L., Bransford, J. D., Ferrara, R. A., & Campione, J. C. (1983). Learning, remembering, and understanding. In P. H. Mussen (Series Ed.), J. H. Flavell & E. M. Markman (Vol. Eds.), *Handbook of child psychology: Vol. 3. Cognitive development* (4th ed., pp. 77–166). New York: Wiley.

Chen, Z., & Siegler, R. S. (2000). Across the great divide: Bridging the gap between understanding of toddlers' and older children's thinking. *Monographs of the Society for Research in Child Development, 65* (2, Whole No. 261).

Coyle, T. R., & Bjorklund, D. F. (1997). Age differences in, and consequences of, multiple- and variable-strategy use on a multiple sort-recall task.

Developmental Psychology, 33, 372–380.

Dowker, A., Flood, A., Griffiths, H., Harriss, L., & Hook, L. (1996). Estimation strategies of four groups. *Mathematical Cognition, 2,* 113–135.

Fischer, K. W., & Biddell, T. R. (1998). Dynamic development of psychological structures in action and thought. In W. Damon (Series Ed.) & R. Lerner (Vol. Ed.), *Handbook of child psychology: Vol. 1. Theoretical models of human development* (5th ed., pp. 467–562). New York: Wiley.

Flavell, J. (1963). *The developmental psychology of Jean Piaget.* Princeton, NJ: Van Nostrand.

Gauvain, M. (2001). *The social context of cognitive development.* New York: Guilford.

Geary, D. C., & Brown, S. C. (1991). Cognitive addition: Strategy choice and speed-of-processing differences in gifted, normal, and mathematically disabled children. *Developmental Psychology, 27,* 398–406.

Geary, D. C., & Burlingham-Dubree, M. (1989). External validation of the strategy choice model for addition. *Journal of Experimental Child Psychology, 47,* 175–192.

Goldman, S. R., Mertz, D. L., & Pellegrino, J. W. (1989). Individual differences in extended practice functions and solution strategies for basic addition facts. *Journal of Educational Psychology, 81,* 481–496.

Granott, N. (1998). A paradigm shift in the study of development: Essay review of *Emerging Minds* by R. S. Siegler. *Human Development, 41,* 360–365.

Groen, G. J., & Parkman, J. M. (1972). A chronometric analysis of simple addition. *Psychological Review, 79,* 329–343.

Holland, J. H. (1986). Escaping brittleness: The possibilities of general purpose machine learning algorithms applied to parallel rule-based systems. In R. S. Michalski, J. G. Carbonell, & T. M. Mitchell (Eds.), *Machine learning: An artificial intelligence approach* (pp. 593–624). Los Altos, CA: Kaufmann.

Johnson, M. H. (1998). The neural basis of cognitive development. In W. Damon (Series Ed.), D. Kuhn & R. S. Siegler (Vol. Eds.), *Handbook of child psychology: Vol. 2. Cognition, perception, and language* (5th ed., pp. 1–50). New York: Wiley.

Klahr, D., & Wallace, J. G. (1976). *Cognitive development: An information processing view.* Hillsdale, NJ: Erlbaum.

Lefevre, J. A., Sadesky, G. S., & Bisanz, J. (1996). Selection of procedures in mental addition: Reassessing the problem-size effect in adults. *Journal of Experimental Psychology: Learning, Memory, and Cognition, 22,* 216–230.

Lemaire, P., & Siegler, R. S. (1995). Four aspects of strategic change: Contributions to children's learning of multiplication. *Journal of Experimental Psychology: General, 124,* 83–97.

Marcus, G. F., Pinker, S., Ullman, M., Hollander, M., Rosen, T. J., & Xu, F. (1992). Over-regularization in language acquisition. *Monographs of the Society for Research in Child Development, 57* (4, Serial No. 228).

McGilly, K., & Siegler, R. S. (1989). How children choose among serial recall strategies. *Child Development, 60,* 172–182.

Miller, P. H., & Aloise-Young, P. (1996). Preschoolers' strategic behaviors and performance on a same-different task. *Journal of Experimental Psychology, 60,* 284–303.

Miller, P. H., & Coyle, T. R. (1999). Developmental change: Lessons from microgenesis. In E. K. Scholnick, K. Nelson, S. A. Gelman, & P. H. Miller (Eds.), *Conceptual development: Piaget's legacy* (pp. 209–239). Mahwah, NJ: Erlbaum.

Munakata, Y., & McClelland, J. L. (2003). Connectionist models of development. *Developmental Science, 6,* 413–429.

Neches, R. (1987) Learning through incremental refinement of procedures. In D. Klahr, P. Langley, & R. Neches (Eds.), *Production system models of learning and development* (pp. 163–219). Cambridge, MA: MIT Press.

Newell, A., & Rosenbloom, P. S. (1981). Mechanisms of skill acquisition and the law of practice. In J. R. Anderson (Ed.), *Cognitive skills and their acquisition.* Hillsdale, NJ: Erlbaum.

Opfer, J. E., & Siegler, R. S. (2004). Revisiting preschoolers' living things concept: A microgenetic analysis of conceptual change in basic biology. *Cognitive Psychology, 49,* 301–332.

Perry, M., & Lewis, J. L. (1999). Verbal imprecision as an index of knowledge in transition. *Developmental Psychology, 25,* 749–759.

Piaget, J. (1964). Development and learning. In T. Ripple & V. Rockcastle (Eds.), *Piaget rediscovered* (pp. 7–19). Ithaca, NY: Cornell University Press.

Schauble, L. (1996). The development of scientific reasoning in knowledge-rich contexts. *Developmental Psychology, 32,* 102–119.

Shrager, J., & Siegler, R. S. (1998). SCADS: A model of children's strategy choices and strategy discoveries. *Psychological Science, 9,* 405–410.

Siegler, R. S. (1981). Developmental sequences within and between concepts. *Society for Research in Child Development Monographs, 46* (Whole no. 189).

Siegler, R. S. (1987). The perils of averaging data over strategies: An example from children's addition. *Journal of Experimental Psychology: General, 116,* 250–264.

Siegler, R. S. (1995). How does change occur: A microgenetic study of number conservation. *Cognitive Psychology, 25,* 225–273.

Siegler, R. S. (2000). The rebirth of children's learning. *Child Development, 71,* 26–35.

Siegler, R. S., & Chen, Z. (1998). Developmental differences in rule learning: A microgenetic analysis. *Cognitive Psychology, 36,* 273–310.

Siegler, R. S., & Jenkins, E. A. (1989). *How children discover new strategies.* Hillsdale, NJ: Erlbaum.

Siegler, R. S., & Lemaire, P. (1997). Older and younger adults' strategy choices in multiplication: Testing predictions of ASCM via the choice/no-choice method. *Journal of Experimental Psychology: General, 126,* 71–92.

Siegler, R. S., & McGilly, K. (1989). Strategy choices in children's time-telling. In I. Levin & D. Zakay (Eds.), *Time and human cognition: A life-span perspective* (pp. 185–218). Amsterdam: Elsevier Science.

Siegler, R. S., & Shrager, J. (1984). Strategy choices in addition and subtraction: How do children know what to do? In C. Sophian (Ed.), *Origins of cognitive skills* (pp. 229–293). Hillsdale, NJ: Erlbaum.

Siegler, R. S., & Svetina, M. (2002). A microgenetic/cross-sectional study of matrix completion: Comparing short-term and long-term change. *Child Development, 73,* 793–809.

Smith, L. B., Thelen, E., Titzer, R., & McLin, D. (1999). Knowing in the context of acting: The task dynamics of the A-not-B error. *Psychological Review, 106,* 235–260.

Sodian, B., Zaitchik, D., & Carey, S. (1991). Young children's differentiation of hypothetical beliefs from evidence. *Child Development, 62,* 753–766.

Stevenson, H. W. (1970). Learning in children. In P. H. Mussen (Ed.), *Carmichael's manual of child psychology* (3rd ed., Vol. 1, pp. 849–938). New York: Wiley.

Stevenson, H. W. (1983). How children learn: The quest for a theory. In P. H. Mussen (Series Ed.) & W. Kessen (Vol. Ed.), *Handbook of child psychology: Vol. 1. History, theory, and methods* (4th ed., pp. 213–236). New York: Wiley.

Zernicke, R. F., & Schneider, K. (1993). Biomechanics and developmental neuromotor control. *Child Development, 64,* 982–1004.

6

Temperament and the Pursuit of an Integrated Developmental Psychology

Mary K. Rothbart

Historical Trends and Perspectives

When I began work in psychology in the late 1950s, social learning approaches dominated the field of developmental psychology. Individual differences were most often explained in terms of the child's history of rewards and punishments, and little was said about the initial state of individual differences in infants or about influences other than social learning on developmental change. In the 1960s cognitive development views became dominant. These approaches were based on a developmental theory but one limited to cognition and language. They stressed how the developing child represents objects, events, and people but often neglected the child's emotion, motivation, and even behavior.

Once the cognitive development area gained popularity, training and research in developmental psychology split into the two main areas of cognitive/language development and social-emotional development, sometimes coming together in social cognition. Working in the relative shadows were other contributors to an understanding of child development: psychobiology, emotional development, temperament-personality and individual differences, and motivation. This fragmentation in the field served to limit the scope of our thinking. In retrospect it may have been preferable to continue to offer general training in developmental psychology, with specializations organized around research questions rather than area boundaries.

More recently, we have seen renewed interest in the emotions and emotional development. The study of temperament and personality development has also experienced a renaissance, although frequently the dimensions of temperament studied have not differed from those put forward by Thomas and Chess (1977) in the New

York Longitudinal Study. More recent data have nevertheless suggested that changes in the original list are appropriate (Rothbart & Bates, 1998, 2006), and I will discuss a revised list later in this chapter. Since the mid-1980s neuroscience approaches to human brain imaging and the mapping of the human genome have also provided increased opportunities for studying the psychobiology of development and individual differences.

Throughout the period of emphasis on cognitive development, *Merrill-Palmer Quarterly* continued to publish papers in social-emotional areas and to emphasize developmental processes. In 1984 my colleagues and I published a paper in the journal on the development of inhibitory control that was not of immediate interest to the mainstream, in part because it did not fit neatly into cognitive or social development categories (Reed, Pien, & Rothbart, 1984). Interest in the topic of inhibitory and effortful control took decades to grow. Recent interest in brain development has now given topics like this a credibility they did not previously possess.

Temperament: An Integrative Construct

The area that my colleagues and I investigate, temperament, gives an example of an integration of social, cognitive, and personality development (Posner & Rothbart, in press). The study of temperament, which is defined as individual differences in constitutionally based reactivity and self-regulation (Rothbart & Derryberry, 1981), allows us to consider both the initial state of individual differences and the early development of emotional and attentional systems basic to development. *Reactivity* refers to individual differences in motor arousability, emotionality, and orienting. *Self-regulation* refers to processes that moderate this reactivity. Tendencies toward approach, avoidance (or behavioral inhibition), and temperamental effortful control all serve this function.

Temperament refers to behavioral tendencies and attentional capacities that form the early core of individual differences in personality. Beyond temperament, *personality* also refers to the content of cognitions and attitudes concerning the self, others, and the physical world, as well as general attitudes, goals, and values. Personality characteristics will be further shaped by experience, reward, and punishment, and temperament will be linked to the relative degree of influence of rewards and punishments (Gray, 1987; Rothbart, Ahadi, & Hershey, 1994). Because the mood and conduct disorders are closely linked to negative affect and attentional control, these temperament dimensions provide obvious connections to the development of psychopathology (Murray & Kochanska, 2002; Rothbart & Posner, 2006; Posner & Rothbart, 2007, in press).

Finally, because of connections between the temperament dimensions and affective and cognitive neuroscience, it has been possible to study links between behavior, experience, and brain functioning (e.g., Caspi et al., 2002; Schwartz, Wright, Shin, Kagan, & Rauch, 2003). Temperament has also been linked to later personality (McCrae et al., 2000; Rothbart, Ahadi, & Evans, 2000) and to the development of conscience, empathy, and other prosocial behaviors.

Recent Breakthroughs in the Study of Temperament

IDENTIFYING BASIC TEMPERAMENT DIMENSIONS

A major breakthrough in the study of temperament has been refinement of our understanding of basic dimensions of temperament. Thomas and Chess (1977) and their colleagues defined temperament as behavioral style, the "how" rather than the "what" or "why" of behavior, including such dimensions as intensity, threshold, and rhythmicity. In factor analytic research, however, dimensions of intensity, threshold, and rhythmicity have not proved to be substantial or reliable (Rothbart & Mauro, 1990). Instead, reactivity of quite specific emotional, motor, and attentional systems appeared to represent the structure of early individual differences, along with attentional characteristics (Rothbart & Bates, 1998, 2006). Thomas and Chess (1977) had also proposed several bipolar dimensions of temperament, such as approach versus withdrawal and positive versus negative mood, and this structure has also not received support. Instead, approach is separable from withdrawal and related to positive mood, whereas withdrawal is related to fear and negative affect (Rothbart & Mauro, 1990).

A hierarchical structure to temperament has also been identified, with evidence in childhood for broad factors of extraversion/surgency, including positive anticipation, impulsivity, activity level, and sensation seeking; negative affectivity, including fear, frustration, sadness, and discomfort; and effortful control, including attentional focusing and shifting, inhibitory control, perceptual sensitivity, and low-intensity pleasure (Rothbart, Ahadi, Hershey, & Fisher, 2001). Broad factors in childhood have been further related to the Big Five and Five Factor Model personality trait factors (Halverson, Kohnstamm, & Martin, 1994; McCrae et al., 2000; Rothbart, 1989; Rothbart, Ahadi, & Evans, 2000).

These findings are important to developmental psychology, because although temperament researchers set out to discover the basic dimensions of temperament, in so doing they identified basic processes of social, personality, and cognitive development. These include the emotions and related motivation systems, motor activity, and attention. While we all share the psychological processes on which temperament dimensions are based, individuals differ in their reactivity on each dimension and on the broad reactive factors, as measured by latency to reaction, overall and peak intensity of reaction, and recovery time of reaction (Rothbart & Derryberry, 1981), as well as in their effortful capacities to moderate those reactions.

The reactive dimensions identified also bear important similarities to those found in nonhuman animals (Panksepp, 1998). Temperament dimensions appear to be evolutionarily conserved systems, so animal studies can link temperamental dispositions and capacities to both underlying neural architecture and the effects of experience. It is important to recognize that, as evolutionarily prepared systems, temperament processes are open systems: experience influences their development.

THE STUDY OF EFFORTFUL CONTROL

A second major breakthrough in the area of temperament is the identification of the construct of effortful control. Effortful control, defined as the ability to withhold a dominant response in order to perform a nondominant response, to detect errors, and to engage in planning, involves the voluntary deployment of executive attention, allowing children to come to regulate their more reactive tendencies (Kochanska, Murray, & Harlan, 2000; Rothbart, 1989; Rothbart & Bates, 1998). Individual differences in attention influence children's capacity to suppress their more reactive tendencies, to stop and take in additional sources of information, to activate responses that will not receive immediate reward, and to plan and execute efficient strategies for coping.

In two large longitudinal studies involving children from 9 to 45 months of age, Kochanska and her colleagues assessed five effortful control skills involving the capacity to suppress a dominant response in order to perform a subdominant response (Kochanska, Murray, & Coy, 1997; Kochanska, Murray, & Harlan, 2000; Kochanska, Murray, Jacques, Koenig, & Vandegeest, 1996). These included delay (e.g., waiting for candy displayed under a transparent cup), slowing down motor movement (drawing a line slowly), suppressing and initiating responses to changing signals (go/no-go games), effortful attention (recognizing small shapes hidden within a dominant large shape), and lowering the voice. Batteries of tests were designed for developmental periods ranging from 22 to 66 months. Beginning at 30 months, children's performance was found to be highly consistent across tasks, indicating that all the batteries appeared to measure a common underlying quality that had developed over time. Children were also remarkably stable on their effortful control scores over time (Kochanska, Murray, & Harlan, 2000). Kochanska and Knaack (2003) further followed up on this longitudinal sample, reporting that "by 45 months, effortful control became a highly coherent and highly stable personality characteristic" (p. 1099). Early effortful control also predicted fewer behavior problems at 73 months.

Six- to seven-year-olds high in effortful control have also been found to be high in empathy and guilt/shame and low in aggressiveness (Rothbart, Ahadi, & Hershey, 1994). In addition, Eisenberg and her colleagues have found that 4- to 6-year-old boys with good attentional control tend to deal with anger by using nonhostile verbal methods rather than overtly aggressive methods (Eisenberg, Fabes, Nyman, Bernzweig, & Pinulas, 1994). Effortful control may support empathy by allowing attention to the thoughts and feelings of another person without becoming overwhelmed by one's own reactive distress. Similarly, effortful control may contribute to feelings of guilt by allowing the child to notice negative feelings in others and to relate them to feelings of responsibility for one's own actions and their negative consequences for another (Derryberry & Reed, 1994, 1996).

As might be expected from these findings, effortful control is also important in the development of conscience. The internalization of moral principles is related to fear in preschoolage children, especially when their mothers use gentle discipline (Kochanska 1991, 1995, 1997). In addition, internalized control is greater in children who are high in effortful control (Kochanska et al., 1996, 1997, 2000; Kochanska & Knaack, 2003). There appear to be two separable control systems regulating the development of conscience. Although fear may provide reactive inhibition and the negative affect that can be associated with moral principles and guilt feelings, effortful control provides the attentional flexibility to link negative affect, action, and moral principles. In addition, effortful control allows the application of moral injunctions and other rules without the necessity for intervening affect.

Low effortful control has been linked to maladaptive outcomes as well, including externalizing and antisocial behavior, drug use, and aggression (Rothbart & Bates, 1998, 2006). Valiente and colleagues (2003), for example, have found that effortful control at age 7 predicted low externalizing problems at age 11, with the strongest effects for children high in negative emotion.

Individual differences in effortful control are also related to aspects of metacognitive knowledge, such as theory of mind, that is, knowing that people's behavior is guided by their beliefs, desires, and other mental states (Carlson & Moses, 2001). Tasks requiring inhibition of prepotent responses are positively correlated with performance on theory-of-mind tasks, even when other factors—such as age, intelligence, and working memory—are factored out (Carlson & Moses, 2001). Inhibitory control and theory of mind also share a similar developmental time course, with advances in both areas between the ages of 2 and 5.

Why is effortful control of such basic importance to thinking about temperament and development? Early theoretical models of temperament stressed the way we are moved by our positive and negative emotions or level of arousal, with our actions driven by these tendencies. Using effortful control, however, we can more flexibly approach the situations we fear, inhibit the actions we desire, and activate the activities we would prefer not to engage in. The efficiency of control will nevertheless depend on the strength of the emotional processes against which effort is exerted.

Advances from Neuroscience

Two breakthroughs in neuroscience are making major contributions to our understanding of temperament and development. The first of these is the ability to image the functioning human brain, and the second is the mapping of the human genome. Imaging studies have provided exciting developmental data. For example, in comparison with adults who had been uninhibited as children, adults who had been inhibited as young children showed greater fMRI activation in the amygdala to novel faces than to familiar faces (Schwartz et al., 2003).

Model tasks related to brain imaging have also been used to assess the executive attention capacities likely to underlie effortful control (Posner & Rothbart, 1998). When a task activates a given brain region or network in adults, we can adapt it to children. It is then possible to trace the development of function in the brain areas through children's performances on the marker tasks. A basic measure of executive attention, the Stroop task, requires subjects to report the color of ink that a word is written in, when the color word (e.g., blue) conflicts with the color of ink (e.g., red). We know from adult brain imaging studies that Stroop tasks activate a midline brain structure, the anterior cingulate cortex, that is also associated with other executive attention activities. In a meta-analysis of imaging studies an area of the anterior cingulate was found to be activated in cognitive conflict tasks using variants of the Stroop task (Bush, Luu, & Posner, 2000). An adjacent area of the anterior cingulate was activated by emotional tasks and emotional states. When the effortful control area was activated, the emotion area tended to be deactivated, and vice versa, suggesting the possibility of reciprocal effortful and emotional controls on attention.

The spatial conflict task was thus developed as a measure of executive attention in young children who cannot read and perform the classic Stroop task (Gerardi-Caulton, 2000; Posner & Rothbart, 1998; Rothbart, Ellis, Rueda, & Posner, 2003). In the spatial conflict task the child must respond to a spatially conflicting stimulus by inhibiting a dominant response and executing a subdominant response. Imaging studies of adults performing this task found it activated the same frontal network as the Stroop and other conflict tasks (Fan, Flombaum, McCandliss, Thomas, & Posner, 2003). Performance on the task improves considerably between 27 and 36 months, with older children showing less perseveration of the previous response. Children who performed well on the task were also described by their parents as more skilled at effortful control subscales of attentional shifting and focusing, lower in impulsivity, and lower in proneness to frustration. Using a very similar task with adults, subjects who performed poorly on the task tended to be high in anxiety and low in self-reported attentional control (Derryberry & Reed, 1998). These findings are consistent with the idea that effortful attention may help individuals moderate negative emotion.

We have hypothesized that children's effortful control is based on the executive attention skills developing during the early years, and another skill related to executive attention is the detection and correction of errors. In the spatial conflict task reaction times following an error were 200 ms longer than those following a correct trial for 30-month-old children, and more than 500 ms longer at 36 months, indicating that children were noticing their errors and correcting them (Jones, Rothbart, & Posner, 2003). No evidence of slowing following an error was found at 24 months. A flanker task called the Attention Network Task, or ANT (Rueda et al., 2004), has also been developed that is appropriate for use with children as young as 4 years of age. In this task a row of five fish appear in the center of the screen, and the child's task is to identify the direction in which the middle fish is pointing by pressing a key. On half the trials the flanker fish are pointing in the same direction as the middle fish (congruent trials); on the other half the flanker fish are pointing in the opposite direction (incongruent trials). Using this task, there is considerable development of conflict resolution up to 7 years of age but a striking consistency in performance after this age up to adulthood (Rueda et al., 2004).

We have long known from studies of behavior genetics that the heritable contributions to temperament are strong. Now the breakthrough mapping of the human genome allows us to look at relationships between variability in specific genes and temperament at different points in the developmental process. This work was begun by Auerbach and Ebstein and their associates (Auerbach et al., 2001; Ebstein et al., 1998). More recently, Caspi and colleagues (2002) studied a functional polymorphism of the gene that codes the enzyme monoamine oxidase (MAOA), which they found to moderate effects of family maltreatment in children's development of conduct disorder and the disposition to commit violence. With genes conferring low MAOA expression, early maltreatment had no effect, and the low MAOA group had low antisocial outcomes. With genes conferring high MAOA expression, early maltreatment predicted later antisocial behavior.

Genetic links to attention and sensation seeking have also been found. DNA from cheek swabs of subjects who performed the Attention Network Task has been used to examine candidate differences in gene polymorphisms related to dopamine. At least two candidate genes were related to the executive network to a greater degree than to overall performance or to efficiency measures of any other network, as measured by reaction time and accuracy (Fossella, Posner, Fan, Swanson, & Pfaff, 2002). One of these genes was the dopamine D4 receptor (DRD4) gene, widely reported to be associated with ADHD and with the temperament trait of sensation seeking (Swanson et al., 2000). The other was the MAOA gene studied by Caspi and colleagues (2002), which is related both to dopamine and to norepinephrine.

Neuroimaging can also serve as a tool for examining the role of genetic variation in influencing brain networks. The two genes associated with differences in conflict reaction time (DRD4 and

MAOA) also produced differences in brain activation within the anterior cingulate gyrus (Fan, Fossella, Sommer, & Posner, 2003). We expect that molecular genetics and imaging research, along with imaging studies and the development of further model tasks, will provide important neuroscience links to temperament in future years.

Prospects for Temperament and Personality

SEEKING A UNIFIED LANGUAGE

Another advance in the study of temperament is possible, although it has not yet taken place. We may be able to make use of psychobiology to get beyond a current problem in the naming of temperamental dimensions. Different names have frequently been proposed for very similar temperament constructs, suggesting disagreement in the field that may not exist. In the animal literature, on the other hand, a term such as fear has a standard meaning. Behaviorally and cognitively, fear involves body and vocal expression, response preparation (escape, inhibition, or attack), and attention toward the fear-inducing stimulus and/or toward potential escape routes (Davis, Hitchcock, & Rosen, 1987). Instead of focusing on a potential single construct such as fear, however, temperament researchers have often focused on components of the fear response. Some have been concerned with fear's motivational aspects in terms such as approach/withdrawal and avoidance. Others have been concerned with its emotional aspects, as in emotionality; with its relation to inhibited motor reaction, as in behavioral inhibition; or with its relation to others' response to the characteristic, as in difficult temperament.

At first the proliferation of temperament terms seems to suggest that the field is in disagreement about what constitutes temperament. If we consider a biologically based view of temperament, however, there may be more agreement than we might have thought. If we choose a general term like *fear*, which has long been used by biologists and students of animal behavior, we can then study its components and their relations to one another, as well as the relation of fear and/or its components to other negative affects, including frustration, sadness, shyness, and anxiety. This will allow an empirically based, bottom-up approach to the study of temperament. Substantial intercorrelations among scales with different names further support the helpfulness of adopting a standard terminology (Goldsmith, Rieser-Danner, & Briggs, 1991).

In a biologically based view fear can be seen as an inherited system activated by novelty, sudden or intense stimuli, evolutionarily prepared dangers (e.g., snakes or falling), interactions with unfamiliar conspecifics, and conditioned responses to punishment (Gray, 1987). Individuals vary in the threshold, intensity, and duration of their responses to these conditions. Do individual differences in fear reactivity show consistency across these elicitors? This is an empirical question, and to answer it, fear reactivity in a large group of subjects would be measured under each of these conditions, testing to see whether individual responsiveness is related across the elicitors. We could then use a bottom-up strategy to support (or fail to support) the use of the more general construct. This kind of research will be extremely important in the near future, allowing us to have a better view of what we mean by fear reactivity or more general constructs such as negative affectivity.

Developing Links Between Temperament and Personality

Stronger links between temperament and personality across the life span can also be pursued within a coherent framework of individual differences (Caspi, 1998). To accomplish this we need to continue to develop an empirically based general theory of temperament, as I indicated earlier, and to connect it with other influences on personality, including the development of concepts of the self and others. We have already recognized that temperament involves organized systems rather than separate traits and that it includes both emotional and attentional processes. When these processes can be considered both in concert and in interaction with other cognitive and social influences, we will have a much richer view of development. Researchers at Hampton University and the University of Oregon have recently undertaken an investigation of children's temperament and personality as seen by the mother (Victor, Rothbart, & Baker, 2003). One interesting finding in this work has been that mothers' views of the personality of temperamentally extraverted/surgent children appear to vary depending on the effectiveness of the child's socialization.

Ultimately, the pathways between early temperament and future personality are likely to be complex, because children's development unfolds through genetic inheritance in the context of social relationships, cognition, and experience, and because both continuity and change must eventually be understood in these contexts. Functional brain imaging and the mapping of the human genome allow further links between inherited structure, temperament, and the effects of experience. To understand developmental pathways involving temperament predispositions, socialization processes, relationships, cognition, and culture, we will also require a more unified developmental psychology, one that *Merrill-Palmer Quarterly* has encouraged throughout its notable history.

References

Auerbach, J., Faroy, M., Kahana, M., Ebstein, R., & Levine, J. (2001). The association of dopamine D4 receptor gene (DRD4) and the serotonin transporter promoter gene (5-HTTLPR) with temperament in 12-month-old infants. *Journal of Child Psychology and Psychiatry, 42,* 777–783.

Bush, G., Luu, P., & Posner, M. I. (2000). Cognitive and emotional influences in anterior cingulate cortex. *Trends in Cognitive Sciences, 4,* 215–222.

Carlson, S. M., & Moses, L. J. (2001). Individual differences in inhibitory control and children's theory of mind. *Child Development, 72,* 1032–1053.

Caspi, A. (1998). Personality development across the life course. In W. Damon (Series Ed.) & N. Eisenberg (Vol. Ed.), *Handbook of child psychology: Vol. 3. Social, emotional, and personality development* (5th ed., pp. 311–388). New York: Wiley.

Caspi, A., McClay, J., Moffitt, T. E., Mill, J., Martin, J., Craig, I. W., Taylor, A., & Poulton, R. (2002). Role of genotype in the cycle of violence in maltreated children. *Science, 297,* 851–854.

Davis, M., Hitchcock, J. M., & Rosen, J. B. (1987). Anxiety and the amygdala: Pharmacological and anatomical analysis of the fear-potentiated startle paradigm. In G. H. Bower (Ed.), *The psychology of learning and motivation: Advances in research and theory* (Vol. 2, pp. 263–305). New York: Academic Press.

Derryberry, D., & Reed, M. A. (1994). Temperament and the self-organization of personality. *Development and Psychopathology, 6,* 653–676.

Derryberry, D., & Reed, M. A. (1996). Regulatory processes and the development of cognitive representations. *Development and Psychopathology, 8,* 215–234.

Derryberry, D., & Reed, M. A. (1998). *Individual differences in attentional control: Adaptive regulation of response interference.* Unpublished manuscript.

Ebstein, R. P., Levine, J., Geller, V., Auerbach, J., Gritsenko, I., & Belmaker, R. H. (1998). Dopamine D4 receptor and serotonin transporter promoter in the determination of neonatal temperament. *Molecular Psychiatry, 3,* 238–246.

Eisenberg, N., Fabes, R. A., Nyman, M., Bernzweig, J., & Pinulas, A. (1994). The relations of emotionality and regulation to children's anger-related reactions. *Child Development, 65,* 109–128.

Fan, J., Flombaum, J. I., McCandliss, B. D., Thomas, K. M., & Posner, M. I. (2003). Cognitive and brain mechanisms of conflict. *Neuroimage, 18,*

42–57.

Fan, J., Fossella, J. A., Sommer, T., & Posner, M. I. (2003). Mapping the genetic variation of executive attention onto brain activity. *Proceedings of the National Academy of Sciences of the United States of America, 100,* 7406–7411.

Fossella, J., Posner, M. I., Fan, J., Swanson, J. M., & Pfaff, D. W. (2002). Attentional phenotypes for the analysis of higher mental function. *Scientific World.* Retrieved October 22, 2003, from http://www.sacklerinstitute.org/cornell/online_papers/ant-phenotype.pdf.

Gerardi-Caulton, G. (2000). Sensitivity to spatial conflict and the development of self-regulation in children 24–36 months of age. *Developmental Science, 3,* 397–404.

Goldsmith, H. H., Rieser-Danner, L. A., & Briggs, S. (1991). Evaluating convergent and discriminant validity of temperament questionnaires for preschoolers, toddlers, and infants. *Developmental Psychology, 27,* 566–579.

Gray, J. A. (1987). The *psychology of fear and stress* (2nd ed.). Cambridge, England: Cambridge University Press.

Halverson, C. F., Jr., Kohnstamm, G. A., & Martin, R. P. (1994). *The developing structure of temperament and personality from infancy to adulthood.* Hillsdale, NJ: Erlbaum.

Jones, L. B., Rothbart, M. K., & Posner, M. I. (2003). Development of executive attention in preschool children. *Developmental Science, 6,* 498–504.

Kochanska, G. (1991). Socialization and temperament in the development of guilt and conscience. *Child Development, 62,* 1379–1392.

Kochanska, G. (1995). Children's temperament, mothers' discipline, and security of attachment: Multiple pathways to emerging internalization. *Child Development, 66,* 597–615.

Kochanska, G. (1997). Multiple pathways to conscience for children with different temperaments: From toddlerhood to age 5. *Developmental Psychology, 33,* 228–240.

Kochanska, G., & Knaack, A. (2003). Effortful control as a personality characteristic of young children: Antecedents, correlates, and consequences. *Journal of Personality, 71,* 1087–1112.

Kochanska, G., Murray, K., & Coy, K. C. (1997). Inhibitory control as a contributor to conscience in childhood: From toddler to early school age. *Child Development, 68,* 263–277.

Kochanska, G., Murray, K. T., & Harlan, E. T. (2000). Effortful control in early childhood: Continuity and change, antecedents, and implications for social development. *Developmental Psychology, 36,* 220–232.

Kochanska, G., Murray, K. T., Jacques, T. Y., Koenig, A. L., & Vandegeest, K. A. (1996). Inhibitory control in young children and its role in emerging internalization. *Child Development, 67,* 490–507.

McCrae, R. R., Costa, P. T., Jr., Ostendorf, F., Angleitner, A., Hrebickova, M., Avia, M. D., Sanz, J., Sanchez-Bernardos, M. L., Kusdil, M. E., Woodfield, R., Saunders, P. R., & Smith, P. B. (2000). Nature over nurture:

Temperament, personality, and life span development. *Journal of Personality and Social Psychology, 78,* 173–186.

Murray, K. T., & Kochanska, G. (2002). Effortful control: Factor structure and relation to externalizing and internalizing behaviors. *Journal of Abnormal Child Psychology, 30,* 503–514.

Panksepp, J. (1998). *Affective neuroscience: The foundations of human and animal emotions.* New York: Oxford University Press.

Posner, M. I., & Rothbart, M. K. (1998). *Attention, self-regulation, and consciousness.* Philosophical Transactions of the Royal Society of London, B, 353: 1915–1927.

Posner, M. I., & Rothbart, M. K. (2007). *Educating the human brain.* Washington, DC: American Psychological Association Books.

Posner, M. I., & Rothbart, M. K. (in press). Research on attention networks as a model for the integration of psychological science. *Annual Review of Psychology.*

Reed, M., Pien, D., & Rothbart, M. K. (1984). Inhibitory self-control in preschool children. *Merrill-Palmer Quarterly, 30,* 131–148.

Rothbart, M. K. (1989). Temperament and development. In G. Kohnstamm, J. Bates, & M. K. Rothbart (Eds.), *Temperament in childhood* (pp. 187–248). New York: Wiley.

Rothbart, M. K., Ahadi, S. A., & Evans, D. E. (2000). Temperament and personality: Origins and outcomes. *Journal of Personality and Social Psychology, 78,* 122–135.

Rothbart, M. K., Ahadi, S. A., & Hershey, K. L. (1994). Temperament and social behavior in childhood. *Merrill-Palmer Quarterly, 40,* 21–39.

Rothbart, M. K., Ahadi, S. A., Hershey, K., & Fisher, P. (2001). Investigations of temperament at three to seven years: The Children's Behavior Questionnaire. *Child Development, 72,* 1394–1408.

Rothbart, M. K., & Bates, J. E. (1998). Temperament. In W. Damon (Series Ed.) & N. Eisenberg (Vol. Ed.), *Handbook of child psychology: Vol. 3. Social, emotional, and personality development* (5th ed., pp. 105–176). New York: Wiley.

Rothbart, M. K., & Bates, J. E. (2006). Temperament. In W. Damon & R. Lerner (Series Eds.) & N. Eisenberg (Vol. Ed.), *Handbook of child psychology: Vol. 3. Social, emotional, and personality development* (6th ed, pp. 99–166). New York: Wiley.

Rothbart, M. K., & Derryberry, D. (1981). Development of individual differences in temperament. In M. E. Lamb & A. L. Brown (Eds.), *Advances in developmental psychology* (Vol. 1, pp. 37–86). Hillsdale, NJ: Erlbaum.

Rothbart, M. K., Ellis, L. K., Rueda, M. R., & Posner, M. I. (2003). Developing mechanisms of temperamental effortful control. *Journal of Personality, 71,* 1113–1143.

Rothbart, M. K., & Mauro, J. A. (1990). Questionnaire approaches to the study of infant temperament. In J. W. Fagen & J. Colombo (Eds.), *Individual differences in infancy: Reliability, stability and prediction* (pp. 411–429). Hillsdale, NJ: Erlbaum.

Rothbart, M. K., & Posner, M. I. (2006). Temperament, attention, and developmental psychopathology. In Dante Cicchetti & Donald J. Cohen (Eds.), *Developmental psychopathology* (2nd ed., pp. 465–501). Hoboken, NJ: Wiley.

Rueda, M. R., Fan, J., McCandliss, B., Halparin, J. D., Gruber, D. B., Pappert, L., & Posner, M. I. (2004). Development of attentional networks in childhood. *Neuropsychologia, 42,* 1029–1040.

Schwartz, C. E., Wright, C. I., Shin, L. M., Kagan, J., & Rauch, S. L. (2003). Inhibited and uninhibited infants "Grown Up": Adult amygdalar response to novelty. *Science, 300,* 1952–1953.

Swanson, J., Oosterlaan, J., Murias, M., Moyzis, R., Schuck, S., Mann, M., Feldman, P., Spence, M. A., Sergeant, J., Smith, M., Kennedy J., & Posner, M. I. (2000). ADHD children with 7-repeat allele of the DRD4 gene have extreme behavior but normal performance on critical neuropsychological tests of attention. *Proceedings of the National Academy of Sciences, USA, 97,* 4754–4759.

Thomas, A., & Chess, S. (1977). *Temperament and development.* New York: Bruner/Mazel.

Valiente, C., Eisenberg, N., Smith, C. L., Reiser, M., Fabes, R. A., Losoya, S., Guthrie, I. K., & Murphy, B. C. (2003). The relations of effortful control and reactive control to children's externalizing problems: A longitudinal assessment. *Journal of Personality, 71,* 1171–1196.

Victor, J. B., Rothbart, M. K., & Baker, S. R. (2003, April). *Developing an Integrated Assessment of Children's Temperament and Personality.* Paper presented at the Biennial meeting of the Society for Research in Child Development, Tampa, FL.

7

Emotion-Related Regulation
An Emerging Construct

Nancy Eisenberg, Claire Champion, and Yue Ma

Emotion regulation is a major topic of study in developmental psychology and related disciplines or subdisciplines. Its dominance is reflected in the number of books and monographs that have been published about emotion regulation since the mid-1990s (e.g., Baumeister & Vohs, 2004; Fox, 1994; Philippot & Feldman, 2004).

However, the topic was not always a popular one. Before the mid-1980s discussion of emotion by developmentalists was relatively limited; even more rare were writings on emotion regulation. For example, in 1981, at the biennial meeting of the Society for Research in Child Development, no entries appeared in the program index for the terms *emotion regulation* or *delay tasks*, and only one paper was listed under the term *self-regulation*. In 1989 the category of emotion regulation did not appear in the index; three abstracts were listed under *regulation*, three abstracts were listed under *self-regulation*, and one abstract was listed under *delay tasks*. Fourteen years later, in 2003, the category of emotion regulation included 53 entries and self-regulation had 36 entries.

Similarly, only recently has emotion regulation been covered in any depth in developmental psychology or child development textbooks. For example, in two textbooks from the mid- to late 1970s (Gardner, 1978; Schell, 1975) cognitive development dominated the contents, and the chapters related to social-emotional development pertained primarily to attachment relationships. In three textbooks in the early 1980s (Clarke-Stewart & Koch, 1983; Kopp & Krakow, 1982; Mussen, Conger, Kagan, & Huston, 1984) sections on emotion were very limited, although some included chapters on social and emotional development (Clarke-Stewart & Koch, 1983; Mussen et al., 1984). Topics such as attachment, moral development, and aggression dominated the space devoted to social and emotional development. However, one book of that era (Mussen et al., 1984) included three pages on self-control.

In the late 1980s to early 1990s sections on social, emotional, and personality development were larger than previously (Berk, 1991; M. Cole & Cole, 1989; Shaffer, 1989). However, the topic of emotion regulation still usually was not included, aside from the early childhood chapter in the Cole and Cole textbook, which had a three-page subsection titled "Developing the Ability to Regulate Oneself."

Only recently have textbooks routinely included content on emotion regulation. For example, three recent textbooks (Berger, 2003; Shaffer, 2002; Siegler, Deloache, & Eisenberg, 2003) all include at least one section on emotion regulation, and all contain chapters or parts of chapters on emotional development.

Despite the relatively recent surge of theory and research on emotion regulation, work on the topic did not emerge from a total theoretical vacuum. For example, Freud (1997) argued that the ego regulates impulses and drives (often involving emotion), which are housed in the id, for the purpose of obtaining more pleasure in the long run. Moreover, in Freud's theory the emergence of the super-ego adds to the ego a new type of control, one that is based on guilt and the internalization of values and standards of the same-sex parent. Erikson (1950/1963) also discussed the emergence of emotion regulation. In regard to the infant stage of trust versus basic mistrust, he noted, "The [infant's] experience of a mutual regulation of his increasingly receptive capacities with the maternal techniques of provision gradually helps him to balance the discomfort caused by the immaturity of homeostasis with which he was born" (1950/1963, p. 147).

Erikson discussed the importance of firm, reassuring outer control for structuring and regulating children's early emotion and argued that his second psychosocial stage, autonomy versus shame and doubt, was "decisive for the ration of . . . freedom of self-expression and its suppression" (1950/1963, p. 264). Further, investigators studying coping in the 1960s and 1970s also dealt with the issue of regulation. Haan (1963, 1977), for example, developed elaborate systems of coding ego-related coping behaviors and argued that coping involves "purpose, choice, and flexible shift, adheres to intersubjective reality and logic, and allows and enhances proportionate affective expression" (1977, p. 34). She differentiated coping from ego defenses, which were viewed as more rigid and irrational and as involving covert expression of impulses. Furthermore, Lazarus's

(1966) early work on coping, influenced by even earlier work on stress and cognitive appraisals, pertained to the management of emotion and behavior when an individual is stressed. Indeed, Lazarus and Folkman (1984) defined coping as "constantly changing cognitive and behavioral efforts to manage specific external and/or internal demands that are appraised as taxing or exceeding the resources of the person" (p. 141). Thus coping generally is viewed as including attempts to modulate the effects of stressful circumstances (which generally elicit emotion).

It is not clear how much the aforementioned (and other) early lines of work stimulated more recent interest in the construct of emotion regulation. Much of the initial surge of interest in emotion regulation in the 1970s and 1980s was in the area of infancy (see Campos, Barrett, Lamb, Goldsmith, & Stenberg, 1983). For example, Kopp in 1982 outlined stages of emotion-related regulation in the early years of life, especially as exhibited in young children's compliance. Around the same time Rothbart and Derryberry (1981) cited the regulation of reactivity as one of the two major constructs of temperament, and their conception of temperament came to dominate work on temperament in infants and young children (e.g., Fox, 1989; Rothbart, 1989).

In general, in early studies on regulation or self-control in infancy, regulation was assessed with measures of infants' coping with distress or with obstructions to their desires or movement (e.g., Fox, 1989), infants' reactions during peek-a-boo, separations from mother (e.g., Braungart & Stifter, 1991; Stifter & Moyer, 1991), the still-face situation (Gianino & Tronick, 1988), or measures of temperament (Rothbart, 1981). In early research and theory self-regulation or self-control after infancy sometimes was operationalized as compliance (especially willing compliance; e.g., Kopp, 1982) or socially appropriate behavior (e.g., not disrupting games or breaking rules; e.g., Block & Block, 1980, in their rating scale; Kendall & Wilcox, 1979). The use of behavioral measures of regulation was less frequent in early studies of children than in studies of infants and toddlers, although research by Mischel (Mischel & Baker, 1972; Mischel & Ebbesen, 1970) and Block and Block (1980) were two notable exceptions. For example, Mischel and his colleagues measured children's abilities to delay gratification (e.g., eating a treat) when doing so would result in receiving a larger amount of the desirable commodity.

In early studies of the correlates of children's emotion-related regulation, investigators tended to use the same person—often the parent—to report on children's regulation (often as part of their temperament) and their adjustment or social functioning (Barron & Earls, 1984; Teglasi & MacMahon, 1990). The issue of reporter bias is, consequently, an important limitation to consider when interpreting the results of some early research. Moreover, because of the goals of the researchers at the time of data collection, the construct of emotion regulation sometimes was not differentiated much from emotion: measures of anger, other negative emotions, or emotional lability, for example, often were viewed as an index of low regulation (Pulkkinen, 1982; Pulkkinen & Hamalainen, 1995; also see Caspi, Henry, McGee, Moffitt, & Silva, 1995). Nonetheless, some of the early work was groundbreaking in that it established links (often over time) between constructs related to or partly reflecting regulation and the quality of children's social functioning (such as their aggression; e.g., Block & Block, 1980; Pulkkinen, 1982). The demonstration of the relevance of regulation to children's adjustment and social competence was, in all likelihood, one of the major factors fueling the sharp increase in interest in regulation in the late 1980s and 1990s.

In the early studies of children's emotion regulation, theoretical models, and especially empirical research linking regulation to other domains of children's functioning, generally examined simple, direct relations (see Block & Block, 1980; Fox, 1989; Pulkkinen, 1982, 1986, for some exceptions). Typically, correlations between some measure of regulation and an aspect of socioemotional functioning (e.g., compliance, externalizing problems) were examined. Factors that mediated or moderated the relation of regulation to developmental outcomes were seldom examined, nor was regulation likely to be examined as a mediating variable between other variables (e.g., demographic variables or parenting) and children's socioemotional functioning.

Around 1990 and thereafter the literature saw a dramatic increase in the number of chapters, books, and articles on the topic of children's emotion-related regulation (e.g., Eisenberg & Fabes, 1992; Fox, 1994; Garber & Dodge, 1991; the special issues of *Developmental Psychology* and *Merrill-Palmer Quarterly* edited by Dodge [1989] and Eisenberg [1994], respectively). By the mid-1990s emotion regulation was arguably one of the most popular topics in developmental psychology (Dunn, 1996). Moreover, the central importance of regulation has been widely recognized. For example, a National Academy of Sciences (NAS) committee report in 2000, *From Neurons to Neighborhoods*, concluded, "The growth of self-regulation is a cornerstone of early childhood development that cuts across all domains of behavior" (Shonkoff & Phillips, 2000, p. 3).

Now

On average, research and theory on emotion regulation have increased in quality as well as quantity since the mid-1990s. On the conceptual front developmentalists have devoted considerable time and energy to the issues of defining emotion regulation or self-regulation (e.g., Campos, Mumme, Kermoian, & Campos, 1994; Cicchetti, Ganiban, & Barnett, 1991; P. Cole, Martin, & Dennis, 2004; P. Cole, Michel, & Teti, 1994; Eisenberg, 2002; Kopp & Neufeld, 2003; Thompson, 1994) and to delineating the complex ways in which regulation might be linked to the quality of children's social functioning (e.g., P. Cole, Martin, & Dennis, 2004; Eisenberg & Fabes, 1992; Eisenberg, Fabes, Guthrie, & Reiser, 2000; Thompson & Calkins, 1996). Although there is still no consensus, issues related to the role of intent, external agents, motivation, physiology, and many other factors in emotion-related regulation are topics of intense discussion. Two examples of definitions of emotion regulation are "extrinsic and intrinsic processes responsible for monitoring, evaluating, and modifying emotional reactions, especially their intensive and temporal features, to achieve one's goals" (Thompson, 1994, pp. 27–28), and "the process of initiating, avoiding, inhibiting, maintaining, or modulating the occurrence, form, intensity, or duration of internal feeling states, emotion-related physiological, attentional processes, motivational states, and/or the behavioral concomitants of emotion in the service of accomplishing affect-related biological or social adaptation or achieving individual goals" (Eisenberg & Spinrad, 2004).

Investigators generally agree that emotion regulation often involves internal processes related to emotion. Some, but not all, investigators appear to believe that the intent often is important (e.g., Eisenberg & Spinrad, 2004; Thompson, 1994). Many would likely include regulation imposed or fostered by other people (e.g., parents) as part of emotion-related regulation, if not part of emotion self-regulation. Some include the regulation of behavior that is an external manifestation of emotion (e.g., emotional expressions) or is fueled by emotion (e.g., some acts of aggression) as part of emotion regulation (e.g., Campos, Mumme, et al., 1994; Eisenberg, Fabes, Guthrie, Murphy, et al., 1996); it is not clear whether all investigators would agree on this point. Some researchers (e.g., Gross, 1999) have included behaviors that preclude the actual experience of emotion in their definitions of emotion regulation (or related coping behaviors; see Aspinwall & Taylor, 1997); others do not discuss this possibility. Perhaps of most relevance to our discussion, the centrality of these aspects of functioning to a definition of emotion regulation is a topic of considerable debate (see the special section of *Child Development*, March 2004, including commentaries accompanying the lead article by P. Cole, Martin, & Dennis).

In regard to methods researchers currently tend to use a wide array of measures of emotion regulation and multiple methods (e.g., questionnaires, behavioral measures, physiological measures) and/or multiple reporters (self-reports, parents' reports, teachers' reports). An array of behavioral measures exists for assessing children's self-regulation, even in the second to fifth year of life (e.g., P. Cole, Martin, & Dennis, 2004; Kochanska, Murray, & Coy, 1997; Kochanska, Murray, & Harlan, 2000; Mangelsdorf, Shapiro, & Marzolf, 1995), as well as in the school years (e.g., Lengua, 2002; Mezzacappa, Kindlon, Saul, & Earls, 1998; Olson, Schilling, & Bates, 1999; White et al., 1994). These measures typically assess the children's abilities to effortfully manage their attention, soothe themselves, enlist support, inhibit behavior when needed or on command, or activate behavior as required to behave in the desired or appropriate way. Although these aspects of regulation are not used solely for the regulation of emotion, they are processes that often are part of an effort to modulate emotional experience and expression. In addition, investigators have used vagal tone (Fox, 1989; Porges, Doussard-Roosevelt, & Maiti, 1994) and cortisol responding (Stansbury & Gunnar, 1994) as measures of regulation (or related constructs).

Current research on emotion regulation often involves longitudinal data, which are desirable for assessing various complex ways of conceptualizing the role of regulation in socioemotional development. As Rothbart and Bates (1998) noted, temperament (including aspects of temperamentally based regulation) may relate to adjustment (or other aspects of development) through direct relations, indirect relations, or moderated relations. An example of indirect or mediated relations is that investigators have found that individual differences in personality resiliency mediate relations of emotion-related regulation to children's social competence (e.g., Eisenberg, Fabes, Guthrie, & Reiser, 2000), agreeableness (Cumberland, Eisenberg, & Reiser, 2004), and internalizing problems (Eisenberg, Spinrad, Fabes, et al., 2004). Moreover, coping can mediate the relations of regulation to adjustment (Lengua & Long, 2002). In addition, emotion-related regulation has been found to mediate relations of such socialization variables as attachment (Contreras, Kerns, Weimer, Gentzler, & Tomich, 2000), parental expression of emotion (Eisenberg, Gershoff, et al., 2001; Eisenberg, Valiente, Morris, et al., 2003), parental philosophy of emotion (Gottman, Katz, & Hooven, 1997), nurturant-response, sensitivity, conflicted or harsh parenting (Braungart-Rieker, Garwood, Powers, & Wang, 2001; Brody & Ge, 2001; also see Wills, DuHamel, & Vaccaro, 1995), or parental temperament-personality (Cumberland-Li, Eisenberg, Champion, Gershoff, & Fabes, 2003) to social competence, adjustment, and alcohol use. Thus findings show that emotion-related regulation or related constructs are involved in chains of potentially causal relations.

Further, a number of studies have demonstrated that various indexes of regulation interact with other variables when predicting outcomes such as social competence, adjustment, and substance/alcohol problems. For example, some investigators have found that regulation and negative emotionality interact when predicting children's social competence, coping, or adjustment (e.g., Belsky, Friedman, & Hsieh, 2001; Colder & Stice, 1998; Diener & Kim, 2004; Eisenberg, Fabes, Guthrie, & Reiser, 2000; Lengua & Long, 2002; Valiente et al., 2003; also see Colder & Chassin, 1997; Lengua, Wolchik, Sandler, & West, 2000). In many instances regulation is a stronger predictor of outcomes for children prone to experience negative emotions than for less emotional children. Moreover, in other studies self-regulation has moderated the association between multiple risk and adjustment (such that children low in self-regulation were more vulnerable to multiple risk; Lengua, 2002) and between coping and adjustment in children of divorce (Lengua & Sandler, 1996). These studies are representative of the nonlinear relations that have been obtained in a number of recent studies.

Central to many recent studies on emotion-related work have been theory and empirical data on effortful control, an aspect of temperament that is believed to involve executive functioning. Effortful control is defined as "the ability to inhibit a dominant response to perform a subdominant response" (Rothbart & Bates, 1998, p. 137) or as the "efficiency of executive attention—including the ability to inhibit a dominant response and/or to activate a subdominant response, to plan, and to detect errors" (Rothbart & Bates, 2006, p. 129). Effortful control pertains to the ability to willfully or voluntarily inhibit, activate, or change (modulate) attention and behavior. Measures of effortful control often include indexes of attentional regulation (e.g., the ability to voluntarily focus or shift attention as needed, called attentional control) and behavioral regulation (e.g., the ability to effortfully inhibit behavior as appropriate, especially when one does not feel like doing so, called inhibitory control). Executive skills involved in the integration of information and planning are also involved. Evidence is mounting that effortful control is related to problems with adjustment and social competence (e.g., Eisenberg, Cumberland, Spinrad, et al., 2001; Gilliom, Shaw, Beck, Schonberg, & Lukon, 2002; Kochanska & Knaack, 2003; Lemery, Essex, & Snider, 2002; see Eisenberg, Fabes, Guthrie, & Reiser, 2000; Rothbart & Bates, 1998, 2006).

Investigators are also beginning to examine the relations of different aspects of emotion-related regulation (including aspects of effortful control) to various aspects of socioemotional functioning. For example, internalizing problems, because they often involve problems with anxiety (including social anxiety) and depression, likely involve deficits in the ability to modulate internal emotional and emotion-related physiological states. Attentional control—especially the ability to focus on nonthreatening stimuli and to shift attention—may be especially important for minimizing internalizing tendencies (Derryberry & Reed, 2002). Because many individuals with internalizing problems tend to be inhibited, rigid, and inflexible in their behavior, one also might expect them to exhibit high levels of problems with activational control. In contrast, children with externalizing problems, especially those associated with anger and frustration, would be expected to exhibit deficits in attentional control and inhibitory control. There is some initial support for these predictions: Both internalizing children and externalizing children tend to be low in attentional control (e.g., Eisenberg, Cumberland, Spinrad, et al., 2001; Lengua, West, & Sandler, 1998; Oldehinkel, Hartman, Winter, Veenstra, & Ormel, 2004; cf. Lemery et al., 2002), although it is possible that this deficit declines with age (Eisenberg, Sadovsky, et al., 2005). Moreover, children also tend to be low to average in inhibitory control (and high in impulsivity; Eisenberg, Cumberland, Spinrad, et al., 2001; Lemery et al., 2002; Lengua, West, & Sandler, 1998; Oldehinkel et al., 2004). Thus investigators are beginning to chart relations between different aspects of regulation (including some executive functioning skills related to regulation) and different aspects of children's socioemotional functioning.

Although numerous studies since the late 1980s have linked problems in emotion-related regulation with adjustment and social competence, it is difficult to prove causality with correlational relations. The increase in longitudinal research on this issue has made it possible at least to examine prediction over time. For example, there is evidence that effortful control and related constructs are related to guilt, social competence, compliance, and adjustment several or even more years in the future (e.g., Eisenberg, Fabes, Guthrie, Reiser, 2000; Eisenberg, Guthrie, et al., 2000; Kochanska & Knaack, 2003; Kochanska, Tjebkes, & Forman, 1998; Mischel, Shoda, & Peake, 1988; Murphy, Shepard, Eisenberg, & Fabes, 2004; Olson et al., 1999; also see Caspi, 2000; Shoda, Mischel, & Peake, 1990). Thus, even if the direction of causality between emotion-related regulation and aspects of socioemotional functioning has not been proved, it is clear that these aspects of functioning are interrelated.

The Future

DEFINITIONAL ISSUES

An important goal for the future is to develop greater consensus about the definition of emotion (or emotion-related) regulation. Even though there are numerous commonalities in the definitions used by different theorists and investigators, there are also important differences that lead to problems. Often the results of studies examining emotion regulation cannot be directly compared, in part because the lack of consensus on the definition of emotion regulation results in investigators' using quite different measures of the construct. As P. Cole, Martin, and Dennis (2004) suggest, a common definition of emotion regulation would foster progress in the field and contribute to the validity of emotion regulation as a scientific construct.

A number of key distinctions should be considered when constructing a definition of emotion regulation. Researchers generally agree that emotion regulation involves internal processes related to emotion. However, they do not agree on whether emotion regulation involves primarily effortful (i.e., voluntary, albeit not necessarily conscious) processes or also includes involuntary, more reactive processes such as inhibition from subcortical motivational (e.g., approach or inhibition) systems (see Eisenberg & Morris, 2002; Eisenberg & Spinrad, 2004). In addition, as we have already noted, definitions of emotion regulation vary in regard to their inclusion of (a) processes used to regulate emotion-related behavior such as emotional expression and emotionally driven aggression (rather than only internal emotion-related states), and their inclusion of (b) instances of external regulation (e.g., by parents) of children's emotion-related responding. Even though external regulation of emotion by socializers likely promotes internal regulation, it may be fruitful to differentiate between emotion self-regulation—that is, emotion-relevant regulatory processes that are generated primarily by the target individual—and regulation that is primarily accomplished through the efforts of others (e.g., a parent soothing an infant). Moreover, definitions of emotion regulation differ in regard to their inclusion of proactive coping ("efforts undertaken in advance of a potentially stressful event to prevent it or to modify its form before it occurs" [Aspinwall & Taylor, 1997, p. 417]) or antecedent emotion regulation (managing emotional reactions before they occur by using proactive coping or attentional and cognitive processes to choose the situations that are focused upon and how they are interpreted [Gross, 1999]). In the future, researchers should strive to clarify their conceptions of emotion regulation, especially if they do not achieve consensus on the term. Unfortunately, investigators often do not define emotion regulation at all, or they include elements of other constructs (e.g., negative emotionality, adjustment, or social competence) in their operationalizations of emotion-related regulation.

Topics of Study

Currently, there is relatively little published longitudinal work on emotion-related regulation's precursors, development, stability, and relations with other emerging processes such as language and an understanding of emotion. For example, although cognition and attention obviously play important roles in emotion regulation, the role of cognitive processes (and their emergence and development) in emotion-related regulation has suffered from benign neglect. Coping theorists have addressed this issue to some degree because of their focus on planning, positive cognitive restructuring, cognitive distraction, and other cognitive coping mechanisms (e.g., Sandler, Tein, & West, 1994; see Compas, Connor-Smith, & Saltzman, 2001). In addition, Mischel and colleagues (e.g., Mischel & Baker, 1972; Mischel & Ebbeson, 1970) examined the role of cognitive transformations and distraction in delay of gratification. Other investigators have included emotion knowledge in interventions that were designed to promote regulated behavior (e.g., Greenberg, Kusche, Cook, & Quamma, 1995; see Denham & Burton, 2003). Crick and Dodge's 1994 work on processes involved in aggression also is of some relevance; their conceptual model includes the role of cognitive processes such as attributions about others and generating and prioritizing strategies for dealing with potential social conflicts in aggression (often a dysregulated behavior). However, we know relatively little about the role of children's understanding of their own (as well as others') feeling states in self-regulation when emotionally aroused, how the need to regulate is internally calculated, how regulation strategies are weighed and selected, and how cognitive processes are harnessed to modulate attention and effortfully activate or inhibit behavior.

Physiological correlates of effortful control and less voluntary reactive processes also are of considerable interest, but they seldom have been studied. It is likely, for example, that effortful control and reactive processes are most closely associated with different parts of the brain (see Derryberry & Reed, 1996; Eisenberg & Morris, 2002). Moreover, vagal modulation of respiratory-driven, high-frequency heart rate variability has been associated with executive control (i.e., effortful control) on behavioral tasks, whereas motivational or reactive processes involved in reactive control (e.g., passive avoidance, avoidance of punishment, and low reward dominance) have been correlated with sympathetic modulation of heart-rate variability (Mezzacappa et al., 1998).

Moreover, although children's emotion-related regulation has been a popular topic of study in recent years, most investigators have focused primarily on parental socialization, such as parenting style, parental expression, acceptance, and discussion of emotion, and parental reactions to children's expression of emotion (see Eisenberg, Cumberland, & Spinrad, 1998; Eisenberg, Spinrad, & Cumberland, 1998; Gottman et al., 1997). Socialization influences on emotion-relevant regulation in day care, kindergarten, and elementary school, as well as in other contexts external to the home, seldom have been studied. These potential sources of influence likely play an important role in the socialization of regulation, especially for older children. Moreover, research on this issue is of practical significance for education.

Culture has been a growing topic of interest in the field of psychology in recent years. Unfortunately, most studies on emotion regulation have been conducted in Western cultures, especially in North America, and clearly a need exists for studies in different cultures and subcultures. In this type of research it would be useful to explore such issues as similarities and differences across cultures in conceptions of regulated behavior, when regulation is desirable, and how it is achieved; the applicability of measures of emotion-related regulation across cultures and how they can be adapted to be culturally sensitive and valid; cultural differences in commonly enacted regulation styles and strategies; and cultural differences in the relations between regulation and other psychological variables, such as parenting socialization, social competence, and psychological adjustment. Although cross-cultural studies can contribute greatly to our understanding of the role of context in conceptions and instantiations of emotion-related regulation, within-culture studies in non-Western societies or subcultures in Western societies that examine the correlates or predictors of individual differences in emotion regulation can also be informative (see Eisenberg, Pidada, & Liew, 2001; Zhou, Eisenberg, Wang, & Reiser, 2004, for examples of studies conducted in Indonesia and China, respectively).

In addition, although behavioral geneticists are researching processes or dispositions involved in infants' and toddlers' emotion regulation (e.g., attention focusing, inhibitory control [Goldsmith, Buss, & Lemery, 1997]), few investigators are doing analogous work in older children, especially involving both questionnaire and behavioral indexes. Studies that examine age-related change in the contributions of genetic and environmental factors to regulation are an example of behavioral genetics research that would be especially informative (see Plomin et al., 1993).

Measurement Challenges

Several challenges in regard to the measurement of emotion-related regulation are evident (see P. Cole, Martin, & Dennis, 2004). First, investigators need purer measures of emotion regulation. Some measures of emotion regulation likely measure emotion, social competence, or adjustment as much (or more) than regulation. Moreover, measures of regulation often may inadvertently tap relatively involuntary behavioral inhibition resulting from children's inhibition in novel situations; others may assess a combination of effortful control and impulsivity (i.e., the relatively involuntary pull toward a reward such as food). Inhibition tasks that assess children's behavioral inhibition when confronted with novel objects or people might be used in combination with effortful control to assess the unique relations of both constructs. Moreover, although voluntary attention focusing has been studied frequently, aspects of attention focusing that are involuntary (e.g., rumination) have been examined less frequently in children. Information about these processes might help investigators to differentiate between effortful attentional processes and more involuntary attentional responses (see, e.g., Derryberry & Reed, 2002; Vasey, El-Hag, & Daleiden, 1996).

As P. Cole, Martin, and Dennis (2004) suggested, researchers should strive, when possible, to use independent measurements for the activated emotion and the regulatory process. Because emotion regulation often is inferred from the expression of low levels of emotion, measures of emotion regulation and emotionality often are confounded. This is one reason that it is useful to assess processes that often are involved in emotion-related regulation (e.g., attentional control, inhibition of behavior) rather than trying to assess the regulation of the emotion itself. One approach that P. Cole, Martin, and Dennis (2004) suggested for separating emotion regulation from emotion is to analyze temporal relations between emotions and regulatory processes (e.g., behaviors such as self-comforting or distracting oneself).

In addition, investigators need new measures for tapping neglected aspects of emotion regulation such as antecedent emotion regulation or proactive coping (see earlier discussion). Most researchers have focused on regulation processes that occur during the elicitation of emotion or its physiological concomitants (and related action tendencies) or after an emotion is presumed to have been elicited. One reason for the lack of research on antecedent types of regulation is that they are difficult to observe and measure. Perhaps some aspects of antecedent regulation or proactive coping could be assessed by measuring attentional and cognitive processes (and perhaps physiological reactions) that proceed (or portent) potentially stressful events. For example, one could assess attempts to avoid allocating attention to cues regarding threatening events using Strooplike and other attentional tasks (see Derryberry & Reed, 2002). One might also try to assess (e.g., with interviews or thought-reporting procedures) children's attempts to plan ahead in order to prevent or minimize exposure to stressful or negative circumstances (or maximize positive emotion; see Eisenberg, Morris, & Spinrad, 2005). Similar procedures could be used to assess cognitive activities that adjust or alter goals when doing so is likely to reduce distress. Investigators might also construct situations in which they can observe behavioral instances of avoiding or modifying potentially evocative contexts (before they become distressing).

Further investigation of the relative effectiveness of different regulatory strategies or processes for modulating different specific emotions (e.g., anger, sadness, fear) would also contribute to an understanding of emotion-related regulation. Such information has theoretical and applied implications. For example, when considering intervention studies or clinical work, after determining the negative emotion(s) to which an individual or a population is most prone, clinicians could foster adequate behavioral or cognitive strategies. The work of Beck (e.g., Beck & Freeman, 1990) and others on the cognitive control of depression represents attempts to use cognitive strategies to regulate thoughts linked with certain emotional experiences. Similarly, information about the regulatory behaviors associated with specific emotions could be useful in prevention and intervention programs with children.

Finally, many studies of older children's and adolescents' emotion-related regulation used only self-report questionnaires because it is difficult to elicit sufficient emotion to observe adolescents' emotion regulation. The use of other-report measures is a partial remedy (e.g., Lengua, West, & Sandler, 1998), but more studies involving behavioral measures of adolescents' emotion-related regulation (e.g., White et al., 1994) are needed.

DESIGN ISSUES

Most studies of emotion-related regulation involve correlational, often concurrent, data, so inferences in regard to causality are unwarranted. Sometimes investigators have used longitudinal methods, especially to study the relation of children's emotion-related regulation at one age to their psychological adjustment, such as internalizing problems, externalizing problems, and social competence, at an older age. However, because these studies are expensive and have attrition problems, most longitudinal studies of regulation span only a few years.

In addition, although the causal relation of earlier regulation to later psychological outcomes cannot be clearly demonstrated from longitudinal correlational data, certain analytic procedures can provide evidence regarding the plausibility of particular causal sequences. For example, an investigator can take into account earlier levels of variables when examining relations among variables at a later assessment in order to assess whether relations between regulation and other variables seem to be simply the result of earlier levels of those variables (and their possible interrelations at a younger age [Eisenberg, Valiente, Fabes, et al., 2003]). When regulation relates to subsequent social functioning even when controlling for levels of functioning at the time regulation was assessed (or taking into account consistency in measures over time in structural equation models), regulation's having a causal effect on social functioning is more likely (e.g., Eisenberg, Spinrad, Fabes, et al., 2004). In addition, in structural equation modeling one can test the plausibility of bidirectional relations over time or whether a path from emotion-related regulation to an aspect of socioemotional functioning occurring later in time is stronger or more distinct than a path from such functioning to emotion-related regulation at the later assessment (see Eisenberg, Spinrad, Fabes, et al., 2004, for an example).

In the future the field would benefit from greater use of studies involving the assessment of at least two points and the use of sophisticated statistical tools such as structural equation modeling. A related statistical tool that could be used to greater advantage is growth curve analysis, which can help identify different developmental trajectories for emotion regulation and relations among the developmental trajectories of regulation and other aspects of socioemotional functioning.

However, even correlational longitudinal data cannot prove causality. Experimental intervention or prevention studies that train children to be more regulated and then test their social competence and adjustment are the best way to unravel causal relations and test theoretical propositions (e.g., Greenberg et al., 1995).

The experimental intervention work by people such as Greenberg (Greenberg et al., 1995; Kam, Greenberg, & Walls, 2003) and others using his Promoting Alternative Thinking Strategies curriculum (PATHS; Conduct Problems Prevention Research Group, 1999a, 1999b) is an example of programs in which teaching regulation is part of an intervention. This program likely promotes children's regulation because it can reduce the level of externalizing behavior, especially for those children who are lowest in adjustment (e.g., Greenberg et al., 1995). However, in general, interventions of this sort have included so many components that it is impossible to know which aspects of the intervention were responsible for changes in regulation or related social behaviors (e.g., changes in aggression). For example, the PATHS curriculum involves teaching children to understand their own and others' emotions, to stop before reacting when emotionally aroused, and to think about appropriate strategies for dealing with their emotions and with stressful situations, as well as other elements. Moreover, the PATHS curriculum often is used in combination with other intervention techniques. In the future it would be useful to examine the effects of interventions specifically and primarily targeted at promoting regulation (not in combination with other interventions) on children's regulation and related social behaviors.

Despite the lack of reseach demonstrating that fostering regulation promotes children's adjustment and social and emotional competence, the relatively consistent and often strong association between children's emotion-related regulation and their socioemotional competence suggests that practitioners and researchers who wish to promote adjustment should target regulatory processes in their interventions. Indeed, it is likely that many successful intervention programs are effective partly because of their effect on children's abilities to manage their internal emotional states and the external expression of these states.

In summary, the topic of emotion regulation has moved to center stage in developmental psychology in recent years. Building on early pioneers in the field, we have made considerable progress in understanding this crucial aspect of development. Nonetheless, many challenges related to defining, measuring, and understanding emotion-related regulation and its associations with other aspects of development remain. If investigators address these challenges, we are likely to see further significant strides in our understanding of emotion regulation in coming decades.

References

Aspinwall, L. G., & Taylor, S. E. (1997). A stitch in time: Self-regulation and proactive coping. *Psychological Bulletin, 121,* 417–436.

Barron, A. P., & Earls, F. (1984). The relation of temperament and social factors to behavior problems in three-year-old children. *Journal of Child Psychology and Psychiatry, 25,* 23–33.

Baumeister, R. F., & Vohs, K. D. (Eds.). (2004). *Handbook of self-regulation: Research, theory, and applications.* New York: Guilford.

Beck, A. T., & Freeman, A. (1990). *Cognitive theory of personality disorders.* New York: Guilford.

Belsky, J., Friedman, S. L., & Hsieh, K. H. (2001). Testing a core emotion-regulation prediction: Does early attentional persistence moderate the effect of infant negative emotionality on later development? *Child Development, 72,* 123–133.

Berger, K. S. (2003). *The developing person through childhood to adolescence.* New York: Worth.

Berk, L. E. (1991). *Child Development* (2nd ed.). New York: Allyn and Bacon.

Block, J. H., & Block, J. (1980). The role of ego-control and ego-resiliency in the organization of behavior. In W. A. Collins (Ed.), *The Minnesota Symposia on Child Psychology: Vol. 13. Development of cognition, affect, and social relations* (pp. 39–101). Hillsdale, NJ: Erlbaum.

Braungart, J. M., & Stifter, C. A. (1991). Regulation of negative reactivity during the strange situation: Temperament and attachment in 12-month-old infants. *Infant Behavior and Development, 14,* 349–364.

Braungart-Rieker, J., Garwood, M. M., Powers, B. P., & Wang, X. (2001). Parental sensitivity, infant affect, and affect regulation: Predictors of later attachment. *Child Development, 72*, 252–270.

Brody, G. H., & Ge, X. (2001). Linking parenting processes and self-regulation to psychological functioning and alcohol use during early adolescence. *Journal of Family Psychology, 15*, 82–94.

Campos, J. J., Barrett, K. C., Lamb, M. E., Goldsmith, H. H., & Stenberg, C. (1983). Socioemotional development. In P. H. Mussen (Series Ed.), M. Haith & J. Campos (Vol. Eds.), *Handbook of Child Psychology: Vol. 2. Infancy and developmental psychobiology* (4th ed., pp. 783–915). New York: Wiley.

Campos, J. J., Mumme, D. L., Kermoian, R., & Campos, R. G. (1994). A functionalist perspective on the nature of emotion. *Monographs of the Society for Research in Child Development, 59* (Serial No. 240), 284–303.

Caspi, A. (2000). The child is the father of the man: Personality continuities from childhood to adulthood. *Journal of Personality and Social Psychology, 78*, 158–172.

Caspi, A., Henry, B., McGee, R. O., Moffitt, T. E., & Silva, P. A. (1995). Temperamental origins of child and adolescent behavior problems: From age three to age fifteen. *Child Development, 66*, 55–68.

Cicchetti, D., Ganiban, J., & Barnett, D. (1991). Contributions from the study of high risk populations to understanding the development of emotion regulation. In K. Dodge & J. Garber (Eds.), *The development of emotion regulation* (pp. 15–48). New York: Cambridge University Press.

Clarke-Stewart, A., & Koch, J. B. (1983). *Children: Development through adolescence.* New York: Wiley.

Colder, C. R., & Chassin, L. (1997). Affectivity and impulsivity: Temperament risk for adolescent alcohol involvement. *Psychology of Addictive Behaviors, 11*, 83–97.

Colder, C. R., & Stice, E. (1998). The moderating effect of impulsivity on the relationship between anger and adolescent problem behavior: Cross-sectional and prospective findings. *Journal of Youth and Adolescence, 27*, 255–274.

Cole, M., & Cole, S. R. (1989). *The development of children.* New York: Scientific American.

Cole, P. M., Martin, S. E., & Dennis, T. A. (2004). Emotion regulation as a scientific construct: Methodological challenges and directions for child development research. *Child Development, 75*, 317–333.

Cole, P. M., Michel, M. K., & Teti, L. O. (1994). The development of emotion regulation and dysregulation: A clinical perspective. *Monographs of the Society for Research in Child Development, 59* (Serial No. 240), 73–100.

Compas, B. E., Connor-Smith, J. K., & Saltzman, H. (2001). Coping with stress during childhood and adolescence: Problems, progress, and potential in theory and research. *Psychological Bulletin, 127*, 87–127.

Conduct Problems Prevention Research Group. (1999a). Initial impact of the Fast Track Prevention Trial for conduct problems: I. The high-risk sample. *Journal of Consulting and Clinical Psychology, 67,* 631–647.

Conduct Problems Prevention Research Group. (1999b). Initial impact of the Fast Track Prevention Trial for conduct problems: II. Classroom effects. *Journal of Consulting and Clinical Psychology, 67,* 648–657.

Contreras, J., Kerns, K. A., Weimer, B. L., Gentzler, A. L., & Tomich, P. L. (2000). Emotion regulation as a mediator of associations between mother-child attachment and peer relationships in middle childhood. *Journal of Family Psychology, 14,* 111–124.

Crick, N. R., & Dodge, K. A. (1994). A review and reformulation of social information-processing mechanisms in children's social adjustment. *Psychological Bulletin, 115,* 74–101.

Cumberland, A., Eisenberg, N., & Reiser, M. (2004). Relations of young children's agreeableness and resiliency to effortful control, impulsivity, and social competence. *Social Development, 13,* 191–212.

Cumberland-Li, A., Eisenberg, N., Champion, C., Gershoff, E. T., & Fabes, R. A. (2003). The relation of parental emotionality and related dispositional traits to parental expression of emotion and children's social functioning. *Motivation and Emotion, 2,* 27–56.

Denham, S., & Burton, R. (2003). *Social and emotional prevention and intervention programming for preschoolers.* New York: Kluwer Academic/ Plenum.

Derryberry, D., & Reed, M. A. (1996). Regulatory processes and the development of cognitive representations. *Development and Psychopathology, 8,* 215–234.

Derryberry, D., & Reed, M. A. (2002). Anxiety-related attentional biases and their regulation by attentional control. *Journal of Abnormal Psychology, 111,* 225–236.

Diener, M. L., & Kim, D. Y. (2004). Maternal and child predictors of preschool children's social competence. *Applied Developmental Psychology, 25,* 3–24.

Dodge, K. A. (Ed.). (1989). Development of emotion regulation. Special issue, *Developmental Psychology, 25,* 339–402.

Dunn, J. (1996). The Emanuel Miller Memorial Lecture 1995: Children's relationships: Bridging the divide between cognitive and social development. *Journal of Child Psychology and Psychiatry and Allied Disciplines, 37,* 507–518.

Eisenberg, N. (Ed.). (1994). Children's emotions and social competence. Special issue, *Merrill-Palmer Quarterly, 40,* 1–169.

Eisenberg, N. (2002). Emotion-related regulation and its relation to quality of social functioning. In W. W. Hartup & R. A. Weinberg (Eds.), *Child psychology in retrospect and prospect: In celebration of the 75th anniversary of the Institute of Child Development* (pp. 133–171). Mahwah, NJ: Erlbaum.

Eisenberg, N., Cumberland, A., & Spinrad, T. L. (1998). Parental socialization of emotion. *Psychological Inquiry, 9,* 241–273.

Eisenberg, N., Cumberland, A., Spinrad, T. L., Fabes, R. A., Shepard, S. A.,

Reiser, M., Murphy, B. C., Losoya, S. H., & Guthrie, I. K. (2001). The relations of regulation and emotionality to children's externalizing and internalizing problem behavior. *Child Development, 72,* 1112–1134.

Eisenberg, N., & Fabes, R. A. (Eds.). (1992). Emotion and its regulation in early development. *New Directions in Child Development, 55,* 1–110.

Eisenberg, N., Fabes, R. A., Guthrie, I., Murphy, B. C., Maszk, P., Holmgren, R., & Suh, K. (1996). The relations of regulation and emotionality to problem behavior in elementary school children. *Development and Psychopathology, 8,* 141–162.

Eisenberg, N., Fabes, R. A., Guthrie, I. K., & Reiser, M. (2000). Dispositional emotionality and regulation: Their role in predicting quality of social functioning. *Journal of Personality and Social Psychology, 78,* 136–157.

Eisenberg, N., Gershoff, E. T., Fabes, R. A., Shepard, S. A., Cumberland, A. J., Lososya, S. H., Guthrie, I. K., & Murphy, B. C. (2001). Mothers' emotional expressivity and children's behavior problems and social competence: Mediation through children's regulation. *Developmental Psychology, 37,* 475–490.

Eisenberg, N., Guthrie, I. K., Fabes, R. A., Shepard, S., Losoya, S., Murphy, B. C., Jones, S., Poulin, R., & Reiser, M. (2000). Prediction of elementary school children's externalizing problem behaviors from attentional and behavioral regulation and negative emotionality. *Child Development, 71,* 1367–1382.

Eisenberg, N., & Morris, A. S. (2002). Children's emotion-related regulation. In R. Kail (Ed.), *Advances in child development and behavior* (Vol. 30, pp. 190–229). San Diego: Academic Press.

Eisenberg, N., Morris, A. S., & Spinrad, T. L. (2005). Emotion-related regulation: The construct and its measurement. In D. Teti (Ed.), *Handbook of research methods in developmental psychology* (pp. 423–442). Oxford, England: Blackwell.

Eisenberg, N., Pidada, S., & Liew, J. (2001). The relations of regulation and negative emotionality to Indonesian children's social functioning. *Child Development, 72,* 1747–1763.

Eisenberg, N., Sadovsky, A., Spinrad, T. L., Fabes, R. A., Losoya, S. H., Valiente, C., Reiser, M., Cumberland, A., & Shepard, S. A. (2005). The relations of problem behavior status to children's negative emotionality, effortful control, and impulsivity: Concurrent relations and prediction of change. *Developmental Psychology, 41,* 193–211.

Eisenberg, N., & Spinrad, T. L. (2004). Emotion-related regulation: Sharpening the definition. *Child Development, 75,* 334–339.

Eisenberg, N., Spinrad, T. L., & Cumberland, A. (1998). Socialization of emotion: Reply to reviewers. *Psychological Inquiry, 9,* 317–333.

Eisenberg, N., Spinrad, T. L., Fabes, R. A., Reiser, M., Cumberland, A., Shepard, S. A., Valiente, C., Losoya, S. L., Guthrie, I. K., & Thompson, M. (2004). The relations of effortful control and impulsivity to children's resiliency and adjustment. *Child Development, 75,* 25–46.

Eisenberg, N., Valiente, C., Fabes, R. A., Smith, C. L., Reiser, M., Shepard, S.

A., Losoya, S. H., Guthrie, I. K., Murphy, B. C., & Cumberland, A. J. (2003). The relations of effortful control and ego control to children's resiliency and social functioning. *Developmental Psychology, 39,* 761–776.

Eisenberg, N., Valiente, C., Morris, A. S., Fabes, R. A., Cumberland, A., Reiser, M., Gershoff, E. T., Shepard, S. A., & Losoya, S. (2003). Longitudinal relations among parental emotional expressivity, children's regulation, and quality of socioemotional functioning. *Developmental Psychology, 39,* 2–19.

Erikson, E. (1950/1963). *Childhood and society.* New York: Norton.

Fox, N. A. (1989). Psycho-physiological correlates of emotional reactivity during the first year of life. *Developmental Psychology, 25,* 364–372.

Fox, N. A. (1994). Emotion regulation: Behavioral and biological considerations. *Monographs of the Society for Research in Child Development, 59* (Serial No. 240), 167–186.

Freud, S. (1997). Beyond the pleasure principle. In *Sigmund Freud: Selected writings* (pp. 235–310). New York: Norton. (Reprinted from *Civilization and its discontents,* [J. Strachey, Trans., 1961]).

Garber, J., Dodge, K. A. (Eds.). (1991). *The development of emotion regulation and dysregulation.* Cambridge, England: Cambridge University Press.

Gardner, H. (1978). *Developmental Psychology: An introduction.* Boston: Little, Brown.

Gianino, A., & Tronick, E. Z. (1988). The mutual regulation model: The infant's self- and interactive regulation, coping, and defense. In T. Field, P. McCabe, & N. Schneiderman (Eds.), *Stress and coping* (pp. 47–68). Hillsdale, NJ: Erlbaum.

Gilliom, M., Shaw, D. S., Beck, J. E., Schonberg, M. A., & Lukon, J. L. (2002). Anger regulation in disadvantaged preschool boys: Strategies, antecedents, and the development of self-control. *Developmental Psychology, 38,* 222–235.

Goldsmith, H. H., Buss, K. A., & Lemery, K. S. (1997). Toddler and childhood temperament: Expanded content, stronger genetic evidence, new evidence for the importance of environment. *Developmental Psychology, 33,* 891–905.

Gottman, J. M., Katz, L. F., & Hooven, C. (1997). *Meta-emotion: How families communicate emotionally.* Mahwah, NJ: Erlbaum.

Greenberg, M. T., Kusche, C. A., Cook, E. T., Quamma, J. P. (1995). Promoting emotional competence in school-aged children: The effects of the PATHS curriculum. *Development and Psychopathology, 7,* 117–136.

Gross, J. J. (1999). Emotion and emotion regulation. In L. A. Pervin & O. P. John (Eds.), *Handbook of personality: Theory and research* (2nd ed.; pp. 525–552). New York: Guilford.

Haan, N. (1963). An investigation of the relationship of Rorschach scores, patterns, and behavior to coping and defense mechanisms. *Journal of Projective Techniques, 28,* 429–441.

Haan, N. (1977). *Coping and defending: Processes of self-environment organization.* New York: Academic Press.

Kam, C-M., Greenberg, M. T., & Walls, C. T. (2003). Examining the role of implementation quality in school-based prevention using the PATHS curriculum. *Prevention Science, 4,* 55–63.

Kendall, P. C., & Wilcox, L. E. (1979). Self-control in children: The development of a rating scale. *Journal of Consulting and Clinical Psychology, 47,* 1020–1030.

Kochanska, G., & Knaack, A. (2003). Effortful control as a personality characteristic of young children: Antecedents, correlates, and consequences. *Journal of Personality, 71,* 1087–1112.

Kochanska, G., Murray, K. T., & Coy, K. C. (1997). Inhibitory control as a contributor to conscience in childhood: From toddler to early school age. *Child Development, 68,* 263–277.

Kochanska, G., Murray, K. , & Harlan, E. T. (2000). Effortful control in early childhood: Continuity and change, antecedents, and implications for social development. *Developmental Psychology, 36,* 220–232.

Kochanska, G., Tjebkes, T. L., & Forman, D. R. (1998). Children's emerging regulation of conduct: Restraint, compliance, and internalization from infancy to the second year. *Child Development, 69,* 1378–1389.

Kopp, C. B. (1982). Antecedents of self-regulation: A developmental perspective. *Development Psychology, 18,* 199–214.

Kopp, C. B., & Krakow, J. B. (1982). *The child: Development in a social context.* Reading, MA: Addison-Wesley.

Kopp, C. B., & Neufield, S. J. (2003). Emotional development during infancy. In R. Davidson, K. R. Scherer, & H. H. Goldsmith (Eds.), *Handbook of Affective Sciences* (pp. 347–374). Oxford, England: Oxford University Press.

Lazarus, R. S. (1966). *Psychological stress and the coping process.* New York: McGraw-Hill.

Lazarus, R. S., & Folkman, S. (1984). *Stress, appraisal, and coping* (pp. 282–325). New York: Springer.

Lemery, K. S., Essex, M. J., & Snider, N. A. (2002). Revealing the relation between temperament and behavior problem symptoms by eliminating measurement confounding: Expert ratings and factor analyses. *Child Development, 73,* 867–882.

Lengua, L. J. (2002). The contribution of emotionality and self-regulation to the understanding of children's response to multiple risk. *Child Development, 73,* 144–161.

Lengua, L. J., & Long, A. C. (2002). The role of emotionality and self-regulation in the appraisal-coping process: Tests of direct and moderating effects. *Journal of Applied Developmental Psychology, 23,* 471–493.

Lengua, L. J., & Sandler, I. N. (1996). Self-regulation as a moderator of the relation between coping and symptomatology in children of divorce. *Journal of Abnormal Child Psychology, 24,* 681–701.

Lengua, L. J., West, S. G., & Sandler, I. N. (1998). Temperament as a predictor of symptomatology in children: Addressing contamination of measures. *Child Development, 69,* 164–181.

Lengua, L. J., Wolchik, S. A., Sandler, I. N., & West, S. G. (2000). The additive and interactive effects of parenting and temperament in predicting problems of children of divorce. *Journal of Clinical Child Psychology, 29,* 232–244.

Mangelsdorf, S. C., Shapiro, J. R., & Marzolf, D. (1995). Developmental and temperamental differences in emotion regulation in infancy. *Child Development, 66,* 1817–1828.

Mezzacappa, E., Kindlon, D., Saul, J. P., & Earls, F. (1998). Executive and motivational control of performance task behavior, and autonomic heart-rate regulation in children: Physiological validation of two-factor solution inhibitory control. *Journal of Child Psychology and Psychiatry, 39,* 525–531.

Mischel, W., & Baker, N. (1972). Cognitive appraisals and transformations in delay behavior. *Journal of Personality and Social Psychology, 31,* 254–261.

Mischel, W., & Ebbesen, E. B. (1970). Attention in delay of gratification. *Journal of Personality and Social Psychology, 16,* 329–337.

Mischel, W., Shoda, Y., & Peake, P. K. (1988). The nature of adolescent competencies predicted by preschool delay of gratification. *Journal of Personality and Social Psychology, 54,* 687–696.

Murphy, B. C., Shepard, S. A., Eisenberg, N., & Fabes, R. A. (2004). Concurrent and across time prediction of young adolescents' social functioning: The role of emotionality and regulation. *Social Development, 13,* 56–86.

Mussen, P. H., Conger, J. J., Kagan, J., & Huston, A. C. (1984). *Child development and personality.* New York: Harper & Row.

Oldehinkel, A. J., Hartman, C. A., Winter, A. F. D., Veenstra, R., & Ormel, J. (2004). Temperament profiles associated with internalizing and externalizng problems in preadolescence. *Development and Psychopathology, 16,* 421–440.

Olson, S. L., Schilling, E. M., & Bates, J. E. (1999). Measurement of impulsivity: Construct coherence, longitudinal stability, and relationship with externalizing problems in middle childhood and adolescence. *Journal of Abnormal Child Psychology, 27,* 151–165.

Philippot, P., & Feldman, R. S. (Eds.). (2004). *The regulation of emotion.* Mahwah, NJ: Erlbaum.

Plomin, R., Emde, R. N., Braungart, J. M., Campos, J., Kagan, J., Reznick, J. S., Robinson, J., Zahn-Waxler, C., & Defries, J. C. (1993). Genetic change and continuity from fourteen to twenty months: The MacArthur Longitudinal Twin Study. *Child Development, 64,* 1354–1376.

Porges, S. W., Doussard-Roosevelt, J. A., & Maiti, A. K. (1994). Vagal tone and the physiological regulation of emotion. *Monographs of the Society for Research in Child Development, 59* (Serial No. 240), 167–186.

Pulkkinen, L. (1982). Self-control and continuity from childhood to late adolescence. In P. B. Baltes & O. Brim, Jr. (Eds.), *Life-span development and behavior* (Vol. 4., pp. 63–105). New York: Academic Press.

Pulkkinen, L. (1986). The role of impulse control in the development of antisocial and prosocial behavior. In D. Olweus, J. Block, & M. Radke-Yarrow (Eds.), *Development of antisocial and prosocial behavior: Research, theories, and issues* (pp. 149–206). Orlando, FL: Academic Press.

Pulkkinen, L., & Hamalainen, M. (1995). Low self-control as a precursor to crime and accidents in a Finnish longitudinal study. *Criminal Behaviour and Mental Health, 5,* 424–438.

Rothbart, M. K. (1981). Measurement of temperament in infancy. *Child Development, 52,* 569–578.

Rothbart, M. K. (1989). Temperament and development. In G. A. Kohnstamm, J. E. Bates, & M. K. Rothbart (Eds.), *Temperament in childhood* (pp. 187–248). New York: Wiley.

Rothbart, M. K., & Bates, J. E. (1998). Temperament. In W. Damon (Series Ed.) & N. Eisenberg (Vol. Ed.), *Handbook of child psychology: Vol. 3. Social, emotional, and personality development* (5th ed., pp. 105–176). New York: Wiley.

Rothbart, M. K., & Bates, J. E. (2006). Temperament. In W. Damon & R. Lerner (Series Eds.), N. Eisenberg (Vol. Ed.), *Handbook of Child Psychology: Vol. 3. Social, emotional, and personality development* (6th ed., pp. 99–166). New York: Wiley.

Rothbart, M. K., & Derryberry, D. (1981). Development of individual differences in temperament. In M. E. Lamb & A. L. Brown (Eds.), *Advances in developmental psychology* (Vol. 1, pp. 37–86). Hillsdale, NJ: Erlbaum.

Sandler, I. N., Tein, J., & West, S. G. (1994). Coping, stress, and the psychological symptoms of children of divorce: A cross-sectional and longitudinal study. *Child Development, 65,* 1744–1763.

Schell, Robert E. (Chief academic adviser and coordinator). (1975). *Developmental Psychology Today.* New York: Random House.

Shaffer, D. R. (1989). *Developmental psychology: Childhood and adolescence* (2nd ed.). Belmont, CA: Brooks/Cole.

Shaffer, D. R. (2002). *Developmental psychology: Childhood and adolescence* (6th ed.). Belmont, CA: Wadsworth.

Shoda, Y., Mischel, W., & Peake, P. K. (1990). Predicting adolescent cognitive and self-regulatory competencies from preschool delay of gratification: Identifying diagnostic conditions. *Developmental Psychology, 26,* 978–986.

Shonkoff, J. P., & Phillips, D. A. (Eds.), & Committee on Integrating the Science of Early Childhood Development. (2000). *From neurons to neighborhoods: The science of early childhood development.* Washington DC: National Academy of Science.

Siegler, R., Deloache, J., & Eisenberg, N. (2003). *How children develop.* New York: Worth.

Society for Research in Child Development. (1981, April). *Program book.* Biennial meeting, Boston.

Society for Research in Child Development. (1989, April). *Abstracts (Vol. 6).* Biennial meeting, Kansas City, MO.

Society for Research in Child Development. (2003, April). *Program book.* Biennial meeting, Tampa, FL.

Stansbury, K., & Gunnar, M. R. (1994). Adrenocortical activity and emotion regulation. *Monographs of the Society for Research in Child Development, 59* (Serial No. 240), 108–134.

Stifter, C. A., & Moyer, A. (1991). The regulation of positive affect: Gaze aversion activity during mother-infant interaction. *Infant Behavior and Development, 14,* 111–123.

Teglasi, H., & Macmahon, B. H. (1990). Temperament and common problem behaviors of children. *Journal of Applied Developmental Psychology, 11,* 331–349.

Thompson, R. A. (1994). Emotion regulation: A theme in search of definition. *Monographs of the Society for Research in Child Development, 59* (Serial No. 240), 25–52.

Thompson, R. A., & Calkins, S. D. (1996). The double-edged sword: Emotional regulation for children at risk. *Development and Psychopathology, 8,* 163–182.

Valiente, C., Eisenberg, N., Smith, C. L., Reiser, M., Fabes, R. A., Losoya, S., Guthrie, I. K., & Murphy, B. C. (2003). The relations of effortful control and reactive control to children's externalizing problems: A longitudinal assessment. *Journal of Personality, 71,* 1171–1196.

Vasey, M. W., El-Hag, N., & Daleiden, E. L. (1996). Anxiety and the processing of emotionally threatening stimuli: Distinctive patterns of selective attention among high- and low-test-anxious children. *Child Development, 67,* 1173–1185.

White, J. L., Moffitt, T. E., Caspi, A., Bartusch, D. J., Needles, D. J., & Stouthamer-Loeber, M. (1994). Measuring impulsivity and examining its relationship to delinquency. *Journal of Abnormal Psychology, 103,* 192–205.

Wills, T. A., Duhamel, K., & Vaccaro, D. (1995). Activity and mood temperament as predictors of adolescent substance use: Test of a self-regulation mediational model. *Journal of Personality and Social Psychology, 68,* 901–916.

Zhou, Q., Eisenberg, N., Wang, Y., & Reiser, M. (2004). Chinese children's effortful control and dispositional anger/frustration: Relations to parenting styles and children's social functioning. *Developmental Psychology, 40,* 352–366.

8

The Role of Mental Representation in Social Development

Carol S. Dweck and Bonita E. London

Since the 1950s one of the most important advances has been the introduction of mental representation as a means of understanding development. Across all areas of developmental psychology, starting in earnest in the 1970s and 1980s, came the idea that children's mental representations and concepts—number concepts, object concepts, representations of grammatical rules, self-conceptions, attachment/relationship conceptions, causal conceptions, and the like—could give us unique insights into how experience is registered and how it goes on to shape the child's subsequent interactions with the physical and social world.

Mental representations are the means through which children package their experiences and carry them forward. As we will show, notable advances in the last few decades have been made in identifying the kinds of mental representations that can play a key role in social development. However, except for attachment researchers, much of the field remains relatively unconcerned with concepts and beliefs as carriers of experience and as mediators of the effects of experience on subsequent functioning. An examination of the tables of contents of the major journals in developmental psychology in recent years documents this trend. Most articles on predictors of children's personal and social functioning look at some potentially formative experience (e.g., exposure to aggression or maternal depression) and then track children's outcomes (e.g., aggression or depression), often seeking to understand the relation between the experience and the outcome in terms of nonpsychological variables (e.g., the child's age, the presence of siblings, the neighborhood), or they identify some characteristic of the child and evaluate how it predicts the child's future outcomes. Mediators and moderators are statistical but often not psychological.

We do not wish to deny the enormous importance of the many findings this approach has yielded. It has contributed invaluable information about the antecedents of important emotional and behavioral patterns and about the conditions under which they are likely to emerge. We do wish to argue, however, that that approach cannot give us a full understanding of social development and of the impact of experience on social development. Thus in this chapter we will show:

1. How children's mental representations (their beliefs or concepts) influence the social and self-related outcomes that we are most interested in—achievement, self-esteem, depression, and peer relations—and how they do so by shaping the ways in which children interact with their worlds.

2. That these beliefs can be the carriers of socialization and thus a means through which experience affects outcomes. For example, there is now evidence that the impact of exposure to violence, abuse, or parental depression can depend on how that experience is represented by the child. This supports the idea that understanding the impact of parents requires attention to children's beliefs.

3. How this approach has key implications for socialization practices and interventions, for example, by showing how relatively modest, belief-targeted interventions can have surprisingly powerful effects, while other seemingly worthy ones may have little discernable impact.

We also suggest that the study of mental representations can link social development to other areas of psychology. Social development has surprisingly few links to other areas of psychology. In some ways this may be necessitated by the complex, real-world nature of our subject matter, but it is nonetheless something that impoverishes all parties. By encouraging a common and mutually interesting set of ideas and findings, the study of mental representations could create a much-needed bridge to other areas, such as social psychology, personality psychology, cognitive psychology, and cognitive neuroscience. At the heart of cutting-edge approaches in all these areas is the idea that people mentally represent their experiences (including their emotional experiences) and that studying these representations and their organization can illuminate the processes that we all seek to understand.

Mental Representations and Social Development

Children's underlying beliefs and concepts have been shown to play key roles across many areas of developmental psychology, illuminating such diverse areas as the study of self and identity (e.g., Bandura, 1986; Harter, 2003; Martin, Ruble, & Szkrybalo, 2002), attachment relationships (e.g., Main, Kaplan, & Cassidy, 1985; Thompson, 2000; cf. Bowlby, 1969/1982), peer relations and stereotyping (e.g., Crick & Dodge, 1996; Dodge, 1980; Downey, Lebolt, Rincon, & Freitas, 1998; Hirschfeld, 1995; Levy & Dweck, 1999), and coping and achievement processes (Cain & Dweck, 1995; Dweck & Reppucci, 1973; Fincham, Hokoda, & Sanders, 1989; Nolen-Hoeksema, Girgus, & Seligman, 1992; Skinner, Zimmer-Gembeck, & Connell, 1998). Even many researchers who do not typically study children's beliefs have recently called attention to the importance of studying beliefs in order to understand development. These include such personality, temperament, and emotion researchers as Jack Block (1993), Mary Rothbart (Rothbart & Ahadi, 1994), and Michael Lewis (1999; Lewis & Sullivan, 2005). Block proposed that internal models, schema, and premise systems are major links between early experiences with parents and later personality functioning. Rothbart acknowledges that personality consists of much more than temperament and, it is important to note, includes the ways in which one perceives the self, others, and events. Lewis suggests that children's experiences, including traumatic ones, affect not only their emotions but also, what may be more important, how they think about themselves; these emotions and beliefs then work together to determine future adjustment.

Moreover, in recent articles about the attachment literature, Thompson (2000; Thompson & Raikes, 2003) has pointed to mental representations as a bridge between children's early experiences and their later expectations and behavior, eloquently arguing for a clearer understanding of the nature, development, and workings of these representations. Near the end of his life even Piaget (Piaget & Garcia, 1989) conceded that the worldviews that children develop might guide their behavior in ways that are perhaps as important as their logical thinking.

In this chapter, for simplicity and clarity, we will focus primarily on one class of beliefs, namely, attributions—beliefs about the causes of outcomes and behavior. Specifically, we will carry through our arguments using illustrations from the literature on children's attributions for their own outcomes and children's attributions for the behavior of others. Both strands of research arose in the 1970s and 1980s, have had rich and continuing lives, and have shown the power of even one belief to influence important behavior and predict important outcomes.

What These Beliefs Predict

SELF-ATTRIBUTIONS

Here we focus on children's attributions for their own outcomes, particularly blaming their global traits for their failures. By preschool and kindergarten children's attributions are already exerting important influences on their affect and persistence in the face of obstacles (Dweck, 1999; Heyman, Dweck, & Cain, 1992; Ziegert, Kistner, Castro, & Robertson, 2001; see also Alessandri & Lewis, 1993), with the global negative self-attributions predicting shame and sadness as well as helpless reactions to criticism or failure. Moreover, the helpless patterns seen in kindergarten have been shown to be relatively stable over a 5-year period (Ziegert et al., 2001). It is critical to note that none of the effects we report are the result of differences in children's actual ability.

Several years later, by mid- to late grade school, children's global negative self-attributions begin to reliably predict their vulnerability to depression (Cole & Turner, 1993; Fincham, Diener, & Hokoda, 1987) and to declining school achievement (Fincham, Hokoda, & Sanders, 1989). This relation becomes even stronger and more consistent as children move into adolescence (Garber, Keiley, & Martin, 2002; Hankin, Abramson, & Siler, 2001; Nolen-Hoeksema, Girgus, & Seligman, 1992; Robinson, Garber, & Hilsman, 1995).

These kinds of attributions also play a role in peer relations (Erdley, Cain, Loomis, Dumas-Hines, & Dweck, 1997; Fincham & Hokoda, 1987; Giles & Heyman, 2003; Goetz & Dweck, 1980), predicting a helpless reaction to social setbacks or peer rejection. Indeed, Graham and Juvonen (1998), in a study of adolescents, showed that global self-blame exacerbated the effects of peer victimization. Over and above the severity of victimization, global self-blame strongly predicted loneliness and social anxiety and was, in fact, a mediator of the impact of victimization on these social adjustment variables.

Building on the attribution work, recent research has identified a related class of beliefs (children's self-theories) that appear to generate these global self-attributions in the achievement domain: the belief that one's intelligence is a fixed trait rather than a malleable quality that can be developed. That is, students who believe in fixed intelligence are more prone to blaming that fixed intelligence (as opposed to their effort) when they encounter failure (Blackwell, Dweck, & Trzesniewski, in press; Henderson & Dweck, 1990; Robins & Pals, 2002; Trzesniewski & Robins, 2002; cf. Hong, Chiu, Dweck, Lin, & Wan, 1999). Those who believe their intelligence is a more malleable quality that they can develop tend to focus on effort and strategy attributions when they fail.

In several studies of school transitions, the fixed theory of intelligence, by giving rise to global ability attributions for setbacks, predicted declining grades as well as declining self-esteem, in contrast to the malleable theory of intelligence, which, by fostering the more mastery-oriented effort attributions, predicted rising grades (Blackwell et al., in press; Henderson & Dweck, 1990; Trzesniewski & Robins, 2002) and rising self-esteem (Robins and Pals, 2002; Trzesniewski & Robins, 2002). This research highlights the robust effect of adolescent beliefs on their adjustment in critical areas.

ATTRIBUTIONS ABOUT OTHERS

Here we will focus on the hostile attributional bias, identified by Dodge and his colleagues (Dodge, 1980; Dodge & Frame, 1982). This attributional bias occurs when, in response to ambiguous provocation, children attribute hostile intent to the provocateur. From early grade school on, this hostile attributional bias is found among aggressive children and leads to anger and aggressive retaliation in the face of perceived provocation (e.g., Dodge & Frame, 1982; Graham, Hudley, & Williams, 1992). Moreover, this attributional bias appears to mediate increases in aggression over time (Zelli, Dodge, Lochman, Laird, and the Conduct Problems Prevention Group, 1999), primarily by creating greater accessibility of aggressive responses.

Recently, Orobio de Castro, Veerman, Koops, Bosch, and Monshouwer (2002) performed a meta-analysis of 41 studies with 6,017 participants and found a robust, significant relationship between hostile attributions and aggressive behavior, providing further evidence for the impact of attributions on behavioral outcomes.

In summary, there is impressive evidence that children's beliefs play a highly important role in their coping, adjustment, and achievement in major areas of their lives. These beliefs are not only related to children's contemporaneous functioning but are also predictive of their functioning over time.

Beliefs as the Carriers of Socialization and Experience

It is often difficult to detect the effects of children's socialization experiences on their developmental outcomes. Some children who experience abuse or have depressed mothers have obvious adjustment problems, whereas others do not. This is perhaps why some authors are moved to claim that parenting makes little difference (e.g., Harris, 1998).

However, the way in which an experience affects children can depend on how they mentally represent it, that is, how it changes their beliefs. The research that we review next suggests that, indeed, negative experiences appear to have clearer or more major consequences for adjustment and well-being when they affect children's beliefs. We focus on studies that examine relatively extreme experiences, for they serve to highlight the importance of beliefs as carriers of experience.

SELF-ATTRIBUTIONS

Maternal depression

Maternal depression is known to have widespread effects on the development of children and to predict their later vulnerability to depression. Yet research suggests that maternal depression per se may be less influential in predicting children's depression than are maternal practices that convey a sense of control or lack of control (Nolen-Hoeksema, Wolfson, Mumme, & Guskin, 1995) or that impart negative attributions (Crossfield, Alloy, Gibb, & Abramson, 2002).

More evidence that it is not simply maternal depression but rather experiences that mold attributions comes from a recent 5-year longitudinal study of children in 6th through 11th grade. In this study Garber, Keiley, and Martin (2002) found that although maternal depression did predict children's initial levels of depression, children's attributions predicted the trajectory of depression: growth in negative self-attributions foreshadowed growth in depression, whereas a decline in these attributions foreshadowed a decline in depression.

Abuse

Feiring, Taska, and Lewis (2002) studied adjustment following sexual abuse. When they controlled for initial adjustment, they found that shame and attributional style (not abuse severity) predicted long-term adjustment. (Abuse severity predicted depression and low self-esteem only for children who already had global negative self-attributions.) And, as in the 2002 study by Garber, Keiley, and Martin, change in attributional style predicted improvement or worsening of adjustment, including changes in post-traumatic stress disorder symptoms.

Domestic violence between parents

Parents who engage in violent acts toward each other clearly provide their children with a highly negative rearing experience. Grych, Jouriles, Swank, McDonald, and Norwood (2000) examined the impact of domestic violence on children's adjustment. First, 31% of the children in this sample did not exhibit clear signs of maladjustment on the measures of internalizing and externalizing symptoms. What is important to note is that how the children represented the experience consistently predicted their adjustment. In particular, self-blame distinguished the "multi-problem internalizing group" from other groups. This group had by far the most severe depressive symptoms and by far the lowest self-esteem of the five groups considered. Moreover, children's cognitive appraisals (both of threat and self-blame) distinguished the groups better than the frequency, intensity, and resolution of parental violence (see also Grych, Fincham, Jouriles, & McDonald, 2000).

ATTRIBUTIONS ABOUT OTHERS

Having established the role of hostile attributions in the generation of aggression, Dodge and his colleagues went on to examine the role of children's experiences in fostering hostile attributions. They found that several types of negative childhood experiences, such as physical abuse (Dodge, Pettit, Bates, & Valente, 1995), harsh discipline (Weiss, Dodge, Bates, & Pettit, 1992), or peer rejection (Dodge, Lansford, et al., 2003), resulted in clear increases in the tendency toward hostile attributions. Although the resulting hostile attributions did not always directly mediate the path to future conduct problems, the findings are consistent with the idea that harsh treatment "shape[s] the child's knowledge structures, which are stored in memory and which, in turn, shape the manner in which a child processes information in future social interactions" (Dodge, Pettit, et al., 1995, p. 641).

Of course, not all maltreated children develop deviant attributional styles, but Dodge, Pettit, and colleagues (1995) found that the odds of doing so were far greater for them than for nonabused children, and this may represent an important way that abuse experiences are carried forward.

EMOTIONAL EXPERIENCES AFFECT MENTAL REPRESENTATIONS

There is growing evidence that children's own emotional experiences can play a powerful role in molding their beliefs. That is, in addition to socialization experiences from the outside, experiences from the inside (e.g., shame, distress, or depression) can foster the development of attributions, which then, together with the emotion, can go on to drive behavior. Much current developmental research focuses on the affect and affect regulation part of the picture but not on the mutual influence of affect and mental representation, either contemporaneously or over time.

Lewis and his colleagues (Feiring et al., 2002; see also Lewis, 1999; Lewis & Sullivan, 2005) propose that early experiences with intense negative emotions (such as shame) predict later negative self-attributions, which then go to produce helplessness. Data from other sources are supportive of this proposal. For example, Nolen-Hoeksema, Girgus, and Seligman (1992) showed that when children suffered periods of depression, their tendency to make negative self-attributions increased and remained higher even after the depression lifted, which put them at increased risk for future depression. In a recent study Pomerantz and Rudolph (2003) followed more than 900 late-grade-school children, examining the impact that experiences of emotional distress (depression or anxiety) had on their later views of their competence. They found that in both the academic and social realms, children's emotional distress led to more negative attributions, which then led to poorer views of their competence over time.

In summary, much evidence is emerging that children's experiences mold their beliefs and that through these beliefs their experiences affect their future functioning.

New Insights into Socialization Practices

As we suggested earlier, the impact of parenting cannot be fully understood until researchers take account of children's beliefs. This is not only because different children may mentally represent their experiences in different ways, but also because until we understand children's mental representations, we will not know what particular parenting practices to look for. Researchers have often tended to look at broad dimensions of child-rearing practices, such as parental responsiveness, because these dimensions have been seen as relevant to the child's acquisition of overall competence and security. Very early on this may be exactly what matters, but later on children may be forming much more fine-grained, specific beliefs about themselves and the world.

This is when thinking about practices that can lead to particular self-attributions or self-theories can lead us to look beyond the general positivity-negativity or responsiveness of parental feedback or practices. Instead, it leads us to think about the attribution that is taught or the message that is sent by the parental practice. For example, in attempting to understand why girls often make more global self-attributions for their failures than do boys, Alessandri and Lewis (1993) found that parents give significantly more specific feedback to boys than to girls, and Dweck, Davidson, Nelson, and Enna (1978) found that teachers made more effort attributions for boys' difficulties than they did for girls'.

Recent work by Mueller and Dweck (1998) even more clearly illustrates how this analysis can lead one to look in unlikely places. Common sense suggests that praising children's intelligence when they succeed on a challenging task can only build their confidence and enjoyment, leading to more positive achievement outcomes. However, thinking about the messages behind intelligence praise gives one pause. By praising children's intelligence, one may be telling them that some fixed inner quality is causing their performance (rather than their effort or strategies). In a series of six studies with late-grade-school children, Mueller and Dweck indeed found that intelligence praise (which, by the way, children loved) led to a host of negative effects when children later encountered more difficult problems. Interestingly, they made global negative self-attributions for their difficulty, for if success meant they were smart, then failure meant they were not. In addition, they showed a steep decline in their task enjoyment and in their subsequent performance. In contrast, students who had been praised for their effort remained focused on effort when they hit difficulty, maintained their enjoyment of the task, and showed enhanced performance on subsequent trials.

In the same vein preliminary work (Dweck & Lennon, 2001) suggests that students who perceive their parents to be giving them person-focused feedback (such as the intelligence praise) versus process-focused feedback (such as the effort praise) show more fixed self-theories, more global self-attributions for failure, and more academic difficulties across the transition to junior high school (controlling for entering achievement). It is interesting to note that the tendency toward process-focused feedback was related to authoritative rearing practices (à la Baumrind, 1968), but it was the process-focused (versus person-focused) feedback, and not the authoritative rearing, that accounted for the differences in beliefs and academic performance. This is important, since there are many cultural groups in which authoritative rearing practices, however desirable we think them to be, are incompatible with the prevailing customs. However, incorporating process-focused feedback could be accomplished without changing the structure and philosophy of the family.

Thus, although much further work needs to be done, this research suggests that looking for practices that foster particular beliefs can lead us beyond broad styles of child rearing to pinpoint critical ingredients in socialization practices.

Beliefs Have Implications for Targeted Interventions

If beliefs control important aspects of children's functioning, it follows that changing these beliefs should result in changes in functioning. This is good news, since beliefs can be changed. Indeed, one may get even more benefit from a belief-changing intervention than might seem plausible given the magnitude of the child's problem (relatively large) and the magnitude of the intervention (relatively small).

In line with this, Dweck (1975), working with extremely academically helpless children, showed that changing their global negative self-attributions for failure (from blaming their ability to focusing on their effort) resulted in enhanced persistence in the face of failure, both on experimental tasks and in the classroom.

Recently, several interventions have focused on students' self-theories, since self-theories affect not only students' attributions but also their achievement goals (e.g., whether they value learning versus looking smart) and their beliefs about the efficacy of their effort. In a recent study Blackwell, Dweck, and Trzesniewski (in press) worked with seventh-grade students who had recently made the transition to junior high and were suffering steep declines in their grades. Both the experimental group and the control group received an 8-session multifaceted intervention that, among other things, taught them study skills, discussed their academic problems, and delivered strong antistereotyping messages. This message taught the students—mostly minority group members—not to let stereotypes and labels limit them. However, in addition, the experimental group received several sessions on the malleable theory of intelligence, learning how the brain grows new connections and makes them smarter every time they learn, and learning how to apply this lesson to their schoolwork. At the end of the semester the intervention group had earned significantly higher grades than the control group and were reported by their teachers (who were blind to their experimental condition) to have shown marked changes in motivation.

A similar intervention study by Good, Aronson, and Inzlicht (2003), also with students making the transition to junior high school, showed increased math and verbal achievement test scores for those in the experimental group. In both studies, then, a targeted belief-changing intervention had far more impact than one might expect, given the scope of the intervention. In both studies, as well, a highly worthy control intervention had little or no beneficial impact.

In the social arena Hudley and Graham (1993) set out to change the hostile attributions of aggressive boys. In a series of sessions the experimental group received instruction in how to identify peers' intent, how to generate nonhostile attributions, and how to respond appropriately to ambiguous provocation. Posttraining measures showed these children to be significantly less aggressive and more prosocial than the control groups, both in the face of peer provocation in a laboratory setting and on teacher ratings of aggression in the classroom (with teachers, again, being blind to the children's experimental condition).

Although researchers need to determine whether these gains are lasting and, if not, how to sustain them, knowledge of the beliefs that guide children's behavior has clear promise as a means to designing effective interventions.

The work we have reviewed underscores the importance of children's mental representations for their personal and social functioning. Children's beliefs predict such critical things as their achievement, self-esteem, depression, and peer relations over time. Major socialization experiences appear to affect children most when they have an impact on their beliefs. Focusing on children's beliefs can also provide new insights into socialization practices and into interventions that are likely to be maximally effective.

Taken together, these findings about the importance of beliefs in shaping children's adjustment and achievement over time raise important issues for developmental psychology. First, different developmental trajectories are typically understood in terms of different skill levels—either intellectual skills or coping and self-regulatory skills. The work reviewed here has shown that children's beliefs can also govern their trajectories. This is an exciting topic for future research.

Second, the issue of continuity and change is one that has always intrigued and plagued developmental psychology. We wish to heartily echo Thompson (2000), who suggests that children's representations of their experience hold a key to understanding continuity and change (cf. Westen, 1998). When children's experiences consolidate or strengthen their existing beliefs, we should expect continuity, but when their experiences instill new beliefs, we should expect change. This important point was highlighted by the studies that tracked children's beliefs over time and by the interventions that altered children's beliefs.

Finally, as we proposed at the outset, giving mental representation its due could provide a stronger link between social development and other areas of psychology. For example, some of the most exciting current approaches to personality (e.g., Mischel & Shoda, 1995), emotion (Barrett & Gross, 2001; Clore & Colcombe, 2003), and cognitive neuroscience (Damasio, 1994) are built around people's mental representations, often enriching our understanding of how these mental representations work in concert with emotional processes to affect behavior (e.g., Ochsner, Bunge, Gross, & Gabrieli, 2002). Social development has much to offer these other areas—rich findings and big-picture wisdom that would greatly inform their research—and social development, in turn, would profit from the conceptual and methodological advances that are emerging from these areas.

In closing, we hope that the next 50 years of *Merrill-Palmer Quarterly* will be filled with articles that illuminate how children represent and carry forward their experience, and we hope that these articles are fully as exciting as we expect them to be.

References

Alessandri, S. M., & Lewis, M. (1993). Parental evaluation and its relation to shame and pride in young children. *Sex Roles, 29,* 335–343.
Bandura, A. (1986). *Social foundations of thought and action: A social cognitive theory.* Englewood Cliffs, NJ: Prentice-Hall.
Barrett, L. F., & Gross, J. J. (2001). Emotional intelligence: A process model

of emotion representation and regulation. In T. J. Mayne & G. A. Bonanno (Eds.), *Emotions: Current issues and future directions* (pp. 286–310). New York: Guilford.

Baumrind, D. (1968). Authoritarian vs. authoritative parental control. *Adolescence, 3*, 255–272.

Blackwell, L. S., Dweck, C. S., & Trzesniewski, K. (in press). Implicit theories of intelligence predict achievement across an adolescent transition: A longitudinal study and an intervention. *Child Development.*

Block, J. (1993). Studying personality the long way. In D. C. Funder, R. D. Parke, C. Tomlinson-Keasey, & J. Block (Eds.), *Studying lives through time: Personality and development* (pp. 9–41). Washington, DC: American Psychological Association.

Bowlby, J. (1969/1982). *Attachment and loss: Vol. 1. Attachment.* New York: Basic Books.

Cain, K., & Dweck, C. S. (1995). The development of children's achievement motivation patterns and conceptions of intelligence. *Merrill-Palmer Quarterly, 41*, 25–52.

Clore, G. L., & Colcombe, S. (2003). The parallel worlds of affective concepts and feelings. In J. Musch & K. C. Klauer (Eds.), *The psychology of evaluation: Affective processes in cognition and emotion* (pp. 335–369). Mahwah, NJ: Erlbaum.

Cole, D. A., & Turner, J. E. (1993). Models of cognitive mediation and moderation in child depression. *Journal of Abnormal Psychology, 102*, 271–281.

Crick, N. R., & Dodge, K. A. (1996). Social information-processing mechanisms in children's social adjustment. *Child Development, 67*, 993–1002.

Crossfield, A. G., Alloy, L. B., Gibb, B. E., & Abramson, L. Y. (2002). The development of depressogenic cognitive styles: The role of negative childhood life events and parental inferential feedback. *Journal of Cognitive Psychotherapy, 16*, 487–502.

Damasio, A. R. (1994). *Descartes' error: Emotion, reason, and the human brain.* New York: Grosset/Putman.

Dodge, K. A. (1980). Social cognition and children's aggressive behavior. *Child Development, 51*, 162–170.

Dodge, K. A., & Frame, C. L. (1982). Social cognitive biases and deficits in aggressive boys. *Child Development, 53*, 620–635.

Dodge, K. A., Lansford, J. E., Burks, V. S., Bates, J. E., Pettit, G. S., Fontaine, R., & Price, J. M. (2003). Peer rejection and social information-processing factors in the development of aggressive behavior problems in children. *Child Development, 74*, 374–393.

Dodge, K. A., Pettit, G. S., Bates, J. E., & Valente, E. (1995). Social information-processing patterns partially mediate the effect of early physical abuse on later conduct problems. *Journal of Abnormal Psychology, 104*, 632–643.

Downey, G., Lebolt, A., Rincon, C., & Freitas, A. (1998). Rejection sensitivity and children's interpersonal difficulties. *Child Development, 69*, 1074–1091.

Dweck, C. S. (1975). The role of expectations and attributions in the alleviation of learned helplessness. *Journal of Personality and Social Psychology, 31*, 674–685.

Dweck, C. S. (1999). *Self-theories: Their role in motivation, personality and development.* Philadelphia: Psychology Press.

Dweck, C. S., Davidson, W., Nelson, S., & Enna, B. (1978). Sex differences in learned helplessness: (II) The contingencies of evaluative feedback in the classroom and (III) An experimental analysis. *Developmental Psychology, 14*, 268–276.

Dweck, C. S., & Lennon, C. (2001, April). *Person vs. process-focused parenting styles.* Paper presented at the Meeting of the Society for Research in Child Development, Minneapolis.

Dweck, C. S., & Reppucci, N. D. (1973). Learned helplessness and reinforcement responsibility in children. *Journal of Personality and Social Psychology, 25*, 109–116.

Erdley, C., Cain, K., Loomis, C., Dumas-Hines, F., & Dweck, C. S. (1997). The relations among children's social goals, implicit personality theories, and response to social failure. *Developmental Psychology, 33*, 263–272.

Feiring, C., Taska, L., & Lewis, M. (2002). Adjustment following sexual abuse discovery: The role of shame and attributional style. *Developmental Psychology, 38*, 79–92.

Fincham, F. D., Diener, C. I., & Hokoda, A. (1987). Attributional style and learned helplessness: Relationship to the use of causal schemata and depressive symptoms in children. *British Journal of Social Psychology, 26*, 1–7.

Fincham, F. D., & Hokoda, A. (1987). Learned helplessness in social situations and sociometric status. *European Journal of Social Psychology, 17*, 95–111.

Fincham, F. D., Hokoda, A., & Sanders, R. (1989). Learned helplessness, test anxiety, and academic achievement: A longitudinal analysis. *Child Development, 60*, 138–145.

Garber, J., Keiley, M. K., & Martin, N. C. (2002). Developmental trajectories of adolescents' depressive symptoms: Predictors of change. *Journal of Consulting and Clinical Psychology, 70*, 79–95.

Giles, J. W., & Heyman, G. D. (2003). Preschoolers' beliefs about the stability of antisocial behavior: Implications for navigating social challenges. *Social Development, 12*, 182–197.

Goetz, T. E., & Dweck, C. S. (1980). Learned helplessness in social situations. *Journal of Personality and Social Psychology, 39*, 246–255.

Good, C., Aronson, J., & Inzlicht, M. (2003). Improving adolescents' standardized test performance: An intervention to reduce the effects of stereotype threat. *Journal of Applied Developmental Psychology, 24*, 645–662.

Graham, S., Hudley, C., & Williams, E. (1992). Attributional and emotional determinants of aggression among African-American and Latino young adolescents. *Developmental Psychology, 28*, 731–740.

Graham, S., & Juvonen, J. (1998). Self-blame and peer victimization in middle school: An attributional analysis. *Developmental Psychology, 34*, 587–599.

Grych, J. H., Fincham, F. D., Jouriles, E. N., & McDonald, R. (2000). Interparental conflict and child adjustment: Testing the mediational role of appraisals in the cognitive-contextual framework. *Child Development, 71*, 1648–1661.

Grych, J. H., Jouriles, E. N., Swank, P. R., McDonald, R., & Norwood, W. D. (2000). Patterns of adjustment among children of battered women. *Journal of Consulting and Clinical Psychology, 68*, 84–94.

Hankin, B. L., Abramson, L. Y., & Siler, M. (2001). A prospective test of the hopelessness theory of depression in adolescence. *Cognitive Therapy and Research, 25*, 607–632.

Harris, J. (1998). *The nurture assumption.* New York: Free Press.

Harter, S. (2003). The development of self-representations during childhood and adolescence. In J. P. Tangney & M. R. Leary (Eds.), *Handbook of self and identity* (pp. 610–642). New York: Guilford.

Henderson, V., & Dweck, C. S. (1990). Achievement and motivation in adolescence: A new model and data. In S. Feldman and G. Elliott (Eds.), *At the threshold: The developing adolescent* (pp. 308–329). Cambridge, MA: Harvard University Press.

Heyman, G. D., Dweck, C. S., & Cain, K. (1992). Young children's vulnerability to self-blame and helplessness. *Child Development, 63*, 401–415.

Hirschfeld, L. A. (1995). Do children have a theory of race? *Cognition, 54*, 209–252.

Hong, Y. Y., Chiu, C., Dweck, C. S., Lin, D., & Wan, W. (1999). Implicit theories, attributions, and coping: A meaning system approach. *Journal of Personality and Social Psychology, 77*, 588–599.

Hudley, C., & Graham, S. (1993). An attributional intervention to reduce peer-directed aggression among African-American boys. *Child Development, 64*, 124–138.

Levy, S. R., & Dweck, C. S. (1999). Children's static vs. dynamic person conceptions as predictors of their stereotype formation. *Child Development, 70*, 1163–1180.

Lewis, M. (1999). The role of the self in cognition and emotion. In T. Dalgleish & M. J. Power (Eds.), *Handbook of cognition and emotion* (pp. 125–142). New York: Wiley.

Lewis, M., & Sullivan, M. W. (2005). The development of self-conscious emotions. In A. Elliot & C. Dweck (Eds.), *Handbook of competence and motivation* (pp. 185–201). New York: Guilford.

Main, M., Kaplan, N., & Cassidy, J. (1985). Security of infancy, childhood, and adulthood: A move to the level of representation. *Monographs of the Society for Research in Child Development, 50* (Serial No. 209), 66–106.

Martin, C. L., Ruble, D. N., & Szkrybalo, J. (2002). Cognitive theories of early gender development. *Psychological Bulletin, 128*, 903–933.

Mischel, W., & Shoda, Y. (1995). A cognitive-affective systems theory of personality: Reconceptualizing the invariances in personality and the role of situations. *Psychological Review, 102,* 246–268.

Mueller, C. M., & Dweck, C. S. (1998). Intelligence praise can undermine motivation and performance. *Journal of Personality and Social Psychology, 75,* 33–52.

Nolen-Hoeksema, S., Girgus, J., & Seligman, M. E. (1992). Predictors and consequences of childhood depressive symptoms: A 5-year longitudinal study. *Journal of Abnormal Psychology, 101,* 405–422.

Nolen-Hoeksema, S., Wolfson, A., Mumme, D., & Guskin, K. (1995). Helplessness in children of depressed and nondepressed mothers. *Developmental Psychology, 31,* 377–387.

Ochsner, K. N., Bunge, S. A., Gross, J. J., & Gabrieli, J. D. (2002). Rethinking feelings: An fMRI study of the cognitive regulation of emotion. *Journal of Cognitive Neuroscience, 14,* 1215–1229.

Orobio de Castro, B., Veermen, J. W., Koops, W., Bosch, J. D., & Monshouwer, H. J. (2002). Hostile attributional intent and aggressive behavior: A meta-analysis. *Child Development, 73,* 916–934.

Piaget, J., & Garcia, R. (1989). *Psychogenesis and the history of science* (H. Feider, Trans). New York: Columbia University Press.

Pomerantz, E. M., & Rudolph, K. D. (2003). What ensues from emotional distress? Implications for competence estimation. *Child Development, 74,* 329–345.

Robins, R. W., & Pals, J. L. (2002). Implicit self-theories in the academic domain: Implications for goal orientation, attributions, affect, and self-esteem change. *Self and Identity, 1,* 313–336.

Robinson, N. S., Garber, J., & Hilsman, R. (1995). Cognitions and stress: Direct and moderating effects on depressive versus externalizing symptoms during the junior high school transition. *Journal of Abnormal Psychology, 104,* 453–463.

Rothbart, M. K., & Ahadi, S. A. (1994). Temperament and the development of personality. *Journal of Abnormal Psychology, 103,* 55–66.

Skinner, E. A., Zimmer-Gembeck, M. J., & Connell, J. P. (1998). Individual differences and the development of perceived control. *Monographs of the Society for Research in Child Development, 63* (2–3).

Thompson, R. A. (2000). The legacy of early attachments. *Child Development, 71,* 145–152.

Thompson, R. A., & Raikes, H. A. (2003). Toward the next quarter century: Conceptual and methodological challenges for attachment theory. *Development and Psychopathology, 15,* 691–718.

Trzesniewski, K., & Robins, R. W. (2002, April). *Integrating self-esteem into a process model of academic achievement.* Paper presented at the biennial meeting of the Society for Research in Child Development, Tampa, FL.

Weiss, B., Dodge, K. A., Bates, J. E., & Pettit, G. S. (1992). Some consequences of early harsh discipline: Child aggression and a maladaptive social information processing style. *Child Development, 63,* 1321–1335.

Westen, D. (1998). The scientific legacy of Sigmund Freud: Toward a psychodynamically informed psychological science. *Psychological Bulletin, 124,* 333–371.

Zelli, A., Dodge, K. A., Lochman, J. E., Laird, R. D., & Conduct Problems Prevention Group. (1999). The distinction between beliefs legitimizing aggression and deviant processing of social cues: Testing measurement validity and the hypothesis that biased processing mediates the effects of beliefs on aggression. *Journal of Personality and Social Psychology, 77,* 150–166.

Ziegert, D. I., Kistner, J. A., Castro, R., & Robertson, B. (2001). Longitudinal study of young children's responses to challenging achievement situations. *Child Development, 72,* 609–624.

9

Children's Friendships
Shifts Over a Half-Century in Perspectives on Their Development and Their Effects

Thomas J. Berndt

Provocative ideas about the nature, development, and effects of children's friendships were included in the lectures of Harry Stack Sullivan, which were edited and published in the 1950s. Sullivan emphasized the love, intimacy, and collaboration found in the close friendships that children form around 8 to 10 years of age. Subsequent research has shown that close friendships have both a positive dimension, with features such as intimacy, and a negative dimension, with features such as rivalry. However, close friendships do not emerge suddenly at 8 to 10 years of age. Rather, the closeness of children's friendships increases gradually during middle childhood and adolescence. Recent studies suggest that having close, high-quality friendships increases children's success in the peer social world. Having high-quality friendships could magnify the positive or negative influence of friends with positive or negative characteristics, but this hypothesis needs to be evaluated more thoroughly in the future.

The 1950s, when *Merrill-Palmer Quarterly* was founded, was far from a golden age for research either on friendships or on the broader topic of peer relationships. No article with some form of *friend* or *peer* in the title was published in any *MPQ* issue during the entire decade. Moreover, the same neglect of peer relationships characterized the rest of the field of child development during the 1950s. The landmark 1954 *Manual of Child Psychology*, edited by Leonard Carmichael, included no chapter on peer relationships and only a few paragraphs on popularity, friendship, and the peer group in other chapters. Even in those cases most references were to studies published in the 1930s or 1940s rather than to contemporary research.

A half-century later, research on peer relationships is clearly in the mainstream of the field of child development. Between 2000 and

2002 more than a dozen articles in *MPQ* had forms of *friend* or *peer* in their title. An entire special issue on peer influences in childhood and adolescence was published in January 1999. Likewise, the latest edition of Carmichael's manual, now retitled as *Handbook of Child Psychology* (the sixth edition, edited by William Damon and Richard Lerner, appeared in 2006), includes a chapter on peer relationships that is more than 70 pages long (Rubin, Bukowski, & Parker, 2006).

My focus is on the closest of children's peer relationships, those with their best friends. I consider three questions about friendships: what best friendships are like in childhood and adolescence, how these friendships change with age, and what effects they have on children's and adolescents' development. In addressing each question I briefly review early writings on the question, present some major conclusions that derive from recent research, and then discuss some issues that remain to be resolved in future research. That is, I examine the past, present, and potential future of research on children's friendships.

What Are Best Friendships Like?

Although child development researchers largely ignored children's friendships during the 1950s, an important theoretical statement about these friendships was published at the time. Students of Harry Stack Sullivan, a neo-Freudian psychiatrist, edited and published *The Interpersonal Theory of Psychiatry* (1953) based on lectures that Sullivan gave shortly before his death in 1949. In these lectures Sullivan traced the development of individuals from infancy to adulthood, and he tried to explain adult personality in terms of earlier social relationships. Most important, he attempted to answer each of the questions about children's friendships that I stated earlier. Research during the decades since has shed light on several of his answers, showing the accuracy of some but casting doubt on others. Consequently, a careful examination of his writings can clarify how perspectives on children's friendships have shifted in the last 50 years and what issues remain unresolved.

Sullivan argued that friendships are particularly crucial during a phase of life that he called preadolescence, the years just before the onset of puberty. Sullivan's initial statement about preadolescent friendships is provocative and has been widely quoted. He said that the beginning of preadolescence is marked by the appearance of "a specific new type of interest in a *particular* member of the same sex who becomes a chum or a close friend" (Sullivan, 1953, p. 245; emphasis in original). He described this new interest as follows:

> All of you who have children are sure that your children love you; when you say that, you are expressing a pleasant illusion. But if you will look very closely at one of your children when he finally finds a chum—somewhere between eight-and-a-half and ten—you will discover something very different in the relation—namely, that your child begins to develop a real sensitivity to what matters to another person. And this is not in the sense of "what should I do to get what I want," but instead "what should I do to contribute to the happiness or to support the prestige and feeling of worth-whileness of my chum." So far as I have been able to discover, nothing remotely like this appears before the age of, say, eight-and-a-half, and sometimes it appears decidedly later. (pp. 245–246)

Sullivan explained the origins of close friendships in the preadolescent years by saying that they reflect "the coming of the integrating tendencies which, when they are completely developed, we call love, or, to say it another way, by the manifestation of the need for interpersonal intimacy" (p. 246). He clarified that intimacy means "closeness, without specifying that which is close other than the persons. Intimacy is that type of situation involving two people which permits validation of all components of personal worth. Validation of personal worth requires a type of relationship which I call collaboration, by which I mean clearly formulated adjustments of one's behavior to the expressed needs of the other person in the pursuit of increasingly identical—that is, more and more nearly mutual—satisfactions" (p. 246).

In these statements Sullivan made two types of proposals about children's friendships. First, he proposed that close friendships between children have several positive features, including sensitivity to another person's needs and desires, intimacy, and efforts by the friends to make their interactions mutually satisfying. That is, he tried to describe what children's friendships are like, at least during the preadolescent years and later. Second, he proposed that close friendships are first formed between 8 and 10 years of age. Let me consider the accuracy of his description before I address the ages at which Sullivan assumed that these first friendships are formed.

The Positive Dimension of Friendship Quality

Perhaps because Sullivan's disciplinary affiliation was psychiatry, developmental researchers ignored his ideas about children's friendships for many years. A 1966 monograph on adolescence that included an extensive discussion of friendships (Douvan & Adelson, 1966) did not cite his book, and it was not cited in the peer-interaction chapter (Hartup) in the 1970 edition of the *Manual of Child Psychology*. But during the 1970s a few researchers began to test Sullivan's hypotheses systematically (e.g., Mannarino, 1976), and by 1980 Sullivan and Jean Piaget were linked together as foundational thinkers on the development of peer relationships (Youniss, 1980).

The researchers who rediscovered Sullivan's writings emphasized his construct of interpersonal intimacy, but they usually defined intimacy more narrowly than he did. In particular, they adopted the definition of intimacy in contemporary social-psychological research that emphasized the disclosure of personal and private information about the self (e.g., Rubin & Shenker, 1978). Thus during the 1970s many researchers asked children open-ended questions about what makes a best friendship or what their own friendships were like. The children's responses were coded into categories for distinct features of friendship, and comments about the self-disclosure of personal thoughts and feelings among friends were placed in the category labeled intimacy (see Berndt, 1986).

Ultimately, however, these studies led back to the broader conception of closeness in friendship that Sullivan had proposed. They did so because researchers discovered that children expect close friendships to have all the positive features that Sullivan mentioned (Berndt, 1986; Youniss, 1980). Children expect friends to "contribute to their happiness" by helping and sharing with them. Children expect friends to "support their prestige and feelings of worth-while-ness" by expressing their acceptance of them or enhancing their self-esteem in other ways. Children expect friends to be companions for one another in activities that are mutually satisfying.

As researchers were learning about the variety of positive features of close friendships, they were exploring various theories of close relationships. Some researchers noted that the positive features of children's friendships are similar to the positive features of supportive social relationships among adults (e.g., Berndt, 1989). Some researchers linked the features of children's friendships to Weiss's (1974) model of the provisions that can be obtained from involvement in social relationships (Furman & Buhrmester, 1985). Others examined the connections between the emerging description of children's friendships and prominent theories of other types of social relationships (see Furman, 1996).

After completing this empirical and theoretical work, researchers took on the methodological challenge of devising interviews and questionnaires to assess the positive features of specific friendships. Subsequent research reports have described several of these measures. A consistent finding is that most children who describe their best friendships as high in one positive feature, such as intimacy, describe those friendships as high in other positive features too. As a result researchers often have used a composite score for all positive features to assess a positive dimension of friendship quality (Berndt, 1996, 2002). The availability of valid measures of this dimension has been vital to the field, because these measures have been used to test various hypotheses about friendships, especially for examining how friendships change with age and how the quality of children's friendships affects their social adjustment and development.

Conflicts and Rivalry: The Dark Side of Friendship

For several years researchers focused exclusively on the positive features of children's friendships, not even mentioning that close friendships can have negative features. However, the occurrence of negative interactions between friends was implicit in Sullivan's (1953) comments about the emergence of close friendships. He implied that before preadolescents find a close friend, their interactions with peers are governed by the question, "What should I do to get what I want?" That is, children's actions are motivated by self-interest rather than concern for others.

When children motivated by self-interest interact, conflicts between them are inevitable. Moreover, these conflicts are unlikely to disappear when children enter the preadolescent years. The existence and persistence of conflicts between friends have now been thoroughly documented (e.g., Laursen, 1996). In addition, items about the frequency and intensity of conflicts have been included in instruments to assess friendship quality (see Furman, 1996).

Sullivan described another type of negative interaction among peers as occurring early in the elementary school years. He suggested that competition with peers can become so pervasive during these years that for some children it becomes a central trait: "One sees a competitive way of life in which nearly everything that has real importance is part of a process of getting ahead of the other person." In the worst cases "getting the other fellow down becomes the outstanding pattern in the integration of interpersonal relations" (p. 232).

"Getting the other fellow down" can be defined as the goal of rivalry. When children describe friendships, they acknowledge that friends sometimes engage in intense rivalry (Berndt, 1986). Thus rivalry must be regarded as another negative feature of friendship. Although few measures of friendship quality include items to assess the degree of rivalry between friends, when both rivalry and conflicts between friends are measured, scores for the two are strongly correlated. The correlation suggests that these features define a negative dimension of friendship quality. Somewhat surprisingly, scores for the negative dimension of particular friendships are not strongly correlated with those for the positive dimension of the same friendships. Stated differently, friendships that are high in positive features may be either high or low in negative features.

All the current measures of friendship quality include more items for assessing positive friendship features than for assessing negative friendship features. This imbalance is troubling because it may reduce researchers' ability to find out how children are affected when their friendships are high in negative features. More generally, the negative dimension of friendships deserves more careful attention than it has received thus far. To guide future research this dimension would benefit from the in-depth theoretical analysis that the positive dimension has already received. Researchers should no longer overlook or minimize the significance of the dark side of friendships.

How Do Best Friendships Change With Age?

When Sullivan (1953) presented his lectures about personality development, almost nothing was known about the development of children's friendships. Thus Sullivan was charting new territory when he proposed that close friendships first emerge when children are between 8 and 10 years of age. As I mentioned earlier, the first empirical research on Sullivan's proposals focused on his statements about intimacy in friendships, but most researchers defined intimacy in terms of the self-disclosure of personal thoughts and feelings. Many studies showed that elementary school children, when asked open-ended questions about friendships, rarely mention intimate self-disclosure between friends. But during the adolescent years comments about friends' intimate self-disclosure are frequent (Berndt, 1986).

Initially, these findings led researchers to conclude that Sullivan was incorrect about the age at which close friendships emerge (e.g., Berndt, 1982). Close friendship seemed to emerge in early adolescence, not preadolescence. This conclusion seemed more doubtful as data became available from later research with structured interviews and questionnaires that provided information about other features of friendship besides intimacy. Mean scores on other positive features rarely showed the same increase between childhood and adolescence as scores for intimacy did. In one study, for example, boys judged companionship with friends as equally great in the second, fifth, and eighth grades (Buhrmester & Furman, 1987).

Even when the mean scores for specific features of friendship changed significantly with age, the age changes were modest rather than dramatic. Thus, as the research data accumulated, few investigators echoed Sullivan's words that "something very different" becomes apparent in friendships around 8 to 10 years of age—or at any other age. Instead, researchers began to draw conclusions about gradual increases in friendship quality during childhood and early adolescence (e.g., Furman & Buhrmester, 1992). This shift in perspectives on the age changes in friendships probably was accelerated by the decrease in developmental researchers' acceptance, during the same period, of all theories of developmental stages (e.g., Flavell, 1982).

Unfortunately, the decrease in acceptance of stage theories has been accompanied by a dramatic decrease in the investigation of normative development, or how children's thinking, behavior, and relationships typically change with age. Research on most topics in the area of social development, including peer relationships, is now focused almost exclusively on the exploration of individual differences rather than the description of normal development (see Rubin et al., 1998).

Determining the correlates and consequences of individual differences in friendship quality is obviously valuable, but further exploration of the normative development of friendships would also be valuable. In particular, more research is needed on the friendships of children in the preschool and early school years. Research on children of these ages is complicated by the children's inability to respond to the questionnaires used most often to assess friendship quality. But excellent research on preschoolers' friendships has been done with observational measures and with parent and teacher reports (see Howes, 1996; Kerns, 1996). Excellent research on preschool and kindergarten children's friendships has been done by interviewing these children about their friendships (e.g., Ladd, Kochenderfer, & Coleman, 1996). More research of these types is needed to understand the age changes in young children's friendships.

Also needed are data on friendships near the end of adolescence and the transition to adulthood. It is unclear whether same-sex friendships continue to be very close and supportive during these years (Sharabany, Gershoni, & Hofman, 1981) or whether they become less close and supportive as the second decade of life ends (Furman & Buhrmester, 1992). Romantic relationships with boyfriends or girlfriends do increase substantially in closeness during the adolescent years (Furman, Brown, & Feiring, 1999), but the effect of this increase on same-sex friendships is unclear. One hypothesis implicit in many theories, including Sullivan's, is that same-sex friendships provide a foundation for but are later supplanted by romantic relationships.

Still, same-sex friendships remain important to most adults (Hartup & Stevens, 1997). How these friendships are coordinated with romantic relationships in late adolescence and in adulthood is not well understood. Some conflicts between the two types of relationships are certainly possible but so are conflicts between two friendships—or two romantic relationships. More evidence about the usual connections between friendships and romantic relationships in late adolescence and early adulthood would help not only in understanding the development of personal relationships but also in evaluating deviations from the norm.

Finally, additional research on the development of children's friendships would reduce the chances of a premature narrowing of focus. Most recent studies of individual differences in friendships have focused on the correlations of variations in friendship quality (e.g., Rose, 2002). Other studies have focused on whether a child has at least one reciprocal (or mutual) best friendship or on how many reciprocal friendships a child has (e.g., Ladd & Troop-Gordon, 2003).

Less often examined are how friends typically interact with one another at different ages. Systematic observations of the differences between friends' and nonfriends' interactions were common in the 1970s and 1980s, as researchers tried to determine what is distinctive about friends' interactions (see Newcomb & Bagwell, 1995). But few studies involving direct observations of friends' interactions have been reported recently (but see, e.g., Parker & Herrera, 1996), and those studies have rarely been designed to document how friendships normally change with age.

More research on the activities of children and their friends would also be desirable. Friends spend a significant amount of time conversing or socializing with each other, playing games or sports, going to movies, and participating in other leisure-time activities (e.g., Larson, Kubey, & Colletti, 1989). In addition, friends spend time doing homework and working on other school-related tasks together (Leone & Richards, 1989).

Knowing what friends do together may be extremely important in understanding how these friendships affect their behavior and development. For example, socializing with friends in settings not supervised by adults apparently contributes directly to delinquent behavior in adolescence (Osgood, Wilson, O'Malley, Bachman, & Johnston, 1996). Not yet known is whether other types of activities with friends have desirable or undesirable effects on children's and adolescents' behavior.

Future investigations of friends' interactions and friends' activities could give researchers information essential for describing what best friendships are like and how they change with age. These investigations would add context and concreteness to studies of friendship quality or the number of reciprocal friends that children have. Without data on friends' interactions and activities, measures of friendship quality and numbers of friends would remain as they are today, largely disconnected from their foundation in actual events. Consequently, more systematic investigation of friends' interactions and activities should be a high priority.

How Do Best Friendships Affect Children's Development?

In Sullivan's description of the preadolescent era, hypotheses about the nature of friendships are not always clearly distinguished from hypotheses about the effects of friendships. Perhaps for that reason many later writers have interpreted his statements about children's motivation "to support the prestige and feeling of worth-whileness of my chum" not as a description of one feature of close friendships but as a hypothesis about how these friendships enhance children's self-esteem. Initial evidence consistent with this hypothesis came from correlational studies showing that children and adolescents whose friendships were higher in positive quality also were higher in self-esteem (Berndt, 1996, 2002), but longitudinal studies have not provided support for the hypothesis.

Keefe and Berndt (1996) assessed seventh- and eighth-graders' self-esteem and the quality of their friendships in both the fall and spring of the school year. Then these researchers examined whether the quality of the students' friendships in the fall was a significant predictor of the changes in their self-esteem during the year. The answer was a definite no. Although students' self-esteem was positively correlated with the quality of their friendships in both the fall and the spring, variations in friendship quality were unrelated to the changes over time in students' self-esteem. Comparable results were reported in two previous studies (cited in Keefe and Berndt, 1996) and at least one subsequent study (Berndt, Hawkins, & Jiao, 1999).

Furthermore, an argument can be made that Sullivan did not believe good friendships would always enhance children's self-esteem. When talking about the effects of friendships, he said that children who have developed a habit of derogating others may, with a close friend, "discuss these other unpleasant people who don't seem to like them, in a fashion that is illuminating, both as to the real worth of the others and as to some of their own traits which may not be very endearing" (1953, p. 253). He later summarized the beneficial effects of close friendships by saying, "One gets a look at oneself through the chum's eyes. To the extent that this is accomplished, the self-system concerned is definitely expanded, and its more troublesome, inadequate, and inappropriate functions are reduced to the point that they become unnecessary" (pp. 254–255).

Taken together, these comments cast doubt on the hypothesis that having close and intimate friendships inevitably makes children feel more positively about themselves. For individuals with an exaggerated sense of their own worth, conversations with close friends may have the opposite effect. Sullivan certainly believed that close friendships help children and adolescents form a more realistic and adaptive self-concept, but that hypothesis would be difficult to test with existing self-concept and self-esteem measures.

At other points Sullivan suggested that close friendships are important because they affect children's relationships with other members of their peer group. For example, he proposed that close friendships in childhood are a requirement for developing a "capacity for ease, [and] for maximum profit from experience, in carrying on the conventional business of life with members of one's own sex" (1953, p. 248). He also proposed that self-centered children may, after forming a close friendship, become "very much less inclined to expect unlimited services from others, very much nearer the ideal of a good sport." These children then "become less objectionable to the prevailing preadolescent society and may actually get to be quite well esteemed in the gang," or friendship group (p. 252).

Findings consistent with these speculations have been reported for young children and for adolescents. In one study (Ladd et al., 1996), kindergarten children who had high-quality friendships in January of the school year improved by the end of the year in their perceptions of all their classmates' support. In another study (Berndt, Hawkins, & Jiao,, 1999) sixth-graders in their last semester of elementary school reported on the quality of their friendships, and their classmates rated their sociability and leadership. These reports and ratings were repeated after the students made the transition to seventh grade in junior high school. Students whose sixth-grade friendships were higher in quality improved after the school transition in their sociability and leadership as rated by classmates but only if most of their sixth-grade friendships were stable over time.

Both studies suggest that close friendships can affect children's and adolescents' relationships with the rest of their peers. In particular, having supportive friendships may help students make positive contacts with other classmates. Those positive contacts may lead to positive relationships that are not as close as best friendships but that still enhance the students' social adjustment in the world of peers. The importance of having friends who facilitate the formation of positive relationships with other classmates is confirmed by the evidence that high-quality friendships help students adjust after a school transition only if those friendships are stable. Apparently, those friendships form the center of a circle of positive peer relationships that widens over time. With the widening of this circle, students' attitudes toward their classmates and their classmates' attitudes toward them become more positive.

Obviously, the findings of these two studies need to be replicated in future research. Nonetheless, they are broadly consistent with other evidence of positive effects of close friendships on children's peer relationships. For example, having loyal friends reduces the chances that elementary school children will be victimized by their classmates (Hodges, Boivin, Vitaro, & Bukowski, 1999). One goal for future research should be to determine how the quality of children's friendships affects their relationships with other peers. Stated differently, identifying the processes responsible for these effects is essential. An equally important goal is to explore the limits of these processes, the situations in which having high-quality friendships does not improve some important element of peer relationships.

As I noted earlier, best friendships also have a negative dimension, and the limited available data suggest that highly negative friendships can be very damaging. In one study (Berndt & Keefe, 1995) seventh- and eighth-graders reported on the levels of conflicts and rivalry in their three closest friendships. Students who described their friendships as higher in these negative features were higher in self-reported disruptive behavior in the fall of the school year, and their level of disruptive behavior increased during the year. Surprisingly, the increase in disruptive behavior was greatest for students who also perceived their friendships as high in positive features. These results suggest that negative interchanges with friends are especially likely to lead to negative interchanges with other peers and teachers when students also view their friendships as intimate and supportive.

Finally, it's important to keep in mind that children are affected by other aspects of their best friendships besides their quality. Hartup (1996) argued that the developmental significance of friendships cannot be fully understood unless researchers distinguish the effects of friendship quality from the effects of having (reciprocal) friends at all and the effects of the identity (or characteristics) of those friends. For example, one effect of not having friends during the early years of elementary school is to increase children's anxiety, depression, and social withdrawal (Ladd & Troop-Gordon, 2003).

Research on the identity of children's friends typically examines the characteristics on which children are similar to their friends and the degree to which this similarity reflects the friends' influence on one another. Many studies have established that friends influence important attitudes (e.g., students' attitudes toward school), socially relevant behaviors (e.g., adolescents' drug use), and many other characteristics of great significance for children's and adolescents' adjustment and development (e.g., students' academic achievement) (Berndt, 1999; Berndt & Murphy, 2002).

A full review of the effects of having friends and of the influence of friends' characteristics would be impossible in this brief commentary. This discussion of the effects of friendship quality would be seriously incomplete, however, if I omitted discussion of the possibility of interactions between friendship quality and friends' characteristics. Many theories of social influence include some form of what can be called the magnification hypothesis, which asserts that the influence of a friend's characteristics is magnified when a child's relationship with that friend is higher in quality. In social learning theory, for example, the hypothesis is that children will learn more from observing a friend's behavior if they have a more positive relationship with that friend (Bandura, 1977).

The magnification hypothesis may seem like common sense, but it implies that interventions to improve the quality of children's friendships may have negative effects on children's behavior and adjustment if their friends' characteristics are negative. These interventions may be harmful because they may increase the degree to which children are influenced by their friends' characteristics and so develop more negative characteristics themselves. Even interventions not intended to improve children's friendships may have negative effects if they lead to the formation of high-quality friendships among children high in antisocial behavior (Dishion, McCord, & Poulin, 1999).

Not all theories of social influence include a version of the magnification hypothesis. In particular, theories of social support (see Berndt, 1989, 2002) include a hypothesis that supportive social relationships are beneficial regardless of the characteristics of the supporters. These theories imply that high-quality friendships should always have positive effects on children's behavior and adjustment. Stated more formally, the theories imply that the effects of friendship quality should not interact with the influences of friends' characteristics. Evidence consistent with these theories and inconsistent with the magnification hypothesis has been obtained in two recent studies (Berndt & Keefe, 1995; Poulin, Dishion, & Haas, 1999), and a third study provided only equivocal support for the hypothesis (Berndt, Hawkins, & Jiao, 1999).

Nevertheless, additional tests of the hypothesis are needed, for both theoretical and practical reasons. If future studies provide no support for the hypothesis, some general theories of social influence will need to be revised. If future studies support the hypothesis, interventions that bring together groups of at-risk children will need to be designed to ensure that they do not foster or strengthen friendships among these children, because doing so would magnify their negative influence on one another.

Finally, evidence about the magnification hypothesis is scanty because researchers who study friends' influence have rarely assessed the quality of these friendships. Conversely, researchers who study friendship quality have rarely assessed the characteristics of the friends. Bridging the gap between these two research traditions might reveal interactions between friendship quality and friends' characteristics that are different from those implied by the magnification hypothesis. For example, one study indicated that high-quality friendships seemed to reduce adolescents' tendencies toward shy and withdrawn behavior even when their friends were high in shyness and social withdrawal (Berndt, Hawkins, & Jiao, 1999). This kind of protective effect of high-quality friendships can be identified only if researchers evaluate possible interactions between the effects of friendship quality and the influence of friends' characteristics.

A Final Look Back and Look Forward

It is gratifying to see how dramatically knowledge about children's friendships, their development, and their effects has increased during the past half-century. Systematic research on children's friendships was virtually nonexistent in the 1950s but is extremely vigorous today. Sullivan's writings on friendship, published in the 1950s, have proved to be a rich source of ideas for developmental researchers, but the limitations of his work should not be overlooked. His writings actually belong to the prescientific era of scholarly work. His statements about children's friendships derived primarily from his reading of other psychiatrists' writings and his own practice of psychiatry. In the half-century since his book was published, researchers have supplemented rational analysis of early writings with experimental tests of hypotheses in explicit theories; researchers have discounted conclusions based on one individual's clinical practice in favor of conclusions based on sophisticated statistical analyses of data from large samples of children. In short, the increase in knowledge of children's friendships has resulted largely from the application of the latest and best methods of psychological science.

Will the next half-century be a golden age for research on children's friendships? Trying to make predictions 50 years into the future would be foolish, but the near-term challenges facing researchers are clear. A large body of research has established what the most important positive features of children's friendships are, and reliable and valid measures of an overarching positive dimension of friendship quality have been devised. This research has also established that scores on measures of this positive dimension increase from middle childhood into at least middle adolescence.

However, less is known about conflicts and rivalry in friendships. These features are elements of an overarching negative dimension of friendship quality that needs more careful theoretical analysis. In addition, the measures used to assess the position of particular friendships on this dimension need more thorough validation. To fully describe the development of friendships in childhood and adolescence, researchers also need to give more attention to the earliest friendships among preschool children and to the changes in same-sex friendships in late adolescence, when romantic relationships become more common and significant.

Another challenge for future research is charting the developmental changes in friends' interactions and in the activities in which they engage when they are together. Researchers have been very successful in defining and measuring friendship quality and the degree to which children have reciprocal best friendships. But in recent years researchers have seldom directly observed the age changes in friends' interactions and seldom obtained information about the age changes in friends' activities. Yet these interactions and activities are the reality out of which children construct their judgments about who their best friends are and what the quality of those friendships is. Consequently, research on friends' interaction and activities is needed to complete the picture of how friendships develop.

Finally, recent studies strongly suggest that close friendships do not have a significant effect on children's general self-esteem, but the quality of these friendships can affect children's success in forming positive relationships with the rest of their peers. Conversely, having friendships high in conflicts and rivalry can reinforce a negative pattern of social interaction that becomes the pattern for interactions with other peers and with teachers. Still more alarming is the hypothesis, implicit in many theories of social influence, that friendships high in positive features can have negative effects on children's behavior by magnifying the negative influence of friends whose attitudes and behaviors are socially undesirable. The magnification hypothesis describes a link that may exist between two traditions of research on friendship, one focusing on the quality of friendship and the other focusing on the influence of friends' characteristics. Partly for this reason, and partly because the hypothesis has great theoretical and practical significance, determining the validity of that hypothesis should be given a high priority. If researchers in the future can meet this challenge and the others that I have outlined here, the next few decades will be a golden age for research on children's friendships.

References

Bandura, A. (1977). *Social learning theory.* Englewood Cliffs, NJ: Prentice-Hall.

Berndt, T. J. (1982). The features and effects of friendships in early adolescence. *Child Development, 53,* 1447–1460.

Berndt, T. J. (1986). Children's comments about their friendships. In M. Perlmutter (Ed.), *The Minnesota Symposia on Child Psychology: Vol. 18. Cognitive perspectives on children's social and behavioral development* (pp. 189–212). Hillsdale, NJ: Erlbaum.

Berndt, T. J. (1989). Obtaining support from friends in childhood and adolescence. In D. Belle (Ed.), *Children's social networks and social supports* (pp. 308–331). New York: Wiley.

Berndt, T. J. (1996). Exploring the effects of friendship quality on social development. In W. M. Bukowski, A. F. Newcomb, & W. W. Hartup (Eds.), *The company they keep: Friendship in childhood and adolescence* (pp. 346–365). New York: Cambridge University Press.

Berndt, T. J. (1999). Friends' influence on children's adjustment to school. In W. A. Collins & B. Laursen (Eds.), *The Minnesota Symposia on Child Psychology: Vol. 30. Relationships as developmental contexts* (pp. 85–107). Mahwah, NJ: Erlbaum.

Berndt, T. J. (2002). Friendship quality and social development. *Current Directions in Psychological Science, 11,* 7–10.

Berndt, T. J., Hawkins, J. A., & Jiao, Z. (1999). Influences of friends and friendship on adjustment to junior high school. *Merrill-Palmer Quarterly, 45,* 13–41.

Berndt, T. J., & Keefe, K. (1995). Friends' influence on adolescents' adjustment to school. *Child Development, 66,* 1312–1329.

Berndt, T. J., & Murphy, L. M. (2002). Influences of friends and friendships: Myths, truths, and research recommendations. In R. Kail (Ed.), *Advances in child development and behavior* (Vol. 30, pp. 275–310). San Diego: Academic Press.

Buhrmester, D., & Furman, W. (1987). The development of companionship and intimacy. *Child Development, 58,* 1101–1113.

Carmichael, L. (Ed.). (1954). *Manual of child psychology* (2nd ed.). New York: Wiley.

Dishion, T. J., McCord, J., & Poulin, F. (1999). When interventions harm: Peer groups and problem behavior. *American Psychologist, 54,* 755–764.

Douvan, E., & Adelson, J. (1966). *The adolescent experience.* New York: Wiley.

Flavell, J. H. (1982). Structures, stages, and sequences in cognitive development. In W. A. Collins (Ed.), *The Minnesota Symposia on Child Psychology: Vol. 15. The concept of development* (pp. 1–28). Hillsdale, NJ: Erlbaum.

Furman, W. (1996). The measurement of friendship perceptions: Conceptual and methodological issues. In W. M. Bukowski, A. F. Newcomb, & W. W. Hartup (Eds.), *The company they keep: Friendship in childhood and adolescence* (pp. 41–65). New York: Cambridge University Press.

Furman, W., Brown, B. B., & Feiring, C. (Eds.). (1999). *The development of romantic relationships in adolescence.* Cambridge, England: Cambridge University Press.

Furman, W., & Buhrmester, D. (1985). Children's perceptions of the personal relationships in their social networks. *Developmental Psychology, 21,* 1016–1024.

Furman, W., & Buhrmester, D. (1992). Age and sex differences in perceptions of networks of personal relationships. *Child Development, 63,* 103–115.

Hartup, W. W. (1970). Peer interaction and social organization. In P. H. Mussen (Ed.), *Carmichael's manual of child psychology* (3rd ed., Vol. 2, pp. 361–456). New York: Wiley.

Hartup, W. W. (1996). The company they keep: Friendships and their developmental significance. *Child Development, 67,* 1–13.

Hartup, W. W., & Stevens, N. (1997). Friendships and adaptation in the life course. *Psychological Bulletin, 121,* 355–370.

Hodges, E. V., Boivin, M., Vitaro, F., & Bukowski, W. M. (1999). The power of friendship: Protection against and escalating cycle of peer victimization. *Developmental Psychology, 35,* 94–101.

Howes, C. (1996). The earliest friendships. In W. M. Bukowski, A. F. Newcomb, & W. W. Hartup (Eds.), *The company they keep: Friendship in childhood and adolescence* (pp. 66–86). New York: Cambridge University Press.

Keefe, K., & Berndt, T. J. (1996). Relations of friendship quality to self-esteem in early adolescence. *Journal of Early Adolescence, 16,* 110–129.

Kerns, K. A. (1996). Individual differences in friendship quality: Links to child-mother attachment. In W. M. Bukowski, A. F. Newcomb, & W. W. Hartup (Eds.), *The company they keep: Friendship in childhood and adolescence* (pp. 137–157). New York: Cambridge University Press.

Ladd, G. W., Kochenderfer, B. J., & Coleman, C. C. (1996). Friendship quality as a predictor of young children's early school adjustment. *Child Development, 67,* 1103–1118.

Ladd, G. W., & Troop-Gordon, W. (2003). The role of chronic peer difficulties in the development of children's psychological adjustment problems. *Child Development, 74,* 1344–1367.

Larson, R. W., Kubey, R., & Colletti, J. (1989). Changing channels: Early adolescent media choices and shifting investments in family and friends. *Journal of Youth and Adolescence, 18,* 583–599.

Laursen, B. (1996). Closeness and conflict in adolescent peer relationships: Interdependence with friends and romantic partners. In W. M. Bukowski, A. F. Newcomb, & W. W. Hartup (Eds.), *The company they keep: Friendship in childhood and adolescence* (pp. 186–210). New York: Cambridge University Press.

Leone, C. M., & Richards, M. H. (1989). Classwork and homework in early adolescence: The ecology of achievement. *Journal of Youth and Adolescence, 18,* 531–548.

Mannarino, A. P. (1976). Friendship patterns and altruistic behavior in preadolescent males. *Developmental Psychology, 12,* 555–556.

Newcomb, A. F., & Bagwell, C. L. (1995). Children's friendship relations: A meta-analytic review. *Psychological Bulletin, 117,* 306–347.

Osgood, D. W., Wilson, J. K., O'Malley, P. M., Bachman, J. G., & Johnston, L. D. (1996). Routine activities and individual deviant behavior. *American Sociological Review, 61*, 635–655.

Parker, J. G., & Herrera, C. (1996). Interpersonal processes in friendship: A comparison of abused and nonabused children. *Developmental Psychology, 32*, 1025–1038.

Poulin, F., Dishion, T. J., & Haas, E. (1999). The peer influence paradox: Friendship quality and deviancy training within male adolescent friendships. *Merrill-Palmer Quarterly, 45*, 42–61.

Rose, A. J. (2002). Co-rumination in the friendships of girls and boys. *Child Development, 73*, 1830–1843.

Rubin, K. H., Bukowski, W., & Parker, J. G. (2006). Peer interactions, relationships, and groups. In W. Damon & R. Lerner (Series Eds.), N. Eisenberg (Vol. Ed.), *Handbook of child psychology: Vol. 3. Social, emotional, and personality development* (6th ed., pp. 571–645). New York: Wiley.

Rubin, Z., & Shenker, S. (1978). Friendship, proximity, and self-disclosure. *Journal of Personality, 46*, 1–22.

Sharabany, R., Gershoni, R., & Hofman, J. E. (1981). Girlfriend-boyfriend: Age and sex differences in intimate friendships. *Developmental Psychology, 17*, 800–808.

Sullivan, H. S. (1953). The interpersonal theory of psychiatry. New York: Norton.

Urberg, K. A. (1999). Introduction to invitational issue: Some thoughts about studying the influence of peers on children and adolescents. *Merrill-Palmer Quarterly, 45*, 1–12.

Weiss, R. S. (1974). The provisions of social relationships. In Z. Rubin (Ed.), *Doing unto others.* Englewood Cliffs, NJ: Prentice-Hall.

Youniss, J. (1980). *Parents and peers in social development.* Chicago: University of Chicago Press.

10

Paying Attention to and Not Neglecting Social Withdrawal and Social Isolation

Kenneth H. Rubin and Robert J. Coplan

The study of peer interaction has a long and rich history. We have long sought to understand how children learn to get along with one another and why this is important. Implicitly and explicitly enmeshed with our studies of peer interaction is the question of children who tend not to interact with peers. In this commentary we trace some of the origins of research on children's social withdrawal. Significantly, this topic was largely nonexistent in the 1950s, 1960s, and 1970s, but it has more recently emerged as a phenomenon that is publication rich, research supported, and much discussed among parents and teachers. In the latter half of this chapter we take stock of current research issues in the etiology of social withdrawal and outline some future directions for researchers to consider.

Historical Trends in the Study of Peer Interaction

Approximately twenty-five years before the first issue of *Merrill-Palmer Quarterly*, Jean Piaget proposed that children learn a great deal about their social and impersonal worlds through exploration, construction, discussion, negotiation, and the expression and resolution of differences of opinion with age-mates. Moreover, in the 1920s and 1930s researchers were already studying such topics as the social interactions of infants and toddlers, social participation among preschoolers, sympathy and altruism in the peer group, antisocial tendencies, leadership, friendship, and peer-group networks and social structures. Much of this work was developmental in perspective, although the vast majority of published research focused on the early years of childhood.

Of the research conducted on how children spent their lives among peers, few early theorists and researchers speculated about the potential role of individual differences in peer-oriented behaviors or relationships. After World War II, however, a small number of investigators began to use now-familiar labels to identify children who could be "classified" on the basis of their reputation in the peer group. Moreno (1934) wrote about peer-group structure and composition, as well as interpersonal attraction, repulsion, and indifference. Bronfenbrenner (1943) described three sociometric status groups within which children might fall—high, average, and low. But other than Piaget, Mead, and Sullivan, few reflected on the significance of peer exchange for normal growth and development. Interacting with peers was viewed as developmentally appropriate insofar as everyday life is concerned. In many ways peer interaction, like play, was either neglected in its entirety or deemed superfluous. Consequently, those seriously interested in the socialization of adaptive thinking, feeling, and doing kept their investigatory efforts focused on the child's home life and, more specifically, on the mother-child relationship or on maternal behavior. And those seriously interested in developmental psychology as science pursued the understanding of children's development in such "measurable" and "controllable" areas as learning, memory, perception, cognition, intelligence, and achievement. A quick glance at the content of *Merrill-Palmer Quarterly* in the 1950s, 1960s, and 1970s supports these reflections on the relatively short history of our science.

Eventually, however, researchers outgrew the once-beloved "marble-dropping," learning theory–derived experiments of the 1960s and moved forward into studying learning in social contexts. After all, all learning does take place in a more or less social environment. Schools are filled not only with teachers and counselors but also with children, many of whom share a given classroom for seven hours per day, five days per week. In addition to parents, many homes also contain younger and older siblings—other children! With the recognition of the putative significance of children's peers, both directly (as in reinforcing or punishing one another on continuous or partial reinforcement schedules) and indirectly (as in seeing how others are reinforced or punished for various and sundry social behaviors), the field of social development entered an emergent growth period. The strikingly rich work of Bandura, Walters, and their students and protégés led researchers to recognize that peers could serve as both direct and subtle influences. And eventually, with the help of both empirical research and the publication of timely reviews by Campbell (1964) and Hartup (1970), the study of children's interactions, relationships, and groups found itself on a swiftly accelerating trajectory during the last decades of the

20th century. Indeed, the "Bible" of our discipline, the *Handbook of Child Psychology*, has included chapters about children's peer interactions and relationships in the 1970 (Mussen), 1983 (Mussen), 1998 (Damon), and 2006 (Damon and Lerner) editions.

Given the extant attention to the voluminous research on the topic, one must conclude that peers must be of no small significance in the lives of children. Indeed, one of the more controversial arguments proposed in the latter years of the 20th century was that peers mattered in perhaps more significant ways than parents (Harris, 1995). This chapter is not the proper venue for a review of research about the significance of peer interactions, relationships, and groups. However, the space allotted does allow us to reflect on the friendly and intellectually stimulating "battles" fought with other researchers about the developmental significance of not interacting with peers during the childhood years.

A Personal History

The career of Kenneth H. Rubin, the lead author of this chapter, began with an investigation of Piaget's notion that during early childhood, social interaction was constrained by the child's inability to take the social perspective of those in his or her social surround— a construct once known as "egocentrism" and now probabilistically defunct, given contemporary work on theory of mind (see Chapter 3). The premise in Rubin's early work was that young children (4- and 5-year-olds) did, in fact, use egocentric speech but that they could also generally make themselves understood, for example, by using gestures (e.g., Evans & Rubin, 1979). That is, young children may often display speech that is egocentric, and yet most of the time they are actually quite communicatively competent—a message conveyed by other researchers in the 1970s (Garvey & Hogan, 1973; Mueller, 1972; Shatz & Gelman, 1973). Of course, as researchers examined the natural use of egocentric speech in social settings, some noted individual differences in the extent to which children of various ages could make themselves understood by others. Some preschoolers and kindergartners were clearly communicatively competent; others were less so (Levin & Rubin, 1983; Rubin & Borwick, 1984). At the time one natural question for a developmental psychologist to ask was what accounts for these individual differences in this basic social skill—the ability to make oneself understood by others? Certainly, Piaget didn't address the issue of individual differences. Nor did he inform his readers that during interaction, children develop relationships—often with age-mates. It was left to researchers in the 1970s and 1980s to begin to ponder the individual difference and relationships questions.

Other questions posed by "neo-Piagetian" scholars have included the following: What are the putative "causes" of perspective taking and communicative abilities and lags thereof? What are the contemporaneous correlates of perspective taking and related social-cognitive and communicative skills? What is it that results from an ability to take social perspectives? What are the consequences of conversing, negotiating, and compromising with age-mates? Researchers have been addressing these questions since the 1970s. The database is now enormous. For example, throughout the 1970s researchers examined the prevalence, correlates, and consequences of egocentrism in childhood (see Shantz, 1983, for a thorough review of early research on social-cognitive development). We now know that children develop mature ways of thinking about things social and nonsocial through discussion, negotiation, and compromise. Those who fail to overcome their initial developmentally normative egocentricities appear less socially skilled to their peers. They may act aggressively (Dodge, Pettit, McClaskey, & Brown, 1986); they may be less empathic and altruistic (Eisenberg & Miller, 1987; Rubin & Schneider, 1973); they may fail to think through the consequences of their behaviors for themselves and others (Rubin & Krasnor, 1986; Selman, 1980; Weissberg et al., 1981); and by and large, they may be rejected by their age-mates (Rubin, Bukowski, & Parker, 2006). Indeed, in 1983 *Merrill-Palmer Quarterly* published two issues about children's peer relationships; many articles addressed the issues we have just noted (e.g., Coie & Dodge, 1983; Dodge, Schlundt, Schocken, & Delugach, 1983; Rubin & Daniels-Beirness, 1983). More recently, those of us who have continued to pursue the understanding of children's relationships with others have begun to focus on their friendships; children who have difficulties understanding the thoughts, intentions, and emotions of others as well as the consequences of their actions for others and themselves do not make the best relationship partners. They are not sought out as friends (see Bukowski, Newcomb, & Hartup, 1996, for relevant reviews).

All of which is to argue that we have come to know that there is a grand dialectic between interacting with others, most notably peers, and the development of social perspective taking, social information processing, and social-behavioral skills. Those who interact often with others gain experiences in learning to communicate, negotiate, and compromise. Such experiences can lead to positive developments in such social-cognitive skills as perspective taking and social information processing. The latter result in more opportunities for positive social interaction and the development of productive dyadic relationships with peers. And so it goes. But what about those children who, for whatever reason, do not interact with others, either "voluntarily" (i.e., social withdrawal) or by virtue of external "forces" (i.e., social isolation)? In this regard we now turn to a discussion of the many faces of "solitude" in childhood.

The Research Neglect of Social Withdrawal

In the mid-1980s Sroufe and Rutter defined the new field of developmental psychopathology as "the study of the origins and course of individual patterns of behavioral maladaptation, whatever the transformations in behavioral manifestation, and however complex the course of the developmental pattern may be" (1984, p. 18). For the most part the study of developmental psychopathology has concerned two broad forms of maladjustment, namely, those involving difficulties of undercontrol and those involving difficulties of overcontrol. Psychological undercontrol problems, or externalizing difficulties, include attention deficit disorder with hyperactivity, conduct disorder, opposition and defiance, and aggression. Overcontrol problems, or internalizing difficulties, include anxiety, fears, depression, and social withdrawal (Mash & Barkley, 2003).

Until and throughout the 1980s the study of externalizing difficulties in childhood had a broader, richer conceptual and empirical history than that of psychological overcontrol. This predominant interest in externalizing disorders most likely stemmed from several significant factors. First, from the very earliest years of childhood, externalizing problems are easier to detect than internalizing problems. The behavioral manifestations of undercontrol are highly salient and likely to evoke some form of negative affect (e.g., anger) in the perceiver, even during the early preschool period (e.g., Cheah & Rubin, 2004; Mills & Rubin, 1990; Schneider, Attili, Vermigli, & Younger, 1997). Behavioral manifestations of overcontrol, however, are less salient and are less likely to evoke reactive behavior in the perceiver (Mills & Rubin, 1990; Younger, Gentile, & Burgess, 1993).

Second, children in Western cultures attend group care and educational settings at earlier ages and for longer periods of the life span than did children in earlier generations. As such, behavioral and emotional self-regulation in these group settings is an important mandate for caregivers and educators; children who are "out of control" or dysregulated are viewed as serious challenges to the delivery of appropriate group care and/or education. Obviously, it is very difficult to avoid thinking and feeling about, and behaviorally reacting to, children who express aggression, violence, opposition, defiance, and impulsivity at school (as well as at home). Consequently, such children are targeted early and often for ameliorative attention (Conduct Problems Prevention Research Group, 1992, 1999).

In contrast, quiet and overcontrolled young children may represent veritable models of proper school decorum. Often they play in a quiescent fashion on their own or work quietly at their desks. Typically, these are not children who arouse, in their teachers, negative thoughts, feelings, or reactive behaviors. Consequently, these children's internalized difficulties are more likely to go undetected or ignored by the typically harried caregiver/educator.

Third, by the 1980s and for some time thereafter the thriving literature concerning externalizing difficulties suggested that aggressive behavior is not only salient but also highly stable throughout the years of childhood (e.g., Moskowitz, Schwartzman, & Ledingham, 1985). Childhood aggression has been found to predict antisocial behavior and other negative outcomes in adolescence and adulthood (e.g., Dodge, Lochman, Harnish, Bates, & Pettit, 1997; Pulkkinen, 1996; Vitaro, Gendreau, Tremblay, & Oligny, 1998). Externalizers, as a group, have deficits in understanding the perspectives, feelings, and intentions of others (e.g., Crick & Dodge, 1994). They bully their classmates and quickly establish, for themselves, negative reputations among their peers (Ladd & Profilet, 1996; Rubin, Chen, & Hymel, 1993), especially when they are unable to control their anger (Eisenberg, Fabes, et al., 1996). Taken together, given the potential danger of hostile, unthinking aggressive behavior for its victims, it is not surprising that the phenomenon has attracted voluminous and compelling conceptual and empirical treatments (see Dodge & Coie, 1998, for a relevant review).

In contrast, until the 1980s the literature about internalizing disorders in childhood had a rather checkered history. For example, up until the late 1960s prevailing psychoanalytic theory suggested that a child could not experience true depression until the superego was fully developed in adolescence (Kashani et al., 1981). Furthermore, it was reported that behavioral manifestations of psychological overcontrol in childhood were relatively unstable and not significantly predictive of maladjustment during the adolescent and adult periods (Kohlberg, LaCrosse, & Ricks, 1972; Morris, Soroker,

& Buruss, 1954; Robins, 1966). Taken together, during the 1970s and 1980s the prevailing theory and the extant data failed to evoke the same kind of urgency to understand problems of an internalizing nature in childhood as had been the case for externalizing difficulties. In short, because externalizing problems are easier to detect, teachers and other caregivers target disruptive children for attention, and because childhood aggression is predictive of antisocial behavior later on, it is clear why children who rarely interacted with peers, for whatever reason, were neglected by researchers, theorists, parents, and teachers alike.

And yet, despite this neglect, several factors spurred developmental psychologists' persistence in tracking what had been a problem of relatively insignificant proportions. Despite the aforementioned lack of concern among many researchers, by the early 1980s clinical psychologists were insisting that overcontrol and its behavioral manifestations in childhood comprised a major category of disorder (e.g., Achenbach & Edelbrock, 1981) and warranted intervention (e.g., Conger & Keane, 1981). Moreover, during the 1980s researchers were demonstrating that the behavioral manifestations of overcontrol are indeed quite salient to caregivers and age-mates (e.g., Bacon & Ashmore, 1985; Bugental & Shennun, 1984; Younger & Boyko, 1989). From the perspective of developmental psychologists, it seemed that social wariness might make interaction effortful for the child's social partners, whether they were parents or peers. Furthermore, such interactions, or the lack thereof, led us to speculate that social wariness and withdrawal were potential contributors to the development of distant and sometimes difficult relationships. And, from the perspective of dyadic influence, we posited that difficult relationships with primary caregivers in infancy and early childhood might contribute to the formation of a reticent behavioral style and to the development of difficult relationships outside the home.

As we noted earlier, adherents of the more "traditional" theoretical point of view had long proposed that peer interaction represents a social context within which children learn to consider the perspectives of others and coordinate them with their own (e.g., Mead, 1934; Piaget, 1926). Thus we began to think that children who consistently demonstrate the behavior that is paradigmatically "driven by" internalizing problems, that is, social withdrawal, should be at major risk of failing to develop those social and social-cognitive skills that purportedly result from peer interactive experiences (see, for example, Mash & Dozois, 2003).

The conceptual impoverishment of the pre-1980s literature concerning withdrawal in childhood jump-started the determined focus of developmental psychologists on internalizing disorders in general and on the developmental course of social withdrawal in particular. For example, the handful of early prospective longitudinal studies that examined the risk status of childhood social withdrawal (Janes, Hesselbrock, Myers, & Penniman, 1979; John, Mednick, & Schulsinger, 1982; Michael, Morris, & Soroker, 1957; Morris et al., 1954) all shared serious methodological and conceptual flaws. For example, all used clinic or high-risk samples, which tends to result in an attenuated range of observed behavior and an underestimate of the correlation with later outcomes. All used some form of teacher assessment, the validity of which was largely unknown as a measure of social withdrawal. And the outcome measure typically assessed was some form of externalizing disorder. This latter procedure seemed odd to us as researchers, given that withdrawal had been regarded as a reflection of internalizing difficulties.

Finally, in the original research on social withdrawal published in the 1950s, 1960s, and 1970s, the construct of social withdrawal was ill defined. This is the point at which the "new" phase of research emerged. Some researchers argued, for example, that social isolation can occur for a variety of different reasons, ranging from ostracism by the peer group to anxious withdrawal from the peer group to social disinterest in the peer group (e.g., Asendorpf, 1993; Rubin & Mills, 1988). Developmental and clinical psychologists since have found that one explanation for the early lack of evidence that social withdrawal presaged later maladjustment was the failure to differentiate between different subtypes of the phenomenon.

Correlates and Outcomes of Solitude

In response to earlier claims that researchers, parents, and teachers who might worry about shy/withdrawn children were "overconcerned about these personality characteristics" (Morris et al., 1954, p. 753), researchers set out to document the correlates and outcomes associated with social withdrawal across the life span. Although it is certainly not the case that all shy/withdrawn/solitary/inhibited children experience problems (we discuss nomenclature and definitional issues in more detail later in this chapter), results from a growing body of converging literature now indicate that socially withdrawn children are predictively at risk for a host of maladaptive outcomes across the life span (see Rubin, Burgess, & Coplan, 2002, for a recent review).

It has become clear that social withdrawal has negative consequences, even from an early age. Socially withdrawn children in preschool and kindergarten are more likely than their more sociable and socially interactive peers to display signs of anxiety, have lower self-worth, and experience other internalizing problems (e.g., Coplan, Prakash, O'Neil, & Armer, 2004; Rubin, 1982b, 1985; Stevenson-Hinde & Glover, 1996). Socially withdrawn children are also more likely to experience other problems related to early school adjustment, including peer rejection, social isolation, increased teacher attention, academic difficulties, and refusal to attend school (Coplan, Gavinski-Molina, Lagace-Seguin, & Wichmann 2001; Coplan & Prakash, 2003; Gazelle & Ladd, 2003; Hart et al., 2000). Moreover, extremely shy, anxious, and withdrawn children are at increased risk for developing anxiety disorders (particularly social phobia) in later childhood and adolescence (e.g., Rosenbaum, Biederman, Hirshfeld, Bolduc, & Chaloff, 1991; Schwartz, Snidman, & Kagan, 1999).

This negative trajectory for socially withdrawn children appears to worsen with age. In middle and late childhood social withdrawal becomes increasingly associated with peer rejection, loneliness, depressive symptoms, and negative self-regard (e.g., Boivin, Hymel, & Bukowski, 1995; Harrist, Zaia, Bates, Dodge, & Pettit, 1997; Hymel, Bowker & Woody, 1993; Hymel, Rubin, Rowden, & LeMare, 1990; Rubin, Chen, & Hymel, 1993; Rubin, Hymel, & Mills, 1989). In adolescence social withdrawal continues to be associated with loneliness, depression, social anxiety, and lower self-worth (Prior, Smart, Sanson, & Oberklaid, 2000; Rubin, Chen, McDougall, Bowker, & McKinnon, 1995).

Interestingly, in recent years it has become increasingly clear that gender plays an important role in the developmental trajectory of social withdrawal. Growing evidence suggests that from early childhood through to adolescence, social withdrawal is more strongly associated with indexes of maladjustment for boys than for girls (Coplan, Gavinsky-Molina, et al., 2001; Coplan, Prakash, et al., 2004; Eisenberg, Shepard, Fabes, Murphy, & Guthrie, 1998; Morison & Masten, 1991; Rubin, Chen, & Hymel, 1993; Stevenson-Hinde & Glover, 1996). These findings have been attributed in part to the notion that shyness is less socially acceptable for boys than for girls (Sadker & Sadker, 1994). In support of this notion researchers have reported that parents tend to respond more negatively to shy/withdrawn behaviors in boys than in girls (e.g., Radke-Yarrow, Richters,

& Wilson, 1988; Simpson & Stevenson-Hinde, 1985; Stevenson-Hinde, 1989).

For both boys and girls the incidence of social withdrawal appears to be relatively stable (Rubin, 1993; Schneider, Younger, Smith, & Freeman, 1998). Moreover, results from longitudinal research indicate that socially withdrawn children grow up to be adolescents and adults who suffer from feelings of depression and lower self-esteem, lead less active social lives than their peers, and show delays in important life transitions such as getting married, having children, and obtaining a stable career (Caspi, Elder, & Bem, 1998; Gest, 1997; Kerr, Lambert, & Bem, 1996; Rubin, Chen, et al., 1995). Thus there appears to be good reason to pay attention to social withdrawal and social isolation across the life span.

Definitions, Nomenclature, and the Heterogeneity of Solitude

The early study of social withdrawal was severely hampered by the lack of both conceptual and definitional frameworks. Researchers and clinicians have tended to use such terms as *social withdrawal, isolation, shyness,* and *inhibition* interchangeably. In the 1980s and early 1990s theoretical and empirical writings by Rubin (e.g., Rubin, 1982a, 1985; Rubin & Mills, 1988) and Asendorpf (e.g., Asendorpf, 1990, 1993) established the notion that solitude (i.e., a lack of social interaction) in childhood is a heterogeneous construct that varies in terms of behaviors, situational context, motivational tendencies, and developmental consequences. The publication of *Social Withdrawal, Inhibition, and Shyness in Childhood* (Rubin & Asendorpf, 1993) served to further clarify this issue and to focus research attention on a closer examination of the different meanings of *solitude*. Results from more recent research have provided strong support for their conceptualizations of the causes attributed to a child's low rate of social interaction (Coplan, Prakash, et al., 2004; Coplan, Rubin, Fox, Calkins, & Stewart, 1994; Harrist et al., 1997; Hart et al., 2000; Henderson, Marshall, Fox, & Rubin, 2004) and suggest that parents (Coplan, Prakash, et al., 2004), teachers (Rubin & Coplan, 1998), and even young children (Gavinski-Molina, Coplan, & Younger, 2003) can make these more fine-grained distinctions.

The term *active isolation* denotes the process whereby some children play alone because their play partners do not wish to interact with them (Rubin, 1982a). In this case the child's lack of social interaction is attributed to external factors (i.e., the child is isolated by others), perhaps in response to social immaturity and behavioral undercontrol on the part of the child (Rubin, Lemare, & Lollis, 1990). Actively isolated children appear to demonstrate a greater frequency of solitary-active play, which includes boisterous, repetitive sensory-motor behaviors and dramatizing while playing alone while in the company of peers (Coplan, Rubin, et al., 1994; Rubin, 1982a).

The term *social withdrawal* (sometimes called passive withdrawal) denotes a child's isolating him- or herself from the peer group (Rubin, 1982a; Rubin & Mills, 1988) through the consistent (across situations and over time) display of solitary behavior in the presence of peers (Rubin, 1982a; Rubin & Asendorpf, 1993). In this regard social withdrawal is seen as arising from internal factors, with the child opting, for some reason or another, not to interact with peers. Social withdrawal itself can be construed as an umbrella term, encompassing at least two different reasons why children might choose to play alone.

First, some children's social withdrawal is a product of an internal conflict between having high social approach motivation accompanied by wariness at initiating social interaction (high social avoidance motivation). This construct has most recently been labeled "anxious solitude" (Gazelle & Ladd, 2003). Using different nomenclature, researchers have explored conceptually similar constructs related to wariness/anxiety in the face of novelty (e.g., inhibition, Kagan, 1997), social novelty (e.g., fearful shyness, Buss & Plomin, 1984), and perceived social evaluation (e.g., self-conscious shyness, Asendorpf, 1989). In free play situations with peers, shy/anxious children tend to engage in onlooking behaviors or remain unoccupied (i.e., reticent), both in novel and familiar settings (Coplan, Rubin, et al., 1994; Fox, Calkins, Schmidt, Rubin, & Coplan, 1996; Fox, Henderson, Rubin, Calkins, & Schmidt, 2001; Rubin, Burgess, & Hastings, 2002).

Other children may refrain from social interaction because they lack a strong desire to play with others (i.e., low social approach motivation), although they are not strongly averse to peer interaction (i.e., low social avoidance motivation). This nonfearful preference for solitary activities has been labeled unsociability (Asendorpf, 1993) or social disinterest (Coplan, Prakash, et al., 2004) in children and solitropic orientation in adults (Leary, Herbst, & McCrary, 2003). In contrast to other forms of solitude, unsociability has been considered relatively benign, particularly in early childhood (Rubin & Asendorpf, 1993). However, the lack of sociability appears benign only for those young children who are neither emotionally reactive nor unable to regulate their emotions (be soothed) when upset.

For example, in their study of preschoolers in a familiar play setting (preschool or day care), Coplan, Prakash, and colleagues (2004) found that children rated as unsociable were less often observed to initiate social interactions with peers, and teachers viewed these children as more socially withdrawn. Yet ratings of unsociability, in and of themselves, were not significantly associated with the display of solitary-passive behavior, which is characterized by exploratory and constructive activity while playing alone in the presence of peers. Alternatively, Rubin and colleagues reported that unsociable preschoolers who are emotionally regulated (not easily upset and easy to soothe or calm) frequently display solitary-passive behavior (Rubin, Coplan, Fox, & Calkins, 1995). And Henderson and colleagues (2004) have found that a subset of unsociable children is physiologically similar to children who frequently engage in reticent behavior when among unfamiliar peers. Those solitary-passive players who had lower resting heart period were similar to their reticent age-mates in that they were behaviorally inhibited at 24 months. Those solitary-passive players who had higher resting heart period were not behaviorally inhibited as toddlers. In this regard the data suggested that some children may engage in unsociable, solitary-passive behaviors as a strategy for coping with feelings of unease. In short, the frequent expression of quiet, sedentary, constructive solitary activity may have varying psychological and emotional meanings depending on where children are observed and the extent to which children are able to regulate their negative emotions. It is important to note that the longer-term consequences of unsociability remain virtually unexplored.

Current Issues in the Etiology of Social Withdrawal

Since the mid-1980s research related to the development of social withdrawal and social isolation has expanded almost exponentially. The results of this work have led to a greater understanding of the etiology of social withdrawal. Much of this work has focused on issues of nature and nurture and their complex and transactional interaction over time.

THE ROLE OF BIOLOGY

A major advance during the 1990s was the exploration of the biological and physiological underpinnings of social withdrawal. Drawing from early research on temperament and personality by Kagan and his colleagues (Kagan, 1989; Kagan & Moss, 1962), researchers posited that fearfulness (i.e., behavioral inhibition), as it is expressed in infancy and toddlerhood, has a distinctively biological origin. They have since found that toddlers and preschoolers who express fear when in the company of unfamiliar adults and children differ from their uninhibited counterparts in ways that imply variability in the threshold of excitability of the amygdala and its projections to the cortex, hypothalamus, sympathetic nervous system, corpus striatum, and central gray (see Marshall & Stevenson-Hinde, 2001, for a recent review).

For example, a profile of asymmetric resting right frontal EEG activity has consistently been associated with social fear and anxiety in young children (Fox, Calkins, et al., 2001; Fox, Henderson, et al., 1996; Henderson et al., 2004). In addition, vagal tone, an index of the functional status or efficiency of the nervous system (Porges & Byrne, 1992), marking both general reactivity and the ability to regulate one's level of arousal, distinguishes socially fearful from non-fearful toddlers and preschoolers (Anderson, Bohlin, & Hagekull, 1999; Garcia-Coll, Kagan, & Reznick, 1984); children with lower vagal tone (consistently high heart rate due to less parasympathetic influence) tend to be more inhibited. Last, the hypothalamic-pituitary-adrenocortical axis is affected largely by stressful or aversive situations that involve novelty, uncertainty, and/or negative emotions (Levine, 1983); and behaviorally inhibited infants evidence significant increases in cortisol as a function of exposure to stressful social situations (Spangler & Schieche, 1998). Moreover, socially wary, fearful young children have shown elevated home baseline cortisol readings relative to nonwary children, suggesting that wary children are physiologically primed to react with wariness to novel or unsettling social situations (Schmidt, Fox, Rubin, & Sternberg, 1997).

THE ROLE OF PARENTS

Biology clearly plays a contributing role in the development of social withdrawal. However, not all behaviorally inhibited infants and toddlers go on to become shy, withdrawn, and anxious children. In recent years researchers have begun to explore some factors that may moderate the life courses of shy/inhibited children. Not surprisingly, this has led contemporary researchers to significantly re-examine the role of parents.

Attachment theory has influenced some recent advances in this area. For example, we now have evidence linking behavioral inhibition with insecure ambivalent (C) attachment classification (Calkins & Fox, 1992; Stevenson-Hinde & Shouldice, 1993). Stevenson-Hinde and Shouldice (1993) have suggested that unfamiliar situations (including Ainsworth's Strange Situation) activate both the attachment system and the fear behavior system. It is important to note that this link between an insecure attachment relationship and socially fearful, wary behavior appears to be a product of far more than an attachment "main effect." Thus Spangler and Schieche (1998) have reported that the Strange Situation activates the endocrine stress response in ambivalent (C) infants but not in securely attached (B) or avoidant (A) infants.

In the late 1990s and early 2000s, however, we have also witnessed what can only be characterized as a major paradigm shift in the study of parenting styles and the development of social withdrawal. In the past researchers focused on the relation between social withdrawal and authoritarian (i.e., harsh, coercive, punitive) parenting (e.g., Attili, 1989; Baumrind, 1971; Belsky, Rovine, & Taylor, 1984). More recently, support has been increasing for a link between social withdrawal and parenting that can best be described as overprotective, intrusive, and oversolicitous (Barber, Olsen, & Shagle, 1994; Coplan, Prakash, et al., 2004; Hudson & Rapee, 2001; Mills & Rubin, 1998; Rubin, Burgess, & Hastings, 2002; Rubin, Cheah, & Fox, 2001; Rubin, Hastings, Stewart, Henderson, & Chen, 1997). Parents who are overprotective tend to overmanage situations for their child, restrict child behaviors, discourage child independence, and direct child activities. As a result researchers have posited that temperamentally shy/inhibited children who are raised in this environment may not develop the necessary coping and problem-solving strategies in their interpersonal milieu.

Through related longitudinal research, investigators are slowly uncovering the complex and transactional interplay between child characteristics and parenting beliefs and behaviors. For example, parents' perceptions of toddlers' shyness and physiological indexes of shyness (i.e., lower vagal tone) have been found to predict overprotective/overcontrolling parenting 2 years hence (Kennedy, Rubin, Hastings, & Maisel, 2004; Rubin, Nelson, Hastings, & Asendorpf, 1999). These findings suggest that the origins of socially withdrawn behavior are parental reactions to their young children's biologically based characteristics. Moreover, these parental reactions can, in turn, influence the developmental trajectories of temperamentally shy children. For example, Rubin, Burgess, and Hastings (2002) reported that behavioral inhibition at age 2 years was predictive of reticent-anxious play among peers at age 4 years only for those children whose mothers were overprotective and intrusive.

Thus we can postulate that the dialectic between dispositional factors that are biologically driven and experiential factors that are driven by the presence of a fearful and wary infant or toddler may result in psychologically and emotionally negative outcomes for both children and their parents. It remains to be discovered whether variations in parenting styles can alter the physiological responses of dispositionally inhibited or reticent children. This is clearly an exciting path for future study.

Future Directions and Points to Ponder

As we look forward to the next 50 years of *Merrill-Palmer Quarterly*, we can contemplate additional research directions in the study of social withdrawal. This final section describes two broad areas that merit increased research attention.

RISK AND PROTECTIVE FACTORS

In 1990 Rubin, LeMare, and Lollis proposed a theoretical model outlining developmental pathways in the etiology of social withdrawal and internalizing problems. This theoretical framework considers the joint influences of child characteristics, parental socialization practices, the quality of relationships outside the family, and macrosystemic forces. They postulate transactional processes, describing the reciprocal and evolving relations over time between child temperamental predispositions and environmental contexts.

Since the mid-1980s we have come to learn much about the roles of biology and parenting in the etiology of social withdrawal in childhood. We urge researchers to continue to explore these areas but also to consider other factors that either put children at risk or offer them some protection. Few researchers have considered variables that may moderate the relations between social withdrawal and adjustment outcomes over time.

For example, Asendorpf (1994) found that shy children with higher verbal IQ and greater social competence were more likely to become less shy over time than their shy peers who did not share these characteristics. Asendorpf speculated that increased social and communicative competencies might be particularly helpful for shy children in developing effective coping strategies in response to challenging social situations. In a similar vein Coplan and Armer (2005) found that expressive vocabulary moderated the relation between shyness and indexes of adjustment during the transition to preschool—with increased language skills serving to buffer shy children against negative outcomes.

Within the peer domain Gazelle and Ladd (2003) reported that shy/anxious kindergartners who were excluded by peers displayed greater stability in anxious solitude through the fourth grade and had levels of depressive symptoms that were higher than those of shy/anxious peers who did not experience peer exclusion. A "stress-diathesis" model is suggested, whereby the experience of peer exclusion exacerbates the outcomes associated with anxious solitude. Similarly, Gazelle and Rudolph (2004) have found that among fifth- and sixth-graders, anxious solitary youth display maintenance or exacerbation of social avoidance and depression in the context of high exclusion; however, social approach increases when children do not experience peer exclusion or rejection.

Given that peer exclusion and rejection appear to exacerbate problems for anxiously withdrawn children, one might ask whether protective factors can be identified as well. Researchers are only beginning to focus on such protective factors. For example, Oh, Rubin, Burgess, Booth-LaForce, and Rose-Krasnor (2004) used latent growth curve modeling to investigate the extent to which the perceived supportiveness of friendship served as a protective factor in the maintenance, decrease, or increase of anxious withdrawal over five assessments taken between the fifth and eighth grades (10 to 13 years of age). The perceived supportiveness of the child's best friendship was a significant predictor for both the initial level of anxious withdrawal and the rate of change of withdrawal over time. Young adolescents who viewed their friendships as highly supportive were less likely to be socially withdrawn in fifth grade and showed a greater rate of decline in social withdrawal over time.

Drawing upon previous theoretical work (Rubin, Burgess, & Coplan, 2002; Rubin, LeMare, and Lollis, 1990), we can suggest several additional potential risk and protective factors for future investigation. For example, biological factors (brain-wave activity, electrical activity of the heart, cortisol levels) that reflect emotion regulatory skills have been the focus of study in the infant, toddler, and early childhood periods. Few such studies exist in the later years of childhood and adolescence. Thus we do not know whether anxious withdrawal in late childhood and early adolescence is accompanied or predicted by these physiological markers.

Social-cognitive prowess may serve as a protective or exacerbating factor as well. It is well known that aggressive children attribute negative consequences that befall them to the purposeful thoughts of their protagonists; such children respond with anger and hostility (Dodge, Pettit, et al., 1986). Less is known about the social-cognitive processes that may accompany and predict anxious withdrawal. Wichmann, Coplan, and Daniels (2004) have reported that in comparison with their peers, socially withdrawn children displayed a pattern of self-defeating attributions for social situations, reported lower efficacy for assertive goals, and indicated a preference for nonassertive, withdrawn strategies to deal with hypothetical conflict situations. However, many questions remain to be investigated. When socially anxious and withdrawn children experience negative events with ambiguous causes, do they attribute them to intentional acts? How do they feel about such events? And how do they react behaviorally?

Parenting and parent-child relationships may prove important as protective or exacerbating factors. Yet virtually nothing is known about the quality of the parenting experience and the parent-child relationships of anxiously withdrawn children during middle and late childhood and early adolescence. Similarly, the quality of anxiously withdrawn children's relationships with friends is unknown. Typically, do socially withdrawn children have friends? With whom do they make friends? How stable are those friendships, and what role do their friendships play in their developmental trajectories? These are questions that researchers are only now beginning to answer (e.g., Schneider, 1999).

As a final note, it is clear that the etiology of social withdrawal must be considered within cultural context. For example, in an extensive series of studies, Chen and colleagues have demonstrated that mothers, teachers, and peers in the People's Republic of China encourage and accept shy, reticent, reserved behavior, and it is positively associated with social competence, peer acceptance, and academic success (Chen, Chen, & Kaspar, 2001; Chen, Hastings, et al., 1998; Chen, Rubin, & Li, 1995). Chen has argued that the collectivistic values found in Chinese culture place a strong emphasis on group cohesion; consequently, shyness and reservedness are more greatly appreciated there than in Western cultures that espouse individualistic beliefs and norms. Cross-cultural work is underway in a number of countries. In an ongoing study of behavioral inhibition on four continents, Rubin and colleagues have found that as early as 24 months, toddlers exhibit differences in their extent of inhibited behavior in unfamiliar settings. For example, Australian and Italian toddlers were observed to display less inhibited behavior than their

Korean and Chinese age-mates (Rubin, Hemphill, et al., in press).

How parents respond to their inhibited toddlers or socially withdrawn children in cultural context may provide valuable information about why some, but not all, sociocultural environments perceive social withdrawal as an impediment. And it may well be shy reservedness and social withdrawal draw different reactions. Cheah and Rubin (2004) found that Chinese mothers of preschoolers reported greater anger and teaching behaviors in response to the consistent display of social withdrawal than did American mothers. These findings suggest that Chinese parents regard shyness and social withdrawal as rather different constructs. Thus reserved, shy behavior may eventually be conducive to harmonious group interactions, whereas socially withdrawn behavior that removes the child from familiar others could undermine such goals. In this regard Chinese mothers could perceive socially withdrawn behavior as unsocial behavior that undermines the predominant collectivistic teachings of preschool caregivers, as well as the societal goals of group harmony and close interaction (Stimpfl, Zheng, & Meredith, 1997).

INTERVENTION AND PREVENTION

As we mentioned earlier, since the 1980s research into the development and outcomes of social withdrawal in childhood has experienced rapid growth. What is surprising is that, despite the increasing evidence linking social withdrawal to contemporaneous and longitudinal socioemotional difficulties, research related to intervention and prevention appears to have declined during this same time period.

Researchers in the 1970s and 1980s explored a variety of techniques in an effort to increase the social interaction of withdrawn children. This included the use of symbolic modeling (e.g., O'Connor, 1972), "implosion" exposure to group activities (e.g., Lowenstein, 1983), placing the withdrawn child in a classroom manager role (e.g., Sainato, Maheady, & Shook, 1986), and pairing withdrawn children with more sociable peers (Furman, Rahe, & Hartup, 1979). The results of these early attempts were decidedly mixed (see Greco & Morris, 2001, for a recent review).

Also very popular at the time was the use of social skills training, which has demonstrated some moderate effects in enhancing specifically targeted social skills (e.g., Christoff et al., 1985). However, it remains unclear whether the mastery of trained skills and social problem-solving abilities will actually result in enhanced peer relationships. Moreover, there is a lack of convincing evidence that the observed changes in trained behaviors are durable and easily generalized to real-life settings.

Although many intervention programs have demonstrated at least some success, the extant literature in this area is plagued with conceptual and methodological difficulties. These include extremely small sample sizes (e.g., Hodges & McCoy, 1990; Sainato et al., 1986; Sheridan, Kratochwill, & Elliott, 1990); the lack of any control group (e.g., Lewis & Sugai, 1993; Lindeman, Fox, and Redelheim, 1993; Sheridan et al., 1990) or a failure to include a control group of withdrawn children (Hodges & McCoy, 1990; Storey, Smith, & Strain, 1993); and sole reliance on teacher referrals to identify withdrawn children (e.g., Lewis & Sugai, 1993; Lindeman et al., 1993; Storey et al., 1993). Moreover, problems with operational definitions and assessments of social withdrawal likely resulted in the selection of heterogeneous treatment groups.

We are hopeful that recent advances in the conceptualization, assessment, and etiology of social withdrawal will inform subsequent research aimed at ameliorating the life courses of socially withdrawn children. For example, future prevention and intervention programs should begin in early childhood, include a focus not only on teaching skills but also on emotion regulation, involve both familiar and unfamiliar peers, and include a substantive parental component.

Some Final Thoughts

After a long history of research neglect, the study of social withdrawal in childhood has garnered an enormous amount of attention since the 1990s. The dates of the material cited in this chapter attest to this. Much work has been directed toward establishing the developmental origins of social withdrawal and its related constructs, as well as toward examining the contemporaneous and predictive correlates of social withdrawal at different points in childhood and adolescence. Empirical work suggests that the quality of life for the socially withdrawn child on individual, family, and peer levels is less than pleasant. Withdrawn children are socially deferent, anxious, lonely, and insecure in the company of peers and often are rejected by peers. Withdrawn children fail to exhibit age-appropriate interpersonal problem-solving skills and believe themselves to be deficient in social skills and social relationships. These characteristics do not augur well for socially withdrawn children. Whether the constellation of these factors leads inexorably to the development of psychopathology or clinical disorders is not yet known. With regard to the latter, relatively few longitudinal studies exist; therefore, researchers would do well to examine the premise that social withdrawal represents a risk factor in childhood and adolescence. And certainly, it would behoove researchers to investigate potentially protective and exacerbating factors within the cultural context. The field is wide open, and one would hope that within the next 50 years readers will see significant advances in the study of social withdrawal within the pages of *Merrill-Palmer Quarterly.*

References

Achenbach, T. M., & Edelbrock, C. (1981). Behavioral problems and competencies reported by parents of normal and disturbed children aged four through sixteen. *Monographs for the Society for Research in Child Development, 46* (Serial No. 188).

Anderson, K., Bohlin, G., & Hagekull, B. (1999). Early temperament and stranger wariness as predictors of social inhibition in 2 year olds. *British Journal of Developmental Psychology, 17,* 421–434.

Asendorpf, J. B. (1989). Shyness as a final common pathway for two different kinds of inhibition. *Journal of Personality and Social Psychology, 57,* 481–492.

Asendorpf, J. B. (1990). Beyond social withdrawal: Shyness, unsociability and peer avoidance. *Human Development, 33,* 250–259.

Asendorpf, J. B. (1993). Abnormal shyness in children. *Journal of Child Psychology and Psychiatry, 34,* 1069–1081.

Asendorpf, J. B. (1994). The malleability of behavioral inhibition: A study of individual developmental functions. *Developmental Psychology, 30,* 912–919.

Attili, G. (1989). Social competence versus emotional security: The link between home relationships and behavior problems at school. In B. H. Schneider, G. Attili, J. Nadel, & R. P. Weissberg (Eds.), *Social competence in developmental perspective* (pp. 293–311). London: Kluwer.

Bacon, M. K., & Ashmore, R. D. (1985). How mothers and fathers categorized descriptions of social behavior attributed to daughters and sons. *Social Cognition, 3,* 193–217.

Barber, B. K., Olsen, J. E., & Shagle, S. C. (1994). Associations between parental psychological and behavioral control and youth internalized and externalized behaviors. *Child Development, 65,* 1120–1136.

Baumrind, D. (1971). Current patterns of parental authority. *Developmental Psychological Monographs, 4* (1, Pt. 2).

Belsky, J., Rovine, M., & Taylor, D. (1984). The Pennsylvania infant and family development project: III. The origins of individual differences in infant-mother attachment: Maternal and infant contributions. *Child De-*

velopment, 55, 718–728.

Boivin, M., Hymel, S., & Bukowski, W. (1995). The roles of social withdrawal, peer rejection, and victimization by peers in predicting loneliness and depressed mood in childhood. *Development and Psychopathology, 7,* 765–785.

Bronfenbrenner, U. (1943). A constant frame of reference for sociometric research: Pt. 1. Theory and technique. *Sociometry, 6,* 363–397.

Bugental, D. B., & Shennun, W. A. (1984). "Difficult" children as elicitors and targets of adult communication patterns: An attributional-behavioral transactional analysis. *Monographs of the Society for Research in Child Development, 49.*

Bukowski, W. M., Newcomb, A. F., & Hartup, W. W. (Eds.). (1996). *The company they keep: Friendship in childhood and adolescence.* New York: Cambridge University Press.

Buss, A. H., & Plomin, R. (1984). *Temperament: Early developing personality traits.* Hillsdale, NJ: Erlbaum.

Calkins, S. D., & Fox, N. A. (1992). The relations among infant temperament, security of attachment, and behavioral inhibition at 24 months. *Child Development, 63,* 1456–1472.

Campbell, J. D. (1964). Peer relationships in childhood. In M. Hoffman & L. W. Hoffman (Eds.), *Review of child development research* (pp. 289–322). New York: Russell Sage Foundation.

Caspi, A., Elder, G. H., Jr., & Bem, D. J. (1988). Moving away from the world: Life-course patterns of shy children. *Developmental Psychology, 24,* 824–831.

Cheah, C. S. L., & Rubin, K. H. (2004). A cross-cultural examination of maternal beliefs regarding maladaptive behaviors in preschoolers. *International Journal of Behavioral Development, 28,* 83–94.

Chen, X., Chen, H., & Kaspar, V. (2001). Group social functioning and individual socio-emotional and school adjustment in Chinese children. *Merrill-Palmer Quarterly, 47,* 264–299.

Chen, X., Hastings, P., Rubin, K. H., Chen, H., Cen, G., & Stewart, S. L. (1998). Childrearing attitudes and behavioral inhibition in Chinese and Canadian toddlers: A cross-cultural study. *Developmental Psychology, 34,* 677–686.

Chen, X., Rubin, K. H., & Li, B. (1995). Social and school adjustment of shy and aggressive children in China. *Development and Psychopathology, 7,* 337–349.

Christoff, K. A., Scott, W. O. N., Kelley, M. L., Schlundt, D., Baer, G., & Kelly, J. A. (1985). Social skills and social problem-solving training for shy young adolescents. *Behavior Therapy, 16,* 468–477.

Coie, J. D., & Dodge, K. A. (1983). Continuities and changes in children's social status: A five-year longitudinal study. *Merrill-Palmer Quarterly, 29,* 261–281.

Conduct Problems Prevention Research Group. (1992). A developmental and clinical model for the prevention of conduct disorder: The FAST

Track Program. *Development and Psychopathology, 4,* 509–527.

Conduct Problems Prevention Research Group. (1999). Initial impact of the Fast Track Prevention Trial for conduct problems: I. The high-risk sample. *Journal of Consulting and Clinical Psychology, 67,* 631–647.

Conger, J. C., & Keane, S. P. (1981). Social skills interventions in the treatment of isolated or withdrawn children. *Psychological Bulletin, 90,* 478–495.

Coplan, R. J., & Armer, M. (2005). Talking yourself out of being shy: Shyness, expressive vocabulary, and adjustment in preschool. *Merrill-Palmer Quarterly, 51,* 20–41.

Coplan, R. J., Gavinsky-Molina, M. H., Lagace-Seguin, D., & Wichmann, C. (2001). When girls versus boys play alone: Gender differences in the associates of nonsocial play in kindergarten. *Developmental Psychology, 37,* 464–474.

Coplan, R. J., & Prakash, K. (2003). Spending time with teacher: Characteristics of preschoolers who frequently elicit versus initiate interactions with teachers. *Early Childhood Research Quarterly, 18,* 143–158.

Coplan, R. J., Prakash, K., O'Neil, K., & Armer, M. (2004). Do you "want" to play? Distinguishing between conflicted-shyness and social disinterest in early childhood. *Developmental Psychology, 40,* 244–258.

Coplan, R. J., Rubin, K. H., Fox, N. A., Calkins, S. D., & Stewart, S. L. (1994). Being alone, playing alone, and acting alone: Distinguishing among reticence and passive- and active-solitude in young children. *Child Development, 65,* 129–138.

Crick, N. R., & Dodge, K. A. (1994). A review and reformulation of social information-processing mechanisms in children's social adjustment. *Psychological Bulletin, 115,* 74–101.

Damon, W. (Series Ed.). (1998). *Handbook of child psychology.* (5th ed.). New York: Wiley.

Dodge, K. A., & Coie, J. D. (1998). Aggression and antisocial behavior. In W. Damon (Series Ed.) & N. Eisenberg (Vol. Ed.), *Handbook of child psychology: Vol. 3. Social, emotional, and personality development* (5th ed., pp. 779–862). New York: Wiley.

Dodge, K. A., Lochman, J. E., Harnish, J. D., Bates, J. E., & Pettit, G. S. (1997). Reactive and proactive aggression in school children and psychiatrically impaired chronically assaultive youth. *Journal of Abnormal Psychology, 106,* 37–51.

Dodge, K. A., Pettit, G. S., McClaskey, C. L., & Brown, M. (1986). Social competence in children. *Monographs of the Society for Research in Child Development, 51* (Serial No. 213).

Dodge, K. A., Schlundt, D. G., Schocken, I., & Delugach, J. D. (1983). Social competence and children's social status: The role of peer group entry strategies. *Merrill-Palmer Quarterly, 29,* 309–336.

Eisenberg, N., Fabes, R. A., Guthrie, I. K., Murphy, B., Maszk, P., Holmgren, R., & Suh, K. (1996). The relations of regulation and emotionality to problem behavior in elementary school children. *Development and Psy-*

chopathology, 8, 141–162.

Eisenberg, N., & Miller, P. A. (1987). Empathy, sympathy, and altruism: Empirical and conceptual links. In N. Eisenberg & J. Strayer (Eds.), *Empathy and its development* (pp. 292–316). New York: Cambridge University Press.

Eisenberg, N., Shepard, S. A., Fabes, R. A., Murphy, B. C., & Guthrie, I. K. (1998). Shyness and children's emotionality, regulation, and coping: Contemporaneous, longitudinal, and across-context relations. *Child Development, 69,* 767–790.

Evans, M., & Rubin, K. H. (1979). Hand gestures as a communicative mode in school-aged children. *Journal of Genetic Psychology, 135,* 189–196.

Fox, N. A., Calkins, S. D., Schmidt, L. A., Rubin, K. H., & Coplan, R. J. (1996). The role of frontal activation in the regulation and dysregulation of social behavior during the preschool years. *Development and Psychopathology, 8,* 89–102.

Fox, N. A., Henderson, H. A., Rubin, K. H., Calkins, S. D., & Schmidt, L. A. (2001). Stability and instability of behavioral inhibition and exuberance: Psychophysiological and behavioral factors influencing change and continuity across the first four years of life. *Child Development, 72,* 1–21.

Furman, W., Rahe, D. F., & Hartup, W. W. (1979). Rehabilitation of socially withdrawn preschool children through mixed-age and same-age socialization. *Child Development, 50,* 915–922.

Garcia-Coll, C., Kagan, J., & Reznick, J. S. (1984). Behavioral inhibition in young children. *Child Development, 55,* 1005–1019.

Garvey, C., & Hogan, R. (1973). Social speech and social interaction: Egocentrism revisited. *Child Development, 44,* 562–568.

Gavinski-Molina, M. H., Coplan, R. J., & Younger, A. (2003). A closer look at children's knowledge about social isolation. *Journal of Research in Childhood Education, 18,* 93–104.

Gazelle, H., & Ladd, G. W. (2003). Anxious solitude and peer exclusion: A diathesis-stress model of internalizing trajectories in childhood. *Child Development, 74,* 257–278.

Gazelle, H., & Rudolph, K. D. (2004). Moving toward and away from the world: Social approach and avoidance trajectories in anxious solitary youth. *Child Development, 75,* 257–278.

Gest, S. D. (1997). Behavioral inhibition: Stability and association with adaptation from childhood to early adulthood. *Journal of Personality and Social Psychology, 72,* 467–475.

Greco, L. A., & Morris, T. L. (2001). Treating childhood shyness and related behavior: Empirically evaluated approaches to promote positive social interactions. *Clinical Child and Family Psychology Review, 4,* 299–318.

Harris, J. R. (1995). Where is the child's environment? A group socialization theory of development. *Psychological Review, 102,* 458–489.

Harrist, A. W., Zaia, A. F., Bates, J. A., Dodge, K. A., & Pettit, G. S. (1997). Subtypes of social withdrawal in early childhood: Sociometric status and social-cognitive differences across four years. *Child Development,*

68, 278–294.

Hart, C. H., Yang, C., Nelson, L. J., Robinson, C. C., Olsen, J. A., Nelson, D. A., Porter, C. L., Jin, S., Olsen, S. F., & Wu, P. (2000). Peer acceptance in early childhood and subtypes of socially withdrawn behaviour in China, Russia, and the United States. *Journal of Behavioral Development, 24*, 73–81.

Hartup, W. W. (1970). Peer interaction and social organization. In P. H. Mussen (Ed.), *Carmichael's manual of child psychology* (3rd ed., Vol. 2, pp. 361–456). New York: Wiley.

Henderson, H., Marshall, P., Fox, N. A., & Rubin, K. H. (2004). Converging psychophysiological and behavioral evidence for subtypes of social withdrawal in preschoolers. *Child Development, 75*, 251–263.

Hodges, J. B., & McCoy, J. F. (1990). Effects of coaching and per utilization procedures on the withdrawn behaviors of preschoolers. *Child and Family Behavior Therapy, 12*, 25–47.

Hudson, J. L., & Rapee, R. M. (2001). Parent-child interactions and anxiety disorders: An observational study. *Behavior Research and Therapy, 39*, 1411–1427.

Hymel, S., Bowker, A., & Woody, E. (1993). Aggressive versus withdrawn unpopular children: Variations in peer and self-perceptions in multiple domains. *Child Development, 64*, 879–896.

Hymel, S., Rubin, K. H., Rowden, L., & Lemare, L. (1990). Children's peer relationships: Longitudinal predictions of internalizing and externalizing problems from middle to late childhood. *Child Development, 61*, 2004–2021.

Janes, C. L., Hesselbrock, V. M., Myers, D. G., & Penniman, J. H. (1979). Problem boys in young adulthood: Teachers' ratings and twelve-year follow-up. *Journal of Youth and Adolescence, 8*, 453–472.

John, R. S., Mednick, S. A., & Schulsinger, F. (1982). Teacher reports as a predictor of schizophrenia and borderline schizophrenia: A Bayesian decision analysis. *Journal of Abnormal Psychology, 6*, 399–413.

Kagan, J. (1989). Temperamental contributions to social behavior. *American Psychologist, 44*, 668–674.

Kagan, J. (1997). Temperament and reactions to the unfamiliar. *Child Development, 68*, 139–143.

Kagan, J., & Moss, H. A. (1962). *Birth to maturity: A study of psychological development*. New York: Wiley.

Kashani, J. H., Husain, A., Shekim, W. O., Hodges, K. K., Cytryn, L., & McKnew, D. H. (1981). Current perspectives of childhood depression: An overview. *American Journal of Psychiatry, 138*, 143–153.

Kennedy, A. E., Rubin, K. H., Hastings, P., & Maisel, B. (2004). The longitudinal relations between child vagal tone and parenting behavior: 2 to 4 years. *Developmental Psychobiology, 45*, 10–21.

Kerr, M., Lambert, W. W., & Bem, D. J. (1996). Life course sequelae of childhood shyness in Sweden: Comparison with the United States. *Developmental Psychology, 32*, 1100–1105.

Kohlberg, L., Lacrosse, J., & Ricks, D. (1972). The predictability of adult mental health from childhood behavior. In B. B. Wolman (Ed.), *Manual of child psychopathology* (pp. 1217–1284). New York: McGraw-Hill.

Ladd, G. W., & Profilet, S. M. (1996). The child behavior scale: A teacher report measure of young children's aggressive, withdrawn, and prosocial behaviors. *Developmental Psychology, 32,* 1008–1024.

Leary, M. R., Herbst, K. C., & McCrary, F. (2003). Finding pleasure in solitary activities: Desire for aloneness or disinterest in social contact? *Personality and Individual Differences, 35,* 59–68.

Levin, E., & Rubin, K. H. (1983). Getting others to do what you wanted them to do: The development of children's requestive strategies. In K. Nelson (Ed.), *Child language* (Vol. 4, pp. 157–186). Hillsdale, NJ: Erlbaum.

Levine, S. (1983). A psychobiological approach to the ontogeny of coping. In N. Garmezy & M. Rutter (Eds.), *Stress, coping, and development in children* (pp. 107–131). Baltimore: Johns Hopkins University Press.

Lewis, T. J., & Sugai, G. (1993). Teaching communicative alternatives to socially withdrawn behavior: An investigation in maintaining treatment effects. *Journal of Behavioral Education, 3,* 61–75.

Lindeman, D. P., Fox, J. J., & Redelheim, P. S. (1993). Increasing and maintaining withdrawn preschoolers' peer interactions: Effects of double prompting and booster session procedures. *Behavior Disorders, 11,* 54–66.

Lowenstein, L. (1983). Treatment of extreme shyness by implosive, counseling, and conditioning approaches. *Association of Educational Psychologists, 6,* 64–69.

Marshall, P. J., & Stevenson-Hinde, J. (2001). Behavioral inhibition: Physiological correlates. In W. R. Crozier & L. E. Alden (Eds.), *International handbook of social anxiety* (pp. 53–66). New York: Wiley.

Mash, E. J., & Barkley, R. A. (Eds.). (2003). *Child psychopathology* (2nd ed.). New York: Guilford.

Mash, E. J., & Dozois, D. J. A. (2003). *Child psychopathology: A developmental-systems perspective.* In E. J. Mash & R. A. Barkley (Eds.), *Child psychopathology* (2nd ed., pp. 3–71). New York: Guilford.

Mead, G. H. (1934). *Mind, self, and society.* Chicago: University of Chicago Press.

Michael, C. M., Morris, D. P., & Soroker, E. (1957). Follow-up study of shy, withdrawn children—II. Relative incidence of schizophrenia. *American Journal of Orthopsychiatry, 27,* 331–337.

Mills, R. S. L., & Rubin, K. H. (1990). Parental beliefs about problematic social behaviours in early childhood. *Child Development, 61,* 138–151.

Mills, R. S. L., & Rubin, K. H. (1998). Are behavioral control and psychological control both differentially associated with childhood aggression and social withdrawal? *Canadian Journal of Behavioral Sciences, 30,* 132–136.

Moreno, J. L. (1934). *Who shall survive? A new approach to the problem of human inter-relations.* Washington, DC: Nervous and Mental Disease Publishing Co.

Morison, P., & Masten, A. S. (1991). Peer reputation in middle childhood as a predictor of adaptation in adolescence: A seven year follow-up. *Child Development, 62,* 991–1007.

Morris, D. P., Soroker, E., & Buruss, G. (1954). Follow-up studies of shy, withdrawn children—I. Evaluation of later adjustment. *American Journal of Orthopsychiatry, 24,* 743–754.

Moskowitz, D. S., Schwartzman, A. E., & Ledingham, J. E. (1985). Stability and change in aggression and withdrawal in middle childhood and early adolescence. *Journal of Abnormal Psychology, 94,* 30–41.

Mueller, E. (1972). The maintenance of verbal exchanges in young children. *Child Development, 43,* 930–938.

Mussen, P. H. (Ed.). (1970). *Carmichael's manual of child psychology.* New York: Wiley.

Mussen, P. H. (Series Ed.). (1983). *Handbook of child psychology.* New York: Wiley.

O'Connor, R. D. (1972). The relative efficacy of modeling, shaping, and combined procedures. *Journal of Abnormal Psychology, 79,* 327–334.

Oh, W., Rubin, K. H., Burgess, K. B., Booth-Laforce, C., & Rose-Krasnor, L. A. (2004, July). Developmental perspective on social withdrawal across middle childhood and adolescence: Predictions from parental and peer factors. Poster presented at the 18th Biennial Meetings of the International Society for the Study of Behavioral Development, Ghent, Belgium.

Piaget, J. (1926). *The language and thought of the child.* London: Routlege & Kegan Paul.

Porges, S. W., & Byrne, E. A. (1992). Research methods for measurement of heart rate and respiration. *Biological Psychology, 34,* 93–130.

Prior, M., Smart, D., Sanson, A., & Oberklaid, F. (2000). Does shy-inhibited temperament in childhood lead to anxiety problems in adolescence? *Journal of the American Academy of Child and Adolescent Psychiatry, 39,* 461–468.

Pulkkinen, L. (1996). Proactive and reactive aggression in early adolescence as precursors to anti- and prosocial behavior in young adults. *Aggressive Behavior, 22,* 241–257.

Radke-Yarrow, M., Richters, J., & Wilson, W. E. (1988). Child development in a network of relationships. In R. A. Hinde & J. Stevenson-Hinde (Eds.), *Relationships within families: Mutual influences* (pp. 48–67). Oxford, England: Clarendon.

Robins, L. N. (1966). *Deviant children grown up.* Baltimore: Williams & Wilkins.

Rosenbaum, J. F., Biederman, J., Hirshfeld, D. R., Bolduc, E. A., & Chaloff, J. (1991). Behavioral inhibition in children: A possible precursor to panic disorder or social phobia. *Journal of Clinical Psychiatry, 52,* 5–9.

Rubin, K. H. (1982a). Non-social play in preschoolers: Necessary evil? *Child Development, 53,* 651–657.

Rubin, K. H. (1982b). Social and social-cognitive developmental character-istics of young isolate, normal, and sociable children. In K. H. Rubin & H. S. Ross (Eds.), *Peer relationships and social skills in childhood* (pp. 353–374). New York: Springer-Verlag.

Rubin, K. H. (1985). Socially withdrawn children: An "at risk" population? In B. H. Schneider, K. H. Rubin, & J. Ledingham (Eds.), *Children's peer relations: Issues in assessment and intervention* (pp. 125–139). New York: Springer-Verlag.

Rubin, K. H. (1993). The Waterloo Longitudinal Project: Correlates and con-sequences of social withdrawal from childhood to early adolescence. In K. H. Rubin & J. B. Asendorpf (Eds.), *Social withdrawal, inhibition, and shyness in childhood* (pp. 291–314). Hillsdale, NJ: Erlbaum.

Rubin, K. H., & Asendorpf, J. B. (1993). Social withdrawal, inhibition, and shyness in childhood: Conceptual and definitional issues. In K. H. Rubin & J. B. Asendorpf (Eds.), *Social withdrawal, inhibition, and shyness in childhood* (pp. 3–17). Hillsdale, NJ: Erlbaum.

Rubin, K. H., & Borwick, D. (1984). The communication skills of children who vary with regard to sociability. In H. Sypher & J. Applegates (Eds.), *Social cognition and communication* (pp. 152–170). Hillsdale, NJ: Erlbaum.

Rubin, K. H., Bukowski, W., & Parker, J. G. (2006). Peer interactions, rela-tionships, and groups. In W. Damon & R. Lerner (Series Eds.), N. Eisen-berg (Vol. Ed.), *Handbook of child psychology. Vol. 3. Social, emotional, and personality development* (6th ed., pp. 571–645). New York: Wiley.

Rubin, K. H., Burgess, K. B., & Coplan, R. J. (2002). Social withdrawal and shyness. In P. K. Smith & C. H. Hart (Eds.), *Blackwell's handbook of child-hood social development* (pp. 329–352). London: Blackwell.

Rubin, K. H., Burgess, K. B., & Hastings, P. D. (2002). Stability and social-be-havioral consequences of toddlers' inhibited temperament and parent-ing behaviors. *Child Development, 73*, 483–495.

Rubin, K. H., Cheah, C. S. L., & Fox, N. (2001). Emotion regulation, parent-ing, and display of social reticence in preschoolers. *Early Education & Development, 12*, 97–115.

Rubin, K. H., Chen, X., & Hymel, S. (1993). Socioemotional characteristics of withdrawn and aggressive children. *Merrill-Palmer Quarterly, 39*, 518–534.

Rubin, K. H., Chen, X., McDougall, P., Bowker, A., & McKinnon, J. (1995). The Waterloo Longitudinal Project: Predicting internalizing and exter-nalizing problems in adolescence. *Development and Psychopathology, 7*, 751–764.

Rubin, K. H., & Coplan, R. J. (1998). Social and nonsocial play in childhood: An individual differences perspective. In O. N. Saracho & B. Spodek (Eds.), *Multiple perspectives on play in early childhood education* (pp. 144–170). Albany: State University of New York Press.

Rubin, K. H., Coplan, R. J., Fox, N. A., & Calkins, S. D. (1995). Emotionality, emotion regulation, and preschoolers' social adaptation. *Development and Psychopathology, 7*, 49–62.

Rubin, K. H., & Daniels-Beirness, T. (1983). Concurrent and predictive correlates of sociometric status in kindergarten and grade one children. *Merrill-Palmer Quarterly, 29*, 337–352.

Rubin, K. H., Hastings, P. P., Stewart, S. L., Henderson, H. A., & Chen, X. (1997). The consistency and concomitants of inhibition: Some of the children, all of the time. *Child Development, 68*, 467–483.

Rubin, K. H., Hemphill, S. A., Chen, X., Hastings, P., Sanson, A., Lococo, A., Chung, O. B., Park, S. Y., Zappulla, C., Yoon, C. H., & Doh, H. S. (in press). A cross-cultural study of behavioral inhibition in toddlers: East-west-north-south. *International Journal of Behavioral Development.*

Rubin, K. H., Hymel, S., & Mills, R. S. L. (1989). Sociability and social withdrawal in childhood: Stability and outcomes. *Journal of Personality, 57*, 238–255.

Rubin, K. H., & Krasnor, L. R. (1986). Social-cognitive and social behavioral perspectives on problem solving. In M. Perlmutter (Ed.), *The Minnesota Symposia on Child Psychology. Vol. 18. Cognitive perspectives on children's social and behavioral development* (pp. 1–68). Hillsdale, NJ: Erlbaum.

Rubin, K. H., Lemare, L., & Lollis, S. (1990). Social withdrawal in childhood: Developmental pathways to peer rejection. In S. Asher & J. D. Coie (Eds.), *Peer rejection in childhood* (pp. 217–249). New York: Cambridge University Press.

Rubin, K. H., & Mills, R. S. L. (1988). The many faces of social isolation in childhood. *Journal of Consulting and Clinical Psychology, 6*, 916–924.

Rubin, K. H., Nelson, L. J., Hastings, P., & Asendorpf, J. B. (1999). Transaction between parents' perceptions of their children's shyness and their parenting styles. *International Journal of Behavioral Development, 23*, 937–957.

Rubin, K. H., & Schneider, F. W. (1973). The relationship between moral judgment, egocentrism, and altruistic behavior. *Child Development, 44*, 661–665.

Sadker, M., & Sadker, D. (1994). *Failing at fairness: How America's schools cheat girls.* New York: Scribner.

Sainato, D. M., Maheady, L., & Shook, G. L. (1986). The effects of a classroom manager role on the social interaction patterns and social status of withdrawn kindergarten students. *Journal of Applied Behavior Analysis, 19*, 187–195.

Schmidt, L. A., Fox, N. A., Rubin, K. H., & Sternberg, E. M. (1997). Behavioral and neuroendocrine responses in shy children. *Developmental Psychobiology, 30*, 127–140.

Schneider, B. H. (1999). A multimethod exploration of the friendships of children considered social withdrawn by school peers. *Journal of Abnormal Child Psychology, 27(2)*, 115–123.

Schneider, B. H., Attili, G., Vermigli, P., & Younger, A. (1997). A comparison of middle-class English-Canadian and Italian mothers' beliefs about children's peer directed aggression and social withdrawal. *International Journal of Behavioural Development, 21*, 133–154.

Schneider, B. H., Younger, A. J., Smith, T., & Freeman, P. (1998). A longitudinal exploration of the cross-context stability of social withdrawal in early adolescence. *Journal of Early Adolescence, 18,* 734–396.

Schwartz, C. E., Snidman, N., & Kagan, J. (1999). Adolescent social anxiety as an outcome of inhibited temperament in childhood. *Journal of the American Academy of Child & Adolescent Psychiatry, 38,* 1008–1015.

Selman, R. L. (1980). *The growth of interpersonal understanding: Developmental and clinical analyses.* New York: Academic.

Shantz, C. U. (1983). Social cognition. In P. H. Mussen (Series Ed.), J. H. Flavell & E. M. Markman (Vol. Eds.), *Handbook of child psychology. Vol. 3. Cognitive development* (4th ed., pp. 495–555). New York: Wiley.

Shatz, M., & Gelman, R. (1973). The development of communication skills: Modifications of the speech of young children as a function of the listener. *Monographs of the Society for Research in Child Development, 38* (No. 38).

Sheridan, S. M., Kratochwill, T. R., & Elliott, S. N. (1990). Behavioral consultation with parents and teachers: Delivering treatment for socially withdrawn children at home and school. *School Psychology Review, 19,* 33–52.

Simpson, A. E., & Stevenson-Hinde, J. (1985). Temperamental characteristics of three- to four-year-old boys and girls and child-family interactions. *Journal of Child Psychology and Psychiatry, 26,* 43–53.

Spangler, G., & Schieche, M. (1998). Emotional and adrenocortical responses of infants to the Strange Situation: The differential function of emotional expression. *International Journal of Behavioral Development, 22,* 681–706.

Sroufe, L. A., & Rutter, M. (1984). The domain of developmental psychopathology. *Child Development, 55,* 17–29.

Stevenson-Hinde, J. (1989). Behavioral inhibition: Issues of context. In J. S. Reznick (Ed.), *Perspectives on behavioral inhibition* (pp. 125–138). Chicago: University of Chicago Press.

Stevenson-Hinde, J., & Glover, A. (1996). Shy girls and boys: A new look. *Journal of Child Psychology and Psychiatry, 37,* 181–187.

Stevenson-Hinde, J., & Shouldice, A. (1993). Wariness to strangers: A behavior systems perspective revisited. In K. H. Rubin & J. B. Asendorpf (Eds.), *Social withdrawal, inhibition, and shyness in childhood* (pp. 101–116). Hillsdale, NJ: Erlbaum.

Stimpfl, J., Zheng, F., & Meredith, W. (1997). A garden in the motherland: A study of a preschool in China. *Early Child Development and Care, 129,* 11–26.

Storey, K., Smith, D. J., & Strain, P. S. (1993). Use of classroom assistants and peer-mediated intervention to increase integration in preschool settings. *Exceptionality, 4,* 1–16.

Vitaro, F., Gendreau, P. L., Tremblay, R. E., & Oligny, P. (1998). Reactive and proactive aggression differentially predict later conduct problems. *Journal of Child Psychology and Psychiatry and Allied-Disciplines, 39,* 377–385.

Weissberg, R., Gesten, E., Rapkin, B., Cowan, E., Davidson, E., Flores De

Apodica, R., & McKim, M. (1981). Evaluation of a social problem-solving training program for suburban and inner-city third-grade children. *Journal of Consulting Clinical Psychology, 49,* 251–261.

Wichmann, C., Coplan, R. J., & Daniels, T. (2004). The social cognitions of socially withdrawn children. *Social Development, 13,* 377–392.

Younger, A. J., & Boyko, K. A. (1989). Aggression and withdrawal as social schemas underlying children's peer perceptions. *Child Development, 58,* 1094–1100.

Younger, A., Gentile, C., & Burgess, K. (1993). Children's perceptions of social withdrawal: Changes across age. In K. H. Rubin & J. B. Asendorpf (Eds.), *Social withdrawal, inhibition, and shyness in childhood.* Hillsdale, NJ: Erlbaum.

11

The Next 50 Years
Considering Gender as a Context for Understanding Young Children's Peer Relationships

*Richard A. Fabes, Carol Lynn Martin,
and Laura D. Hanish*

The study of children's peer relationships has a long and rich history (see Rubin, Bukowski, & Parker, 1998). This history is represented by investigations spanning such important topics as peer acceptance and rejection, friendship, leadership, peer group structure and formation, social conflict, and social networks, and these topics have permeated the field since its beginning (e.g., Monroe, 1899). *Merrill-Palmer Quarterly* is no exception to this historical trend—during its first 50 years articles about these topics routinely appeared in its pages. Moreover, the last two editors of *Merrill-Palmer Quarterly*, Carolyn Shantz and Gary Ladd, brought to the journal their wealth of knowledge about peer relationships. In fact, one of the initial members of *Merrill-Palmer Quarterly*'s editorial board, Leland H. Stott, had an interest in peer relationships (see Stott & Ball, 1957). Thus it is not surprising that the archives of *Merrill-Palmer Quarterly* reflect the rich tradition of peer relationship research.

Despite the pace and intensity of the research, significant gaps remain. Several have already been identified (see Rubin et al., 1998), and other chapters in this collection discuss additional gaps (e.g., see Chapter 9). In this chapter we focus on an area that we feel has been neglected in the many studies of peer relationships, specifically, the sex-segregated nature of children's peer relationships during early childhood. We believe that research in this area is particularly important for advancing our understanding of the developmental implications of peer relationships because same-sex peer interactions provide the primary peer socialization context for young children. Moreover, boys' and girls' same-sex peer interactions involve different qualities of play, and boys and girls structure their peer relationships and social networks in different ways.

To date, however, studies of young children's peer relationships have often neglected considerations of the organizing role of gender and the implications of these sex differences for children's developmental trajectories. We will review why sex segregation is worthy of further investigation and suggest avenues for integrating this concept into peer relationship research that might appear in future editions of *Merrill-Palmer Quarterly.*

Where Is Gender in the Study of Children's Peer Relationships?

Gender has not been entirely ignored in the peer research literature; a better description is that gender is a topic that has received attention in select domains. For instance, research has emphasized gender in the study of the development of heterosexual relationships that begin to appear in early adolescence and continue to form and mature across later adolescence and adulthood (e.g., Florsheim, 2003; Furman, 2002; Laursen & Jensen-Campbell, 1999). Specifically, a number of researchers have examined how boys and girls, or men and women, come to develop friendships and intimate relationships with one another. This is not a surprising focus for research on adolescence and young adulthood, as these are periods when interest in, and attraction toward, members of the other sex generally increases and becomes more significant. The interest in gender issues is also apparent in the increasing numbers of articles on gay and lesbian intimate relationships (see D'Augelli & Patterson, 2001).

We suggest that what has been neglected in the literature is the role of gender in early peer relationships—before puberty begins and before interest in other-sex peers develops. It is important to note that gender plays a different role in young children's peer relationships than it does for older children, teens, and adults. Specifically, in early childhood the focus is on the role of same-sex peers. With few exceptions (e.g., Leaper, 1994; Maccoby, 1998; Maccoby & Jacklin, 1987), researchers have paid little attention to the role of same-sex peers in early development, even though sex segregation—the tendency to prefer and play with children of one's own sex and avoid members of the other sex—is one of the most noticeable aspects of early peer relationships.

Why Study Sex-Segregated Peer Relationships?

Sex segregation is one of the most powerful and pervasive social phenomena known to exist in childhood (see Leaper, 1994; Maccoby,

1990). Sex segregation begins around the age of 3 and escalates throughout childhood. By the time children enter preschool, boys and girls show strong and consistent preferences for same-sex peers over other-sex peers (Fabes, Martin, & Hanish, 2003; Maccoby & Jacklin, 1987; Martin & Fabes, 2001). Not only do young children show strong preferences for same-sex peers, they also spend relatively little time with children of the other sex. In particular, children spend very little time solely with members of the other sex. By most estimates more than half of all young children's peer interactions involve play with same-sex peers, about 30% involve peers of both sexes (playing with both a boy and a girl, which we call mixed-sex play), and less than 10% of peer interactions involve play only with other-sex peers (play that we call other-sex play) (Fabes, 1994). With age the proportion of same-sex peer preferences increases, at least through the elementary school years. For instance, Maccoby and Jacklin (1987) reported that preschoolers were three times as likely to interact with same-sex peers as with other-sex peers, whereas 6 1/2 year olds interacted with same-sex peers 11 times more often than they interacted with other-sex peers.

How sex differentiated are play partner preferences in children? One way to answer this question is to consider the magnitude of these patterns in relation to other sex differences. For example, in most studies of sex differences in behavior, such as in spatial abilities, language abilities, or mathematical abilities, sex accounts for less than 2% to 5% of the variance (Eagly, 1995; Hyde & Plant, 1995). In contrast, for choices of play partner, sex accounts for 70% to 80% of the variance (Maccoby, 1998; Martin & Fabes, 2001). Data from our own research illustrate this very clearly (see Figures 1a and 1b). In yearlong observations of children's peer play partners, preschool and kindergarten boys and girls (number of subjects = 72 boys and 80 girls, mean age = 57.8 months) exhibited almost completely nonoverlapping distributions of play with boy or girl peer partners (Martin & Fabes, 2001). This same-sex play preference pattern is observed in children not only in the United States but elsewhere. Cross-cultural studies confirm its universality (Omark, Omark, & Edelman, 1975), and these preferences even appear in many other mammal species (Bernstein, Judge, & Ruehlmann, 1993).

Interestingly, same-sex play partner preferences are determined by the children, not their parents or caretakers. That is, the strongest sex segregation occurs in settings where children are allowed to make their own choices. Same-sex peer play is stronger when activities are unstructured and when adults are not immedi-

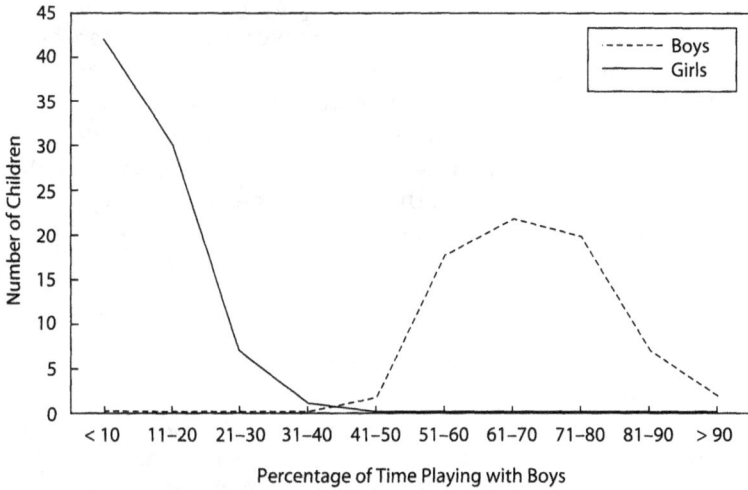

Figure 1a. Time Boys and Girls Were Observed to Play With Boys

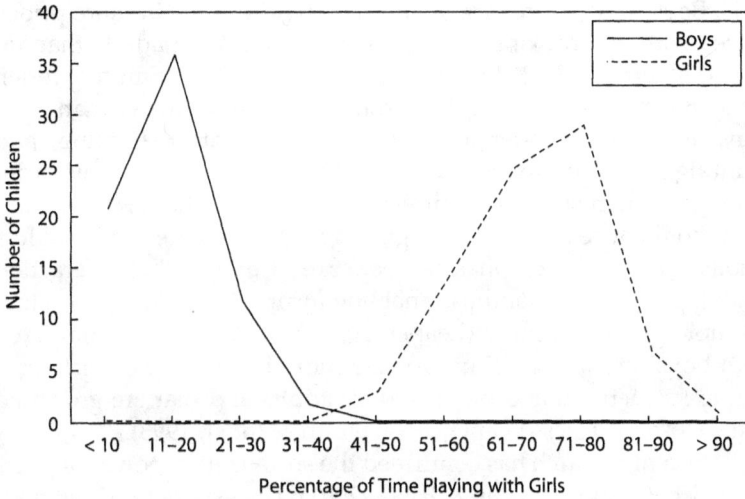

Figure 1b. Time Girls and Boys Were Observed to Play With Girls

ately present or involved in children's play (Maccoby, 1990; Maccoby & Jacklin, 1987; Thorne, 2001). Moreover, these preferences are difficult for adults to change. For instance, when teachers provided reinforcement to preschool children who were seen playing with other-sex peers, the amount of cross-sex play increased while the contingency was in effect. When the reinforcement was discontinued, the children quickly returned to baseline levels of segregated play (Serbin, Tonick, & Sternglanz, 1977).

Sex Segregation and Peer Socialization

The strength of sex segregation has led to speculation about the short- and long-term consequences of these patterns of play (e.g., Leaper, 1994; Maccoby, 1990), but little research has actually addressed this critical issue. Based on the consistency and strength of sex segregation, some researchers have proposed that girls and boys develop within different cultures and that these different cultures provide widely different social experiences.

Research since the mid-1980s has provided information about the qualities of girls' and boys' play groups. Playing with boys provides different opportunities and experiences than playing with girls. Boys' groups are larger, and they tend to play in more public places with less proximity to and supervision from adults than do girls (DiPietro, 1981; Fabes, Martin, & Hanish, 2003; Smith & Inder, 1993). Boys' play also tends to be rougher and more active than girls' play, and it more often involves physical contact, fighting, and taunting. Boys quickly establish a hierarchical order, and this order tends to remain stable over time (Maccoby & Jacklin, 1987). In contrast, dominance hierarchies in girls' groups are more fluid and less stable. Girls often emphasize cooperation and verbal interaction among play partners and use enabling forms of communication that promote group harmony (Leaper, 1994; Maccoby, 1990). Compared with boys' groups, girls' groups are more likely to select activities that are structured and organized by adults and that are governed by strict social rules (Leaper, 1994; Smith & Inder, 1993).

Recent research has confirmed the socialization power of peers in early childhood (Martin & Fabes, 2001). The experiences that boys and girls have in their sex-segregated peer groups contribute to many aspects of their development, and this contribution is likely to be above and beyond the individual difference variables that led children to initially select same-sex peer groups. Experiences gained within boys' and girls' peer groups foster different behavioral norms and interaction styles. Over time repeated exposure to these different behavioral and motivational norms and interaction styles may promote the development of different skills, attitudes, motives, interests, and behaviors (Leaper, 1994). As such, same-sex peer groups represent a potentially powerful context for socialization (Serbin, Moller, Gulko, Powlishta, & Colburne, 1994). However, we believe that this research agenda has not yet received the attention it deserves—particularly as it applies to development in the early years when peer relationships and peer group dynamics are just forming (Fabes, Hanish, & Martin, 2003).

Of course, young children do spend time interacting and playing with members of the other sex. Rarely, however, does this occur when a child is playing only with members of the other sex. When children play with members of the other sex, generally a member of their own sex is also involved in the play (mixed-sex play), and the presence of a same-sex peer has implications for the qualities of the interactions that occur (Fabes, Martin, & Hanish, 2003). As we noted previously, mixed-sex play occurs in about 30% of all interactions that children have in their peer groups. As such, children of the other sex have the potential to be influential. At least in the behaviors we have examined thus far, we have not yet found that play in mixed-sex peer groups produces evidence of socialization effects, whereas we have found such evidence when examining play with same-sex peers (Fabes, Martin, Hanish, Anders, & Madden-Derdich, 2003; Fabes, Shepard, Guthrie, & Martin, 1997). Thus something about the experiences children have in same-sex play appears to be unique. To date, however, this uniqueness has not been clearly identified.

The failure to find evidence of similar mixed-sex socialization effects suggests that children's general sociability is not what accounts for changes in children's behavior over time. Moreover, the lack of significant influences of mixed-sex play reduces the likelihood that selection factors account for findings that we attribute to same-sex peer socialization. That is, when changes occur in a child's behavior as a function of time spent with same-sex peers, one explanation for these changes could be related to the factors that lead children to play with same-sex peers in the first place. Thus selection factors may contribute in some way to developmental changes. We contend that selection effects are likely to be as influential in mixed-sex play as they are in same-sex play. In fact, selection factors may be more influential in mixed-sex play, given that it occurs relatively less often than same-sex play and children who evidence relatively high rates of mixed-sex play may have unique characteristics. Thus it is unlikely that same-sex peer socialization can be explained solely by selection factors.

Individual Variations in the Consequences of Same-Sex Play

Although the sex-segregated pattern of children's play preferences is one of the most recognizable and potentially important features of their play, we understand little about its consequences. The guiding perspective on the causes and consequences of sex segregation has been focused on binary effects—that is, factors that promote virtually universal consequences of these same-sex preferences on children's development. Because all children generally engage in sex-segregated play, a binary view suggests that all children would be exposed to the patterns of interaction that characterize their own sex's play. This, in turn, should provide sufficient levels of gender-typed experiences to promote gender socialization, ultimately changing children's behavior. From this perspective examining the qualities of boys' and girls' play groups has been useful, because these qualities are indicative of the types of changes that might occur with socialization.

Research from our lab suggests that the binary view represents only part of the picture when it comes to understanding the consequences of same-sex play (Martin & Fabes, 2001). Even though most children show distinct patterns of sex-segregated play, the strength of those patterns matters. A complementary view is that children's outcomes vary according to individual differences in degree of exposure to same-sex peers. Although most boys and girls spend considerably more time playing with same- than other-sex peers, we investigated whether the variation in the degree to which children do so would be influential. Although the range in Figures 1a and 1b is restricted, these figures show that children's tendencies to engage same-sex peers varies. As a result we proposed a gradient view, in which same-sex peer effects are dosage dependent—that is, the more exposure a child has to same-sex peers, the more the child will show the influence of these experiences. For example, we found that boys who played more extensively with boys during the fall term of preschool were observed in the spring term with higher levels of activity, rough-and-tumble play, playing apart from adults, and gender-typed play. In contrast, girls who played more with other girls during the fall term of preschool were observed in the spring term with higher levels of playing near adults and gender-typed play (Martin & Fabes, 2001). Thus, in addition to binary effects, gradient effects—individual differences in same-sex peer exposure—must be considered.

Early Sex Segregation and Sex Differences

Children's early sex-segregated peer relationships appear to set the stage for sex differences. Patterns of behavior that are commonly thought of as being boylike or girl-like may in fact be the result of boys' playing with boys in boylike ways, and girls' playing with girls in girl-like ways. Consequently, some sex differences may be a result of group processes (Maccoby & Jacklin, 1987). Defining individual and group contributions to developmental changes is essential in future work in this area (Maccoby, 2002). For example, in some of our observational data we have found that certain sex differences in behavior and activities occur much more frequently in same-sex groups than in other contexts. Specifically, we examined children's activity choices when they were playing with same-sex play partners versus when they were alone, and we found that patterns of sex stereotypic behaviors were most exaggerated when children were playing with members of their own sex. Consider the patterns presented in Figure 2. In this study the percentage of time that young boys and girls were observed in language-related activities (e.g., reading, talking, writing, etc.) varied depending on play partners. Stereotypically, we would expect to observe girls involved in these activities more frequently than boys. As this figure shows, this stereotypic pattern of behavior was evident only when girls were playing with other girls. In general, we found only minor differences in the degree to which boys and girls were involved in language activities when they were alone. The implications of this group-level phenomenon for the development of sex-stereotypic patterns of play and behavior, and the processes through which same-sex peer socialization effects occur, are not well understood. Thus this area is ripe for future research.

Peer Experiences and Gender Development

Surprisingly little is known about the links between early peer relationships and gender development. In the timetable of gender development, children recognize the sexes by approximately 9 months

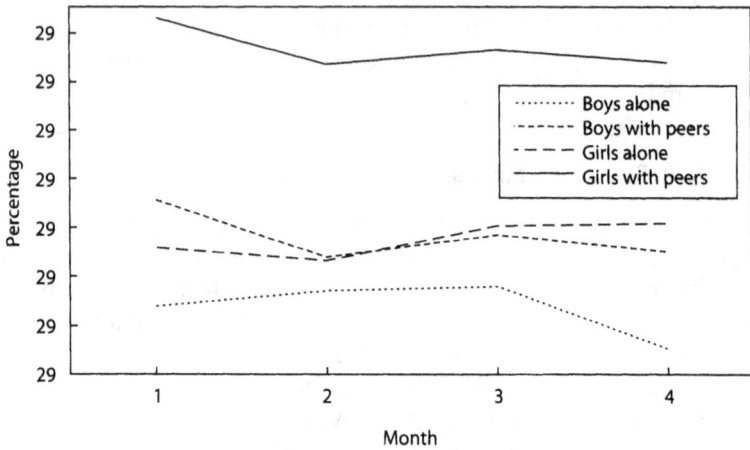

Figure 2. Language-Related Activities Observed for Children Playing Alone or With Peers

of age, they are able to label the sexes by 2 or 3 years, and they begin to show sex segregation at approximately 2 1/2 to 3 years of age (Martin, Ruble, & Szkrybalo, 2002; Ruble & Martin, 1998).

By the age of 4 or 5 years, when many children regularly attend preschool and begin to have increasing sex-segregated play experiences, children also evidence very strong and rigid stereotyping of the sexes and are particularly attuned to gender cues (Martin & Ruble, 2003). Many parents remark that their children became very sensitive about gender issues in preschool. We also know that children's behavior becomes more gender-typed with exposure to same-sex peers during preschool (Martin & Fabes, 2001). These interconnections have led us to speculate about the nature of the links between gender development and peer relationships (Martin & Dinella, 2002; Ruble & Martin, 1998). Clearly, children know about gender before preschool. However, it may be that exposure to same-sex play partners in preschool accelerates the pace of gender development that is already under way. Specifically, playing with same-sex peers may strengthen children's motivation to learn about members of their own sex and may promote stronger adherence to the stereo-types that they know.

Preschool gender-related experiences have the capacity to pro-mote many aspects of gender development: Children learn new stereotypes from peers, they learn to recognize the consequences as-sociated with not complying with stereotypes, and they may di-rectly experience the in-group nature of gender groupings in pre-school. Even in a classroom with only one gender-traditional child, that one child may set the entire class on a more gendered trajectory. This child could play the role of a "gender enforcer" who conveys to the other children the gender-based rules for play among and be-tween girls and boys on the playground. Although these play pat-terns may be difficult to detect in everyday play, there is limited ev-idence that this type of behavior is seen in preschool (see Fagot, 1977).

Studying Early Peer Socialization Processes

The implications of finding that young children's behavior is social-ized by their degree of exposure to peers, particularly same-sex peers, are broad. From the perspective of understanding peer social-ization, the existing theories have been useful for identifying the content likely to be socialized—the types of characteristics that are most typical of each of the gendered cultures of young children's play groups. Much less has been said, however, about how peers might exert their influence. In addition to modeling, engaging in col-laborative tasks, and reinforcement, what mechanisms are involved in early peer socialization? Understanding these mechanisms and how they operate requires more process-oriented data. Furthermore, in future work much more needs to be done to account for individ-ual differences in peer socialization effects. How and why are some young children more vulnerable to peers' influence, or the influence of certain peers, than other children?

To bolster present theoretical accounts requires that re-searchers make forays into the study of how change occurs in com-plex systems. In our view dynamical systems accounts may be promising approaches that could help us understand how children form, structure, and develop peer groups, how peers influence and are influenced by one another, and how children's peer groups and networks change over time (see Dishion, Bullock, & Granic, 2002; Granic & Hollenstein, 2003). For instance, we have found it useful to remember that even very small individual-level differences may interact in ways that lead to a larger and more complex pattern of behavior (Schelling, 1971).

Conclusion: The Importance of Gender in Early Peer Relationships

The pace of research on peer relationships has accelerated since the mid-1990s. In part because of organized forums for making contacts with peer researchers (e.g., the Peer Preconference at the biennial meeting of the Society for Research in Child Development), controversies about the roles of peers and parents in children's development (Harris, 1995, 1998), and the increasing number of research outlets for work on adolescence, the focus on the role of peers has gained momentum, particularly in regard to the development of problem behaviors in later development (Brendgen, Vitaro, Turgeon, & Poulin, 2002; Dishion, Poulin, & Burraston, 2001; Vitaro, Tremblay, Kerr, Pagani, & Bukowski, 1997). Not all areas of peer relationships have seen the same acceleration of interest, however. Our view is that early peer relationships, and in particular the role of sex segregation in those relationships, are still relatively overlooked. This is true even though the work of the National Institute of Child Health and Human Development Early Child Care Research Network (NICHD ECCRN, 2001, 2002a, 2002b) has heightened attention to children's child care experiences as a context for early learning and social development. Even in this work the specific role of peers has been relatively neglected (see Fabes, Hanish, & Martin, 2003). Because child care brings children into contact with many same-age peers—providing greater exposure to other children on a more regular basis than is typically experienced at home or in the neighborhood—peers represent important sources of early socialization.

The simple fact is that being a boy or a girl sets powerful peer group socialization processes in motion early in children's lives (Maccoby & Jacklin, 1987). By the age of 3 years, children spontaneously segregate into same-sex peer groups, and these early sex-segregated relationships likely set the stage for individual and group interactional qualities and trajectories that follow. The potential consequences of the different childhood cultures produced by early sex-segregated play groups are significant not only for development in childhood but considerably beyond, particularly when the two sexes converge in adolescence and adulthood. For example, Maccoby (1998) has argued that the different social histories of males and females affect the relationships of heterosexual couples and the nature of cross-sex interactions that occur in the workplace. With few exceptions the implications of the role of gender as an organizing feature of early peer relationships have rarely been considered. The work of the authors who fill the pages of the next 50 years of *Merrill-Palmer Quarterly* could and should make significant contributions to this important area.

References

Bernstein, I. W., Judge, P. G., & Ruehlmann, T. E. (1993). Sex differences in adolescent rhesus monkey (Macaca mulatta) behavior. *American Journal of Primatology, 31*, 197–210.

Brendgen, M., Vitaro, F., Turgeon, L., & Poulin, F. (2002). Assessing aggressive and depressed children's social relations with classmates and friends: A matter of perspective. *Journal of Abnormal Child Psychology, 30*, 609–624.

D'Augelli, A. R., & Patterson, J. (2001). *Lesbian, gay, and bisexual identities and youth.* London: Oxford University Press.

DiPietro, J. A. (1981). Rough and tumble play: A function of gender. *Developmental Psychology, 17*, 50–58.

Dishion, T. J., Bullock, B. M., & Granic, I. (2002). Pragmatism in modeling peer influence: Dynamics, outcomes, and change processes. *Development and Psychopathology, 14*, 969–981.

Dishion, T. J., Poulin, F., & Burraston, B. (2001). Peer group dynamics associated with iatrogenic effects in group interventions with high-risk young adolescents. In D. W. Nangle & C. A. Erdley (Eds.), *The role of friendship in psychological adjustment* (pp. 79–92). San Francisco: Jossey-Bass.

Eagly, A. H. (1995). The science and politics of comparing women and men. *American Psychologist, 50*, 145–158.

Fabes, R. A. (1994). Physiological, emotional, and behavioral correlates of gender segregation. In C. Leaper (Ed.), *Childhood gender segregation: Causes and consequences* (pp. 19–34). San Francisco: Jossey-Bass.

Fabes, R. A., Hanish, L. D., & Martin, C. L. (2003). Children at play: The role of peers in understanding the effects of child care. *Child Development, 74*, 1039–1043.

Fabes, R. A., Martin, C. L., & Hanish, L. D. (2003). Qualities of young children's same-, other-, and mixed-sex play. *Child Development, 74*, 921–932.

Fabes, R. A., Martin, C. L., Hanish, L. D., Anders, M. C., & Madden-Derdich, D. A. (2003). Early school competence: The roles of sex-segregated play and effortful control. *Developmental Psychology, 39*, 848–859.

Fabes, R. A., Shepard, S. A., Guthrie, I. K., & Martin, C. L. (1997). Roles of temperamental arousal and gender-segregated play in young children's social adjustment. *Developmental Psychology, 33*, 693–702.

Fagot, B. I. (1977). Consequences of moderate cross-gender behavior in pre-school children. *Child Development, 48*, 902–907.

Florsheim, P. (2003). Adolescent romantic and sexual behavior: What we know and where we go from here. In P. Florsheim (Ed.), *Adolescent romantic relations and sexual behavior: Theory, research, and practical implications* (pp. 371–385). Mahwah, NJ: Erlbaum.

Furman, W. (2002). The emerging field of adolescent romantic relationships. *Current Directions in Psychological Science, 11*, 177–180.

Granic, I., & Hollenstein, T. (2003). Dynamic systems methods for models of developmental psychopathology. *Development and Psychopathology, 15*, 641–669.

Harris, J. R. (1995). Where is the child's environment? A group socialization theory of development. *Psychological Review, 102*, 458–489.

Harris, J. R. (1998). *The nurture assumption: Why children turn out the way they do.* New York: Free Press.

Hyde, J. A., & Plant, E. A. (1995). The magnitude of psychological gender differences: Another side to the story. *American Psychologist, 50*, 159–161.

Laursen, B., & Jensen-Campbell, L. A. (1999). The nature and functions of social exchange in adolescent romantic relationships. In W. Furman & B. B. Brown (Eds.), *The development of romantic relationships in adolescence* (pp. 50–74). New York: Cambridge University Press.

Leaper, C. (1994). Exploring the consequences of gender segregation on social relationships. In C. Leaper (Ed.), *Childhood gender segregation: Causes and consequences* (pp. 67–86). San Francisco: Jossey-Bass.

Maccoby, E. E. (1990). Gender as a social category. In S. Chess & M. E. Hertzig (Eds.), *Annual progress in child psychiatry and child development* (pp. 127–150). New York: Brunner/Mazel.

Maccoby, E. E. (1998). *The two sexes: Growing up apart, coming together.* Cambridge, MA: Belknap.

Maccoby, E. E. (2002). Gender and group process: A developmental perspective. *Current Directions in Psychological Science, 11*, 54–58.

Maccoby, E. E., & Jacklin, C. N. (1987). Gender segregation in childhood. In H. W. Reese (Ed.), *Advances in child development and behavior* (Vol. 20, pp. 239–287). Orlando, FL: Academic Press.

Martin, C. L., & Dinella, L. (2002). Children's gender cognitions, the social environment, and sex differences in cognitive domains. In A. V. McGillicuddy-De Lisi & R. De Lisi (Eds.), *Biology, society, and behavior: The development of gender differences in cognition* (pp. 207–239). Westport, CT: Ablex.

Martin, C. L., & Fabes, R. A. (2001). The stability and consequences of young children's same-sex peer interactions. *Developmental Psychology, 37*, 431–446.

Martin, C. L., & Ruble, D. N. (2003). Children's search for gender cues: Cognitive perspectives on gender development. *Current Directions in Psychological Science, 13*, 67–70.

Martin, C. L., Ruble, D. N., & Szkrybalo, J. (2002). Cognitive theories of early gender development. *Psychological Bulletin, 128*, 903–933.

Monroe, W. S. (1899). Play interests of children. *American Educational Review, 4*, 358–365.

NICHD Early Child Care Research Network. (2001). Child care and children's peer interaction at 24 and 36 months: The NICHD study of early child care. *Child Development, 72*, 1478–1500.

NICHD Early Child Care Research Network. (2002a). Early child care and children's development prior to school entry. *American Educational Research Journal, 39*, 133–164.

NICHD Early Child Care Research Network. (2002b). Structure, process, outcome: Direct and indirect effects of caregiving quality on young children's development. *Psychological Sciences, 13*, 199–206.

Omark, D. R., Omark, M., & Edelman, M. (1975). Formation of dominance hierarchies in young children. In T. R. Williams (Ed.), *Psychological anthropology* (pp. 133–156). The Hague: Mouton.

Rubin, K. H., Bukowski, W., & Parker, J. G. (1998). Peer interactions, relationships, and groups. In W. Damon (Series Ed.) & N. Eisenberg (Vol. Ed.), *Handbook of child psychology: Vol. 3. Social, emotional, and personality development* (5th ed., pp. 619–700). New York: Wiley.

Ruble, D. N., & Martin, C. L. (1998). Gender development. In W. Damon (Series Ed.) & N. Eisenberg (Vol. Ed.), *Handbook of child psychology: Vol. 3. Social, emotional, and personality development* (5th ed., pp. 933–1016). New York: Wiley.

Schelling, T. C. (1971). Dynamic models of segregation. *Journal of Mathematical Sociology, 1*, 143–186.

Serbin, L. A., Moller, L. C., Gulko, J., Powlishta, K. K., & Colburne, K. A. (1994). The emergence of gender segregation in toddler playgroups. In C. Leaper (Ed.), *Childhood sex segregation: Causes and consequences* (pp. 7–17). San Francisco: Jossey-Bass.

Serbin, L. A., Tonick, I. J., & Sternglanz, S. H. (1977). Shaping cooperative cross-sex play. *Child Development, 48*, 924–929.

Smith, A. B., & Inder, P. M. (1993). Social interaction in same and cross gender pre-school peer groups: A participant observation study. *Educational Psychology, 13*, 29–42.

Stott, L. H., & Ball, R. S. (1957). Consistency and change in ascendance-submission in the social interaction of children. *Child Development, 28*, 259–272.

Thorne, B. (2001). Girls and boys together but mostly apart: Gender arrangement in elementary school. In R. Satow (Ed.), *Gender and social life* (pp. 152–166). New York: Wiley.

Vitaro, F., Tremblay, R. E., Kerr, M., Pagani, L., & Bukowski, W. M. (1997). Disruptiveness, friends' characteristics, and delinquency in early adolescence: A test of two competing models of development. *Child Development, 68*, 676–689.

12

Understanding Children's Family Worlds
Family Transitions and Children's Outcomes

Judy Dunn

During the last decades of the 20th century and the first decade of the new century, increasing numbers of children have experienced their parents' separation and periods in single-parent families and in stepfamilies, with the dramatic rise in divorce, cohabitation, lone parenting, and repartnering of adults. These patterns of change have been documented around the globe—in North America, in the United Kingdom and Europe, and in Australia and New Zealand (Pryor & Rodgers, 2001). Concern about the impact of these family changes on children, and the effects of the social and financial adversities that frequently accompany such family transitions, has produced a broad and extensive research literature—involving demographers, family sociologists, and developmental and clinical psychologists. This literature reflects changing perspectives on family influence more generally, and the lessons we have learned from it have very general implications for understanding children's development, lessons that go beyond the specific issues concerning parents who separate.

Changing Research Perspectives

While the early research on divorce was often focused on relatively small, clinical groups, rather than representative populations, path-breaking studies in the 1980s and 1990s were conducted within two different disciplines—first, by family sociologists and demographers (e.g., Amato & Booth, 1997; Cherlin et al., 1991; McLanahan & Sandfur, 1994), whose work was based on nationally representative samples and, second, by psychologists, notably Hetherington and her colleagues (Hetherington, 1989; Hetherington & Clingempeel,

1992)—and these have transformed our understanding of the nature and influence of family change.

The demographers documented such changes as the prevalence of child adjustment problems in families with separated parents and the key drop in income experienced by lone parents and its impact. The demographers provided many provocative findings, such as the evidence that in families in which parents divorced, children had shown higher rates of problems before the parental separation as well as after (Cherlin et al., 1991). Hetherington and her colleagues showed how parental separation frequently forms part of an ongoing process of potentially stressful changes for children (for instance, changes in neighborhood and school, dramatic decreases in family finances and in parental well-being and mental health, often the formation of stepfamilies, the experience of living in two households as a result of custody arrangements, and loss of contact with their biological fathers and with paternal grandparents).

The documentation of this complex, changing set of experiences made clear that those attempting to study the impact on children of parental separation faced two sorts of challenges. The first was that this was a moving target and that longitudinal research was essential. The second was that parental separation involved a set of widely differing risk factors for children that ranged from broad social and economic adversities to problems in the intimate relationship processes within the family. The task for researchers was to understand how the broad "distal" risk factors affected children—and to what extent the impact of these risk factors was mediated through more proximal social processes within the family. (This is an issue that takes us beyond parental separation and divorce to such questions as how poverty, social adversity, and parental mental health affect children.)

By the 1990s the number of studies reporting on large representative samples of children who had experienced divorce was sufficient to enable researchers to conduct meta-analyses of the findings on children's outcome. One particularly important contribution was a meta-analysis by Amato and Keith (1991) that established a point of very general significance. This concerned individual differences in children's response to parental separation and the constellation of events that preceded and followed the family change. The focus of the great majority of studies had been on the average prevalence of children's problems following parental separation. They documented that children whose parents separated showed, on average, higher rates of adjustment problems (such as behavior and emotional problems, school failure) than those who had not experienced these transitions. But as Amato (1994) pointed out, although the prevalence of problems was on average double that of children in families that had not gone through such transitions, these average effects were small, and variation among children in their response to family change was great. This established that the key questions that need to be answered are, which children are particularly vulnerable? And which factors in the children's lives increase the risk of problems following family transitions or act to protect children?

Current Perspectives and Challenges

Current research addressing such questions has raised a series of challenges to the ways in which we think about family influence, both following parental separation and more generally. Next we consider some of these issues that have particularly broad implications for understanding family influences.

PARENTING, OR PARENT-CHILD RELATIONSHIPS?

Evidence has increased that the quality of parent-child relationships acts as an important mediator between distal risks and children's outcome following parental separation (Hetherington, Bridges, & Isabella, 1998). However, this needs to be distinguished from the notion of parenting, which has been so often viewed as the proximal process that has immediately influenced children's response to parental separation. Rather, it is the dyadic relationship that is important, and both parent and child will contribute to the quality of that relationship. As an example of the importance of taking account of the contribution of child effects, we know from Hetherington's work that negativity from stepdaughters toward their stepfathers over time contributes to later difficulties in the daughter-stepfather relationship, rather than vice versa (Hetherington & Clingempeel, 1992), and as we noted earlier, a parallel point concerning child effects was established by demographers studying parental divorce and child adjustment. So one key lesson from the recent research is the importance of taking a relationship approach to understanding what happens within families, rather than focusing on parenting per se—a point that is reinforced when we consider the relations among relationships.

THE SIGNIFICANCE OF WITHIN-FAMILY DIFFERENCES

A second lesson—which is of very general significance to the study of family influence—is that children within the same family show marked differences in adjustment outcome following family breakup. Indeed, there is greater variance within than among families (O'Connor, Dunn, Jenkins, Pickering, & Rasbash, 2001). Children within the same family also show marked differences in their relationships with their parents (O'Connor, Dunn, Jenkins, & Rasbash, in press) and differences in the quality of their friendships outside the family. The importance of the latter finding lies in the evidence that friends can be a significant source of support for children facing stressful family change (Dunn & Deater-Deckard, 2001). Behavior geneticists drew attention to the importance of understanding the marked differences in outcome of children growing up within the same family (Plomin & Daniels, 1987). What we are now learning from multilevel modeling approaches is that some key family processes that have been implicated in children's outcome following parental separation, such as exposure to and involvement in parental conflict, are experienced differently by siblings within the same family. Thus parents' arguing about their children is strongly associated with externalizing behavior, and children within the same family have been shown to be differentially exposed to conflict between their parents (Jenkins, Dunn, Rasbash, O'Connor, & Simpson, 2005).

FAMILY TYPE OR BIOLOGICAL RELATEDNESS?

A third lesson from recent research on children's growing up in different family circumstances is that the biological relatedness of child and parent is key. An increasingly extensive literature emphasizes the significance of ownness, or biological relatedness, in family relationships and children's sensitivity to biological relatedness (e.g., Mekos, Hetherington, & Reiss, 1996). In stepfamilies, especially in "complex" stepfamilies, in which each parent has brought children from previous relationships, children may be biologically related to both resident parents, children may be biologically related to the father but not the mother, and children may be biologically related to the mother but not the father. The family may include full siblings, half-siblings, and stepsiblings. For some aspects of family relationships what turns out to be key is whether child and parent, or child and sibling, are biologically related, rather than that the children are growing up in a family setting that is categorized as a stepfamily (see Dunn, Davies, O'Connor, & Sturgess, 2000). However, certain family types are linked with more marked differences between siblings within the same family. So in complex stepfamilies, the differences between siblings are especially marked. A novel contribution to this issue has been made with the evidence that even very young children are notably sensitive to the issue of biological relatedness within stepfamilies (Dunn, Davies, et al., 2000; Dunn, O'Connor, & Levy, 2002).

Parents' Life Histories and Intergenerational Research

Another lesson from recent research into stepfamilies concerns the importance of taking into account the parents' own experiences in childhood and adolescence. Clinicians have long held that individuals' early family experiences can cast a long shadow on their own later relationships as parents; indeed, studies of individuals brought up in institutions (e.g., Quinton & Rutter, 1988) have made some pathbreaking contributions to intergenerational research. From more recent studies we have learned that earlier events, such as unhappy childhood experiences, teenage pregnancy, leaving home early, and having a series of cohabiting relationships, increase the likelihood that a woman will form a partnership with a man who has also experienced a series of cohabiting relationships and frequent earlier negative life events. This echoes the findings on assortative mating for antisocial behavior, depression, and education (see, e.g., Dunn, Davies, et al., 2000). The evidence is important: such selective partnerships lead to less affectionate and supportive relations with their children.

The assortative patterns mean that children of parents with adverse early experiences at risk for a double dose (i.e., from both parents) of less affectionate parent-child relationships within the family. The lesson for researchers studying diverse family settings is that information about the life course of both parents can clarify what contributes to differences in the quality of parent-child relationships (see Amato, 1996, for parallel findings, that the risk of divorce is greatly increased if both partners come from divorced homes in childhood).

Especially intriguing evidence of intergenerational connections has been reported by Amato and his colleagues (Amato & Cheadle, 2003), who used data from a longitudinal study of marital instability over the life course to examine links between divorce in the grandparent generation and outcomes in the grandchild generation. Divorce in the grandparents was associated with less education, more divorce, and weaker ties with both mothers and fathers in the third generation (the grandchildren). The pattern of connections was mediated by what happened in the middle generation, including less education, more marital discord, and more tension in early parent-child relationships. While the details of family process that would explain these links and the role of genetics remain to be further explored, the general lesson—that divorce has consequences for subsequent generations, including those not yet born at the time of the original divorce—certainly deserves further attention.

CHILDREN'S VIEWS: WHAT CAN BE LEARNED?

A fifth important lesson from recent research concerns the significance of including in the studies children's views of the changes in their families. Researchers (e.g., Fine, Coleman, & Ganong, 1999), policy makers, those concerned with care and custody arrangements, and clinicians (e.g., Dowling & Gorrell Barnes, 2000) increasingly stress the importance of understanding children's perspectives of their family situations. Yet most research information on children's responses to family transitions has been based on adults' reports. The changes in children's lives begin early (e.g., 72% of the children living in stepfamilies in the 1993 U.K. Office of National Statistics Survey had begun living in stepfamilies before they were 10 years old). Recently, more studies have included a focus on children's own views. These have included children's accounts of the significant sources of support in times of family change and their views of their various family relationships, their lives in two households, and the particular sources of concern and difficulty they experience in stepfamilies. Methods have been developed for assessing the views of children as young as five, with drawings and family "maps" (Dunn, O'Connor, and Levy, 2002; Sturgess, Dunn, & Davies, 2001) as well as interviews.

The lessons from these studies include some with very practical implications. One lesson concerns communication and confiding—the majority of children felt that changes had not been explained to them, and they were confused. Levels of communication and confiding were particularly low between fathers and their children; in contrast, grandparents (until recently rarely included in studies of the impact of family change on children) were key sources of confiding and communication, and the closeness of children's relationships with their grandparents was related to their adjustment and well-being (Lussier, Deater-Deckard, Dunn, & Davies, 2002). Other lessons concerned practical issues, such as the evidence that giving children a role in decisions about visiting their other household was associated with better adjustment, and that suggestions from the children about practical issues helped children to cope with their divided lives (Dunn & Deater-Deckard, 2001). Finally, the accounts of children themselves—even those 8 to 10 years old—have made clear the importance of friends as confidants and sources of support. And there is growing interest in how children interpret events such as parental conflict, and whether their interpretations mediate the impact of conflict on adjustment (Grych & Cardoza-Fernandes, 2001).

BEYOND THE HOUSEHOLD: CONTACT WITH NONRESIDENT PARENTS AND WITH EXTENDED FAMILIES

If we take account of children's views of their complex family worlds, the issue of contact between children and their nonresident parents (almost always their fathers) cannot be ignored. The literature in this area is growing and has yielded a number of useful meta-analyses (e.g., Amato & Gilbreth, 1999; Whiteside & Becker, 2000). While findings on the connections between frequency of contact and child outcome are mixed, consistent evidence shows that the quality of the relationship between nonresident fathers and their children is related to children's adjustment outcome. These connections are linked in important ways to the quality of the relationship and support between mother and nonresident father. A clear lesson is that it is important to frame research within the network of family relationships and to recognize the mutual influence of these relationships. And here, as in other domains, the particular vulnerability of children in single-mother families to difficulties in the children's relationships with their nonresident fathers is also evident (Dunn, Cheng, O'Connor, & Bridges, 2003).

Since the late 1990s family law, policy, and practice have shifted dramatically on the issue of contact between children and their nonresident parent. In the 1970s the emphasis was on sustaining children's relationships with their custodial parent (usually the mother)—referred to as the "single psychological mother" (Goldstein, Freud, & Solnit, 1979). More recently, however, the balance has changed. The legal presumption usually is that nonresident parents will have contact with their children and that maintaining children's relationships with both parents is important. This shift reflects the increased volume of research on the significance of children's relationships with their nonresident parents as well as the forthright voice of campaign groups (Bainham, Lindley, Richards, & Trinder, 2003).

Researchers have now begun to grapple with the complexity of children's family worlds—not only the complicated set of relationships within one household that is found in many complex stepfamilies but the family ties that extend beyond the household. For many children whose parents have separated and have formed new partnerships, the relationships of three sets of parents may affect the child: the relationship between the child's mother and her former partner, the child's nonresident father; the relationship between the child's mother and her new partner, the child's stepfather; and the relationship between the child's nonresident father and his current partner (the child's nonresident stepmother). Research that includes a focus on all three sets of parents has suggested a number of general principles (Dunn, O'Connor, & Cheng, 2005). First, children's experiences of parental conflict within the three sets of parents are relatively independent. That is, there was little evidence of spillover between the children's various family situations.

In contrast, there was evidence of spillover between family relationships within each household/family: researchers found that interparental conflict affected parent-child relationships, whether the parents in question were biological or biological and stepparents.

Controversies and Future Research

Given the great emotional and developmental significance of parental separation for both parents and children, it is not surprising that particular research findings have generated much controversy and concern about policy implications. Examples from recent research can serve as illustrations. First, the recent findings of Booth and Amato (2001) and their colleagues, that children are especially adversely affected by parental separation in families where parental conflict was low, has resulted in much dispute about the need for policies that discourage family breakup. Second, the inconsistent findings on frequency of contact between children and nonresident fathers have led to lively policy discussions and disagreement. Some reports suggest frequency of contact is associated with better child outcomes; others disagree (Bainham et al., 2003). Third, experts do not agree on the reasons for poor outcomes for children after their parents separate: some claim the main culprit is the loss of income, but others point out that the prevalence of adjustment problems remains high even in stepfamilies where two adults are contributing to family income and children are undoubtedly better off in economic terms than when they were living in single-parent families.

These examples illustrate the need for additional research to help us understand more fully the implications of separation of parents for children. In terms of research design recent research has pointed out the importance of

- Longitudinal, intergenerational research
- Studying more than one child per family, and using multilevel analytic strategies that permit investigation of the relative significance of shared family factors, individual child characteristics, and child-specific experiences
- Assessing the network of family relationships, including associations across generations and across households
- Including children's perspectives and interpretations of family transitions and difficulties

Finally, we are only just beginning to grasp the importance of cultural and community differences in the importance of parental separation and lone parenthood for children. The significance of intergenerational ties is also likely to vary greatly across cultural groups. Now that we have established the impact of parental separation on children and the notable individual differences in how children respond, researchers must turn their attention to the questions of what protects children and what increases their risks as they face these increasingly common changes in their family worlds.

References

Amato, P. R. (1994). The implications of research findings on children in stepfamilies. In A. Booth & J. Dunn (Eds.), *Stepfamilies: Who benefits? Who does not?* (pp. 81–87). Hillsdale, NJ: Erlbaum.

Amato, P. R. (1996). Explaining the intergenerational transmission of divorce. *Journal of Marriage and the Family, 58,* 628–640.

Amato, P. R., & Booth, A. (1997). *A generation at risk: Growing up in an era of family upheaval.* Cambridge, MA: Harvard University Press.

Amato, P. R., & Cheadle, J. (2003). *The legacy of divorce: Tracking the implications of marital dissolution across three generations.* Paper presented at the meeting of the European Developmental Psychological Association, Milan, August.

Amato, P., & Gilbreth, J. G. (1999). Nonresident fathers and children's well-being: A meta-analysis. *Journal of Marriage and the Family, 61,* 557–573.

Amato, P. R., & Keith, B. (1991). Parental divorce and the well-being of children: A meta-analysis. *Psychological Bulletin, 110,* 26–46.

Bainham, A., Lindley, B., Richards, M., & Trinder, E. (2003). *Contact rights and welfare.* Oxford, England: Hart.

Booth, A., & Amato, P. R. (2001). Parental predivorce relations and offspring postdivorce well-being. *Journal of Marriage and Family, 63,* 197–212.

Cherlin, A. J., Furstenberg, F. F., Chase-Lansdale, L. P., Kiernan, K. E., Robins, P. K., Morrison, D. R., & Teitler, J. O. (1991). Longitudinal studies of effects of divorce in Great Britain and the United States. *Science, 252,* 1386–1389.

Dowling, E., & Gorrell Barnes, G. (2000). *Working with children and parents through separation and divorce.* London: Macmillan.

Dunn, J., Cheng, H., O'Connor, T., & Bridges, L. (2003). Children's relationships with their non-resident fathers: Influences, outcomes, and implications. *Journal of Child Psychology and Psychiatry 45,* 553–566.

Dunn, J., Davies, L., O'Connor, T., & Sturgess, W. (2000). Parents' and partners' life course and family experiences: Links with parent-child relationships in different family settings. *Journal of Child Psychology and Psychiatry, 41,* 955–968.

Dunn, J., & Deater-Deckard, K. (2001). *Children's views of their changing families.* York, England: York Publishing Services/Joseph Rowntree Foundation.

Dunn, J., O'Connor, T. G., & Cheng, H. (2005). Children's responses to conflict between their different parents: Mothers, stepfathers, NR fathers, and NR stepmothers. *Journal of Clinical Child and Adolescent Psychology, 34,* 223–234.

Dunn, J., O'Connor, T. G., & Levy, I. (2002). Out of the picture: A study of family drawings by children from step, single-parent, and non-step families. *Journal of Clinical Child and Adolescent Psychology, 31,* 505–512.

Fine, M. A., Coleman, M., & Ganong, L. H. (1999). A social constructionist multi-method approach to understanding the stepparent role. In E. M. Hetherington (Ed.), *Coping with divorce, single parenting, and remarriage* (pp. 273–294). Mahwah, NJ: Erlbaum.

Goldstein, J., Freud, A., & Solnit, A. (1979). *Beyond the best interests of the child.* New York: Free Press.

Grych, J. H., & Cardoza-Fernandes, S. (2001). Understanding the impact of interparental conflict on children: The role of sociocognitive processes. In J. H. Grych & F. D. Fincham (Eds.), *Interparental conflict and child development* (pp. 157–187). Cambridge, England: Cambridge University Press.

Hetherington, E. M. (1989). Coping with family transitions: Winners, losers, and survivors. *Child Development, 60,* 1–14.

Hetherington, E. M., Bridges, M., & Isabella, G. M. (1998). What matters? What does not? Five perspectives on the association between marital transitions and children's adjustment. *American Psychologist, 53,* 167–184.

Hetherington, E. M., & Clingempeel, W. G. (1992). Coping with marital transitions: A family systems approach. *Monographs of the Society for Research in Child Development, 57*, 2–3.

Jenkins, J. M., Dunn, J., Rasbash, J., O'Connor, T. G., & Simpson, A. (2005). *Mutual influence of marital conflict and children's behavior problems: Shared and non-shared family risks. Child Development, 76*, 24–39.

Lussier, G., Deater-Deckard, K., Dunn, J., & Davies, L. (2002). Support across two generations: Children's closeness to grandparents following parental divorce and remarriage. *Journal of Family Psychology, 16*, 363–376.

McLanahan, S., & Sandfur, G. (1994). *Growing up with a single parent: What hurts, what helps?* Cambridge, MA: Harvard University Press.

Mekos, D., Hetherington, E. M., & Reiss, D. (1996). Sibling differences in problem behavior and parental treatment in nondivorced and divorced families. *Child Development, 67*, 2148–2165.

O'Connor, T. G., Dunn, J., Jenkins, J., Pickering, K., & Rasbash, J. (2001). Family settings and children's adjustment: Differential adjustment within and across families. *British Journal of Psychiatry, 179*, 110–115.

O'Connor, T. G., Dunn, J., Jenkins, J., & Rasbash, J. (in press). Predictors of between-family and within-family variation in parent-child relationships. *Journal of Child Psychology and Psychiatry.*

Plomin, R., & Daniels, D. (1987). Why are children in the same family so different from one another? *Behavioural and Brain Sciences, 10*, 1–60.

Pryor, J., & Rodgers, B. (2001). *Children in changing families: Life after parental separation.* Oxford, England: Blackwell.

Quinton, D., & Rutter, M. (1988). *Parenting breakdown: The making and breaking of intergenerational links.* Aldershot, England: Avebury.

Sturgess, W., Dunn, J., & Davies, L. (2001). Young children's perceptions of their relationships with family and friends: Links with family setting and adjustment. *International Journal of Behavioural Development, 25*, 521–529.

Whiteside, M. F., & Becker, B. J. (2000). Parental factors and the young child's postdivorce adjustment: A meta-analysis with implications for parenting arrangements. *Journal of Family Psychology, 14*, 5–26.

13

Fathers, Families, and the Future
A Plethora of Plausible Predictions

Ross D. Parke

For decades family research was synonymous with "mothering," with fathers relegated to the socialization sidelines. Much has been written and much has changed since Lamb's famous pronouncement that fathers were the "forgotten contributors to child development" (1975a, p. 245). In the 21st century fathers are clearly recognized as central players in the family and major contributors to children's social, emotional, and cognitive development. These shifts in paternal roles and the evidence of the importance of fathers as socialization agents are well documented (Lamb, 2004; Parke, 1996).

Several issues remain underdeveloped on the research front, and my goal here is to highlight those topics that are fertile for more theoretical and empirical work. These include the reemergence of interest in the biological determinants of fathering, the cultural constraints on fathering, the impact of fathering on men themselves, the need for an intergenerational examination of fathering, and the challenge of recent work on gay and lesbian parents for our understanding of the father's role.

Rebiologizing Fatherhood

Although much attention has been devoted to the social, demographic, and economic determinants of fathering, the role of biology has been neglected until recently. In part this was because researchers assumed that the lack of biological preparedness accounted for fathers' lack of involvement in caregiving of children. In fact, early evidence (Lamb, 1975b) suggested that the tyranny of hormones as a constraint on father involvement was not well founded and that hormones did not play a necessary role in paternal behavior in either rats or humans. Instead, social factors such as exposure to young offspring increased paternal activity without any changes in hormonal levels in both rats and humans (Fleming & Li, 2002). For example, studies of father-infant relationships in cases of adoption, where the usual hormonal changes accompanying normal biological childbirth are absent, clearly suggest that hormonal shifts are unnecessary for the development of positive father-infant relationships (Brodzinsky & Pinderhughs, 2002).

More recent evidence has challenged the assumption that hormonal levels are unimportant determinants of paternal behavior by examining this issue in species other than rats, which is not a naturally paternal species. In naturally paternal species such as canids, which constitute less than 10% of mammalian species (Storey, Walsh, Quinton, & Wynne-Edwards, 2000), researchers have found that males experience hormonal changes, including increases in prolactin and decreases in testosterone, before the onset of parental behavior and during infant contact (Fleming & Li, 2002; Rosenblatt, 2002). Human fathers also undergo hormonal changes during pregnancy and childbirth. Storey, Walsh, Quinton, and Wynne-Edwards (2000) found that men experienced significant pre-, peri-, and postnatal changes in each of three hormones—prolactin, cortisol, and testosterone—a pattern of results that was similar to that for the women in their study. Specifically, prolactin levels were higher for both men and women in the late prenatal period than in the early postnatal period, and cortisol levels increased just before and decreased in the postnatal period, which corresponds to the first opportunity for interaction with their infants.

Hormonal levels and changes were linked with a variety of social stimuli as well. Men with lower testosterone held test baby dolls longer and were more responsive to infant cues (crying) than were men with higher testosterone. Men who reported a greater drop in testosterone also reported more pregnancy or couvade symptoms. Together these findings suggest that lower testosterone in the postnatal period may increase paternal responsiveness to infant cries and in men reporting more couvade symptoms during pregnancy. Finally, Storey and colleagues argue that the "cortisol increases in late pregnancy and during labor may help new fathers focus on and become attached to their newborns" (2000, p. 91). Men's changes in hormonal levels are linked not only to baby cries and the time in pregnancy cycle but also to the hormonal levels of their partners. Women's hormonal levels were closely linked with the time remaining before delivery, but men's levels were linked with their partner's hormone levels, not with time to birth. This demonstrates that contact with the pregnant partner may play a role in paternal responsiveness, just as the quality of the marital relationship is linked with paternal involvement in later infancy. This suggests that social variables need to be considered in understanding the operation of biological effects. Perhaps intimate ties between partners during pregnancy stimulate hormonal changes that, in turn, are associated with more nurturance toward babies.

Other evidence is consistent with a psychobiological view of paternal behavior. Fleming, Corter, Stallings, and Steiner (2002) found that fathers with lower baseline levels of testosterone are more sympathetic and show a greater need to respond when presented with infant cries than men with higher baseline testosterone levels. Moreover, fathers with higher baseline prolactin levels are more positive and alert in response to infant cries. However, experience also appears to play a role. At two days after the birth of a baby, fathers show lower levels of testosterone than nonfathers. Moreover, fathers who have more experience with babies have lower testosterone and higher prolactin levels than first-time fathers (Corter & Fleming, 2002), even after controlling for paternal age. This perspective recognizes the dynamic or transactional nature of the links between hormones and behavior in which behavior changes can lead to hormonal shifts and vice versa. In contrast to the myth of the biologically unfit father, this work suggests that men may be more prepared—even biologically—for parenting than previously thought. More work is needed to explore the implications of these hormonal changes for the long-term relationship between fathers and their offspring. For example, are the ties between children and fathers who do not experience hormone-related changes at birth weaker, or can experience compensate for this lack of hormonal shift?

The Cultural Embeddedness of Fathers

Cultural factors also play an important role in determining both the quantity and quality of father involvement. Despite this recognition, relatively little is known about the cultural aspects of fatherhood. Numerous reasons account for our lack of a cultural perspective on fathers. First, a universalist assumption underlies much of the theorizing in the social sciences: that the processes noted in studies of Western fathers—or, more narrowly, Euro-American and middle-class fathers—will be generalizable both to other cultures and to non-Euro-American groups in the United States. This assumption has been challenged on several fronts since the last decade of the 20th century. Interest in theories of cross-cultural and intracultural variations has revived, largely as a result of the rediscovery of Vygotskian theory and its strong focus on the cultural embeddedness of families (Rogoff, 2003). This is reflected in renewed interest in cross-cultural variations in parenting more generally (Bornstein, 1991; Parke & Buriel, 2006) and in fathering more specifically (Hewlett, 1991).

A cross-cultural perspective on fathers has not only forced us to confront the variability in fathering behaviors but also challenged some of our assumptions about central features of the father role. For example, the well-established finding that physical play is the hallmark of fathers' interactive style has been questioned (Parke, 2002a). In a variety of cultures (Taiwan, India, Africa, and Thailand) fathers rarely engage in physical play and few mother-father differences in play style are found (Hewlett, 1991; Sun & Roopnarine, 1996). These cross-cultural observations may lead to a reevaluation of the pathways through which fathers influence their children and may force us to rethink the father's role as a major contributor to children's emotional regulation—at least in non-Western cultures.

Second, demographic shifts in North America have fueled interest in intracultural variation. In 2003, 31% of the population belonged to a racial minority group. According to the U.S. Census Bureau (2003), 13% of the U.S. population is Hispanic (37 million), 12.7% is African American (36.7 million), 1% is Asian American, Indian, or Alaska Native (2.7 million), and another 4.1% is of two or more races (4.1 million). These demographic shifts offer an opportunity to evaluate the generalizability of our assumptions about fathering. However, most of the fatherhood research to date has focused on white middle-class samples. Only limited attention has been paid to fathers in other ethnic groups, and often the focus has been on nonresident or unmarried fathers (Gadsen, 1999). At the same time we have a moral obligation to better understand large segments of our population in order to be able to develop and provide culturally sensitive services, programs, and policies on behalf of children and families of diverse cultural backgrounds. In recognition of intracultural diversity within the United States, there has been a shift away from the cultural deficit model, in which the focus was on majority-minority differences in parenting behavior. Instead, the field has moved toward an understanding of intragroup variation with a focus on understanding the adaptive strategies that ethnic minority fathers and families develop in response to their ecological circumstances and cultural traditions. This new paradigm recognizes the value of intragroup analyses involving a single ethnic group and decreases the attention paid to merely documenting group differences. Unfortunately, relatively little research has documented intragroup variability among fathers.

Despite the importance of addressing these cultural variations in fathering processes and practices, barriers have limited the amount of work that has been devoted to these minority groups. Not only are fathers more difficult to recruit for research participation relative to mothers, but members of ethnic minority groups are especially difficult to enlist in our research projects (Parke, Coltrane, et al., 2004). Members of minority groups are often skeptical about participation in scientific studies for a variety of reasons, including the history of mistreatment of minority research participants. Moreover, in the case of Hispanic American and Asian American groups, some of whom are recent immigrants—sometimes illegal—there is a healthy wariness of official institutions and distrust of unfamiliar individuals. As a result our minority samples are often biased and unrepresentative. Moreover, the biased samples lead to a tendency to pathologize fathers and/or families that do not conform to the structure, role arrangements, or child-rearing practices and values of the majority culture (Gadsen, 1999). For example, most samples of African American fathers involve poor and unmarried fathers who are not living with their children's mother, while few samples include fathers from intact or middle-class African American families. Moreover, this sampling bias leads to a distorted portrait of the full range of African American fathers' involvement and makes comparisons with Euro-American fathers problematic, since most of this work involves intact, middle-class fathers.

A second problem is the establishment of scalar equivalence between fathers in different ethnic groups. Progress has been made on this front but more on mothers than fathers (Knight, Tein, Prost, & Gonzales, 2002). Another problem is "interpretative validity" (Maxwell, 1992), or the need to ensure that our interpretations of fathers' behaviors and utterances are consistent with their own understanding of those displays. The increased use of focus groups (Silverstein & Auerbach, 1999) with fathers of different ethnic backgrounds has been valuable in addressing these issues. The next few decades will be increasingly devoted to the elaboration of how culture conditions fathers' roles and behavior. Just as Kessen (1979) argued that the child is a "cultural invention," the future will confirm that fathers (and families) are "cultural inventions" as well. Our challenge for the future will be to include fathers from a wider range of cultural backgrounds in our studies of children and fathers.

Recent Challenges to Fathers as Essential Socialization Agents

Although it is common to assume that fathers are essential to the successful socialization of children, recent evidence concerning the impact of gay and lesbian parents on children's development challenges this basic assumption. Recent work by Golombok, Patterson, and their colleagues suggests that the development of children raised by lesbian parents is well within normal limits (Golombok, 2000, 2006; Patterson, 1995, 2002). Although the amount of research on the effects of being reared by two male parents is even more limited than the work on two female parents, the limited available data suggest that the gender identities of children of gay fathers are similar to those of children of heterosexual fathers (Bailey, Bobrow, Wolfe, & Mikach, 1995). Moreover, as Bozett (1987) reported, the relationships that children develop with their gay fathers are positive. One important challenge faced by children of gay and lesbian parents, however, is that they may be stigmatized by others. One issue that requires concerted attention in this debate is the role of social norms and attitudes toward children who are growing up in same-gender child-rearing unions. Beyond acknowledging the theoretical plausibility of successful adaptation of this type of child-rearing arrangement, our field needs to devote more attention to the level of societal acceptance of these family types as a critical factor that can either facilitate or disrupt the successful adaptation of children in these families (Patterson & Chan, 1997).

If children reared in homes with two parents of the same gender are developing well, are fathers or mothers necessary in the socialization mix? As Silverstein (2002) and Golombok (2000) suggest, our focus on the gender of the parent may be too narrow a conceptualization of the issue. Instead, it may be helpful to recast the issue to ask whether exposure to male and female parents is the key or whether exposure to the interactive style typically associated with either mothers or fathers is what matters. A study by Ross and Taylor (1989) is relevant. They found that boys prefer the "paternal" play style, whether it is mothers or fathers who engage in the physical and active stimulation. The work of Ross and Taylor suggests that boys may not necessarily prefer their fathers but rather their physical style of play. Another body of work relevant to this issue looked at fathers and mothers who reversed their customary roles

(Radin, 1993). In this case men undertook the primary caregiving functions typically fulfilled by women.

Evidence from both the United States (Field, 1978) and Australia (Russell, 1984) suggests that the style of interaction of primary-caregiving fathers is more like that of primary-caregiving mothers. For example, Russell found that role-sharing fathers engaged in a less stereotypically masculine style of parenting and instead exhibited a more maternal interactive style (e.g., more indoor recreational activities and less exclusive focus on roughhousing and outdoor games). Finally, Israeli primary-caregiving fathers were more nurturing than traditional fathers, according to both their self-reports and reports from their children (Sagi, 1982). Together this evidence indicates that the style of parenting is at least somewhat independent of the gender of the parent who delivers or enacts this style. These types of data will help us eventually address the uniqueness of fathers' and mothers' roles in the family and in their children's development, and they will help provide clarity on the important issue of how essential fathers (Silverstein & Auerbach, 1999) or mothers (Parke, 2002b) are for children's development.

At the same time it seems premature to conclude that fathers or mothers are replaceable based on this evidence. Studies have relied largely on small samples of highly educated individuals in stable relationships. Furthermore, two key issues need to be addressed in ongoing work. More needs to be understood about the extent to which role division in lesbian or gay families approximates role division in heterosexual families, and more needs to be understood about the degree to which same-gender couples expose their children to opposite-sex role models. In the first case evidence suggests that lesbian couples share household tasks and decision-making responsibilities more equally than do heterosexual couples (Patterson, 1995). Similarly, gay parental couples are more likely to share child-rearing duties evenly (McPherson, 1993). At the same time, however, lesbian biological mothers viewed their parental role as more salient relative to other roles, such as worker, than did either nonbiological lesbian mothers or heterosexual mothers (Hand, 1991). Moreover, despite the more egalitarian divisions of household labor in lesbian households, there also exists some traditionalism in roles. Biological lesbian mothers are more involved in child care than are their partners; nonbiological lesbian mothers spend more time working outside the family (Patterson, 2002).

This raises the possibility that even in same-gender families, the role division concerning child care that characterizes heterosexual partnerships may be evident. Whether the nonbiological mothers enact other aspects of more traditional male roles, such as a physical play style, remains to be established. Moreover, we know little about the ways in which gay men enact their family roles and whether one partner is likely to enact a more traditional maternal role. In short, children may be afforded opportunities to experience both maternal and paternal interactive styles in same-gender households, but more work is needed to evaluate this possibility.

Parents have increasingly been recognized as managers of their children's social environments (Furstenberg, Cook, Eccles, Elder, & Sameroff, 1999; Parke, Killian, et al., 2003). In this role they can choose to deliberately expand their children's range of experiences with male or, in the case of gay parents, female figures. At this point we simply do not have extensive data on how much exposure children raised by lesbian or gay couples have to males or females outside the family or whether lesbian mothers intentionally provide this exposure as a means of compensating for the absence of a male figure in the household (Parke, 2002b). Moreover, nothing is known about the duration and frequency necessary to confer any potential developmental advantage if such exposure were found to be beneficial.

Perhaps most fundamentally, we lack data on the kind of relationship needed if exposure is to prove beneficial for the child's development. And of course the larger question is whether this exposure, after controlling for parent effects, makes a difference in child outcomes. Recent work on adult mentors confirms conventional wisdom and past research on nonparental adult influence: the effect of nonfamilial mentors on adolescents' social behavior is independent of the effect of parent-child relationships (Greenberger, Chen, & Beam, 1998).

New Routes to Fatherhood (and Motherhood)

Recent studies of the new reproductive technologies raise important questions for fatherhood research. These new technologies are expanding the ways that individuals become parents. Recent changes in childbearing include in vitro fertilization, anonymous and nonanonymous sperm donors, and surrogate mothers (Golombok, 2000, 2006). Djerassi (1999) argued that just as "technology's gift to women (and men) during the latter half of the 20th century was contraception, the first 50 years of the new millennium may well be considered the decades of conception" (p. 53).

Various scenarios that may alter our usual ways of conceptualizing families and parenthood are possible. Assisted reproductive technology (ART), including in vitro fertilization, has produced more than 3 million babies since 1977. Although evidence suggests that children conceived by donor insemination are developing well within normal limits (Golombok, 2000), less is known about the father's role in these families. We do not know whether important issues such as the disclosure of identity of donors or donor involvement with the family interact with family structural variables (e.g., lesbian or gay versus heterosexual partnerships). Other questions remain as well. Does it make a difference if the identity of the donor is known or unknown? What is the effect of disclosing or not disclosing the nature of the child's conception to the child? What is the effect of disclosing or keeping confidential the identity of the donor? Does the availability of the donor to the child after the birth make a difference in the child's adjustment? Are patterns of parent-child relationships different in couples who have achieved parenthood through in vitro fertilization after a long period of infertility? Do such parents develop closer relationships with their children? Are they overprotective of their offspring? It would also be important to understand how the partner-partner relationship is altered by this sequence leading to parenthood.

A variant of the new ART is the increased use of surrogate mothers. This innovation raises questions about the effect of this choice on parent-parent, parent-child, and couple–surrogate mother relationships. Again, issues of disclosure arise. Is there any meaningful developmental effect of the child's learning she or he was born to a surrogate mother? What are the implications for the child's adjustment of contact between the surrogate mother and the child? What is the effect of continuing contact between the surrogate mother and the child-rearing family on the parent-parent relationship? Is the father-child relationship altered in these types of families? Our scientific knowledge about these issues is still limited but growing (Golombok, 2006; Hahn & DiPietro, 2002). Moreover, there is an accumulating and thoughtful clinical literature that can serve as a guide for research in this area and as a helpful map for practitioners and policy and legal scholars (see Paulson & Sachs, 1999; Robertson, 1994).

These recent advances in reproductive technologies remind us that fatherhood (and, more generally, family) is a socially constructed category. Moreover, this work challenges the traditional conception of fathers and families as both biological and social units.

Reproduction can clearly be independent of the social responsibilities of parenthood, and this clearly underscores the lack of necessity of the family as central for reproduction and child rearing. We are only beginning to appreciate the implications of this "divorce" between the procreative and child-rearing aspects of families. How will this alter marriage rates in the future? Will the number of men and women who choose to be solo parents increase? And, of course, as the numbers shift and these routes become more normative, will the effects of discrimination and prejudice decrease as well?

Fathering and Men's Development

Becoming a father affects a man's own psychological development and well-being. As I noted more than 25 years ago, "the father-child relationship is a two-way process and children influence their fathers just as fathers alter their children's development" (Parke, 1981, p. 9). Several aspects of this issue have been examined, especially marital relationships and societal generativity. Some progress has been made on both issues. For example, the literature on the impact of fatherhood on marital satisfaction is sizable (Cowan & Cowan, 1992). However, most of the earlier work focused on infancy, and more attention to the long-term impact of fatherhood on marital relationships is needed (for an exception, see Snarey, 1993). Moreover, the earlier long-term studies are based on cohorts studied several decades ago, and new studies that recognize the changing roles of men and women in both the home and the workplace are needed to adequately evaluate the links between fatherhood and marital satisfaction. Family role shifts for fathers have focused largely on short-term shifts associated with the onset of new parenthood in infancy (Cowan & Cowan, 1992), and more recently more attention has been given to shifts in fathers' roles during adolescence (Larson & Richards, 1994). The implications of these shifts in roles across children's development are still poorly understood and require more attention, especially as these shifts interact with ongoing biological changes in adolescents (e.g., puberty).

The most provocative new direction concerns the links between fathering and generativity, a term introduced by Erikson (1975) and expanded by Snarey (1993), who described three types of generativity that apply to fathers: biological generativity, parental generativity, and societal generativity (indicated by caring for the next generation by mentoring, providing leadership). Using an older cohort of fathers, Snarey (1993) has presented evidence that men who were involved in their children's lives were themselves more generative in areas outside the family, such as community and neighborhood organizations and activities. Similarly, Palkovitz (2002) more recently provided confirmation of this conclusion based on a qualitative analysis of men's views of how fatherhood changed a wide number of aspects of their lives, including health, moral and religious beliefs, marital relationships, and work. Less is known about how these perceived shifts in men's views of themselves and their relationships with others alter their roles as parents, which, in turn, alter children's development. Studies that trace shifts in men's lives as a consequence of fatherhood, with resulting shifts in their parenting practices, will permit us to connect this new work in men's generativity with children's development.

Toward an Intergenerational Examination of the Father's Role

Another issue that needs more attention is the study of men in life-span perspective, especially as they shift their roles and responsibilities as their children develop and become parents themselves. Both intergenerational ties between fathers and their adult children and men's roles as grandfathers merit more research. Several recent reviews have highlighted the issues (see Dunn, Fergusson, & Maughan, 2006; Smith & Drew, 2002), and several topics merit underscoring as directions for future research in this area, including the consistency of child-rearing style across generations of fathers, the impact of grandfathers on children's development, and the role of culture in shaping grandfather roles. Such work will underscore that fathering is a lifelong process and not a role that ends when children reach maturity.

To adequately address these emerging and continuing concerns about father's roles and their impact on children's development, a variety of methodological innovations are needed.

First, we shoud be using qualitative as well as quantitative approaches. Especially in our efforts to understand fathers in different cultural contexts, we need fathers' own voices and perspectives to guide the research agenda. Focus groups can be useful in generating the right questions, in identifying new variables, in the scale production and refinement process, and in ensuring "interpretative validity" (Maxwell, 1992) after the data have been collected (for examples of focus-group approaches with Latino and African American fathers, see Hunter & Davis, 1994; Parke, Coltrane, et al., 2004; Silverstein, 2002). Qualitative and quantitative approaches should not be viewed as mutually exclusive. Instead, both are useful at different stages of the research process in our attempts to better understand fathering (Parke, 2004).

Second, the fathering literature has largely been a correlational one, and reliance on nonexperimental strategies may be insufficient to address the important issue of direction of effects on the impact of fathers on children and families. Experimental strategies have been underused in studies of fathers to date. By experimental modification of either the type of paternal behavior or the level of father involvement, firmer conclusions concerning the direct, causative role that fathers play in modifying their children's and their wives' development will be possible. Intervention studies (e.g., Fagan & Hawkins, 2000) aimed at modifying fathering behaviors provide models for this type of work, and if these studies include measures of child outcomes, they could provide valuable evidence of the impact of fathers on children's development. Moreover, these experimentally based interventions have clear policy implications by exploring the degree of plasticity of fathering behaviors and by illustrating the beneficial impact of father-friendly policies that support increased involvement in children's development (Parke & Brott, 1999). Finally, these interventions can serve as vehicles for evaluation of competing theoretical views of fatherhood.

In conclusion, the role of fathers in children's lives is now more widely recognized and better understood than even a few decades ago. As I have argued in this chapter, a variety of issues still remain and require our attention in future conceptual and empirical work. Addressing these issues will not only increase our understanding but potentially benefit children and families as well as fathers themselves.

References

Bailey, J. M., Bobrow, D., Wolfe, M., & Mikach, S. (1995). Sexual orientation of adult sons of gay fathers. *Developmental Psychology, 31,* 124–129.

Bornstein, M. H. (Ed.). (1991). *Cultural approaches to parenting.* Hillsdale, NJ: Erlbaum.

Bozett, F. W. (1987). Children of gay fathers. In F. W. Bozett (Ed.), *Gay and lesbian parents* (pp. 39–57). New York: Paper.

Brodzinsky, D. M., & Pinderhughes, E. (2002). Parenting and child development in adoptive families. In M. H. Bornstein (Ed.), *Handbook of parenting* (2nd ed., Vol. 1, pp. 279–312). Mahwah, NJ: Erlbaum.

Corter, C., & Fleming, A. S. (2002). Psychobiology of maternal behavior in human beings. In M. H. Bornstein (Ed.), *Handbook of Parenting* (2nd ed., Vol. 2, pp. 141–182). Mahwah, NJ: Erlbaum.

Cowan, P. A., & Cowan, C. P. (1992). *When parents become partners.* New York: Basic Books.

Djerassi, C. (1999). Sex in an age of mechanical reproduction. *Science, 285,* 53–54.

Dunn, J., Fergusson, E., & Maughan, B. (2006). Grandparents, grandchildren and family change in contemporary Britain. In A. Clarke-Stewart & J. Dunn (Eds.), *Families count: Effects on child and adolescent development* (pp. 299–320). Cambridge, England: Cambridge University Press.

Erikson, E. (1975). *Life history and the historical moment.* New York: Norton.

Fagan, J., & Hawkins, A. J. (Eds.). (2000). *Clinical and educational interventions with fathers.* New York: Haworth.

Field, T. M. (1978). Interaction behaviors of primary versus secondary caretaker fathers. *Developmental Psychology, 14,* 183–185.

Fleming, A. S., Corter, C., Stallings, J., & Steiner, M. (2002). Testosterone and prolactin are associated with emotional response to infant cries in new fathers. *Hormones and Behavior, 42,* 399–413.

Fleming, A. S., & Li, M. (2002). Psychobiology of maternal behavior and its early determinants in nonhuman mammals. In M. H. Bornstein (Ed.), *Handbook of parenting* (2nd ed., Vol. 2, pp. 62–98). Mahwah, NJ: Erlbaum.

Furstenberg, F. F., Cook, T. D., Eccles, J., Elder, G. H., & Sameroff, A. J. (1999). *Managing to make it.* Chicago: University of Chicago Press.

Gadsen, V. (1999). Black families in intergenerational and cultural perspective. In M. E. Lamb (Ed.), *Parenting and child development in "nontraditional" families* (pp. 221–246). Mahwah, NJ: Erlbaum.

Golombok, S. (2000). *Parenting: What really counts?* London: Routledge.

Golombok, S. (2006). New family forms. In A. Clarke-Stewart & J. Dunn (Eds.), *Families count: Effects on child and adolescent development* (pp. 273–298). Cambridge, England: Cambridge University Press.

Greenberger, E., Chen, C., & Beam, M. R. (1998). The role of "very important" nonparental adults in adolescent development. *Journal of Youth and Adolescence, 27,* 321–343.

Hahn, C., & Dipietro, J. A. (2002). In-vitro fertilization and the family: Quality of parenting, family functioning, and child psychological adjustment. *Developmental Psychology, 37,* 37–48.

Hand, S. I. (1991). *The lesbian parenting couple.* Unpublished doctoral dissertation, California School of Professional Psychology, San Francisco.

Hewlett, B. S. (1991). *Intimate fathers.* Ann Arbor: University of Michigan Press.

Hunter A. G., & Davis, J. E. (1994). Hidden voices of black men: The meaning, structure, and complexity of manhood. *Journal of Black Studies, 25,* 20–40.

Kessen, W. (1979). The American child and other cultural inventions. *American Psychologist, 34,* 815–820.

Knight, G., Tein, J., Prost, J. H., & Gonzales, N. A. (2002). Measurement equivalence and research on Latino children and families: The importance of culturally informed theory. In J. M. Contreras, K. K. Kerns, & A. M. Neal-Barnett (Eds.), *Latino children and families in the United States* (pp. 181–202). Westport, CT: Praeger.

Lamb, M. E. (1975a). Fathers: Forgotten contributors to child development. *Human Development, 16,* 245–266.

Lamb, M. E. (1975b). Physiological mechanisms in the control of maternal behavior in rats: A review. *Psychological Bulletin, 82,* 104–119.

Lamb, M. E. (Ed.). (2004). *The role of the father in child development* (4th ed.). New York: Wiley.

Larson, R., & Richards, M. (1994). *Divergent realities.* New York: Basic Books.

Maxwell, J. A. (1992). Understanding validity in qualitative research. *Harvard Educational Review, 62,* 279–300.

McPherson, D. (1993). *Gay parenting couples: Parenting arrangements, arrangement satisfaction, and relationship satisfaction.* Unpublished doctoral dissertation, California School of Professional Psychology, San Francisco.

Palkovitz, R. (2002). *Involved fathering and men's adult development.* Mahwah, NJ: Erlbaum.

Parke, R. D. (1981). *Fathers.* Cambridge, MA: Harvard University Press.

Parke, R. D. (1996). *Fatherhood.* Cambridge, MA: Harvard University Press.

Parke, R. D. (2002a). Fathers and families. In M. H. Bornstein (Ed.), *Handbook of parenting* (2nd ed., Vol. 3, pp. 27–73). Mahwah, NJ: Erlbaum.

Parke, R. D. (2002b). Parenting in the new millennium: Prospects, promises, and pitfalls. In J. P. McHale & W. S. Grolnick (Eds.), *Retrospect and prospect in the psychological study of families* (pp. 65–93). Mahwah, NJ: Erlbaum.

Parke, R. D. (2004). The Society for Research in Child Development at 70: Progress and promise. *Child Development, 75,* 1–24.

Parke, R. D., & Brott, A. (1999). *Throwaway dads.* Boston: Houghton-Mifflin.

Parke, R. D., & Buriel, R. (2006). Socialization in the family: Ecological and ethnic perspectives. In W. Damon & R. Lerner (Series Eds.) & N. Eisenberg (Vol. Ed.), *Handbook of child psychology* (6th ed., Vol. 3, pp. 429–504). New York: Wiley.

Parke, R. D., Coltrane, S., Borthwick-Duffy, S., Powers, J., Adams, M., Fabricius, W., Braver, S., & Saenz, D. (2004). Assessing father involvement in Mexican-American families. In R. Day & M. E. Lamb (Eds.), *Conceptualizing and measuring paternal involvement* (pp. 17–38). Mahwah, NJ: Erlbaum.

Parke, R. D, Killian, C. M., Dennis, J. Flyr, M. L., McDowell, D. M., Simpkins, S., Kim, M., & Wild, M. (2003). Managing the external environment: The parent and child as active agents in the system. In L. Kuczynski (Ed.), *Handbook of dynamics in parent-child relations* (pp. 247–270). Thousand Oaks, CA: Sage.

Patterson, C. J. (1995). Gay and lesbian parents. In M. H. Bornstein (Ed.), *Handbook of parenting* (Vol. 3, pp. 255–274). Mahwah, NJ: Erlbaum.

Patterson, C. J. (2002). Lesbian and gay parenthood. In M. H. Bornstein (Ed.), *Handbook of parenting* (2nd ed., Vol. 3, pp. 317–338). Mahwah, NJ: Erlbaum.

Patterson, C. J., & Chan R. W. (1997). Gay fathers. In M. E. Lamb (Ed.), *The role of the father in child development* (3rd ed., pp. 245–260). New York: Wiley.

Paulson, R. J., & Sachs, J. (1999). *Rewinding your biological clock: Motherhood late in life: Options, issues, and emotions.* San Francisco: Freeman.

Radin, N. (1993). Primary caregiving fathers in intact families. In A. E. Gottfried & A. W. Gottfried (Eds.), *Redefining families* (pp. 11–54). New York: Plenum.

Robertson, J. A. (1994). *Children of choice: Freedom and the new reproductive technologies.* Princeton, NJ: Princeton University Press.

Rogoff, B. (2003). *The cultural nature of human development.* New York: Oxford University Press.

Rosenblatt, J. (2002). Hormonal basis of parenting in mammals. In M. H. Bornstein (Ed.), *Handbook of parenting* (2nd ed., Vol. 2, pp. 3–25). Mahwah, NJ: Erlbaum.

Ross, H., & Taylor, H. (1989). Do boys prefer daddy or his physical style of play? *Sex Roles, 20,* 23–33.

Russell, G. (1984). *The changing role of fathers.* St. Lucia, Australia: Queensland University Press.

Sagi, A. (1982). Antecedents and consequences of various degrees of paternal involvement in childrearing: The Israeli project. In M. E. Lamb (Ed.), *Nontraditional families: Parenting and child development* (pp. 205–232). Hillsdale, NJ: Erlbaum.

Silverstein, L. B. (2002). Fathers and families. In J. P. McHale & W. S. Grolnick (Eds.), *Retrospect and prospect in the psychological study of families* (pp. 35–64). Mahwah, NJ: Erlbaum.

Silverstein, L. B., & Auerbach, C. F. (1999). Deconstructing the essential father. *American Psychologist, 54,* 397–407.

Smith, P. K., & Drew, L. M. (2002). Grandparenthood. In M. H. Bornstein (Ed.), *Handbook of parenting* (2nd ed., Vol. 3, pp. 141–172). Mahwah, NJ: Erlbaum.

Snarey, J. (1993). *How fathers care for the next generation.* Cambridge, MA: Harvard University Press.

Storey, A. E., Walsh, C. J., Quinton, R. L., & Wynne-Edwards, D. E. (2000). Hormonal correlates of paternal responsiveness in new and expectant fathers. *Evolution and Human Behavior, 21,* 79–95.

Sun, L. C., & Roopnarine, J. L. (1996). Mother-infant, father-infant interaction and involvement in childcare and household labor among Taiwanese families. *Infant Behavior and Development, 19,* 121–129.

U.S. Census Bureau. (2003). *Population in the United States: Population characteristics,* June 2002. Washington, DC: U.S. Government Printing Office.

14

Progress and Prospects in the Psychology of Moral Development

Lawrence J. Walker

Since the 1970s the psychology of moral development has rightly come to occupy a position of central concern in the field. The vigorous research activity and scholarly debates reflect the significance of the study of morality both for developmental science and for practical applications to broader society. Morality is important for developmental science because it pervades human functioning; thus moral psychology is relevant to many different theoretical perspectives, processes, and content areas across developmental psychology. Morality is also obviously important for broader society because it is essential to the human condition; thus moral psychology has the potential to make vital contributions to parenting, education, corrections, and other areas of intervention. The intent of this commentary is twofold: to reflect upon our progress in the psychology of moral development and provide a critical analysis of some significant theoretical trends and empirical advances; and to gaze forward at our prospects and provide some suggestions for future directions for the field.

First, my arguments require that I comment briefly on the scope of the moral domain. As will become evident in what follows, I contend that we suffer from a conceptual skew that yields an inadequate and incomplete depiction of moral functioning and that what the field needs is a more balanced and comprehensive account of the scope of the moral domain and moral functioning, along with a more realistically attainable depiction of moral maturity. Basic to this enterprise is some common and shared understanding of what is meant by "morality"—and that issue has been largely ignored. The recurrent controversies in moral philosophy regarding its definition and the historically changing and culturally variable boundaries of the moral domain suggest that any agreed-upon definition will not be easily achieved. By proposing a definition, I am only trying to provide a framework for the discussion.

My view, then, is that morality is a fundamental and pervasive aspect of human functioning with both interpersonal and intrapsychic components; more specifically, it refers to voluntary behaviors that have, at least potentially, some social and interpersonal implications and are governed by internal psychological (i.e., both cognitive and affective) mechanisms.

This perspective on morality holds that it entails not only the interpersonal aspects of life (in that it regulates our interactions, orders our relationships, and adjudicates our conflicts) but also the intrapsychic aspects (in that it also references our fundamental goals and values, lifestyle, and identity). These intrapsychic aspects of moral functioning have obvious implications for our interpersonal interactions because our values, goals, and character are directly played out in our relationships with others. Also, this definition of morality claims that moral functioning is inherently multifaceted, involving the dynamic interplay of thought, emotion, and behavior. For example, moral emotions such as empathy or guilt always occur with some accompanying cognitions. Thoughts about one's personal values or one's relationships always have some emotional tone. Thoughts do have an impact on behavior, either directly in overt action or indirectly through behavioral dispositions. Voluntary behaviors always have some intentional basis that determines their moral quality. Furthermore, this definition holds that everyday life is infused with moral implications, that morality is a pervasive feature of human functioning, and that defining the domain in an overly constrictive manner is ill advised (both conceptually and practically). My basic concern is that we have lost a sense of the breadth and complexity of the moral domain—a loss of perspective that occurs as we focus on and become invested in a particular theory, aspect of development, or intervention program.

Progress

Two centuries of modernity have bequeathed to the field of moral development a legacy that is rich in understandings of moral rationality but rather impoverished in terms of its appreciation of other aspects of moral functioning. The formalist philosophical tradition of the Enlightenment era (which has pervasively influenced moral psychology) contributed to this conceptual skew in two ways. One is that it regarded moral issues primarily as those pertaining to interpersonal conflicts and relationships, and hence it framed modern ethical thinking with an emphasis on individualism, justice, rights, duties, and welfare. The consequence of this focus on the interpersonal aspects of moral functioning is that it marginalized the intrapsychic aspects that involve the characteristics of the good person and the aim of the good life. The other way that the formalist tradition contributed to this conceptual skew is that its understanding of human nature was unremittingly dualistic—reason versus passion—with rationality forming the core of moral functioning and with the "passions" (emotions, personality, personal projects, etc.) regarded with suspicion, as corrupting biases that must be overcome.

Dominant models in moral psychology have implicitly assumed these emphases with their focus on moral reasoning in regard to interpersonal problems. The widespread interest in Kohlberg's cognitive-developmental model (1984) exemplifies this trend. Kohlberg's conceptual, empirical, and applied contributions to the field have been monumental, and he can be credited with legitimizing moral development as a field of psychological inquiry. His affinity to the formalist tradition in moral philosophy and to the structuralistic tradition in developmental psychology led him to explicate an account of moral functioning that was defined by reason and revealed through the developmental process, and to advocate a vision of moral maturity that featured principled moral judgment, an ideal ethical stance involving abstracted impartiality and universality.

Kohlberg's legacy is primarily in his delineation of six stages of moral reasoning across the life span and his explication of disequilibrium as the process that motivates development (Walker, 1996). Much of the interest in his model was prompted by the bold empirical claims he made regarding moral development—the structural integrity of the stages, their invariant order and hierarchical nature, and the cross-cultural applicability of the model—claims that were largely substantiated by the now extensive empirical evidence (Walker, 1988). But one of the practical impediments to research in this area was Kohlberg's individually administered moral judgment interview and laborious scoring system (Colby & Kohlberg, 1987), and one of the conceptual impediments was his (1981) insistence that the justice principle was the epitome of moral reasoning. These practical and conceptual issues led to some important challenges and innovations that prompted the field to evolve.

The practical problem of measurement was addressed by Rest (1979), who developed the Defining Issues Test (DIT), an objective measure of moral judgment based loosely on Kohlberg's stages and one that can be administered to groups of individuals and scored by computer. The DIT has become the instrument of choice in the area (by far) and has instigated numerous studies of the development of moral judgment. The extensive research with the DIT eventually prompted some significant conceptual reformulations—what Rest, Narvaez, Bebeau, and Thoma (1999) labeled the neo-Kohlbergian approach. First, the new approach abandoned Kohlberg's hard-stage model in favor of a view of development that entailed gradually shifting distributions of reasoning toward more developed forms. Second, it recast Kohlberg's stages into three developmental schemas: personal interest, maintaining norms, and postconventional morality. Third, and particularly significant here, the new approach reconceptualized the developmental end point as a postconventional morality, which avoids the philosophically constrained foundational principlism of Kohlberg's model in favor of a more common morality—yet one that goes beyond conventional understandings.

Another challenge to the adequacy of Kohlberg's model came from domain theorists (Nucci, 2001; Turiel, 1983) who argued that his model and moral stages confuse domains of social understanding, particularly that his moral Stages 3 and 4 reify social conventions as moral guidelines. Domain theorists contend that social understandings can be parsed into separate domains, notably, the moral, social-conventional, and personal-prudential. In this perspective the moral domain refers to justice, rights, and welfare concerns; the conventional domain refers to arbitrary but shared uniformities in social norms; and the personal domain refers to actions that pertain primarily to oneself and that preclude justifiable social regulation. An example of a prototypic moral violation might be punching someone; an example of a violation of conventional norms might be eating with your hands in a cultural context that prescribes the use of utensils; and an example of a behavior that is frequently judged to be in the personal domain is alcohol and drug use.

A considerable amount of research activity in this area has demonstrated that both children and adults tend to regard prototypic moral rules as generalizable, obligatory, and independent of authority dictates, whereas prototypic conventional norms are judged to be relativistic, contingent upon rules, and subject to authorities. While it is readily acknowledged that many people do make such distinctions on occasion, particularly with simple prototypic examples, I would contend that domain theory defines morality too narrowly in that it fails to recognize the moral implications of conventional and personal behaviors. A violation of a conventional norm (e.g., eating with your hands at a formal dinner) can provide moral offense. Likewise, the judgment that substance use (and abuse) is simply a matter of personal preference and jurisdiction fails to recognize that its consequences can affect others adversely. It is difficult to limit the moral domain if people believe that injustice or harm will follow from an action (regardless of how seemingly trivial it may be). Finally, such a circumscribed definition of morality fails to acknowledge that the domain includes the intrapsychic aspects of moral functioning, such as the development of our basic values, lifestyle, and character.

Kohlberg's interest in reasoning in the resolution of moral conflicts led him to focus on obligatory moral judgments. Soon, however, researchers noted that other aspects of moral functioning are important, notably, prosocial behavior and empathy. Such behaviors often represent a conceptual conundrum for theoretical perspectives that assume that humans are primarily self-interested. Two programs of research are particularly important in this regard. One is Eisenberg's theory of prosocial development (1995), which initially proposed levels of prosocial reasoning and related sociocognitive skills (e.g., perspective taking). Later the theory evolved into a more multifaceted model that incorporated affective motivation (empathy, sympathy, personal distress, and guilt), personality factors, and socialization and situational influences. The other program of research involves Hoffman's theory regarding the development of empathy (2000). His model involves a developmental synthesis of empathic emotions and the development of a cognitive sense of others (as distinct from self) and highlights the parenting practices that foster moral internalization in children.

Perhaps the strongest challenge to Kohlberg's model, and certainly the one to incite the most controversy, was articulated by Gilligan (1982), who advanced well-publicized arguments that Kohlberg's paradigm is insensitive to females' mode of reasoning and caricatures them as morally deficient. Gilligan's contentions were actually twofold. The first was that Kohlberg's model (as well as most theories in developmental psychology) has a masculine bias and that this gender bias leads to scores for females that indicate their moral reasoning is less mature than males'. Her second contention was that moral decision making has two distinct and gender-related orientations: an ethic of justice, which is typical of males and well represented in moral psychology, and an ethic of care, which is typical of females and underrepresented and undervalued in moral psychology. Gilligan's claim that Kohlberg's model maligns and downscores the moral reasoning of females did not stand up to empirical scrutiny (Walker, 1984).

Gilligan's other claim advanced the notion of gender-related moral orientations, orientations that arise in differential early parent-child experiences of detachment and inequality. The claim of gender-related moral orientations also failed to garner empirical support in several regards (Walker, 2006). First, individuals do not show the consistency in orientation that Gilligan claimed and that the notion implies; instead, people evidence considerable variability across contexts and over time. Second, the orientations have not been found to be clearly gender related. Gender differences are rarely evidenced on standard moral problems or within types of real-life problems. Third, preference for orientations seems to be strongly influenced by situational factors; in other words, the nature of the problem under consideration influences the moral framework brought to bear to a much greater extent than does an individual's gender.

Despite the unequivocal lack of evidence for Gilligan's allegations of gender bias within Kohlberg's approach and her claim of gender relatedness for moral orientations, many regarded his model as tainted. Gilligan's theorizing, however, did contribute to the growing realization that Kohlberg's model does not represent the full scope of the moral domain and that other aspects of moral functioning need to be incorporated into our understanding, particularly the relational aspects of personal morality, care, and commitment.

Much more could be said about progress in the field of moral development since the 1970s, but readers who are interested in more detail should consult the handbooks by Killen and Smetana (2006) and Kurtines and Gewirtz (1991), which provide comprehensive overviews. Bearing in mind the context that I have provided, let us now to turn to a perspective on future prospects for this field.

Prospects

Perhaps the primary item on the research agenda for moral psychology would be to move beyond single-variable theories to ones that provide a more balanced, coherent, and comprehensive account of moral functioning. The tendency has been for the major theoretical perspectives to obfuscate the interdependent and interactive nature of various aspects of moral functioning in that each approach has regarded a different aspect (be it thought, emotion, or behavior) as constituting the essence of morality. These different emphases have imparted the view that these are separable aspects of moral functioning when instead they are necessarily interdependent. Single-variable theories of moral psychology are untenable in the face of the complexity of moral functioning and only serve to trivialize our understanding of the domain.

An example of a helpful corrective in this regard is the four-component model proposed by Rest, Narvaez, Bebeau, and Thoma (1999). This model is intended to describe the major psychological processes (with both cognitive and affective elements) that, in complex interaction, contribute to observed moral action. The four psychological components underlying moral action are held to be moral sensitivity, moral judgment, moral motivation, and moral character. Moral sensitivity entails interpretation of the situation, awareness of the relevant moral factors and implications, comprehension of how various potential actions would affect the parties involved, empathy and role taking, and understanding of one's own intuitions and emotional reactions. Moral judgment entails deliberation of the various considerations relevant to different courses of action and making a judgment regarding which of the available actions would be the most morally justifiable. Moral motivation entails giving moral values priority over other competing concerns, making a commitment to the moral course of action, and taking responsibility for the outcome. Moral character refers to the implementation skills and strategies that support the moral choice, and it includes the characterological dispositions that engender effective action. Note that moral failure can be a consequence of a deficiency in any component. Although there is an obvious logical sequence to these four components, naturalistic moral functioning is not necessarily logical, deliberate, or linear; there are many complex feedback loops and interactions.

Walker (2002) has extensively reviewed the research on the component model. Obviously, the model provides a valuable heuristic in positing a framework that could synthesize the field, but considerable conceptual and empirical work is now necessary to assimilate within this model the various theoretical traditions and research paradigms within moral psychology; to develop reliable and valid measures of each component; and to assess the interactive contribution of multiple components in explaining differing types of moral behavior.

The conceptual skew noted earlier reflects the field's preoccupation with the development of moral judgments in regard to interpersonal conflicts. Another way to provide a more balanced account of moral functioning is to accord greater conceptual and empirical attention to moral personality and character and to similar aspects of the intrapsychic side of morality that have been long eschewed. This will entail careful empirical study of morally relevant personality traits and dispositions. What are the socialization factors that foster the development of such traits? How do these character traits optimally interact in development to contribute to positive moral action? What are the risks of moral failure associated with excesses or imbalances in these traits? And what is the role of intuition in moral functioning (Haidt, 2001), and how can it best be cultivated? The very early days of research in moral psychology focused on moral character (Hartshorne, May, & Shuttleworth, 1930), but disappointing findings led to its abandonment. With the benefit of hindsight and the advantage of better conceptual and empirical tools, it is now appropriate to take another look.

Another problem that warrants our attention is deriving a more realistic depiction of moral maturity, because that is what defines our developmental models and our intervention efforts. Kohlberg's (1981) depiction of moral maturity featured dilemma-busting principles of justice wherein people don the "veil of ignorance," divorcing themselves from their own personalities and interests in order to adhere to the dictates of universal moral principles. Interview data have yielded only suggestive evidence for this elusive Stage 6, but more problematic is the sense that this vision of moral maturity is barren, unrealistic, and far from compelling. Most other major theories in contemporary moral psychology have paid scant attention to a full explication of the moral-developmental end point.

In response to the conceptual skew that characterizes the field and the perceived need to provide a broader and perhaps more veridical perspective on moral maturity, two programs of research should be undertaken: to examine people's ordinary conceptions of moral excellence (e.g., Walker & Pitts, 1998) and to examine the psychological functioning of actual moral exemplars, people who have been identified as leading lives of moral virtue, integrity, and commitment (e.g., Colby & Damon, 1992). By examining people's conceptions of moral excellence, notions that are embedded in common understandings, it may be possible to broaden the domain and reveal aspects of morality that dominant models have perhaps ignored.

People's notions about morality are important not only as complements to philosophically derived theories but also because such notions are operative and influential in everyday life. By examining the psychological functioning of moral exemplars, using the template of the most valid models and measures of human development, it may be possible to reveal, in a more full-bodied way, those aspects of psychological development that contribute to extraordinary moral action. These different empirical strategies are mutually informative and should provide convergent evidence regarding aspects of moral functioning that are significant in everyday life and that should be incorporated into our models of moral development. For example, both these approaches will help to identify some personality traits (or virtues) and aspects of character that have long been ignored in the psychology of moral development.

The early roots and precursors of moral internalization and mature moral functioning are another area that warrants increased attention. A consequence of the field's focus on moral cognition is that it required research participants who could be somewhat articulate about their own judgments and reasoning, with the attendant implication that toddlers and preschoolers are essentially amoral and that little of significance is happening in terms of their moral development. Evidence is beginning to accumulate that such a view is badly misguided, that young children evidence acute moral understandings, display a range of moral emotions and sentiments, engage in morally appropriate behaviors, and otherwise demonstrate the hallmarks of a developing conscience. The research programs of Kochanska (Kochanska & Thompson, 1997) and Hoffman (2000) are exemplary in their attention to early moral development; a promising future direction for the field is to further develop the conceptual and empirical tools to examine the roots of moral maturity.

Finally, the discipline of psychology has generally disregarded the significance of religion and spirituality in moral functioning, either by a blanket denial of their importance in the daily lives of the vast majority of people or by a universal focus on their negative manifestations. This secular skew has remained unchanged even though moral guidelines (both intrapsychic and interpersonal) obviously are central to the teachings of all religious traditions and despite the consistent evidence that religious commitment and participation surface as positive contributors to quality-of-life indexes (Koenig, 1998). Kohlberg (1967) reinforced that secular skew within moral psychology by his claim that the moral and religious domains are essentially independent, a claim that perhaps arose from the perceived need to establish the legitimacy of his enterprise in the antagonistic academic climate of the 1960s and 1970s and because the American doctrine of the separation of church and state precluded religious "contamination" of school-based moral education programs.

Evidence is beginning to emerge regarding the potential significance of religion and spirituality in moral functioning (e.g., Colby & Damon, 1992; Matsuba & Walker, 2004; Walker & Pitts, 1998)—a relationship that needs to be explored more systematically and incorporated into our models of moral development. Religion and spirituality are evidently foundational, at least for some people, for their understanding of morality, their everyday processes of moral decision making, and their moral action. A further complication is that the relationship between morality and religion may be culturally variable. The research of Shweder (Shweder, Much, Mahapatra, & Park, 1997) suggests that three ethical frameworks are differentially salient across cultures: an ethic of autonomy, which references notions of freedom, harm, rights, and justice; an ethic of community, which references notions of duty, hierarchy, and interdependence; and an ethic of divinity, which references notions of natural and sacred order, tradition, sin, and sanctity. Thus the role of the cultural context in informing moral understandings should become an important feature of future research directions in moral psychology (Turiel, 2002).

The field faces many obvious and difficult challenges in developing comprehensive and coherent models of moral functioning, yet the future holds numerous positive prospects for significant advances in our understanding of this fundamental aspect of human development.

References

Colby, A., & Damon, W. (1992). *Some do care: Contemporary lives of moral commitment.* New York: Free Press.

Colby, A., & Kohlberg, L. (1987). *The measurement of moral judgment* (Vols. 1–2). New York: Cambridge University Press.

Eisenberg, N. (1995). Prosocial development: A multifaceted model. In W. M. Kurtines & J. L. Gewirtz (Eds.), *Moral development: An introduction* (pp. 401–429). Boston: Allyn and Bacon.

Gilligan, C. (1982). *In a different voice: Psychological theory and women's development.* Cambridge, MA: Harvard University Press.

Haidt, J. (2001). The emotional dog and its rational tail: A social intuitionist approach to moral judgment. *Psychological Review, 108,* 814–834.

Hartshorne, H., May, M. A., & Shuttleworth, F. K. (1930). *Studies in the nature of character: Vol. 3. Studies in the organization of character.* New York: Macmillan.

Hoffman, M. L. (2000). *Empathy and moral development: Implications for caring and justice.* Cambridge, England: Cambridge University Press.

Killen, M., & Smetana, J. G. (Eds.). (2006). *Handbook of moral development.* Mahwah, NJ: Erlbaum.

Kochanska, G., & Thompson, R. A. (1997). The emergence and development of conscience in toddlerhood and early childhood. In J. E. Grusec & L. Kuczynski (Eds.), *Parenting and children's internalization of values: A handbook of contemporary theory* (pp. 53–77). New York: Wiley.

Koenig, H. G. (Ed.). (1998). *Handbook of religion and mental health.* San Diego: Academic Press.

Kohlberg, L. (1967). Moral and religious education and the public schools: A developmental view. In T. Sizer (Ed.), *Religion and public education* (pp. 164–183). Boston: Houghton Mifflin.

Kohlberg, L. (1981). *Essays on moral development: Vol. 1. The philosophy of moral development.* San Francisco: Harper and Row.

Kohlberg, L. (1984). *Essays on moral development: Vol. 2. The psychology of moral development.* San Francisco: Harper and Row.

Kurtines, W. M., & Gewirtz, J. L. (Eds.). (1991). *Handbook of moral behavior and development* (Vols. 1–3). Hillsdale, NJ: Erlbaum.

Matsuba, M. K., & Walker, L. J. (2004). Extraordinary moral commitment: Young adults working for social organizations. *Journal of Personality, 72,* 413–436.

Nucci, L. P. (2001). *Education in the moral domain.* Cambridge, England: Cambridge University Press.

Rest, J. R. (1979). *Development in judging moral issues.* Minneapolis: University of Minnesota Press.

Rest, J. R., Narvaez, D., Bebeau, M. J., & Thoma, S. J. (1999). *Postconventional moral thinking: A neo-Kohlbergian approach.* Mahwah, NJ: Erlbaum.

Shweder, R. A., Much, N. C., Mahapatra, M., & Park, L. (1997). The "big three" of morality (autonomy, community, divinity) and the "big three" explanations of suffering. In A. Brandt & P. Rozin (Eds.), *Morality and health* (pp. 119–169). Florence, KY: Taylor & Francis/Routledge.

Turiel, E. (1983). *The development of social knowledge: Morality and convention.* Cambridge, England: Cambridge University Press.

Turiel, E. (2002). *The culture of morality: Social development, context, and conflict.* Cambridge, England: Cambridge University Press.

Walker, L. J. (1984). Sex differences in the development of moral reasoning: A critical review. *Child Development, 55,* 677–691.

Walker, L. J. (1988). The development of moral reasoning. *Annals of Child Development, 5,* 33–78.

Walker, L. J. (1996). Kohlberg's cognitive-developmental contributions to moral psychology. *World Psychology, 2,* 273–296.

Walker, L. J. (2002). The model and the measure: An appraisal of the Minnesota approach to moral development. *Journal of Moral Education, 31,* 353–367.

Walker, L. J. (2006). Gender and morality. In M. Killen & J. G. Smetana (Eds.), *Handbook of moral development* (pp. 93–115). Mahwah, NJ: Erlbaum.

Walker, L. J., & Pitts, R. C. (1998). Naturalistic conceptions of moral maturity. *Developmental Psychology, 34,* 403–419.

15

Conscience in Childhood
Past, Present, and Future

Grazyna Kochanska and Nazan Aksan

Conscience, the inner guidance system, is perhaps the single most powerful factor that underpins individuals' sociomoral competence and prevents destructive and callous conduct. Conscience is a core component of the child's overall profile of mental health, sociomoral competencies, and vulnerabilities. A mature conscience is associated with adaptive functioning. A deficient conscience is characterized by callous, disruptive, aggressive, antisocial, and underregulated behavior. Such behavior is the most common mental health concern in children and adolescents.

Conscience has a rich conceptual history in human thought. For centuries we have wondered how individuals internalize the values of their families and societies and how those values become a reliable inner guiding system for conduct and a vehicle for the intergenerational transmission of values (Grusec, 1997). Developmentalists have pondered when and how children come to feel moral emotions, such as guilt associated with trangressions and empathy toward others; how they become capable and willing to behave according to rules and values without a need for external control; and how they come to appreciate and reason about right and wrong (Grusec, 1997; Kagan, 2005).

Research on conscience has focused on several perennial core questions: What are the components of conscience? How are they organized? How does conscience develop—when does it first emerge, what determines individual differences, and what are the implications of early conscience for future adjustment and psychopathology?

What are the components of conscience? In the past the "grand theories" have tended to focus mostly on one element. Psychoanalysts were concerned mainly with the moral emotion of guilt. Social learning researchers focused mostly on moral conduct, although they considered multiple types of moral behavior. The influential Piagetian-Kohlbergian cognitive-developmental approach focused almost entirely on moral cognition and discounted moral emotions or moral conduct. Contemporary scholars influenced by the cognitive tradition have proposed more differentiated views of morality that concern separate domains of rules and values, such as conventional, moral, personal, and prudential domains (Smetana, 1997; Turiel, Killen, & Helwig, 1987).

The psychoanalytic influence, and its focus on moral emotion, reappeared in the 1950s and 1960s in the work of Sears, who revisited the questions about the structure of conscience from the neo-Hullian standpoint. Attempting to integrate the psychoanalytic and learning views, Sears, Rau, and Alpert (1965) considered both moral emotions and moral conduct, finding them only modestly related.

The work since the mid-1970s has been, and most likely will continue to be, influenced by an increasing recognition that the multiple components of conscience—emotion, conduct, and cognition—have to be considered together in a comprehensive manner (Burton, 1984; Dienstbier, Hillman, Lehnhoff, Hillman, & Valkenaar, 1975; Grusec & Goodnow, 1994; Grusec & Kuczynski, 1997; Hoffman, 1983; Kagan, 2005; Radke-Yarrow, Zahn-Waxler, & Chapman, 1983; Thompson, 1998; Turiel, 1998). In his groundbreaking work Hoffman (1983) proposed an elegant model that brought together moral emotions of guilt and empathy, moral conduct, and the cognitive processing of information inherent in moral socialization messages. Emotion researchers have proposed the moral self—a system incorporating the do's and don'ts of early socialization—as a core component of conscience (Emde, Biringen, Clyman, & Oppenheim, 1991; Emde, Johnson, & Easterbrooks, 1987; Kochanska, 2002a).

The question about the components of conscience leads to a related question regarding their organization. How is conscience organized? Are moral emotions, conduct, and cognition all part of a coherent system, or are they loosely related or even unrelated? Are children who feel more remorseful after a transgression also more likely to comply with rules of conduct and to show more mature moral judgment? Are children who are more empathic also more likely to refrain from cheating?

Because the grand developmental theories have usually focused predominantly on one aspect of conscience—emotion, conduct, or cognition—they sidestepped the question of whether those components cohere within an individual child. Hartshorne and May

(1928–1930) were the first to address this issue, in their pioneering study of the structure of character. They examined whether different manifestations of conscience, such as honesty, deceit, self-control, and altruism, were interrelated in a large sample of elementary and high school students, and they found these manifestations to be only weakly related.

Two subsequent investigations (Burton, 1963; Rushton, Brainerd, & Pressley, 1983) reexamined Hartshorne and May's (1928–1930) original data, using newer statistical techniques. These more recent studies showed that the early claims of the relative lack of coherence of different aspects of character had been overstated and that, in similar contexts, individuals did show a modest degree of consistency, or a "latent general moral character factor." In our research we have also often found that moral emotion, conduct, and cognition are intercorrelated (Kochanska, Padavich, & Koenig, 1996). Other studies that have addressed the issues of consistency among different aspects of conscience yielded variable results, from absent or low consistency to substantial (for reviews, see Eisenberg & Fabes, 1998; Grusec & Lytton, 1988; Radke-Yarrow et al., 1983).

The questions about the organization of conscience remain to be answered. Future investigations will need to go beyond the issue of whether moral emotions, conduct, cognition, and self cohere within an individual child. More important, we will need to address the causal relations among conscience components. For example, moral emotions of guilt and empathy have been long seen as inhibitors of antisocial behavior (Blair, Monson, & Frederickson, 2001; Hoffman, 1983), but few studies have actually tested whether such models fit the empirical data.

We have begun to address those questions in our research program, and our work has indeed supported causal links among children's guilt, moral self, and moral conduct. Mediational analyses indicated that children's predisposition to experience discomfort after a transgression serves to inhibit behavior that violates rules (Kochanska, Gross, Lin, & Nichols, 2002). We have also shown that children's early wholehearted, committed compliance with their parents results in children's forming a view of themselves as good and moral—a moral self—which, in turn, promotes future rule-compatible behavior (Kochanska, 2002a). This is consistent with the model of Emde, Biringen, and colleagues (1991).

Perhaps the most important set of questions concerns the development of conscience. How early does it emerge? What determines differences in its outcomes? What are its implications for future adjustment?

The views of how soon young children show signs of conscience have varied. The early psychoanalytic theory and the theories influenced by it emphasized the preschool age as the time of the emerging superego. The cognitive theories considered young children essentially amoral and selfish (Piaget, 1932; Kohlberg, 1969).

The 1980s and 1990s ushered in a renewed appreciation of the early years. The interest in conscience has shifted to toddlerhood, stimulated in part by the work on emotional development during the transition from infancy to early childhood. For example, social referencing has been portrayed as an effective process whereby parents convey to their young children emotional valuations of acts of behavior (Emde, Biringen, et al., 1991). Research on early compliance and self-regulation has uncovered an early form of internalization, committed compliance, which clearly serves as a developmental precursor of future, more mature forms of conscience (Kochanska, 2002a). Research on the emerging self led to the focus on self-conscious emotions (Lewis, Sullivan, Stanger, & Weiss, 1989). The accumulating empirical evidence revealed young children's capacity to experience guilt and discomfort after transgressions, empathy toward others, awareness of right and wrong, sensitivity to rule violations, and the emerging ability to regulate their own behavior (Eisenberg & Fabes, 1998; Emde, Biringen, et al., 1991; Kagan, 1981; Kagan & Lamb, 1987; Kochanska, 1994; Kochanska, Gross, et al., 2002; Kochanska & Thompson, 1997; Radke-Yarrow et al., 1983; Stipek, Gralinski, & Kopp, 1990; Thompson, 1998). The contemporary generation of cognitive researchers described young children's abilities to make subtle distinctions among types of transgressions (Smetana, 1997; Turiel, 1998).

What determines individual differences among children regarding the development of conscience? Psychoanalytic and learning theories emphasized parental socialization. The two major dimensions were warmth and control, particularly the use of power and punishment. Depending on the theoretical orientation, the mechanism of internalization was seen as the child's identification (Sears et al., 1965) or learning (Parke, 1974). Hoffman (1983) proposed a more differentiated view of parental discipline that encompassed power, the withdrawal of love (two factors that engender varying levels of arousal in the child), and reasoning, which carries the informational content of moral socialization messages.

Newer approaches to discipline have shifted from the top-down, parent-to-child perspective to a bidirectional view. The child is now seen as an agent in moral socialization who actively processes parental moral messages and exercises a sense of choice and autonomy while engaging in moral behavior (Hoffman, 1983; Grusec & Goodnow, 1994; Maccoby, 1992). The views of the contexts of moral socialization have expanded to include not only discipline situations surrounding the child's immediate misbehavior but also parent-child discourse, during which the parent and the child jointly review specific instances of the child's past conduct (Kochanska, Aksan, & Nichols, 2003; Thompson, Laible, & Ontai, 2003). Variations in the parental style of such moral discourse have been associated with differences in the maturity of children's conscience (Laible & Thompson, 2000; Walker & Taylor, 1991).

The relationship-based approach to socialization continues to gain momentum (Collins & Laursen, 1999; Collins, Maccoby, Steinberg, Hetherington, & Bornstein, 2000; Kochanska, 2002b; Maccoby, 1992; Reis, Collins, & Berscheid, 2000; Thompson, 1998). In that approach a child's conscience is seen as emerging in the context of mutually responsive orientation between the parent and the child (Kochanska, 2002b). The child's willingness to embrace parental values is seen as flowing out of the shared history of a close, responsive relationship. For example, securely attached children, who likely have experienced more responsive care, are more eager to internalize parental rules and demands (Kochanska & Thompson, 1997; Londerville & Main, 1981).

The quality of the relationship may also moderate the effectiveness of specific discipline techniques. For example, we have shown that a history of a warm, mutually responsive relationship enhances the effectiveness of parental discipline and modeling efforts (Kochanska, 2002b; Kochanska, Aksan, Knaack, & Rhines, 2004). Patterson and his colleagues have amply demonstrated that negative, adversarial relationships undermine the effectiveness of parental discipline (Patterson, DeBaryshe, & Ramsey, 1989).

Parallel to the growing emphasis on relationships has been a renewed interest in recent decades in child temperament. Temperament has emerged as a critical set of influences on conscience development (Kagan, 1998, 2005; Rothbart & Bates, 1998). That research has built bridges to the large body of empirical data on adults with seriously impaired consciences. Those individuals—psychopaths—have been long known for their very low level of fear and autonomic hyporeactivity (Fowles, 1993, 1994, 1998; Lykken, 1957; Quay, 1993).

Recent research has extended the inquiry into the links between temperament and conscience to normative populations of very young children and to multiple temperament dimensions.

Consistent with the findings for adults, growing evidence across multiple studies suggests that fearful children develop more internalized consciences (for reviews, see Kagan, 1998, 2005; Rothbart & Bates, 1998). They are more guilt prone and engage in more rule-compatible conduct (Kochanska, Gross, et al., 2002). Temperamental qualities assessed as early as infancy predicted moral emotions several years later (Rothbart, Ahadi, & Hershey, 1994).

Temperament research has also elucidated qualities other than fear as influences on conscience. In particular, effortful control—a capacity to suppress the dominant behavior and to perform instead a subdominant behavior, a characteristic that is linked to early attentional capacities (Rothbart & Ahadi, 1994; Rothbart & Bates, 1998)—has been strongly associated in multiple studies, concurrently and longitudinally, with conscience development (Kochanska & Knaack, 2003; Kochanska & Thompson, 1997).

Future research will almost certainly continue to consider long proposed, and recently demonstrated, interactions between socialization and temperament. Several investigations have shown that those two broad sets of influences may act as moderators for each other. Similar socialization and relationship factors operate differently in children with different temperaments, and similar temperamental predispositions have different effects under varying socialization conditions (Bates, Pettit, Dodge, & Ridge, 1998; Belsky, Hsieh, & Crnic, 1998; Kochanska & Thompson, 1997; Rothbart & Bates, 1998).

What are the developmental implications of early conscience for future adjustment? The study of conscience extends beyond normative development into the purview of developmental psychopathology. An impaired conscience is a core aspect of conduct disorders, antisocial development, and psychopathy (Lykken, 1995). Conversely, the capacity for remorse and empathy, an appreciation of right and wrong, and engaging in behavior compatible with rules all mark successful adaptation. A large body of developmental research shows that early disturbances in conscience development are important portents of future risks and that early moral emotions and self-regulated behavior serve as early protective factors against future antisocial trajectories.

The relations between early conscience and future adjustment are complex. For example, Frick and colleagues (Frick et al., 2003;

Frick & Ellis, 1999) have shown that early callous-unemotional traits—severely impaired guilt and empathy—strongly predict future compromised conscience and serious conduct problems. On the other hand, Zahn-Waxler and Kochanska (1990) have demonstrated that early excessive guilt may also lead to detrimental outcomes. Future work will likely focus on such nonlinear developmental predictions and on the delicate balance of adaptive and maladaptive processes.

What are some of the promising new directions of research on conscience? One avenue involves contemporary analytic methodologies. Rich longitudinal databases with panel design can now use structural modeling to address both the structure of conscience and causal links among its components in ways not adequately addressed with traditional regression and correlational analyses (Bollen, 1989). For example, confirmatory factor-analytic techniques can directly test the plausibility of substantively driven models of how various components of conscience are organized, examine the stability of that organization, and quantify method variance with multitrait multimethod models in a less arbitrary fashion than exploratory factor-analytic techniques (Aksan & Kochanska, 2005). Further, because structural modeling techniques allow researchers to construct a closer representation of causal links among various constructs, they also afford us more direct ways of thinking about and testing both development within each construct and relations among constructs than those offered by the traditional regression-based methods.

More research is needed to understand the links between the parent-child relationship and conscience. Whereas research has repeatedly shown associations between a positive, mutually responsive relationship and children's early conscience (Kochanska, 2002b), the specific mechanisms behind those links are poorly understood. We have proposed, and preliminarily supported, a view that a mutually responsive orientation may promote conscience because it enhances the child's enjoyment of the interactions with the parent, which in turn leaves the child more open to embrace parental values and rules (Kochanska, Forman, Aksan, & Dunbar, 2005).

Future research will also need to consider the network of early relationships in a broader ecology of development. Almost nothing is known about the differential impact of mothers, fathers, and other caregivers, such as grandparents or day care providers, on the child's conscience.

Further, growing connections with affective neuroscience will increasingly inform research on conscience. According to Damasio and his research team (Damasio, 1994), damage to certain brain areas, particularly the prefrontal cortex, results in dysfunction of the "somatic marker system." This, in turn, causes associated deficits in emotion, response to punishment and reward, and response inhibition. Those impairments are particularly severe in empathy and other moral emotions, moral reasoning, and moral conduct, and they are often referred to as acquired psychopathy (Anderson, Bechara, Damasio, Tranel, & Damasio, 1999; Anderson, Damasio, Tranel, & Damasio, 2000). Earlier lesions are linked to more severe deficits in moral emotions and conduct than later lesions, consistent with a view that the early years are critical for the emerging conscience.

Few questions are as important as how young children gradually internalize values and norms of their families and society and how they move toward internally regulated conduct. Rapid progress in contemporary analytic techniques, as well as a growing understanding of links among the brain, psychophysiology, emotions, and conduct hold promise for exciting breakthroughs in delineating processes and mechanisms responsible for children's emerging conscience. We have much to look forward to in the coming years.

References

Aksan, N., & Kochanska, G. (2005). Conscience in childhood: Old questions, new answers. *Developmental Psychology, 41,* 506–516.

Anderson, S. W., Bechara, A., Damasio, H., Tranel, D., & Damasio, A. R. (1999). Impairment of social and moral behavior related to early damage in human prefrontal cortex. *Nature Neuroscience, 2,* 1032–1037.

Anderson, S. W., Damasio, H., Tranel, D., & Damasio, A. R. (2000). Long-term sequelae of prefrontal cortex damage acquired in early childhood. *Developmental Neuropsychology, 18,* 281–296.

Bates, J. E., Pettit, G. S., Dodge, K. A., & Ridge, B. (1998). Interaction of temperamental resistance to control and restrictive parenting in the development of externalizing behavior. *Developmental Psychology, 34,* 982–995.

Belsky, J., Hsieh, K.-H., & Crnic, K. (1998). Mothering, fathering, and infant negativity as antecedents of boys' externalizing problems and inhibition at age 3 years: Differential susceptibility to rearing experience? *Development and Psychopathology, 10,* 301–319.

Blair, R. J. R., Monson, J., & Frederickson, N. (2001). Moral reasoning and conduct problems in children with emotional and behavioural difficulties. *Personality and Individual Differences, 31,* 799–811.

Bollen, K. A. (1989). *Structural equations with latent variables.* New York: Wiley.

Burton, R. V. (1963). The generality of honesty reconsidered. *Psychological Review, 70,* 481–499.

Burton, R. V. (1984). A paradox in theories and research in moral development. In W. M. Kurtines & J. L. Gewirtz (Eds.). *Morality, moral behavior, and moral development* (pp. 193–207). New York: Wiley.

Collins, W. A., & Laursen, B. (Eds.). (1999). *Relationships as developmental contexts.* Hillsdale, NJ: Erlbaum.

Collins, W. A., Maccoby, E. E., Steinberg, L., Hetherington, E. M., & Bornstein, M. H. (2000). Contemporary research on parenting: The case for nature and nurture. *American Psychologist, 55,* 218–232.

Damasio, A. R. (1994). *Descartes' error: Emotion, reason, and the human brain.* New York: Grosset/Putnam.

Dienstbier, R. A., Hillman, D., Lehnhoff, J., Hillman, J., & Valkenaar, M. C. (1975). An emotion-attribution approach to moral behavior: Interfacing cognitive and avoidance theories of moral development. *Psychological Review, 82,* 299–315.

Eisenberg, N., & Fabes, R. A. (1998). Prosocial development. In W. Damon (Series Ed.) & N. Eisenberg (Vol. Ed.), *Handbook of child psychology: Vol. 3. Social, emotional, and personality development* (5th ed., pp. 701–778). New York: Wiley.

Emde, R. N., Biringen, Z., Clyman, R. B., & Oppenheim, D. (1991). The moral self of infancy: Affective core and procedural knowledge. *Developmental Review, 11,* 251–270.

Emde, R. N., Johnson, W. F., & Easterbrooks, A. (1987). The do's and don'ts of early moral development: Psychoanalytic tradition and current research. In J. Kagan & S. Lamb (Eds.), *The emergence of morality in young children* (pp. 245–276). Chicago: University of Chicago Press.

Fowles, D. C. (1993). Electrodermal activity and antisocial behavior: Empirical findings and theoretical issues. In J. C. Roy, W. Boucsein, D. Fowles, & J. Gruzelier (Eds.), *Progress in electrodermal research* (pp. 223–238). London: Plenum.

Fowles, D. C. (1994). A motivational theory of psychopathology. In W. Spaulding (Ed.), *Nebraska Symposium on Motivation, 1993: Vol. 41. Integrated views of motivation and emotion* (pp. 181–228). Lincoln: University of Nebraska Press.

Fowles, D. C. (1998). Psychophysiology and psychopathology: A motivational approach. *Psychophysiology, 25,* 373–391.

Frick, P. J., Cornell, A. H., Bodin, S. D., Dane, H. E., Barry, C. T., & Loney, B. R. (2003). Callous-unemotional traits and developmental pathways to severe conduct problems. *Developmental Psychology, 39,* 246–260.

Frick, P. J., & Ellis, M. L. (1999). Callous-unemotional traits and subtypes of conduct disorder. *Clinical Child and Family Psychology Review, 2,* 149–168.

Grusec, J. E. (1997). A history of research on parenting strategies and children's internalization of values. In J. E. Grusec & L. Kuczynski (Eds.), *Parenting and children's internalization of values: A handbook of contemporary theory* (pp. 3–22). New York: Wiley.

Grusec, J. E., & Goodnow, J. J. (1994). The impact of parental discipline methods on the child's internalization of values: A reconceptualization of the current points of view. *Developmental Psychology, 30,* 4–19.

Grusec, J. E., & Kuczynski, L. (Eds.). (1997). *Parenting and children's internalization of values: A handbook of contemporary theory.* New York: Wiley.

Grusec, J. E., & Lytton, H. (1988). *Social development: History, theory, and research.* New York: Springer-Verlag.

Hartshorne, H., & May, M. S. (1928–1930). *Studies in the nature of character* (Vols. 1–3). New York: Macmillan.

Hoffman, M. L. (1983). Affective and cognitive processes in moral internalization. In E. T. Higgins, D. Ruble, & W. W. Hartup (Eds.), *Social cognition and social development* (pp. 236–274). New York: Cambridge University Press.

Kagan, J. (1981). *The second year: The emergence of self-awareness.* Cambridge, MA: Harvard University Press.

Kagan, J. (1998). Biology and the child. In W. Damon (Series Ed.) & N. Eisenberg (Vol. Ed.), *Handbook of child psychology. Vol. 3. Social, emotional, and personality development* (5th ed., pp. 177–235). New York: Wiley.

Kagan, J. (2005). Human morality and temperament. In G. Carlo & C. Pope-Edwards (Eds.), *Nebraska Symposium on Motivation: Vol. 51. Moral motivation through the life span.* Lincoln: University of Nebraska Press.

Kagan, J., & Lamb, S. (Eds.). (1987). *The emergence of morality in young children.* Chicago: University of Chicago Press.

Kochanska, G. (1994). Beyond cognition: Expanding the search for the early roots of internalization and conscience. *Developmental Psychology, 30,* 20–22.

Kochanska, G. (2002a). Committed compliance, moral self, and internalization: A mediational model. *Developmental Psychology, 38,* 339–351.

Kochanska, G. (2002b). Mutually responsive orientation between mothers and their young children: A context for the early development of conscience. *Current Directions in Psychological Science, 11,* 191–195.

Kochanska, G., Aksan, N., Knaack, A., & Rhines, H. M. (2004). Maternal parenting and children's conscience: Early security as moderator. *Child Development, 75,* 1229–1242.

Kochanska, G., Aksan, N., & Nichols, K. E. (2003). Maternal power assertion in discipline and moral discourse contexts: Commonalities, differences, and implications for children's moral conduct and cognition. *Developmental Psychology, 39,* 949–963.

Kochanska, G., Forman, D. R., Aksan, N., & Dunbar, S. B. (2005). Pathways to conscience: Early mother–child mutually responsive orientation and children's moral emotion, conduct, and cognition. *Journal of Pschology and Psychiatry, 46,* 19–34.

Kochanska, G., Gross, J. N., Lin, M.-H., & Nichols, K. E. (2002). Guilt in young children: Development, determinants, and relations with a broader system of standards. *Child Development, 73*, 461–482.

Kochanska, G., & Knaack, A. (2003). Effortful control as a personality characteristic of young children: Antecedents, correlates, and consequences. *Journal of Personality, 71*, 1087–1112.

Kochanska, G., Padavich, D. L., & Koenig, A. L. (1996). Children's narratives about hypothetical moral dilemmas and objective measures of their conscience: Mutual relations and socialization antecedents. *Child Development, 67*, 1420–1436.

Kochanska, G., & Thompson, R. A. (1997). The emergence and development of conscience in toddlerhood and early childhood. In J. E. Grusec & L. Kuczynski (Eds.), *Parenting and children's internalization of values: A handbook of contemporary theory* (pp. 53–77). New York: Wiley.

Kohlberg, L. (1969). Stage and sequence: The cognitive developmental approach to socialization. In D. A. Goslin (Ed.), *Handbook of socialization theory and research* (pp. 347–480). Chicago: Rand McNally.

Laible, D. J., & Thompson, R. A. (2000). Mother-child discourse, attachment security, shared positive affect, and early conscience development. *Child Development, 71*, 1424–1440.

Lewis, M., Sullivan, M. W., Stanger, C., & Weiss, M. (1989). Self-development and self-conscious emotions. *Child Development, 60*, 146–156.

Londerville, S., & Main, M. (1981). Security of attachment, compliance, and maternal training methods in the second year of life. *Developmental Psychology, 17*, 289–299.

Lykken, D. T. (1957). A study of anxiety in the sociopathic personality. *Journal of Abnormal and Social Psychology, 55*, 6–10.

Lykken, D. T. (1995). *The antisocial personalities.* Hillsdale, NJ: Erlbaum.

Maccoby, E. E. (1992). The role of parents in the socialization of children: An historical overview. *Developmental Psychology, 28*, 1006–1017.

Parke, R. D. (1974). Rules, roles, and resistance to deviation: Recent advances in punishment, discipline, and self-control. In A. D. Pick (Ed.)., *Minnesota Symposium on Child Psychology* (Vol. 8, pp. 111–143). Minneapolis: University of Minnesota Press.

Patterson, G. R., Debaryshe, B. D., & Ramsey, E. (1989). A developmental perspective on antisocial behavior. *American Psychologist, 44*, 329–335.

Piaget, J. (1932). *The moral judgment of the child.* London: Kegan Paul.

Quay, H. C. (1993). The psychobiology of undersocialized aggressive conduct disorder: A theoretical perspective. *Development and Psychopathology, 5*, 165–180.

Radke-Yarrow, M., Zahn-Waxler, C., & Chapman, M. (1983). Children's prosocial dispositions and behavior. In P. Mussen (Series Ed.) & E. M. Hetherington (Vol. Ed.), *Handbook of child psychology: Vol. 4. Socialization, personality, and social development* (4th ed., pp. 469–545). New York: Wiley.

Reis, H. T., Collins, W. A., & Berscheid, E. (2000). Relationships in human behavior and development. *Psychological Bulletin, 126*, 844–872.

Rothbart, M. K., & Ahadi, S. A. (1994). Temperament and the development of personality. *Journal of Abnormal Psychology, 103,* 55–66.

Rothbart, M. K., Ahadi, S. S., & Hershey, K. L. (1994). Temperament and social behavior in childhood. *Merrill-Palmer Quarterly, 40,* 21–39.

Rothbart, M. K., & Bates, J. (1998). Temperament. In W. Damon (Series Ed.) & N. Eisenberg (Vol. Ed.), *Handbook of child psychology: Vol. 3. Social, emotional, and personality development* (5th ed., pp. 105–176). New York: Wiley.

Rushton, J. P., Brainerd, C. J., & Pressley, M. (1983). Behavioral development and construct validity: The principle of aggregation. *Psychological Bulletin, 94,* 18–38.

Sears, R. R., Rau, L., & Alpert, R. (1965). *Identification and child rearing.* Stanford, CA: Stanford University Press.

Smetana, J. G. (1997). Parenting and the development of social knowledge reconceptualized: A social domain analysis. In J. E. Grusec & L. Kuczynski (Eds.), *Parenting and children's internalization of values: A handbook of contemporary theory* (pp. 162–192). New York: Wiley.

Stipek, D. J., Gralinski, J. H., & Kopp, C. B. (1990). Self-concept development in the toddler years. *Developmental Psychology, 26,* 972–977.

Thompson, R. A. (1998). Early sociopersonality development. In W. Damon (Series Ed.) & N. Eisenberg (Vol. Ed.), *Handbook of child psychology: Vol. 3. Social, emotional, and personality development* (5th ed., pp. 25–104). New York: Wiley.

Thompson, R. A., Laible, D. J., & Ontai, L. L. (2003). Early understanding of emotion, morality, and self: Developing a working model. *Advances in Child Development and Behavior, 31,* 137–171.

Turiel, E. (1998). The development of morality. In W. Damon (Series Ed.) & N. Eisenberg (Vol. Ed.), *Handbook of child psychology: Vol. 3. Social, emotional, and personality development* (5th ed., pp. 863–932). New York: Wiley.

Turiel, E., Killen, M., & Helwig, C. C. (1987). Morality: Its structure, functions, and vagaries. In J. Kagan & S. Lamb (Eds.), *The emergence of morality in young children* (pp. 155–244). Chicago: University of Chicago Press.

Walker, L. J., & Taylor, J. H. (1991). Family interactions and the development of moral reasoning. *Child Development, 62,* 264–283.

Zahn-Waxler, C., & Kochanska, G. (1990). The origins of guilt. In R. A. Thompson (Ed.), *Nebraska Symposium on Motivation, 1988: Vol. 6. Socioemotional development* (pp. 183–258). Lincoln: University of Nebraska Press.

16

Genetics and Developmental Psychology

Robert Plomin

The 50th anniversary of *Merrill-Palmer Quarterly* provides an occasion to look back on the history of genetic research in developmental psychology and to look forward to its future. This anniversary coincides with the 50th anniversary of the single most important event in the history of genetic research: the discovery of the structure of DNA (Watson & Crick, 1953), which identifies the mechanisms underlying Mendel's laws of inheritance, published in 1866.

This brief chapter outlines what I see as the major accomplishments in past and present genetic research in developmental psychology and considers its future. Space does not permit me to discuss background issues (such as genetic research's focus on individual differences within the human species rather than the normative development of our species), describe methodological issues (such as the twin and adoption methods), or document thoroughly the research that supports my assertions (for details, see Plomin, DeFries, McClearn, & McGuffin, 2001).

Past

The first attempt to study nature and nurture in the development of behavioral traits was published a year before Mendel's paper (Galton, 1865). The first twin and adoption studies in developmental psychology were published more than 80 years ago (Merriman, 1924; Theis, 1924). Nonetheless, in the 1950s developmental psychologists largely ignored genetic research for three reasons. First, the word *genetics* had become associated with the horrors of Nazi Germany. Second, behaviorism emerged at the same time as the early genetic studies (Watson, 1930). Behaviorism had a much greater impact on psychology, leading to the dominance of an environmental paradigm that assumed that we are what we learn. The third reason was that there were relatively few genetics studies until the last 50 years—the first textbook on behavioral genetics was published only in 1960, and it focused largely on research with nonhuman animals (Fuller & Thompson, 1960).

One of the most dramatic shifts in developmental psychology during the past 50 years has been toward acceptance of a more balanced view that recognizes the importance of genetics as well as environment. This shift can be seen in the growing number of genetic papers in mainstream developmental psychology journals and in funded research grants. The public also accepts a major contribution of genetics. For example, a recent poll found that more than 90% of parents and teachers reported that they believed that genetics is at least as important as environment for mental illness, personality, learning difficulties, and intelligence (Walker & Plomin, 2005).

For nearly every area of psychology that has been studied, twin and adoption studies have shown genetic as well as environmental influence (Plomin, DeFries, McClearn, & McGuffin, 2001). Genetic research has consistently shown heritable influence in many traditional areas of psychological research, such as psychopathology, personality, cognitive disabilities and abilities, and drug use and abuse. Some areas showing strong genetic influence may be more surprising, such as self-esteem, interests and attitudes, and school achievement. Moreover, the influence of genetic factors is substantial, often accounting for as much as half the variance.

Consider schizophrenia. Until the 1960s schizophrenia was thought to be environmental in origin, with theories putting the blame on poor parenting to account for the fact that schizophrenia clearly runs in families. The idea that schizophrenia could run in families for genetic reasons was not seriously considered. Twin and adoption studies changed this view. Twin studies showed that identical twins are much more similar than nonidentical twins, which suggests genetic influence. If one member of an identical twin pair is schizophrenic, the chances are 45% that the other twin is also schizophrenic. For nonidentical twins the chances are 17%. Adoption studies showed that the risk of schizophrenia is just as great when children are adopted away from their schizophrenic parents at birth as when children are reared by their schizophrenic parents, which provides dramatic evidence for genetic transmission. There are now intense efforts to identify some of the specific genes responsible for genetic influence on schizophrenia.

In the 1960s, when schizophrenia was thought to be caused environmentally, it was important to emphasize the evidence for genetic influence, such as the concordance of 45% for identical twins. Now that genetic influence is widely recognized, it is important to emphasize that identical twins are only 45% concordant for schizophrenia, which means that in half the cases these pairs of genetically identical clones are discordant for schizophrenia. This discordance cannot be explained genetically—it must owe to environmental factors. Note that the word *environment* in genetic research really means nongenetic, which is a much broader definition of *environment* than is usually encountered in psychology. That is, environment denotes all nonheritable factors, including biological events such as prenatal and postnatal illnesses, not just psychosocial factors. The point is that genetics often explains half the variance of psychological traits, but this means that the other half of the variance is not the result of genetic factors. As I describe in the next section, one of the directions of current genetic research is to investigate environmental influences in genetically sensitive designs in order to understand the interplay of nature and nurture.

Present

Asking whether and how much genetic factors affect psychological dimensions and disorders are important first steps in understanding the origins of individual differences, but these questions are only a beginning. The next steps involve the question of how—that is, the study of the mechanisms by which genes have their effects. This is the focus of most current genetic research in developmental psychology. Examples include developmental change and continuity, multivariate genetic analysis, and the interplay of genes and environment.

Developmental Change and Continuity

One way in which current genetic research is moving beyond simply demonstrating genetic influence is to ask questions about genetic change and continuity during development (Plomin, 1986). Change in genetic effects from age to age does not necessarily mean that genes are turned on and off during development, although this does happen. Genetic change simply means that genetic effects at one age differ from genetic effects at another age; the same genes could have different effects in the brains of 8-year-olds and 18-year-olds. For example, developmental change in genetic effects is likely to be responsible for the difficulty of finding behavioral markers in childhood for individuals who later become schizophrenic. Although it is possible that "schizophrenia genes" are not turned on until after adolescence, it is more likely that these genes operate the same way before and after adolescence but that they manifest their hallucinatory and paranoid effects only after brain development in adolescence, when the brain becomes capable of such highly symbolic processing.

One of the more striking findings of genetic change involves general cognitive ability, often called intelligence and assessed by IQ tests. The magnitude of genetic influence increases steadily from infancy to childhood to adolescence to adulthood (McGue, Bouchard, Iacono, & Lykken, 1993). This is surprising because most people would think that environmental factors become increasingly important as experiences accumulate during the life course. It is not known why the heritability of general cognitive ability increases during development. It is possible that more genes come into play during development, but it also possible that the same genes have greater effects. This latter hypothesis receives support from longitudinal genetic research on age-to-age change and continuity that suggests that the same genes are largely responsible for genetic influence throughout development. If the same genes are involved, how can genetic influence increase? One possibility is genotype-environment correlation, which, as I discuss later, refers to correlations between genetic propensities and exposure to experiences (Bouchard, Lykken, Tellegen, & McGue, 1996). That is, small genetic differences may snowball as we go through life, creating environments that are correlated with our genetic propensities.

MULTIVARIATE GENETIC ANALYSIS

Another important direction for current research is multivariate genetic analysis, which focuses on the covariance (correlation) between traits rather than variance of each trait considered separately. It estimates the extent to which genetic factors that affect one trait also affect another trait. Multivariate genetic research in psychopathology suggests that genetic diagnoses of disorders often differ greatly from traditional diagnoses based on observable symptoms such as anxiety and depression. For example, several studies have shown that the same genes are largely responsible for anxiety and depression (Kendler, 1996). Recent research suggests that this genetic overlap among mental disorders is even broader in that genetic influences yield two broad domains of common psychopathology: internalizing problems that include anxiety, depression, and phobia, and externalizing problems that include antisocial behavior, conduct disorder, and drug abuse (Kendler, Prescott, Myers, & Neale, 2003).

Broad effects of genes have also been found in the cognitive domain. Despite the obvious differences between cognitive abilities such as verbal, spatial, and memory abilities, the same genes largely affect all these cognitive abilities (Petrill, 1997). Genetic overlap is also substantial across learning disabilities such as language, reading, and mathematics disability (Plomin & Kovas, 2005). Finding such substantial genetic overlap among cognitive abilities and disabilities has far-reaching implications for understanding the brain mechanisms that mediate these genetic effects (Plomin & Spinath, 2002). Multivariate genetic analysis will also be valuable for investigating genetic overlap between behavior and biological processes such as hormones, neurotransmitters, and brain imaging. For example, despite the increasing use of cortisol assays in developmental research, genetic research has only recently begun to consider cortisol and its links to behavior (Bartels, Van den Berg, Sluyter, Boomsma, & de Geus, 2003). Similarly, in the cognitive realm genetic research on neuroimaging measures and their relationship to cognition has just begun (Plomin & Kosslyn, 2001).

Interplay of Genes and Environment

Genetic research is changing the way we think about the environment in development. Two of the most important findings from genetic research involve environmental mechanisms and have come from investigating the environment in genetically sensitive designs. The first finding is that the environment works very differently from the way it has been assumed to work. Instead of making two children growing up in the same family similar to each other, which is what theories of socialization generally assume, genetic research shows that environmental influences that affect behavioral development operate to make children in the same family different (Plomin & Daniels, 1987). We know this, for example, because genetically unrelated children growing up in the same adoptive family scarcely resemble each other for personality, psychopathology, and cognitive abilities after adolescence. Siblings are similar but for genetic rather than environmental reasons. The environment is important, but environmental influences operate to make children in the same family different, not similar. These environmental influences are called nonshared, because they are not shared by children growing up in the same family. Why are children growing up in the same family so different? Although research during the past decade has attempted to identify the specific sources of nonshared environment, only modest progress has been made (Plomin, Asbury, & Dunn, 2001; Turkheimer & Waldron, 2000).

I would like to emphasize that no matter how difficult it may be to find specific nonshared environmental factors within the family, it is clear from the research that such factors exist. Although most research has focused on the family environment, it seems reasonable that experiences outside the family, such as experiences with peers and other life events, might be richer sources of nonshared environment as children make their own way in the world (Harris, 1998). It is also possible that chance contributes to nonshared environment in the sense of random noise, idiosyncratic experiences, or the subtle interplay of a concatenation of events (Plomin, Asbury, & Dunn, 2001; Turkheimer & Waldron, 2000). Compounded over time, small differences in experience might lead to large differences in outcome.

The second finding about environmental mechanisms has been called "the nature of nurture" (Plomin & Bergeman, 1991). Dozens of twin and adoption studies have shown that, when measures of psychological environment (such as parenting, stress, social support) are treated as dependent measures, they show substantial genetic influence (Plomin, 1994). How can this be true, given that environments have no DNA? The answer is that psychological environments can be considered as extended phenotypes of individuals, reflecting genetic differences among individuals as they select, modify, and construct their environments.

Given that environmental as well as behavioral measures show genetic influence, it is reasonable to ask whether associations between environmental measures and behavioral measures are mediated genetically. Multivariate genetic analysis can be used to analyze genetic and environmental contributions to the correlation between environmental measures and behavioral measures. Genetic factors can mediate the correlation between environmental measures and behavioral measures to the extent that the environments respond to genetically influenced characteristics of their children. For example, differences in parenting can be the genetic effect, rather than the environmental cause, of children's psychopathology. A general guideline from multivariate genetic research of this sort is that genetic factors are responsible for about half the phenotypic correlation between measures of the environment and measures of behavior. For this reason environmental measures cannot be assumed to be entirely environmental just because they are called environmental measures. A far-reaching implication of this research is that it supports a shift from thinking about passive models of how the environment affects individuals toward models that recognize the active role we play in selecting, modifying, and constructing our experiences—and reconstructing them in memory (Plomin, 1994).

In summary, genetic research has made some of the most important discoveries about the environment in recent decades, especially about nonshared environment and the role of genetics in experience. More discoveries about environmental mechanisms can be predicted as the environment continues to be investigated in the context of genetically sensitive designs. Much remains to be learned about correlations and interactions between nature and nurture.

Future

The momentum of these findings from current genetic research will carry the field of behavioral genetics well into this new millennium. Twin and adoption studies are called quantitative genetic designs because they can tackle complex traits influenced by multiple genes and multiple environmental factors. The future of genetic research in developmental psychology lies in molecular genetic studies of DNA that will eventually identify specific DNA variants responsible for the widespread influence of genes in psychological development. Identifying these DNA variants will make it possible to address questions about developmental, multivariate, and gene-environment mechanisms with far greater precision and power. For example, in 1993 a gene was identified that increases risk fivefold for dementia later in life (late-onset Alzheimer's disease, or LOAD; Corder et al., 1993). Study of this gene can now be used to investigate its effects earlier in life (developmental), its effect on other types of dementia and other comorbid disorders such as depression (multivariate), and its correlation and interaction with environmental factors, such as its role in worsening the effects of such head injuries as those caused by boxing (gene-environment interplay).

As compared to quantitative genetic studies of twins and adoptees, molecular genetics will have a far greater practical impact on research in developmental psychology because molecular genetic research does not require special populations such as twins or adoptees. In contrast, DNA can be easily and inexpensively obtained (from cheek swabs rather than blood for about $10 per individual), and genotyping of a DNA marker is also inexpensive (about 10¢ per individual). Moreover, devices called gene chips are available that can genotype tens of thousands of genes for an individual in a few hours. Finding genes associated with complex traits is difficult and expensive, but using genes already identified is easy and inexpensive and can add a powerful genetic dimension to any study in developmental psychology (Plomin, DeFries, Craig, & McGuffin, 2003b).

What has happened in the area of dementia in later life will be played out in many areas of developmental psychology. As I mentioned earlier, the only known risk factor for late-onset Alzheimer's disease is a gene, apolipoprotein E, involved in cholesterol transport. A form of the gene called allele 4 increases the risk fivefold for LOAD. Although the association between allele 4 and LOAD was reported only recently (Corder et al., 1993), nearly all research on dementia now genotypes participants for apolipoprotein E in order to ascertain whether the results differ for individuals with and without this genetic risk factor. Genotyping apolipoprotein E will also become routine in clinics if this genetic risk factor is found to predict differential response to interventions or treatments. Several developmental psychology studies are currently obtaining DNA on their samples in anticipation of the time when genes are identified that are relevant to their area of interest.

Note that DNA variation has a unique causal status in explaining behavior. When behavior is correlated with anything else, the adage applies that correlation does not imply causation. For example, parenting is correlated with children's behavioral outcomes, but this does not necessarily mean that the parenting causes the outcome environmentally. As I mentioned earlier, genetic research has shown that parenting behavior in part reflects genetic influences on children's behavior. When it comes to interpreting correlations between biology and behavior, such correlations are often mistakenly interpreted as if biology causes behavior. For example, correlations between neurotransmitter physiology and behavior or between neuroimaging indexes of brain activation and behavior are often interpreted as if brain differences cause behavioral differences. However, these correlations do not necessarily imply causation because behavioral differences can cause brain differences. In contrast, in the case of correlations between DNA variants and behavior, the behavior of individuals does not change their genome. Expression of genes changes but the DNA sequence itself does not change. For this reason correlations between DNA differences and behavioral differences can be interpreted causally: DNA differences cause the behavioral differences but not the other way around.

As I mentioned earlier, the single greatest event in the history of genetics was the discovery of the structure of DNA 50 years ago (Watson & Crick, 1953). Understanding the structure of DNA led directly to understanding the two major functions of DNA. The first is the essence of heredity: how DNA reliably duplicates itself by unzipping and dividing the DNA helix up the middle, with each half of the helix re-creating its complement. The second is how DNA codes for proteins, the building blocks of life, although the actual DNA code was not broken for more than a decade after Watson and Crick's paper—the 4-letter alphabet (G, A, T, C nucleotide bases) of DNA is read as 3-letter words that code for the 20 amino acids that are the building blocks of proteins. The crowning glory of the century and a tremendous start to the new century is the Human Genome Project, which in 2001 provided a working draft of the sequence of the 3 billion bases of DNA. However, there is no single human genome: we each have a unique genome because 1 in 1,000 DNA bases, 3 million bases of DNA, vary for at least 1% of the population. Most life scientists are interested in the generalities of the genome, but medical and behavioral scientists are more interested in the variations in the genome that are responsible for hereditary differences. About 2 million of these DNA variants have already been identified and have made it possible to begin to attempt to find some of the genes that affect psychological development, such as the apolipoprotein E gene that is a risk factor for dementia.

Gene identification has been most successful for the thousands of rare single-gene disorders in which a mutation in a single gene is necessary and sufficient to cause a disorder. Many of these single-gene disorders have psychological effects—for example, more than 200 of these disorders include cognitive effects among their symptoms. However, such single-gene disorders are very rare, with frequencies of 0.0001 or less. The DNA revolution also provides tools to identify genes responsible for the heritability of common psychological disorders and dimensions. These are usually called complex traits, because they are likely to be influenced by multiple genes as well as by multiple environmental factors. Psychological disorders such as schizophrenia, affective disorders, dementia, autism, reading disability, alcoholism, and hyperactivity are the target of much of this DNA research. Although some genes have been identified for these disorders, the process of identifying genes for complex traits in psychology as well as in medicine has been slower and more difficult than anticipated, probably because complex traits are influenced by many more genes of much smaller effect size than has been assumed (Plomin & McGuffin, 2003).

The most far-reaching ramifications for developmental psychology will come after these genes are identified. Psychology will be central to the new era of genetic research, called the postgenomic era, in which the focus will shift from finding genes to understanding how these genes work. Such postgenomic research is usually considered in relation to the bottom-up strategy of molecular biology, in which a gene's product is identified by its DNA sequence and the function of the gene product is traced through cells and then cell systems and eventually the brain. Psychology lies at the other end of the continuum of levels of analysis in the sense that psychology represents an integrationist top-down analysis that begins with the behavior of the whole organism rather than a reductionist bottom-up analysis that begins with a single molecule in a single cell. For example, psychologists can ask how the effects of specific genes unfold in behavioral development and how they interact and correlate with experience (Plomin, DeFries, Craig, & McGuffin, 2003a).

This top-down psychological level of analysis is likely to pay off more quickly in prediction, diagnosis, and intervention and eventually for behavioral preventions that use genes as early warning systems. Bottom-up and top-down levels of analysis of gene-behavior pathways will eventually meet in the brain. The grandest implication is that DNA will serve as an integrating force across all the life sciences, including developmental psychology.

References

Bartels, M., Van Den Berg, M., Sluyter, F., Boomsma, D. I., & De Geus, E. J. (2003). Heritability of cortisol levels: Review and simultaneous analysis of twin studies. *Psychoneuroendocrinology, 28,* 121–137.

Bouchard, T. J., Jr., Lykken, D. T., Tellegen, A., & McGue, M. (1996). Genes, drives, environment, and experience: EPD theory revisited. In C. P. Benbow & D. Lubinski (Eds.), *Intellectual talent: Psychometric and social issues* (pp. 5–43). Baltimore: Johns Hopkins University Press.

Corder, E. H., Saunders, A. M., Strittmatter, W. J., Schmechel, D. E., Gaskell, P. C., Small, G. W., Roses, A. D., Haines J. L., & Perick-Vance, M. A. (1993). Gene dose of apolipoprotein E type 4 allele and the risk of Alzheimer's disease in late onset families. *Science, 261,* 921–923.

Fuller, J. L., & Thompson, W. R. (1960). *Behavior genetics.* New York: Wiley.

Galton, F. (1865). Heredity talent and character. *Macmillan's Magazine, 12,* 157–166, 318–327.

Harris, J. R. (1998). *The nurture assumption: Why children turn out the way they do.* New York: Free Press.

Kendler, K. S. (1996). Major depression and generalised anxiety disorder: Same genes, (partly) different environments—Revisited. *British Journal of Psychiatry Supplement,* 68–75.

Kendler, K. S., Prescott, C. A., Myers, J., & Neale, M. C. (2003). The structure of genetic and environmental risk factors for common psychiatric and substance use disorders in men and women. *Archives of General Psychiatry, 60,* 929–937.

McGue, M., Bouchard, T. J., Jr., Iacono, W. G., & Lykken, D. T. (1993). Behavioral genetics of cognitive ability: A life-span perspective. In R. Plomin & G. E. McClearn (Eds.), *Nature, nurture, and psychology* (pp. 59–76). Washington, DC: American Psychological Association.

Mendel, G. J. (1866). Versuche ueber Pflanzenhybriden. *Verhandlungen des Naturforschunden Vereines in Bruenn, 4,* 3–47.

Merriman, C. (1924). The intellectual resemblance of twins. *Psychological Monographs, 33,* 1–58.

Petrill, S. A. (1997). Molarity versus modularity of cognitive functioning? A behavioral genetic perspective. *Current Directions in Psychological Science, 6,* 96–99.

Plomin, R. (1986). *Development, genetics, and psychology.* Hillsdale, NJ: Erlbaum.

Plomin, R. (1994). *Genetics and experience: The interplay between nature and nurture.* Thousand Oaks, CA: Sage.

Plomin, R., Asbury, K., & Dunn, J. (2001). Why are children in the same family so different? Nonshared environment a decade later. *Canadian Journal of Psychiatry, 46,* 225–233.

Plomin, R., & Bergeman, C. S. (1991). The nature of nurture: Genetic influences on "environmental" measures. *Behavioral and Brain Sciences, 14,* 373–427.

Plomin, R., & Daniels, D. (1987). Why are children in the same family so different from each other? *Behavioral and Brain Sciences, 10,* 1–16.

Plomin, R., Defries, J. C., Craig, I. W., & McGuffin, P. (2003a). *Behavioral genetics in the postgenomic era.* Washington, DC: American Psychological Association.

Plomin, R., Defries, J. C., Craig, I. W., & McGuffin, P. (2003b). Behavioral genomics. In R. Plomin, J. C. DeFries, I. W. Craig, & P. McGuffin (Eds.), *Behavioral genetics in the postgenomic era* (pp. 531–540). Washington, DC: American Psychological Association.

Plomin, R., Defries, J. C., McClearn, G. E., & McGuffin, P. (2001). *Behavioral genetics* (4th ed.). New York: Worth.

Plomin, R., & Kosslyn, S. (2001). Genes, brain and cognition. *Nature Neuroscience, 4,* 1153–1155.

Plomin, R., & Kovas, Y. (2005). Generalist genes for learning disabilities. *Psychological Bulletin, 131,* 592–617.

Plomin, R., & McGuffin, P. (2003). Psychopathology in the postgenomic era.

Annual Review of Psychology, 54, 205–228.

Plomin, R., & Spinath, F. M. (2002). Genetics and general cognitive ability (g). *Trends in Cognitive Science, 6,* 169–176.

Theis, S. V. S. (1924). *How foster children turn out* (Publication No. 165). New York: State Charities Aid Association.

Turkheimer, E., & Waldron, M. (2000). Nonshared environment: A theoretical, methodological, and quantitative review. *Psychological Bulletin, 126,* 78–108.

Walker, S. O., & Plomin, R. (2005). The nature-nurture question: Teachers' perceptions of how genes and the environment influence educationally relevant behavior. *Educational Psychology, 25,* 509–516.

Watson, J. B. (1930). *Behaviorism.* New York: Norton.

Watson, J. D., & Crick, F. H. C. (1953). Genetical implications of the structure of deoxyribonucleic acid. *Nature, 171,* 964–967.

17

The Nature-Nurture Debate and Public Policy

Kenneth A. Dodge

Perhaps the most important, and certainly the most contentious, debate in the history of developmental psychology has concerned the fundamental question of the role of genetic and biological factors versus environmental and learning factors in a child's development. This debate is rooted in philosophical arguments about the nature of the human species as a tabula rasa (Locke, 1690/1913) to be shaped by experience versus a "noble savage" (Rousseau, 1754) to be reined in by environmental constraints on an otherwise biological destiny (Hobbes, 1651/1969). Much of the modern study of individual differences in behavioral development, through longitudinal inquiry in the 1950s and 1960s, inexplicably ignored the role of innate factors but led to unprecedented publicly funded programs (e.g., Head Start) to enrich the early environments of economically disadvantaged children in the War on Poverty (Zigler & Muenchow, 1992). This work had dual premises—that disparities across groups were largely a result of environmental disadvantage and that environmental enrichments could repair this inequity.

The naive hope that early environments could be easily manipulated to alter long-term outcomes inspired a backlash of behavior-genetic studies in the 1980s and 1990s that championed the high percentage of variance in behavior that is accounted for by genes. The legacy of this backlash is the argument that public and private resources (e.g., the best schools and highest incomes) should be administered according to selection of those with the highest (presumably, genetically based) potential to achieve, rather than to compensate for biological or environmental disadvantage (Herrnstein & Murray, 1994). The scholarly anchor for the policy conclusion was exemplified in essays by Scarr (1992), Lytton (1990), and Harris (1995, 1998) that claimed that the environment accounts for little influence on human behavior. After 50 years of study it seemed that little had been learned.

Fortunately, the turn of the 21st century has brought ground-breaking findings that should bring this debate to a rapprochement and new level of sophistication. As highlighted by the National Research Council and Institute of Medicine's panel on early childhood development (National Research Council, 2000), these findings suggest a remarkably intimate relation between genes and the environment that is played out in interaction effects, transaction effects, mediational effects, and even evolutionary effects. In this chapter I will review this progress, forecast the next decades of inquiry, and suggest that these new concepts should direct public policy toward children.

Apportioning the Variance in Human Behavior

One problem with the gene-environment debate has been that scholars have used different ways of aggregating measures of behavior in order to estimate gene and environment effects. By doing so, they have asked different questions, but the debate has failed to capture these nuances. Consider Scarr's 1992 assertion that genes account for more than half the variance in aggressive behavior, and contrast that conclusion with empirical evidence that measures of individual differences in children's aggression are only modestly correlated across home and school settings (r's of about .2; Hope, Bierman, & Conduct Problems Prevention Research Group, 1998), across different peer targets (r's of .1; Hubbard, Dodge, Cillessen, Coie, & Schwartz, 2001), across types of settings such as play versus classrooms (r's of .3; Dodge, Coie, & Brakke, 1982), and across time (r's of .5; Coie & Dodge, 1983). Shouldn't these low cross-setting correlations indicate the strong influence of the environment on behavior? Scarr's conclusion was based on the premise that cross-setting and cross-time differences reflect "error variance" that should be resolved by first aggregating measures across source, setting, and time before conducting a test of genetic versus early family environment. The implication of this aggregation is that, according to the traditional behavior-genetic view, the fundamental gene-environment test concerns the relative proportion of variance accounted for by genes versus early family environment on life-enduring behavior scores that disregard effects of setting, peer target, time, and transient environmental influences. All the latter effects are assumed to be error variance. In such a test genes are indeed shown to exert an important impact.

These assumptions inherent in the behavior-genetic test are simply not consistent with a contemporary view of how the environment exerts an impact on behavior. Virtually no environmental theory posits that early family interaction causes effects on aggressive dispositions that will endure forever, no matter what later environmental or maturational influences occur. Rather, the fundamental nature of environmental theory is that social influences alter behavior patterns only as long as those social influences are still present. When the social influences change, the behavior will change (after a delay, in order for the organism to recalibrate the contingencies of the environment). Social experiments of an A-B-A-B design are premised on the transient nature of environmental impacts. Such a premise does not diminish the importance of the environment; in contrast, it heightens the continuing importance of the environment across the life span.

Consider as a thought experiment a behavior-genetic study in which monozygotic and dizygotic twins of many different ages are sampled from multiple cultures (including the United States, where handgun homicide rates are a thousand times higher than in some European countries, as well as European and Asian countries) and from multiple points in history (including contemporary times as well as times before guns were invented). The behavior-genetic test partitions variance into three components: genetic, nonshared family environment (i.e., the differences between people within the same family), and shared family environment (i.e., differences across families). If the outcome variable is handgun homicide, then no doubt the effect of shared family environment would be more than 90%, because gun laws, the invention and availability of handguns, and social constraints on access to guns exert a large influence on handgun homicide that is shared by members of the same family but varies across secular time and culture.

Why does this obvious effect of the environment not bring down the size of the genetic effect in actual empirical studies? Every behavior-genetic study "controls" for environmental variation that results from secular time and culture (and a host of other environmental factors) by restricting the sample to a single culture or a single point in history. Furthermore, the outcome variable is rarely a score with such strong ecological validity as handgun homicide. Instead, the outcome variables are ironically so calibrated to context that they virtually eliminate context effects (e.g., a parent's rating of a child's level of aggression).

Several conclusions can be drawn from this debate. First, the gene-environment test depends on whether we are interested in understanding specific behavioral events (e.g., Johnny's hitting Daryl on the playground, or Judy's shooting Delilah at a party) or immutable personality propensities (e.g., aggressiveness or extraversion). By studying discrete acts or behavior scores that are so dependent on context (e.g., a law prohibiting handgun ownership), we will privilege the effect of the environment. By dismissing transient environmental variation as error variance, we will privilege the effect of genes.

Second, the magnitude of the effect of genes or the environment on individual differences will vary greatly as a function of the composition of the sample being studied, a point well illustrated by the empirical analyses of Stoolmiller (1999). If the sample includes only a narrow range of environmental differences, such as, say, a sample of Scandinavians (who constitute the majority in studies in behavior genetics because of the ease of tracking children across time in this society, which keeps splendid permanent records of children's whereabouts), then the estimate of genetic effects will be relatively large. In contrast, one could constitute a sample that maximizes environmental differences to yield a relatively large environmental effect. The proportion of variance that genes account for is a description of the sample being studied, with relatively little generalization beyond that sample.

So what is the appropriate sample for these studies? Perhaps we could contemplate the world's entire population. But the population is a moving target. The third assertion that I am making here is that the human species has evolved across generations to maximize biological potential (i.e., the gene pool), environmental affordances (e.g., gains in nutrition and shelter), and the biological-environmental fit for survival. The result may be that the human species as a species has become more influenced by the environment than ever before and than other species (e.g., human infants today are born more dependent on the mother for survival than any other species), but that because of improvements in, and narrowing of, the minimal environmental standard (which generally holds outside third-world countries), individual differences in behavior reflect genes to a greater extent than previously. The search for absolute answers to the question of how much behavior is accounted for by genes versus the environment is a futile exercise.

Gene-Environment Interaction Effects

Scarr (1992) asserted yet another important insight in this debate when she argued that the environment exerts its effect only at the most extreme end of environmental deprivation (e.g., physical abuse). Her intent was to point out the minimal role of the environment, but this assertion grants an exception to the dominance of the gene and illustrates one kind of gene-environment interaction, namely, that genes might have a larger or smaller effect at different points in the environmental continuum. As a result a body of recent studies has revealed that the environment might well exert a stronger effect on poor children than on children in the middle class (National Research Council, 2000).

This discovery is one example of the broader gene-environment interaction effect. Although it was posited decades ago (e.g., Mischel, 1973), recent discoveries have revealed the enormous power of this effect in describing behavior. Among the most remarkable of these findings are those by the team of Caspi and Moffitt (Caspi et al., 2002). Following children from the Dunedin Study, they discovered that genetic vulnerability (i.e., an inherited MAOA deficiency) for conduct disorder is expressed only in the context of the experience of physical abuse (Caspi et al., 2002). Likewise, the experience of physical abuse is manifested in later conduct disorder only among those children who are at genetic risk for this disorder.

Jaffee and colleagues (2005) recently applied similar concepts in the E-Risk Study of 1,116 twin pairs in Great Britain. They used zygosity status (monozygotic versus dizygotic) and the conduct disorder status of one twin, along with evaluations of a history of physical maltreatment, to grade the genetic risk level of a child. They determined that the effect of physical maltreatment on risk for conduct problems is strongest among those at high genetic risk. The experience of maltreatment was associated with an increase of 2% in the probability of a conduct disorder diagnosis among children at low genetic risk for conduct disorder but an increase of 24% among children at high genetic risk.

Dodge, Lansford, and colleagues (2003) demonstrated a similar effect in a different context in a sample of 585 boys and girls followed prospectively from preschool through middle school. Dodge's team examined the effect of the environmental experience of being chronically rejected by one's peer group during early elementary school on growth in aggressive behavior problems by the beginning of middle school. Peer rejection is a major social stressor experienced by 10 to 15% of the school population. Dodge, Lansford, and colleagues

(2003) found that this experience was associated with growth in aggressive behavior only among the subgroup of children who had in early life displayed difficult temperamental behavior patterns. Children without that (presumably biologically mediated) propensity did not react to the stressor of social rejection in an aggressive manner. Again, this interaction effect suggests that environmental effects occur within specific biological contexts and that genetic effects depend on environmental circumstances. These demonstrations of true gene-environment interaction effects render the debate about the relative importance of genes versus the environment moot: both factors are undeniably crucial in understanding how behavior unfolds across development.

The Dynamic Relation Between Biology and the Environment

Another major discovery is the understanding of how biological status and the environment are not static entities unrelated to each other but, rather, operate in dynamic tandem across development (Dodge, 1990). Two concepts are worth highlighting.

First, one of the great insights of developmental psychology is that the environment acts in response to a child's biological affordance (National Research Council, 2000). A young child who displays an aggressive disposition will likely be met with a different environmental response than a child with a calm disposition. In healthy environments the societal response has evolved to compensate for a child's vulnerabilities through extra support, scaffolding, and protection. Thus vulnerable children may receive extra attention and nurturance. Often, however, the social response may well be to act in a way that mediates the very problematic outcome for which the child is vulnerable. A child with a prickly temperament may incite parents to react with physical abuse or peers to react with social rejection. These environmental experiences, in turn, exacerbate the child's behavioral difficulties and potentiate problem outcomes (Dodge & Pettit, 2003). Some behavior geneticists have used such findings to conclude that the environment is incidental in the developmental path of a genetically vulnerable child, whose destiny is inevitable. This conclusion makes no more sense than concluding that the environmental occurrence of nicotine ingestion through cigarette smoking is incidental to the development of lung cancer in an individual who is genetically primed to like and become addicted to cigarettes. The environment is responsive to one's biological dispositions and may well potentiate morbid outcomes.

Second, not only is the environment responsive to biological dispositions, but biological dispositions evolve in response to environmental inputs. De Bellis (2001) has used MRI technology to demonstrate that young children's brain volume and structure are altered as a result of maltreatment. Pollak, Klorman, Thatcher, and Cicchetti (2001) have used priming paradigms and electrophysiological recording to demonstrate that children who have been physically abused become perceptually and psychophysiologically ready to attend to hostile facial displays. This acquired biological disposition mimics the genetically based neurological vulnerability displayed by some children to act impulsively and to display attention deficits, and it may well exacerbate behavioral problems. In this case the psychophysiological reaction to the environmental experience of physical abuse may potentiate the effect of abuse on long-term outcomes.

Thus the environment and one's biologically based dispositional tendencies may dance with each other across development to lead, and, in some cases, to compensate for, each other's vulnerabilities and, in other cases, to potentiate each other's effects.

The Gene-Environment Fit

The gene-environment story gets considerably more complicated when we consider the possibility that the human species has evolved biologically to be especially responsive to differences in the environment that one experiences. Belsky, Steinberg, and Draper (1991) have posited the notion that children are born with the capability to alter their biological development by reading the type of nurturant environment that they experience in early life. If the environment is threatening, nonsupportive, and signaling an early demise, the child may accelerate biological maturation, including puberty, in order to pass along her genes to the next generation before her demise. In contrast, if the environment is safe, nurturant, and signaling a long life, biological maturation may be slowed in favor of higher-quality outcomes and better choices in mating partners for procreation. Evidence has accumulated that is consistent with, but hardly conclusive of, this perspective (Ellis et al., 2003).

Most important, this research has led to the concept of the gene-environment fit, the notion that some children may flourish under one set of environmental conditions but flounder under another set, whereas other children may flounder under the first set while flourishing under the second set. Consider the temperamentally exuberant child who has creative ideas but difficulty holding them back from expression. This child might well flounder in a school environment that requires conformity to a predetermined set of rules; the same child could flourish if exposed to challenging tasks and left alone to explore. Bates, Pettit, Dodge, and Ridge (1998) found that children with difficult temperaments responded to lax parenting with growth in aggressive behavior problems but responded to structured parenting with acceptable behavioral outcomes. These findings suggest that parenting intervention programs should not be directed in an identical manner toward all families but should, instead, be targeted toward specific kinds of families based on fit.

Similar principles apply to children's learning styles. Levine (2002) has found that children with learning disabilities can achieve extraordinary outcomes that one might not expect based solely on a genetically driven assessment of intelligence. These children, however, demonstrate differential responsiveness to various educational interventions as a function of child-specific learning styles. Not all interventions will be equally effective with all children. The task for practitioners is to assess each child's profile of abilities and learning styles and then match interventions to each child's profile.

Transforming Research, Practice, and Policy

The discoveries since the mid-1990s have important implications for research, practice, and public policy through 2015. First, researchers should turn their attention to identifying and understanding the particular ways in which genes and environments interact and transact in particular domains. The nature-nurture debate has been transformed by the concepts described by the National Research Council in its groundbreaking volume *From Neurons to Neighborhoods*. The search for the gene-environment fit is on.

Second, in order to identify strengths and deficits in behavior or learning, practitioners must assess not only an individual child but also the environment in order to identify the child-environment fit that is optimal for development. Psychological assessments must become environmental assessments.

Finally, public policy must shift away from its current main-effects dual foci on early selection of the best and brightest for privileged status and environmental enrichment for all disadvantaged children. Instead, public policy must begin to focus on matching children with the environments in which they will flourish. Education policy must allow for more individualization in curriculum planning. Early childhood care policy must be tailored toward different kinds of family circumstances. Mental health policy must encourage greater matching of interventions with child characteristics. Health policy too must match children with diets and exercise regimens that will optimize healthy outcomes for all children.

Although these reforms will make the world a more complicated place, they will maximize human potential. This legacy is indebted to the contributions of developmental psychology.

References

Bates, J. E., Pettit, G. S., Dodge, K. A., & Ridge, B. (1998). Interaction of temperamental resistance to control and restrictive parenting in the development of externalizing behavior. *Developmental Psychology, 34,* 982–995.

Belsky, J., Steinberg, L., & Draper, P. (1991). Childhood experience, interpersonal development, and reproductive strategy: An evolutionary theory of socialization. *Child Development, 62,* 647–670.

Caspi, A., McClay, J., Moffitt, T. E., Mill, J., Martin, J., Craig, I. W., Taylor, A., & Poulton, R. (2002). Role of genotype in the cycle of violence in maltreated children. *Science, 297,* 851–854.

Coie, J. D., & Dodge, K. A. (1983). Continuities and changes in children's social status: A five-year longitudinal study. *Merrill-Palmer Quarterly, 29,* 261–282.

De Bellis, M. (2001). Developmental traumatology: The psychobiological development of maltreated children and its implications for research, treatment, and policy. *Development and Psychopathology, 13,* 539–564.

Dodge, K. A. (1990). Nature versus nurture in childhood conduct disorder: It's time to ask a different question. *Developmental Psychology, 26,* 698–701.

Dodge, K. A., Coie, J. D., & Brakke, N. P. (1982). Behavior patterns of socially rejected and neglected preadolescents: The roles of social approach and aggression. *Journal of Abnormal Child Psychology, 18,* 389–409.

Dodge, K. A., Lansford, J. E., Burks, V. S., Bates, J. E., Pettit, G. S., Fontaine, R., & Price, J. M. (2003). Peer rejection and social information-processing factors in the development of aggressive behavior problems in children. *Child Development, 74,* 374–393.

Dodge, K. A., & Pettit, G. S. (2003). A biopsychosocial model of the development of chronic conduct problems in adolescence. *Developmental Psychology, 39,* 349–371.

Ellis, B. J., Bates, J. E., Dodge, K. A., Fergussen, D. M., Horwood, L. J., Pettit, G. S., & Woodward, L. (2003). Does early father absence place daughters at special risk for early sexual activity and teenaged pregnancy? *Child Development, 74,* 801–821.

Harris, J. R. (1995). Where is the child's environment? A group socialization theory of development. *Psychological Review, 102,* 458–489.

Harris, J. R. (1998). *The nurture assumption: Why children turn out the way they do.* New York: Free Press.

Herrnstein, R. J., & Murray, C. (1994). *The bell curve: Intelligence and class structure in American life.* New York: Free Press.

Hobbes, T. (1969). *Leviathan.* Cambridge, England: Cambridge University Press. (Original work published 1651)

Hope, T. D., Bierman, K. L., & Conduct Problems Prevention Research Group. (1998). Developmental patterns of home and school behavior in rural and urban settings. *Journal of School Psychology, 36,* 45–58.

Hubbard, J. A., Dodge, K. A., Cillessen, A. H. N., Coie, J. D., & Schwartz, D. (2001). The dyadic nature of social information-processing in boys' reactive and proactive aggression. *Journal of Personality and Social Psychology, 80,* 268–280.

Jaffee, S. R., Caspi, A., Moffitt, T. E., Dodge, K. A., Rutter, M., Taylor, A., & Tully, L. A. (2005). Nature x nurture: Genetic vulnerabilities interact with child maltreatment to promote conduct problems. *Development and Psychopathology, 17,* 67–84.

Levine, M. (2002). *A mind at a time.* New York: Simon and Schuster.

Locke, J. (1913). *Some thoughts concerning education.* London: Cambridge University Press. (Original work published 1690)

Lytton, H. (1990). Child and parent effects in boys' conduct disorder: A reinterpretation. *Developmental Psychology, 26,* 679–697.

Mischel, W. (1973). Toward a cognitive social learning reconceptualization of personality. *Psychological Review, 80,* 252–283.

National Research Council. (2000). *From neurons to neighborhoods: The science of early childhood development.* Washington, DC: National Academies Press.

Pollak, S. D., Klorman, R., Thatcher, J. E., & Cicchetti, D. (2001). P3b reflects maltreated children's reactions to facial displays of emotion. *Psychophysiology, 38,* 267–274.

Rousseau, J. J. (1754). *A discourse on a subject proposed by the Academy of Dijon: What is the origin of inequality among men, and is it authorized by natural law?* Translated by G. D. H. Cole, public domain.

Scarr, S. (1992). Developmental theories for the 1990s: Development and individual differences. *Child Development, 63,* 1–19.

Stoolmiller, M. (1999). Implications of the restricted range of family environments for estimates of heritability and nonshared environment in behavior genetic adoption studies. *Psychological Bulletin, 125,* 392–409.

Zigler, E., & Muenchow, S. (1992). *Head Start: The inside story of America's most successful educational experiment.* New York: Basic Books.

18

Why We Need to Explore Development in Its Cultural Context

Robert J. Sternberg and Elena L. Grigorenko

If children grew up in a world devoid of cultural context, the picture painted of children by developmental psychology textbooks might be quite accurate and therefore adequate. The problem is that not even children confined to so-called bubble worlds because of severely impaired immune systems grow up in such a world. The result is that students of developmental psychology, and even of psychology in general, acquire knowledge structures about development that are incomplete and, in many respects, wrongheaded. We, as developmental psychologists, thereby do our students an injustice.

It is not surprising that much—and arguably, most—research in developmental psychology is done in an acontextual manner. Acontextual research is (a) more easily and quickly completed; (b) easier to divide into least publishable units; (c) highly rewarded because it is usually experimentally more elegant than the mess we confront when we attempt to study children in their natural and diverse sociocultural contexts; and (d) easier to interpret, even if the interpretation is limited to some imaginary microworld in which children do not really live. The thesis of this chapter is that, as developmental psychologists, we have a responsibility at the very least to teach, and ideally also to do our research, in a way that recognizes the complex sociocultural niches in which children live. If we do not do so, we risk coming to conclusions that are incomplete and often wrong.

In this chapter we will describe culturally based research that questions the conclusions that would be reached were the same research conducted in an acultural manner. Because of limited space we shall give only a few brief examples, mostly from our own research program. Research from other groups supports the conclusions we describe here (e.g., Berry, 1974; Greenfield, 1997; Laboratory of Comparative Human Cognition, 1982; Nisbett, 2003; Rogoff, 1990, 2003; Serpell, 2000).

Implicit Lay Theories of Intelligence Around the World

Many developmental psychologists, including some of the most famous, study intellectual development (Piaget, 1972; Vygotsky, 1978; see reviews in Chen & Siegler, 2000; Lutz & Sternberg, 1999; Sternberg & Berg, 1992). But are traditional Western views shared by other cultures? To a large extent, they are not. For example, at the mental level not many cultures share the Western emphasis on speed of mental processing (Sternberg, Conway, Ketron, & Bernstein, 1981). Other cultures may even be suspicious of the quality of work that is done very quickly. Indeed, other cultures emphasize depth rather than speed of processing. They are not alone: some prominent Western theorists have pointed out the importance of depth of processing for full command of material (e.g., Craik & Lockhart, 1972).

Yang and Sternberg (1997a) have reviewed Chinese philosophical conceptions of intelligence. The Confucian perspective emphasizes the characteristic of benevolence and of doing what is right. As in the West, the intelligent person spends a great deal of effort in learning, enjoys learning, and persists in lifelong learning with a great deal of enthusiasm. The Taoist tradition, in contrast, emphasizes the importance of humility, freedom from conventional standards of judgment, and full knowledge of oneself as well as of external conditions.

The difference between Eastern and Western conceptions of intelligence may persist even in the present day. Yang and Sternberg (1997b) studied contemporary Taiwanese Chinese conceptions of intelligence and found five factors underlying these conceptions: a general cognitive factor, much like the g factor in conventional Western tests; interpersonal intelligence; intrapersonal intelligence; intellectual self-assertion; and intellectual self-effacement. In a related study but with different results, Chen (1994) found three factors underlying Chinese conceptualizations of intelligence: nonverbal reasoning ability, verbal reasoning ability, and rote memory. The difference may result from different subpopulations of Chinese, differences in methodology, or differences in when the studies were done.

The factors uncovered in both studies differ substantially from those identified by Sternberg, Conway, and colleagues (1981) in Americans' conceptions of intelligence—practical problem solving, verbal ability, and social competence—although in both cases people's implicit theories of intelligence seem to go quite far beyond what conventional psychometric intelligence tests measure. Of course, comparing the 1994 Chen study to the 1981 study by Sternberg, Conway, and colleagues means comparing studies that vary in both language and culture.

Chen and Chen (1988) varied only language. They explicitly compared the concepts of intelligence of Chinese graduates of Chinese-language schools with those who graduated from English-language schools in Hong Kong. They found that both groups considered nonverbal reasoning skills the most relevant skill for measuring intelligence. Verbal reasoning and social skills came next, followed by numerical skill. Memory was seen as least important. The Chinese-language-schooled group, however, tended to rate verbal skills as less important than did the English-language-schooled group. Moreover, in an earlier study, Chen, Braithwaite, and Huang (1982) found that Chinese students viewed memory for facts as important for intelligence, whereas Australian students viewed these skills as of only trivial importance.

Das (1994), also reviewing Eastern notions of intelligence, has suggested that in Buddhist and Hindu philosophies, intelligence involves waking up, noticing, recognizing, understanding, and comprehending but that it also includes such things as determination, mental effort, and even feelings and opinions in addition to more intellectual elements.

Differences between cultures in conceptions of intelligence have been recognized for some time. Gill and Keats (1980) noted that Australian university students value academic skills and the ability to adapt to new events as critical to intelligence, whereas Malay students value practical skills, as well as speed and creativity. Dasen (1984) found Malay students to emphasize both social and cognitive attributes in their conceptions of intelligence.

The differences between East and West may stem from differences in the kinds of skills valued by the two cultures (Srivastava & Misra, 1996). Western cultures and their schools emphasize what might be called "technological intelligence" (Mundy-Castle, 1974), and so things like artificial intelligence and so-called smart bombs are viewed, in some sense, as intelligent or as smart.

Western schooling also emphasizes other things (Srivastava & Misra, 1996), such as generalization, or going beyond the information given (Connolly & Bruner, 1974; Goodnow, 1976); speed (Sternberg, 1985); minimal moves to a solution (Newell & Simon, 1972); and creative thinking (Goodnow, 1976). Moreover, silence is interpreted as a lack of knowledge (Irvine, 1978). In contrast, the Wolof tribe in Africa views people of higher social class and distinction as speaking less (Irvine, 1978). This difference between the Wolof and Western notions suggests the usefulness of looking at African notions of intelligence as a contrast to U.S. notions.

Studies in Africa in fact provide yet another window on the substantial differences. Ruzgis and Grigorenko (1994) have argued that, in Africa, conceptions of intelligence revolve largely around skills that help to facilitate and maintain harmonious and stable intergroup relations; intragroup relations are probably equally important and at times more important. For example, Serpell (1974, 1982, 1996) found that Chewa adults in Zambia emphasize social responsibilities, cooperativeness, and obedience as important to intelligence; intelligent children are expected to be respectful of adults. Kenyan parents emphasize responsible participation in family and social life as important aspects of intelligence (Super & Harkness, 1982, 1986, 1993). In Zimbabwe the word for intelligence, *ngware*, actually means to be prudent and cautious, particularly in social relationships. Among the Baoule, service to the family and community and politeness toward and respect for elders are seen as key to intelligence (Dasen, 1984).

Similar emphasis on social aspects of intelligence has been found as well among two other African groups—the Songhay of Mali and the Samia of Kenya (Putnam & Kilbride, 1980). The Yoruba, another African tribe, emphasize the importance of depth—of listening rather than just talking—to intelligence and the importance of being able to see all aspects of an issue and of being able to place the issue in its proper overall context (Durojaiye, 1993).

The emphasis on the social aspects of intelligence is not limited to African cultures. Notions of intelligence in many Asian cultures also emphasize the social aspect of intelligence more than does the conventional Western or IQ-based notion (Azuma & Kashiwagi, 1987; Lutz, 1985; Poole, 1985; White, 1985).

Note that neither African nor Asian notions emphasize exclusively social notions of intelligence. These conceptions of intelligence emphasize social skills much more than do conventional U.S. conceptions of intelligence even as they recognize the importance of cognitive aspects of intelligence. A study of Kenyan conceptions of intelligence (Grigorenko, Geissler, et al., 2001) found that four distinct terms constitute conceptions of intelligence among rural Kenyans—*rieko* (knowledge and skills), *luoro* (respect), *winjo* (comprehension of how to handle real-life problems), and *paro* (initiative)—with only the first directly referring to knowledge-based skills (including but not limited to the academic).

It is important to realize, again, that there is no one overall U.S. conception of intelligence. Indeed, Okagaki and Sternberg (1993) found that different ethnic groups in San Jose, California, had rather different conceptions of what it means to be intelligent. For example, Latino parents of schoolchildren tended to emphasize the importance of social competence skills in their conceptions of intelligence, whereas Asian parents tended rather heavily to emphasize the importance of cognitive skills. European American parents also placed a greater emphasis on cognitive than social skills. Teachers, representing the dominant culture, gave greater emphasis to cognitive than social competence skills. The rank order of children of various groups' performance (including subgroups within the Latino and Asian groups) could be perfectly predicted by the extent to which their parents shared the teachers' conception of intelligence. In other words, teachers tended to reward those children who were socialized into a view of intelligence that happened to correspond to the teachers' own. Yet, as we shall argue later, social aspects of intelligence, broadly defined, may be as important as or even more important than cognitive aspects of intelligence in later life. Some, however, prefer to study intelligence not in its social aspect but in its cognitive one.

Explicit Theoretical Investigations of Intelligence Around the World

Many times, investigations of intelligence conducted in settings outside the developed world can yield a picture of intelligence that is quite at variance with the picture one would obtain from studies conducted only in the developed world. In a study in Usenge, Kenya, near the town of Kisumu, Sternberg and his colleagues, who were interested in schoolage children's ability to adapt to their indigenous environment, tested practical intelligence for adaptation to the environment (see Sternberg & Grigorenko, 1997; Sternberg, Nokes, et al., 2001). The test measured children's informal tacit knowledge of natural herbal medicines that the villagers believe can be used to fight various types of infections. Most villagers believe in their efficacy: children in the villages use their knowledge of these medicines an average of once a week in medicating themselves and others. Thus tests of how to use these medicines constitute effective measures of one aspect of practical intelligence as defined by the villagers as well as by their life circumstances in their environmental contexts. Middle-class Westerners might find it quite a challenge to thrive or even survive in these contexts or, for that matter, in the contexts of urban ghettos often not distant from their comfortable homes.

The researchers measured the Kenyan children's ability to identify the medicines, where they come from, what they are used for, and how they are dosed. Based on work the researchers had done elsewhere, they expected that scores on this test would not correlate with scores on conventional tests of intelligence. To test this hypothesis they also administered to the 85 children the Raven Coloured Progressive Matrices Test, which is a measure of fluid, or abstract-reasoning-based, abilities, as well as the Mill Hill Vocabulary Scale, which is a measure of crystallized, or formal-knowledge-based, abilities. In addition, the researchers gave the children a comparable test of vocabulary in their own Dholuo language. The Dholuo language is spoken in the home, English in the schools.

The researchers found statistically significant correlations of the tacit knowledge tests with the tests of crystallized abilities. The correlations, however, were negative. In other words, the higher the children scored on the test of tacit knowledge, the lower they scored, on average, on the tests of crystallized abilities. Correlations with fluid ability tests and school grades were also negative, although not all were significantly so. Nevertheless, the trend toward negative correlations was clear. This surprising result can be interpreted in various ways, but based on the ethnographic observations of the anthropologists on the team, Geissler and Prince, the researchers concluded that a plausible scenario takes into account the expectations of families for their children.

Many children drop out of school before graduation, for financial or other reasons, and many families in the village do not particularly value formal Western schooling. There is no reason they should, as the children of many families will for the most part spend their lives farming or engaged in other occupations that make little or no use of Western schooling. These families emphasize teaching their children the indigenous informal knowledge that will lead to successful adaptation in the environments in which they will really live. Children who spend their time learning the indigenous practical knowledge of the community generally do not invest themselves heavily in doing well in school, whereas children who do well in school generally do not invest themselves as heavily in learning the indigenous knowledge—hence the negative correlations.

The Kenya study suggests that the identification of a general factor of human intelligence may tell us more about how abilities interact with patterns of schooling, and especially Western patterns of schooling, than it does about the structure of human abilities. In Western schooling children typically study a variety of subjects from an early age and thus develop skills in a variety of skill areas. This kind of schooling prepares the children to take a test of intelligence, which typically measures skills in a variety of areas. Often intelligence tests measure skills that children were expected to acquire a few years before taking the intelligence test. But as Rogoff (1990) and others have noted, this pattern of schooling is not universal and has not even been common for much of the history of humankind. Throughout history and in many places still, schooling, especially for boys, takes the form of apprenticeships in which children learn a craft from an early age. They learn what they will need to know in order to succeed in a trade but not a lot more. They are not simultaneously engaged in tasks that require the development of the particular blend of skills measured by conventional intelligence tests. Hence, it is less likely that one would observe a general factor in their scores, much as the investigators discovered in Kenya. Some years back Vernon (1971) pointed out that the axes of a factor analysis do not necessarily reveal a latent structure of the mind but rather represent a convenient way of characterizing the organization of mental abilities. Vernon believed that there was no one right orientation of axes, and, indeed, mathematically, an infinite number of orientations of axes can be fitted to any solution in an exploratory factor analysis. Vernon's point seems perhaps to have been forgotten or at least ignored by later theorists.

We have found related, although certainly not identical, results in a study we have done among Yup'ik Eskimo children in southwestern Alaska (Grigorenko, Meier, et al., 2004). We assessed the importance of academic and practical intelligence in rural and urban Alaskan communities. Adults or peers in the study rated a total of 261 children for practical skills: 69 in grade 9, 69 in grade 10, 45 in grade 11, and 37 in grade 12. Of these children, 145 were females and 116 were males, and they were from 7 different communities, 6 rural and 1 relatively urban. We measured academic intelligence with conventional measures of fluid and crystallized intelligence. We measured practical intelligence with a test of tacit knowledge as acquired in rural Alaskan Yup'ik communities. The urban children generally outperformed the rural children on a measure of crystallized intelligence, but the rural children generally outperformed the urban children on the measure of Yup'ik tacit knowledge. The test of tacit knowledge was superior to the tests of academic intelligence in predicting practical skills of the rural children (for whom the test was created) but not of the urban ones.

The test of practical intelligence developed for use in Kenya might seem more like a test of achievement or of developing expertise (see Ericsson, 1996; Howe, Davidson, & Sloboda, 1998) than of intelligence. But it can be argued that intelligence is itself a form of developing expertise—that there is no clear-cut distinction between the two constructs (Sternberg, 1998, 1999). Indeed, all measures of intelligence, one might argue, measure a form of developing expertise.

An example of how tests of intelligence measure developing expertise rather than some fixed quantity emanates from work done by Sternberg, Grigorenko, and their colleagues in Tanzania. A study done in Tanzania (see Sternberg & Grigorenko, 1997, 2002; Sternberg, Grigorenko, et al., 2002) points out the risks of giving tests, scoring them, and interpreting the results as measures of some latent intellectual ability or abilities. The investigators administered to 358 schoolchildren aged 11 and 13 years near Bagamoyo, Tanzania, tests that included a form-board classification test, a linear syllogisms test, and a Twenty Questions Test, all of which measure the kinds of skills required on conventional tests of intelligence. Of course, the investigators obtained scores that they could analyze and evaluate, ranking the children in terms of their supposed general or other abilities. However, researchers administered the tests dynamically rather than statically (Brown & Ferrara, 1985; Budoff, 1968; Day, Engelhardt, Maxwell, & Bolig, 1997; Feuerstein, 1979; Grigorenko & Sternberg, 1998; Guthke, 1993; Haywood & Tzuriel, 1992; Lidz, 1987, 1991; Tzuriel, 1995; Vygotsky, 1978). Dynamic testing is like conventional static testing in that individuals are tested and inferences about their abilities are made. But dynamic tests differ in that children are given some kind of feedback to help them improve their scores. Vygotsky (1978) suggested that the children's ability to profit from the guided instruction that they received during the testing session could serve as a measure of children's zones of proximal development, or the difference between their developed abilities and their latent capacities. In other words, testing and instruction are treated as being of one piece rather than as being distinct processes. This integration makes sense in terms of traditional definitions of intelligence as the ability to learn ("Intelligence and Its Measurement," 1921; Sternberg & Detterman, 1986). A dynamic test directly measures processes of learning in the context of testing rather than measuring these processes indirectly as the product of past learning. Such measurement is especially important when not all children have had equal opportunities to learn in the past.

In the assessments children took the ability tests first. Then they were given a brief period of instruction in which they were able to learn skills that could enable them to improve their scores. Then they were tested again. Because the instruction for each test lasted only about 5 to 10 minutes, one would not expect dramatic gains. Yet, on average, the gains were statistically significant. More important, scores on the pretest showed only weak although significant correlations with scores on the posttest. These correlations, at about the 0.3 level, suggested that when tests are administered statically to children in developing countries, they may be rather unstable and easily subject to influences of training. The reason could be that the children are not accustomed to taking Western-style tests, and so they profit quickly even from small amounts of instruction as to what is expected from them. Of course, the more important question is not whether the scores changed or even correlated with each other but how they correlated with other cognitive measures. In other words, which test was a better predictor of transfer to other cognitive performance, the pretest score or the posttest score? The investigators found the posttest score to be the better predictor.

In interpreting results, whether from developed or developing cultures, it is always important to take into account the physical health of the participants one is testing. In a study we did in Jamaica (Sternberg, Powell, McGrane, & McGregor, 1997), we found that Jamaican schoolchildren who suffered from parasitic illnesses (for the most part, whipworm or ascaris) did more poorly on higher-level cognitive tests (such as of working memory and reasoning) than did children who did not suffer from these illnesses, even after controlling for socioeconomic status. Why might such a physical illness cause a deficit in higher-level cognitive skills?

Ceci (1996) has shown that increased levels of schooling are associated with higher IQ. Why would there be such a relation? Presumably, in part, because schooling helps children develop the kinds of skills that are measured by IQ tests and that are important, in turn, for survival in school. Children with whipworm-induced and related illnesses are less able to profit from school than are children without these illnesses. Every day that they go to school, they are likely to be experiencing symptoms such as listlessness, stomachache, and difficulties in concentrating. These symptoms reduce the extent to which they are able to profit from instruction and, in turn, reduce their ultimate performance on higher-level cognitive tests.

Crystallized ability tests, such as tests of vocabulary and general information, certainly measure developing and developed knowledge bases. And available data suggest that fluid ability tests, such as tests of abstract reasoning, measure developing and developed expertise even more strongly than do crystallized ability tests. Probably the best evidence for this claim is that fluid ability tests have shown much greater increases in scores over the last several generations than have crystallized ability tests (Flynn, 1984, 1987, 1998; Neisser, 1998). The relatively brief period of time during which these increases have occurred (about 9 points of IQ per generation) suggests an environmental rather than a genetic cause of the increases. And the substantially greater increase for fluid than for crystallized tests suggests that fluid tests, like all other tests, actually measure an expertise acquired through interactions with the environment. This is not to say that genes do not influence intelligence: almost certainly they do (Bouchard, 1997; Plomin, 1997; Scarr, 1997). Rather, the point is that the environment always mediates their influence, and tests of intelligence measure gene-environment interaction effects. The measurement of intelligence is by assessment of various forms of developing expertise.

The forms of developing expertise that are viewed as practically or otherwise intelligent may differ from one society to another or from one sector of a given society to another. For example, procedural knowledge about natural herbal medicines, on the one hand, or Western medicines, on the other, may be critical to survival in one society and irrelevant to survival in another (e.g., where one or the other type of medicine is not available). Whereas what constitutes components of intelligence is universal, the content that constitutes the application of these components to adaptation to, shaping of, and selection of environments is culturally and even subculturally variable. But practical aspects of intelligence are important everywhere, as shown in a study conducted in Russia.

In this study Grigorenko and Sternberg (2001) tested 511 Russian schoolchildren (ranging in age from 8 to 17 years) as well as 490 mothers and 328 fathers of these children. The researchers used entirely distinct measures of analytical, creative, and practical intelligence. Consider, for example, the tests used for adults. Similar tests were used for children.

Two subtests of a test of nonverbal intelligence measured fluid analytical intelligence. The Test of g: Culture Fair, Level II (Cattell & Cattell, 1973) is a test of fluid intelligence designed to reduce, as much as possible, the influence of verbal comprehension, culture, and educational level, although no test eliminates such influences. In the first subtest, Series, individuals were presented with an incomplete, progressive series of figures. The participants' task was to select, from among the choices provided, the answer that best continued the series. In the Matrices subtest the task was to complete the matrix presented at the left of each row.

The test of crystallized intelligence was adapted from existing traditional tests of analogies and synonyms/antonyms used in Russia. Grigorenko and Sternberg used adaptations of Russian rather than American tests because the vocabulary used in Russia differs from that used in the United States. The first part of the test included 20 verbal analogies (KR20 = 0.83). An example is circle—ball = square—? (a) quadrangular, (b) figure, (c) rectangular, (d) solid, (e) cube. The second part included 30 pairs of words, and the participants' task was to specify whether the words in the pair were synonyms or antonyms (KR20 = 0.74). Examples are latent—hidden and systematic—chaotic.

The measure of creative intelligence also comprised two parts. The first part asked the participants to describe the world through the eyes of insects. The second part asked participants to describe who might live and what might happen on a planet called Priumliava. No additional information about the nature of the planet was specified. Each part of the test was scored in three different ways to yield three different scores. The first score was for originality (novelty); the second was for the amount of development in the plot (quality); and the third was for creative use of prior knowledge in these relatively novel kinds of tasks (sophistication). The mean interstory reliabilities were 0.69, 0.75, and 0.75 for the three respective scores, all of which were statistically significant at the $p < .001$ level.

The measure of practical intelligence was self-reported and also comprised two parts. The first part was designed as a 20-item, self-report instrument, assessing practical skills in the social domain (e.g., effective and successful communication with other people), in the family domain (e.g., how to fix household items, how to run the family budget), and in the domain of effective resolution of sudden problems (e.g., organizing something that has become chaotic). For the subscales internal consistency estimates varied from 0.50 to 0.77. In this study only the total practical intelligence self-report scale was used (Cronbach's alpha = 0.71). The second part had four vignettes, based on themes that appeared in popular Russian magazines in the context of discussion of adaptive skills in the current society. The four themes were how to maintain the value of one's savings, what to do when one makes a purchase and discovers that the item one has purchased is broken, how to locate medical assistance in a time of need, and how to manage a salary bonus one has received for outstanding work. Each vignette was accompanied by five choices, and participants had to select the best one. Obviously, there is no one right answer in this type of situation. Hence, Grigorenko and Sternberg used the most frequently chosen response as the keyed answer. To the extent that this response was suboptimal, this suboptimality would work against the researchers in subsequent analyses relating scores on this test to other predictor and criterion measures.

In this study exploratory analysis of the principal components for both children and adults yielded very similar factor structures. Both varimax and oblimin rotations yielded clear-cut analytical, creative, and practical factors for the tests. Thus a sample of a different nationality (Russian), a different set of tests, and a different method of analysis (exploratory rather than confirmatory analysis) again supported the theory of successful intelligence.

In this same study the investigators used the analytical, creative, and practical tests to predict mental and physical health among the Russian adults. Mental health was measured by widely used paper-and-pencil tests of depression and anxiety, and physical health was measured by self-report. The best predictor of mental and physical health was the practical intelligence measure. Analytical intelligence came second, and creative intelligence came third. All three contributed to prediction, however. Thus the researchers again concluded that a theory of intelligence encompassing all three elements provides better prediction of success in life than does a theory comprising just the analytical element.

We have argued in this chapter that doing research in microworlds can tell you a lot—about those microworlds. It does not tell you much about the macroworld of which the various microworlds are a part. People from developed countries, and especially Western ones, can show and have shown a certain kind of arrogance in assuming that concepts (such as implicit theories of intelligence) or results (such as of studies based on explicit theories of intelligence) obtained in one culture—usually, their culture—apply anywhere. In all likelihood they do not. Or at least it cannot be assumed they do until this assumption is tested.

Many results that we have described here are at variance with results typically obtained in Western countries. Other investigators also have obtained results that differ dramatically from those obtained in the developed West. We believe, therefore, that cultural investigations of psychological constructs, such as intelligence, are not just nice but necessary.

Put in concrete terms, the overwhelming majority of studies in developmental psychology are done within a single culture. Results are then published that are taken by authors as well as readers to be generalizable. But generalizable to whom? Our work in a variety of cultures suggests that the generalizability may be considerably more limited than we would like to believe. So the question is whether we want the future of the field to reflect a largely middle-class North American view of North American development that is offered as something more or whether we want the future to reflect an increasingly interconnected set of world cultures that are diverse and that share common aspects but also retain their own unique aspects. The latter seems the better choice.

For the latter choice to be made, certain changes need to occur: more and better rewards for scholars who are willing to spend the time and energy required to do cultural research, especially better funding for such research, and journal referees and editors who are more conscientious in requiring authors to specify exactly to whom they can expect to reasonably apply their generalized results.

As things stand, many scholars are discouraged from doing cultural research on development because it is time consuming, expensive, and extremely demanding. Often one must learn other languages, assemble multinational research teams, and deal with intercultural frustrations that simply do not occur when one does all one's testing locally. Difficult though it may be to deal with school administrators in the United States, it is far more difficult to deal with assorted functionaries from around the globe. And young investigators pressed to publish or perish may be understandably afraid to do such research, because they fear that such studies will take so long that it will cut down on their publication rate and therefore their opportunities for promotion. But such research has the potential to give us unique insights and we should not lose the opportunities.

References

Azuma, H., & Kashiwagi, K. (1987). Descriptions for an intelligent person: A Japanese study. *Japanese Psychological Research, 29*, 17–26.

Berry, J. W. (1974). Radical cultural relativism and the concept of intelligence. In J. W. Berry & P. R. Dasen (Eds.), *Culture and cognition: Readings in cross-cultural psychology* (pp. 225–229). London: Methuen.

Bouchard, T. J., Jr. (1997). IQ similarity in twins reared apart: Findings and responses to critics. In R. J. Sternberg & E.L. Grigorenko (Eds.), *Intelligence, heredity, and environment* (pp. 126–160). New York: Cambridge University Press.

Brown, A. L., & Ferrara, R. A. (1985). Diagnosing zones of proximal development. In J. V. Wertsch (Ed.), *Culture, communication, and cognition: Vygotskian perspectives* (pp. 273–305). New York: Cambridge University Press.

Budoff, M. (1968). Learning potential as a supplementary assessment procedure. In J. Hellmuth (Ed.), *Learning disorders* (Vol. 3, pp. 295–343). Seattle, WA: Special Child.

Cattell, R. B., & Cattell, H. E. P. (1973). *Measuring intelligence with the Culture Fair Tests.* Champaign, IL: Institute for Personality and Ability Testing.

Ceci, S. J. (1996). *On intelligence . . . more or less* (expanded ed.). Cambridge, MA: Harvard University Press.

Chen, M. J. (1994). Chinese and Australian concepts of intelligence. *Psychology and Developing Societies, 6*, 101–117.

Chen, M. J., Braithwaite, V., & Huang, J. T. (1982). Attributes of intelligent behaviour: Perceived relevance and difficulty by Australian and Chinese students. *Journal of Cross-Cultural Psychology, 13*, 139–156.

Chen, M. J., & Chen, H. C. (1988). Concepts of intelligence: A comparison of Chinese graduates from Chinese and English schools in Hong Kong. *International Journal of Psychology, 223*, 471–487.

Chen, Z., & Siegler, R. S. (2000). Intellectual development in childhood. In R. J. Sternberg (Ed.), *Handbook of intelligence* (pp. 92–116). New York: Cambridge University Press.

Connolly, H., & Bruner, J. (1974). Competence: Its nature and nurture. In K. Connolly & J. Bruner (Eds.), *The growth of competence.* New York: Academic Press.

Craik, F. I. M., & Lockhart, R. S. (1972). Levels of processing: A framework for memory research. *Journal of Verbal Learning and Verbal Behavior, 11*, 671–684.

Das, J. P. (1994). Eastern views of intelligence. In R. J. Sternberg (Ed.), *Encyclopedia of human intelligence* (Vol. 1, p. 391). New York: Macmillan.

Dasen, P. (1984). The cross-cultural study of intelligence: Piaget and the Baoule. *International Journal of Psychology, 19*, 407–434.

Day, J. D., Engelhardt, J. L., Maxwell, S. E., & Bolig, E. E. (1997). Comparison of static and dynamic assessment procedures and their relation to independent performance. *Journal of Educational Psychology, 89*,

358–368.

Durojaiye, M. O. A. (1993). Indigenous psychology in Africa. In U. Kim & J. W. Berry (Eds.), *Indigenous psychologies: Research and experience in cultural context*. Newbury Park, CA: Sage.

Ericsson, K. A. (1996). The acquisition of expert performance. In K. A. Ericsson (Ed.), *The road to excellence* (pp. 1–50). Hillsdale, NJ: Erlbaum.

Feuerstein, R. (1979). *The dynamic assessment of retarded performers: The learning potential assessment device theory, instruments, and techniques*. Baltimore: University Park Press.

Flynn, J. R. (1984). The mean IQ of Americans: Massive gains, 1932 to 1978. *Psychological Bulletin, 95*, 29–51.

Flynn, J. R. (1987). Massive IQ gains in 14 nations. *Psychological Bulletin, 101*, 171–191.

Flynn, J. R. (1998). WAIS-III and WISC-III gains in the United States from 1972 to 1995: How to compensate for obsolete norms. *Perceptual and Motor Skills, 86*, 1231–1239.

Gill, R., & Keats, D. M. (1980). Elements of intellectual competence: Judgments by Australian and Malay university students. *Journal of Cross-Cultural Psychology, 11*, 233–243.

Goodnow, J. J. (1976). The nature of intelligent behavior: Questions raised by cross-cultural studies. In L. Resnick (Ed.), *The nature of intelligence* (pp. 169–188). Hillsdale, NJ: Erlbaum.

Greenfield, P. M. (1997). You can't take it with you: Why abilities assessments don't cross cultures. *American Psychologist, 52*, 1115–1124.

Grigorenko, E. L., Geissler, P. W., Prince, R., Okatcha, F., Nokes, C., Kenny, D. A., Bundy, D. A., & Sternberg, R. J. (2001). The organization of Luo conceptions of intelligence: A study of implicit theories in a Kenyan village. *International Journal of Behavior Development, 25*, 367–378.

Grigorenko, E. L., Meier, E., Lipka, J., Mohatt, G., Yanez, E., & Sternberg, R. J. (2004). Academic and practical intelligence: A case study of the Yup'ik in Alaska. *Learning and Individual Differences, 14*, 183–207.

Grigorenko, E. L., & Sternberg, R. J. (1998). Dynamic testing. *Psychological Bulletin, 124*, 75–111.

Grigorenko, E. L., & Sternberg, R. J. (2001). Analytical, creative, and practical intelligence as predictors of self-reported adaptive functioning: A case study in Russia. *Intelligence, 29*, 57–73.

Guthke, J. (1993). Current trends in theories and assessment of intelligence. In J. H. M. Hamers, K. Sijtsma, & A. J. J. M. Ruijssenaars (Eds.), *Learning potential assessment* (pp. 13–20). Amsterdam: Swets and Zeitlinger.

Haywood, H. C., &. Tzuriel, D. (Eds.). (1992). *Interactive assessment*. New York: Springer-Verlag.

Howe, M. J., Davidson, J. W., & Sloboda, J. A (1998). Innate talents: Reality or myth? *Behavioral & Brain Sciences, 21*, 399–442.

Intelligence and its measurement: A symposium. (1921). *Journal of Educational Psychology, 12*, 123–147, 195–216, 271–275.

Irvine, J. T. (1978). Wolof magical thinking: Culture and conservation revisited. *Journal of Cross-Cultural Psychology, 9,* 300–310.

Laboratory of Comparative Human Cognition (1982). Culture and intelligence. In R. J. Sternberg (Ed.), *Handbook of human intelligence* (pp. 642–719). New York: Cambridge University Press.

Lidz, C. S. (Ed.). (1987). *Dynamic assessment.* New York: Guilford.

Lidz, C. S. (1991). *Practitioner's guide to dynamic assessment.* New York: Guilford.

Lutz, C. (1985). Ethnopsychology compared to what? Explaining behaviour and consciousness among the Ifaluk. In G. M. White & J. Kirkpatrick (Eds.), *Person, self, and experience: Exploring Pacific ethnopsychologies* (pp. 35–79). Berkeley: University of California Press.

Lutz, D. J., & Sternberg, R. J. (1999). Cognitive development. In M. H. Bornstein & M. E. Lamb (Eds.), *Developmental psychology: An advanced textbook* (4th ed., pp. 275–311). Mahwah, NJ: Erlbaum.

Mundy-Castle, A. C. (1974). Social and technological intelligence in Western or nonwestern cultures. *Universitas, 4,* 46–52.

Neisser, U. (Ed.). (1998). *The rising curve.* Washington, DC: American Psychological Association.

Newell, A., & Simon, H. A. (1972). *Human problem solving.* Englewood Cliffs, NJ: Prentice-Hall.

Nisbett, R. E. (2003). *The geography of thought: Why we think the way we do.* New York: Free Press.

Okagaki, L., & Sternberg, R. J. (1993). Parental beliefs and children's school performance. *Child Development, 64(1),* 36–56.

Piaget, J. (1972). *The psychology of intelligence.* Totowa, NJ: Littlefield Adams.

Plomin, R. (1997). Identifying genes for cognitive abilities and disabilities. In R. J. Sternberg & E. L. Grigorenko (Eds.), *Intelligence, heredity, and environment* (pp. 89–104). New York: Cambridge University Press.

Poole, F. J. P. (1985). Coming into social being: Cultural images of infants in Bimin-Kuskusmin folk psychology. In G. M. White & J. Kirkpatrick (Eds.), *Person, self, and experience: Exploring Pacific ethnopsychologies* (pp. 183–244). Berkeley: University of California Press.

Putnam, D. B., & Kilbride, P. L. (1980). *A relativistic understanding of social intelligence among the Songhay of Mali and Smaia of Kenya.* Paper presented at the meeting of the Society for Cross-Cultural Research, Philadelphia.

Rogoff, B. (1990). *Apprenticeship in thinking: Cognitive development in social context.* New York: Oxford University Press.

Rogoff, B. (2003). *The cultural nature of human development.* London: Oxford University Press.

Ruzgis, P. M., & Grigorenko, E. L. (1994). Cultural meaning systems, intelligence, and personality. In R. J. Sternberg & P. Ruzgis (Eds.), *Personality and intelligence* (pp. 248–270). New York: Cambridge University Press.

Scarr, S. (1997). Behavior-genetic and socialization theories of intelligence: Truce and reconciliation. In R. J. Sternberg & E. L. Grigorenko (Eds.), *Intelligence, heredity, and environment* (pp. 3–41). New York: Cambridge University Press.

Serpell, R. (1974). Aspects of intelligence in a developing country. *African Social Research, 17,* 576–596.

Serpell, R. (1982). Measures of perception, skills, and intelligence. In W. W. Hartup (Ed.), *Review of child development research* (Vol. 6, pp. 392–440). Chicago: University of Chicago Press.

Serpell, R. (1996). Cultural models of childhood in indigenous socialization and formal schooling in Zambia. In C. P. Hwang & M. E. Lamb (Eds.), *Images of childhood* (pp. 129–142). Mahwah, NJ: Erlbaum.

Serpell, R. (2000). Intelligence and culture. In R. J. Sternberg (Ed.), *Handbook of intelligence* (pp. 549–580). New York: Cambridge University Press.

Srivastava, A. K., & Misra, G. (1996). Changing perspectives on understanding intelligence: An appraisal. *Indian Psychological Abstracts and Review, 3,* 1–34.

Sternberg, R. J. (1985). *Beyond IQ: A triarchic theory of human intelligence.* New York: Cambridge University Press.

Sternberg, R. J. (1998). Abilities are forms of developing expertise. *Educational Researcher, 27,* 11–20.

Sternberg, R. J. (1999). Intelligence as developing expertise. *Contemporary Educational Psychology, 24,* 359–375.

Sternberg, R. J., & Berg, C. A. (Eds.). (1992). *Intellectual development.* New York: Cambridge University Press.

Sternberg, R. J., Conway, B. E., Ketron, J. L., & Bernstein, M. (1981). People's conceptions of intelligence. *Journal of Personality and Social Psychology, 41,* 37–55.

Sternberg, R. J., & Detterman, D. K. (1986). *What is intelligence?* Norwood, NJ: Ablex.

Sternberg, R. J., & Grigorenko, E. L. (Eds.). (1997). *Intelligence, heredity, and environment.* New York: Cambridge University Press.

Sternberg, R. J., & Grigorenko, E. L. (2002). Just because we "know" it's true doesn't mean it's really true: A case study in Kenya. *Psychological Science Agenda, 15,* 8–10.

Sternberg, R. J., Grigorenko, E. L., Ngrosho, D., Tantufuye, E., Mbise, A., Nokes, C., Jukes, M., & Bundy, D. A. (2002). Assessing intellectual potential in rural Tanzanian school children. *Intelligence, 30,* 141–162.

Sternberg, R. J., Nokes, K., Geissler, P. W., Prince, R., Okatcha, F., Bundy, D. A., & Grigorenko, E. L. (2001). The relationship between academic and practical intelligence: A case study in Kenya. *Intelligence, 29,* 401–418.

Sternberg, R. J., Powell, C., McGrane, P. A., & McGregor, S. (1997). Effects of a parasitic infection on cognitive functioning. *Journal of Experimental Psychology: Applied, 3,* 67–76.

Super C. M., & Harkness, S. (1982). The development of affect in infancy and early childhood. In D. Wagnet & H. Stevenson (Eds.), *Cultural perspectives on child development* (pp. 1–19). San Francisco: Freeman.

Super, C. M., & Harkness, S. (1986). The developmental niche: A conceptualization at the interface of child and culture. *International Journal of Behavioral Development, 9,* 545–569.

Super, C. M., & Harkness, S. (1993). The developmental niche: A conceptu-
alization at the interface of child and culture. In R. A. Pierce & M. A.
Black (Eds.), *Life-span development: A diversity reader* (pp. 61–77).
Dubuque, IA: Kendall/Hunt.

Tzuriel, D. (1995). *Dynamic-interactive assessment: The legacy of L. S. Vygotsky
and current developments.* Unpublished manuscript.

Vernon, P. E. (1971). *The structure of human abilities.* London: Methuen.

Vygotsky, L. S. (1978). *Mind in society: The development of higher psychological
processes.* Cambridge, MA: Harvard University Press.

White, G. M. (1985). Premises and purposes in a Solomon Islands ethnopsychology. In G. M. White & J. Kirkpatrick (Eds.), *Person, self, and experience: Exploring Pacific ethnopsychologies* (pp. 328–366). Berkeley: University of California Press.

Yang, S., & Sternberg, R. J. (1997a). Conceptions of intelligence in ancient
Chinese philosophy. *Journal of Theoretical and Philosophical Psychology,
17,* 101–119.

Yang, S., & Sternberg, R. J. (1997b). Taiwanese Chinese people's conceptions
of intelligence. *Intelligence, 25,* 21–36.

19

Historical Lessons
The Value of Pluralism in Psychological Research

Elliot Turiel

The history of psychology includes a characteristic that I think has not served us well. I am referring to a tendency for scholars to proclaim that a particular perspective, theoretical orientation, worldview, or attention to a set of topics is the wave of the future that will transform psychology in the right and necessary direction and move it from its erroneous ways. More often than not, such proclamations have involved proselytizing, in that there are calls for everyone to see the truth of the position, abandon outdated approaches, and embrace research agendas that are within the new perspective. They warn too that the entrenched powers will actively resist the new truths.

As a historical example, behaviorists made such proclamations early in the 20th century. John Watson (1924) boldly asserted that behaviorism was a movement that would replace the prescientific thinking of the great mass of people, which was part and parcel of the ideas of psychologists of the time. He pointed to Wilhelm Wundt, William James, the functionalists, and the Gestaltists, whose concepts, such as consciousness and mind, only paralleled folklore that embraced ideas such as the soul. He also proclaimed the obvious truth of many behaviorist positions, including the environmentalism that he asserted had been neglected in efforts to identify inherited traits—which led him to the famous statement that he could train any healthy infant to become a "doctor, lawyer, artist, merchant-chief and yes, even beggar-man and thief regardless of his talents, penchants, tendencies, abilities, vocations and race of his ancestors" (1924, p. 104). In Watson's perception of the world of the time, behaviorist ideas were not accepted but actively resisted. The resistance was akin to the resistance that had "appeared when Darwin's

'Origin of Species' was first published" (p. v), and because "behaviorism is treading on the hoof of somebody's sacred cow . . . it is threatening the established order of things" (p. vi).

One of Watson's predictions turned out to be correct for a period of time. Behaviorism became the dominant perspective, at least in American psychology, during the first half of the 20th century. Unlike Darwin's *Origin of Species,* however, Watson's *Behaviorism* and other behaviorist writings did not stand the test of time or evidence. It is fortunate, I believe, that the functionalists, Gestaltists, structuralists, and even psychoanalysts did not fold their tents in the wake of the behaviorists' proclamations. Alternative perspectives, theoretical orientations, and research agendas were pursued and, in their offshoots, have proved longer lasting. An interesting question is whether the dominance of behaviorism is attributable to the evidence provided by their research or to the influence of proclamations about the wave of the future. I suspect that the answer is both. Behaviorists did emphasize experimental work and provided a wealth of data (much of it with nonhumans) that influenced many. However, much of the research, especially as it applies to humans, appears to be flawed (see Chomsky, 1959). It is, of course, extremely difficult to estimate the influences of proselytizing by scholars like John Watson.

The types of proclamations and proselytizing evident in Watson's writings continued in the latter part of the 20th century. We have seen it among some proponents of evolutionary psychology and cultural psychology—a contemporary version of the debates about heredity and environment regarded as settled by the behaviorists. Consider proclamations from proponents of each approach. A number of years ago the leading proponent of sociobiology (a precursor to evolutionary psychology), E. O. Wilson (1975), predicted that the social sciences and the humanities would become branches of "neo-Darwinist evolutionary theory." Although that prediction has not panned out in the way Wilson stated so confidently, some evolutionary psychologists claim that matters regarding the evolutionary and genetic bases of many social and personality traits are settled (see Wright, 1994). They assert that many aspects of social relationships, individual dispositions, and morality are based on evolutionary processes. For instance, altruism, conscience, and the sense of justice "can now confidently be said to have a firm genetic basis" (Wright, 1994, p. 12). As a means of conveying the universality of behaviors and social relationships, they also claim that evolutionary psychologists are demonstrating that there is a "psychic unity" to humankind. These claims come with the familiar warnings: "The new Darwinian social scientists are fighting a doctrine that has dominated their fields for much of this century: the idea that biology doesn't matter much—that the uniquely malleable human mind, together with the force of culture, has severed our behavior from its evolutionary roots; that there is no inherent human nature driving human events, but that, rather, our essential nature is to be driven" (Wright, 1994, p. 5).

However, some proponents of another influential movement—cultural psychology (e.g., Shweder, 1990)—have proclaimed a new paradigm that is the wave of the future, to replace, or at least subsume, many social scientific disciplines and subfields of psychology (including developmental psychology). Cultural psychologists say that we now know that cultural traditions and practices regulate and express thoughts, emotions, and actions. Cultural psychology has demonstrated divergence in psychological functioning, so it is futile to search for the psychic unity of humankind (Shweder, 1990; Shweder & Sullivan, 1993). They warn, of course, that because of the vested interests in the dominant paradigm, which is wedded to the proposition of psychic unity and universal psychological processes, the new paradigm will face stiff resistance.

In these proclamations we have, at once, striking similarities and clear differences. The similarities are that each asserts that a dominant paradigm is being displaced by a new paradigm and that proponents of the old paradigm will resist change. The difference, of course, is that the views of what is old and new are opposite.

In addition to proclamations about the settled state of the theoretical direction of the science, we have been subjected to proselytizing with regard to topics that should and should not be studied. Recently, persistent, vociferous calls for the study of "positive psychology" have also influenced funding for research (or is it that funding sources have influenced the positive psychology movement?). As with most proselytizing, these calls invoke supposed ills of the past and of the dominant approach. In this case the claim is that psychology has focused almost exclusively on the negative: maladjustment, mental illness, adversity, conflict, aggression, class conflict, and so on. The call is for research that accentuates the positive, put sometimes in grandiose terms: "Entering a new millennium, Americans face a historical choice. Left alone on the pinnacle of economic and political leadership, the United States can continue to increase its material wealth while ignoring the human needs of its people and those of the rest of the planet. Such a course is likely to lead to increasing selfishness, to alienation between the more or less fortunate, and eventually to chaos and despair" (Seligman & Csikszentmihalyi, 2000, p. 5).

Psychology to the rescue: "The social and behavioral sciences can play an enormously important role. They can articulate a vision of the good life that is empirically sound while being understandable and attractive" (p. 5).

If psychology has not been positive, how is it divined that it can articulate a vision that is empirically sound? An empirical science leads to where it leads and, it is hoped, not to a preordained outcome influenced by what researchers have great stake in finding. Nevertheless, the call is for empirical study of the good life, "a science that takes as its primary task the understanding of what makes life worth living" (Seligman & Csikszentmihalyi, 2000, p. 13). And the prediction is "that positive psychology in this new century will allow psychologists to understand and build those factors that allow individuals, communities, and societies to flourish" (p. 13). These goals will come to fruition if we abandon the predominant concerns with the negative and study instead positive features such as well-being, love, compassion, happiness, harmony, hope, play, responsibility, nurturance, and altruism.

So what is my point? I wish to stress that it is not to argue for eclecticism or relativism. I do believe that researchers should take strong positions within a particular perspective and that it is important to formulate coherent theoretical perspectives. These could emphasize evolution, culture, some coherent combination of the two, or other alternatives, such as a constructivism connected to the interaction of the individual with the environment. Nor do I mean to imply that researchers should not pursue topics that they deem important, such as those they label positive.

However, we do the field a disservice when we substitute the type of proselytizing that comes with assertions about the wave of the future in place of careful research, detailed discussion of the evidence, consideration of the merits of a theoretical perspective, critiques of the substance of alternative theoretical perspectives, and openness to study of a range of topics. All these scholarly and scientific activities contrast with proclamations and proselytizing that continue to occur in psychology with sufficient frequency to impede progress. Progress may be impeded because the state of knowledge within the favored perspective is overblown and it is prematurely claimed that scientific matters are settled. Progress also may be impeded by what must give a false impression of the context of existing knowledge. In these particular examples it cannot be simultaneously true that the dominant paradigm is biological, at the expense of the cultural, and that the dominant view is cultural, at the expense of the biological. An accurate portrayal of the context for our work does matter.

It seems to me that if people centrally involved in psychological research draw opposite conclusions about what is known, it is likely to mean that matters are not settled. In turn, this means that we must be very cautious about reflecting on past achievements and drawing inferences for future directions. Nevertheless, I do think that it is useful, in a measured way, to consider earlier contributions and needed directions. So I will offer some of my own.

Not surprisingly, I will draw primarily from areas of my own research, which include social and moral development, as well as their relations to cultural practices and societal arrangements (Turiel, 2002). In reflecting upon developmental psychology more generally, I believe we need to look to explanations that go beyond genetically based traits, unidirectional influences of culture or experiences, and features seen as positive. The evidence from several areas of investigation suggests that development is a constructive process, broadly defined, stemming from the individual's interactions with a multiplicity of experiences. As is well known, Piaget originally proposed a view of development based on construction. Now a number of researchers are proposing different types of constructive processes in the cognitive and social realms (see a compilation of articles on this topic in Langer & Turiel, 2002). The multiplicity of children's experiences involves interpretations and constructions of meanings that produce the development of a heterogeneous set of nonsocial and social categories, or domains of thinking. Human thought is flexible (Turiel & Perkins, 2004) in that people approach the world in ways that allow them to reflect upon existing conditions and work toward transformation and change (more about this shortly). Such conceptual activities indicate that development is not preformed by biology, nor is it predetermined by social conditions (including culture).

In research on social development these propositions are supported by two interrelated trends—trends that should be attended to in thinking about accomplishments and future challenges. One stems from findings of mutuality and reciprocity in social interactions, such that influences upon children and adolescents cannot be characterized as unidirectional. To put it simply, young people keep demonstrating that they do not just accommodate to others or to environmental pressures. And it is not the case that young people fail to accommodate because they assert their self-interests. A second trend stems from findings that, starting at a young age, children display judgments, emotions, and actions that are not based on self-interest or the gratification of needs. They engage in cooperative and prosocial activities, act in altruistic ways, and experience other-directed emotions such as empathy and sympathy.

All these activities involve positive features. It is, therefore, unclear, to say the least, why proponents of the positive psychology movement assert that the need for a shift "from preoccupation only with repairing the worst things in life to also building positive qualities" (Seligman & Csikszentmihalyi, 2000, p. 5). Indeed, the very concept of development can be seen as positive. Moreover, many other topics traditionally studied by developmental psychologists would fit the label of "positive." These include the many investigations of play, curiosity, exploration, cooperation, altruism, empathy, justice, welfare, rights, and care.

However, the "negative" still looms large. Developmental studies in the latter part of the 20th century also showed that children are not exclusively sociable or positive. Children display opposition to others, engage in socially prohibited acts, and assert their personal interests. Oppositional activities coexist (in the same children) with positive actions and emotions. In the interactions of children and adults there is an interweaving of social harmony and social conflict.

We cannot and should not ignore topics such as conflict and opposition. These are not the inventions of psychologists, and it would be folly to ignore such topics either as scientists or in efforts to improve the conditions of people or societies. Furthermore, seemingly negative activities, such as conflict, opposition, and resistance, can be (and often are) necessary to achieve positive goals, given the social conditions in one's world. It cannot be expected that people or societies will be fulfilled and that communities will "thrive" in conditions of serious injustices and human suffering. In an interesting reversal of how the positive psychology movement couched matters, Martin Luther King Jr. once castigated psychologists for a failure to attend to social problems. In an invited address to the meeting of the American Psychological Association in 1967, King maintained that psychologists paid too much attention to social adaptation and adjustment and said that they need to attend to ways in which "maladjustment" is necessary and morally beneficial. As he put it, "There are some things in our society, some things in our world, to which we should never be adjusted. There are some things to which we must always be maladjusted if we are to be people of good will" (King, 1968, p. 185).

In that perspective it makes little sense to draw a dichotomy between the positive and negative since conditions in the world make for an interweaving in social orientations, as reflected in a statement by Martin Luther King Jr. in another context (while in jail in 1963 for leading a nonviolent demonstration in Birmingham, Alabama): "I have earnestly worked and preached against violent tension, but there is a type of constructive tension that is necessary for growth . . . to create the kind of tension in society that will help men to rise from the dark depths of prejudice and racism to the majestic heights of understanding and brotherhood" (n.d., p. 5).

Of course, Martin Luther King Jr. most frequently discussed and confronted problems of racial prejudice that were not easily resolved (and certainly not by proclaiming that we must look to the positive): "We know from painful experience that freedom is never voluntarily given by the oppressor; it must be demanded by the oppressed. . . . Oppressed people cannot remain oppressed forever. The urge for freedom will come. This is what happened to the American Negro" (King, n.d., pp. 6, 12). Racial prejudice and exclusion certainly are not the only problems of this sort. Problems have long applied to relationships between people of different social castes or classes, and to women, who are most often treated unequally and hold positions of lesser power than men in the social hierarchy. Martha Nussbaum, a philosopher who has studied the plight of women in developing countries, stated the problem in seemingly starkly negative terms: "Women in much of the world lack support for fundamental functions of life. They are less well nourished than men, less healthy, and more vulnerable to physical violence and sexual abuse. They are much less likely than men to be literate. . . . Women have fewer opportunities than men to live free from fear and to enjoy rewarding types of love—especially when, as often happens, they are married without choice in childhood and have no recourse from bad marriages" (Nussbaum, 2000, p. 1).

I believe that the serious social problems identified by Martin Luther King Jr., Martha Nussbaum, and many others pose challenges for researchers of social development. We tend to approach social development as involving cooperation or the formulation of moral prescriptions and actions that make for harmonious social relationships. Researchers have examined awareness of and adherence to norms, customs, and cultural practices. Researchers have also looked at the formation of judgments about a number of moral issues, such as judgments about justice, fairness, rights, caring, and helping. However, we have not been sufficiently concerned with individuals' moral judgments about inequalities, power differences, and practices that benefit some groups to the detriment of other groups (as evident in Nussbaum's characterization of the role and plight of women). Additionally, there is little research on the effect on children's social and moral development of living in conditions of injustice and suffering.

My colleagues and I have, in recent years, begun to explore some of these issues through studies of how people think about cultural practices and societal arrangements that involve inequalities and power differences (Turiel, 2002, 2003; Turiel & Perkins, 2004; Wainryb & Turiel, 1994). The general findings are that children, adolescents, and adults approach their culture with the type of scrutiny that leads them to both accept and critique cultural practices. Social judgments and actions entail, in many instances, opposition, resistance, and subversion. In their everyday lives people come into conflict with others and resist what they perceive to be moral wrongs embedded in practices that serve to further the interests of those in higher positions on the social hierarchy.

I wish to emphasize that opposition, resistance, and subversion are part of people's everyday lives and are not restricted to organized social or political movements or to people with special characteristics (Turiel, 2003). Beginning in childhood, moral judgments of justice and concerns for the welfare and rights of others bring conflicts and opposition in the face of injustices.

There is now enough research in psychology and other social sciences (e.g., Abu-Lughod, 1993; Wikan, 1996) to support the proposition that social opposition and resistance stand alongside harmonious relationships—all as part of the fabric of social lives and communities. Moral and social development are processes of opposing, struggling, and engaging in conflicts, as well as processes of getting along with others. This is not the place to review the findings. I will illustrate with a nonresearch example that comes from recent events in Afghanistan after the fall of the Taliban in late 2001. It is well known that the Taliban imposed severe restrictions on people's activities, banning most forms of entertainment. The restrictions imposed on women were the most severe. Women were confined to their homes unless accompanied by a male relative; when venturing out, women were required to be totally covered by a burka. Females were denied schooling and work.

Immediately after the fall of the Taliban, many women and men felt a striking sense of liberation. As told in media accounts, the reaction was strong and swift. People made widespread use of previously banned objects (e.g., videos, televisions, VCRs, musical instruments), and women mobilized to reopen schools for girls and began looking for work. These actions reveal that the people of Afghanistan had all along engaged in acts of resistance and subversion. They engaged in acts of resistance through deception by hiding the banned objects—which they brought out when it was safe to do so. Women too had engaged in subversive behavior by, for example, running secret schools for girls in their homes.

The examples of how the people of Afghanistan defied and resisted restrictions placed on them are paralleled in many other places. It has been documented that girls and women typically act to get around what they consider to be unfair restrictions and unequal treatment in Western and non-Western societies (Bumiller, 1990; Goodwin, 1994; Nussbaum, 2000; Turiel, 2002; Wikan, 1996, 2002). One of our challenges, then, is to identify the ways societies or cultures are structured with injustices, harm, and even oppression and to make the study of such conditions central in attempts to understand social development. This is not to say that research on problems of justice and inequality is nonexistent. For example, there has been valuable research on the psychology of racial prejudice for a long time. However, very little research has been done on the judgments that people make about injustices in social systems or how they act upon their judgments in efforts to counteract and change social conditions. Since injustices often involve differences in power and privileges between groups (e.g., social class, race, gender), it is especially important to examine the perspectives of those in positions of lesser power and status in social hierarchies. I do not propose that study of these topics and perspectives should displace other topics of interest. However, I do believe these are important and neglected topics. And I venture the prediction that studies of how people in different positions in the social hierarchy think about societal arrangements and cultural practices will lead to transformations of those theories of social development that emphasize compliance and the internalization of societal norms, or the regulation and expression of thoughts and emotions by cultural traditions and practices, or the genetic basis of altruism and a sense of justice.

References

Abu-Lughod, L. (1993). *Writing women's worlds: Bedouin stories.* Berkeley: University of California Press.

Bumiller, E. (1990). *May you be the mother of a hundred sons: A journey among the women of India.* New York: Oxford University Press.

Chomsky, N. (1959). A review of B. F. Skinner's *Verbal Behavior. Language, 35,* 26–58.

Goodwin, J. (1994). *The price of honor: Muslim women lift the veil of silence on the Islamic world.* New York: Norton.

King, M. L., Jr. (n.d.). Letter from a Birmingham jail. In *Loving your enemies, Letter from a Birmingham jail, Declaration of independence from the war in Vietnam.* A. J. Muste Memorial Essay Series, #1. Nyack, NY: Fellowship of Reconciliation.

King, M. L., Jr. (1968). The role of the behavioral scientist in the civil rights movement. *American Psychologist, 23,* 180–186.

Langer, J., & Turiel, E. (Eds.). (2002, September–December). Constructivism today. Special issue, *Cognitive Development, 17.*

Nussbaum, M. C. (2000). *Women and human development: The capabilities approach.* Cambridge, England: Cambridge University Press.

Seligman, E. P., & Csikszentmihalyi, M. (2000). Positive psychology: An introduction. *American Psychologist, 55,* 5–14.

Shweder, R. A. (1990). Cultural psychology—What is it? In J. W. Stigler, R. A. Shweder, & G. Herdt (Eds.), *Cultural psychology: Essays on comparative human development* (pp. 1–43). Cambridge, England: Cambridge University Press.

Shweder, R. A., & Sullivan, M. A. (1993). Cultural psychology: Who needs it? *Annual Review of Psychology, 44,* 497–523.

Turiel, E. (2002). *The culture of morality: Social development, context, and conflict.* Cambridge, England: Cambridge University Press.

Turiel, E. (2003). Resistance and subversion in everyday life. *Journal of Moral Education, 32,* 115–130.

Turiel, E., & Perkins, S. A. (2004). Flexibilities of mind: Conflict and culture. *Human Development, 47,* 158–178.

Wainryb, C., & Turiel, E. (1994). Dominance, subordination, and concepts of personal entitlements in cultural contexts. *Child Development, 65,* 1701–1722.

Watson, J. B. (1924). *Behaviorism.* New York: People's Institute.

Wikan, U. (1996). *Tomorrow, God willing: Self-made destinies in Cairo.* Chicago: University of Chicago Press.

Wikan, U. (2002). *Generous betrayal: Politics of culture in the new Europe.* Chicago: University of Chicago Press.

Wilson, E. O. (1975). *Sociobiology: The new synthesis.* Cambridge, MA: Harvard University Press.

Wright, R. (1994). *The moral animal: The new science of evolutionary psychology.* New York: Pantheon.

Early Child Care
The Known and the Unknown

Deborah Lowe Vandell

The second half of the 20th century witnessed substantial changes in the lives of young children as maternal employment increased and more children participated in nonparental care arrangements. The available evidence indicates that these care arrangements vary widely in quality, amount, and type (NICHD ECCRN, 1996, 2000a; U.S. Census Bureau, 2003). These variations and the large number of children in care (more than 10 million children in the United States in 1999) have raised several questions: Does quality of early child care matter? Do amount and timing of early child care matter? Does type of early child care matter? Answers to these questions are important for parents and policy makers who are interested in the individual and collective well-being of children. The answers also are important for developmental theory because of their relevance to such fundamental issues in the discipline as the role of early versus later experience and the efficacy of enrichment and intervention efforts.

In this chapter I have two goals. The first is to summarize the converging research evidence with respect to the three questions about child care. The evidence from scores of studies represents what we know about the effects of child care on child developmental outcomes. The evidence that I present is not exhaustive but illustrative. My second goal is to consider areas that are unresolved or have not yet been examined. These unknowns, I believe, represent the next steps for child care research.

The need for data to address the questions about early child care was one reason that the National Institute of Child Health and Human Development (NICHD) funded the Study of Early Child Care (SECC) (NICHD ECCRN, 2001c). Key elements in the design of the study included a sample sufficiently large ($n = 1,364$) to detect effects; a diverse sample that included children of color (24%), mothers with less than a high school education (11%), and single-parent households (14%); robust longitudinal measures of child care quality, amount, timing, and type (e.g., center, family day care home, nanny); measures of children's social, cognitive, and language development, obtained during infancy, early childhood, and middle childhood by multiple methods; extensive family measures collected shortly after the child's birth to use as controls for selection bias; and longitudinal family assessments to evaluate changes in family functioning in response to child care.

The NICHD Early Child Care Research Network, the name adopted by the investigators who work collectively on papers from the SECC, has now considered the effects of quality, amount and timing, and types of care in a series of papers that examined children's attachment to mother (1997b, 2001b), mother-child interactions (1999a, 2003c), peer interactions (2001a), behavior problems (1998, 2002b, 2003a), social competence (1998, 2002b, 2003c), and cognitive, language, and preacademic performance (2000b, 2002b). Other investigators (Brooks-Gunn, Han, & Waldfogel, 2002; Sagi, Koren-Karie, Gini, Ziv, & Joels, 2002) have used the SECC data set to address related questions. Instructions for obtaining copies of the public use data set are available at http://secc.rti.org/.

In addition to the SECC, other large, multisite studies include the Cost, Quality, and Outcomes Study (Peisner-Feinberg et al., 2001), the Family and Relative Care Study (Kontos, Howes, Shinn, & Galinsky, 1995), the National Day Care Study (Ruopp, Travers, Glantz, & Coelen, 1979), and the Child-Care Staffing Study (Howes, Phillips, & Whitebook, 1992). These studies have focused on particular types of care.

Challenges and Cautions

Before I examine the progress in answering the child care questions, I should note several overarching challenges and accompanying cautions. The first is that most child care research is correlational. As is the case with any correlational evidence, sample selection and omitted variables may explain the results. For example, if educationally minded parents place their children in more cognitively stimulating child care settings, these preexisting family differences may explain an apparent relation between cognitively stimulating child care and children's academic skills. Or, if parents place children who are challenging or difficult in child care for more hours than less difficult children, this preexisting child difference may explain a relation between child care hours and problem behaviors. The challenge, then, is to reduce the likelihood that these other factors explain child care effects.

One way of addressing this problem has been to adopt experimental designs in which children are randomly assigned to child care of varying types and quality. In several studies that are discussed later in this chapter (e.g., F. A. Campbell & Ramey, 1994; Schweinhart, Weikart, & Larner, 1986), experimental designs were used to examine the effects of high-quality center-based programs for children who were at risk for school failure. In other research also to be reviewed (Ruopp et al., 1979), two aspects of child care quality—child-adult ratio and caregiver education and training—were experimentally manipulated to determine their effects on children's cognitive and social functioning. To my knowledge, no one has studied the effects of amount/timing in an experimental study.

In the absence of random assignment experiments, researchers have adopted other strategies to minimize selection bias and omitted variables. One strategy, which was first used in the 1980s and has since become standard practice, is to include family and child measures as covariates. The early studies typically controlled for a limited number of demographic factors such as maternal education and child gender. Recent research, however, has incorporated extensive covariates.

In the SECC (NICHD ECCRN & Duncan, 2003) the sizes of child care coefficients were compared in statistical analyses that included no covariates, a limited number of family and child covariates, and extensive covariates. The size of the child care coefficients was substantially reduced when the demographic covariates were added to the base model, indicating that the base model containing no covariates was biased. The inclusion of more extensive measures of family functioning in addition to the demographic variables, in contrast, resulted in little or no change in the size of the child care coefficients, suggesting that it was unlikely that unobserved family characteristics could account for the obtained child care effects.

Although the use of multiple covariates reduces the likelihood that obtained relations can be explained by omitted variables, it has its own limitations. Because only the unique variance is attributed to child care and all shared variance is attributed to other factors, the strategy yields a conservative estimate of effects. Thus investigators may be controlling for and thereby removing the very effects of interest (Newcomb, 2003).

Another strategy to minimize the likelihood that omitted or

unmeasured factors account for obtained child care effects has been to use children's earlier performance as a control. Analyses of this sort used in the SECC (NICHD ECCRN& Duncan, 2003) and the Cost, Quality, and Outcomes Study (Peisner-Feinberg et al., 2001) have asked whether quality, amount/timing, or type of care predict a particular child developmental outcome when the child's earlier performance is included as a covariate. These residual change analyses are better able to adjust for observed and unobserved factors but have less power than simply controlling for family and child demographic factors.

A second challenge is that child care is a complex phenomenon that varies along multiple dimensions. Because research initially focused on quality or type or amount, it was not possible to ascertain whether ostensible effects of quality were actually effects of quantity or type or whether ostensible effects of quantity could be explained by the type or quality of the care. Consequently, recent research such as the SECC has sought to examine effects of one aspect of care while controlling for other aspects.

A third challenge and caution is (obviously) that our research evidence is based on the particular samples of children who have been studied in child care of particular quality, amount, and type. If families with impoverished circumstances (or more affluent circumstances) are not included in research studies, our ability to understand child care effects in those circumstances is reduced. Understanding the effects of child care also requires sampling across the full array of child care variations. We are likely to underestimate child care effects if analyses are based on a restricted range of quality, hours, or types of care. One reason that research studies conducted in Sweden generally failed to find quality effects may be that the quality was uniformly high. Consistent with this point, Sagi and colleagues (2002) noted that the child-adult ratio in centers was not related to attachment security in separate analyses involving the NICHD SECC and the Haifa Study of Early Child Care. However, when they combined the two samples and tested a broader range of child-adult ratios, they detected relations between ratios and attachment. In the SECC it is likely that the effects associated with quality were underestimated because refusal rates were higher for informal care settings and settings that were caring for children of low-income families. Consistent with this point, cognitive and language scores were lower in children who had attended child care settings that refused to participate in assessments of child care quality (NICHD ECCRN & Duncan, 2003).

With these challenges, limitations, and caveats in mind, let us now consider the first of our three questions.

Does Quality of Child Care Matter?

An indication of our progress in addressing the quality question is clear when we recall Belsky and Steinberg's classic review, published in 1978. In that review of the extant literature of the time, about 40 studies, Belsky and Steinberg observed, "Our actual knowledge of its [day care's] effects is exceedingly limited. Generally investigations have been conducted within high-quality centers which are not representative of most substitute-care environments" (p. 929). This dearth of research led them to conclude, "The findings from existing research on day care may not be generalizable to the kind and quality of care available to most of the nation's families" (p. 930).

The need to understand the effects of child care quality motivated much of the research during the next 25 years. Early studies by Clarke-Stewart (1987), Howes (1983), Phillips, McCartney, and Scarr (1987), and Vandell and Powers (1983) observed children in child care and recorded their experiences. High-quality child care was conceptualized as involving supportive interactions with caregivers, positive interactions with peers, and opportunities for cognitively stimulating play, whereas poor-quality care was conceptualized as involving negative interactions with caregivers and peers and aimless wandering. From these and other studies during this period, process quality came to refer to the experiences that children have with caregivers, peers, and materials.

Further progress in addressing the quality question occurred with the development and adoption of a common set of measures of process quality. The Early Care Environment Rating Scale (ECERS; Harms & Clifford, 1980) consists of 7-point ratings of the social, language, reasoning, and physical environment in child care centers. The Infant/Toddler Environment Rating Scale (ITERS; Harms, Cryer, & Clifford, 1990) and the Family Day Care Rating Scale (FDCRS; Harms & Clifford, 1989) are related measures of center-based care for children less than 2 1/2 years and child care homes, respectively. The Observational Record of the Caregiving Environment, developed by the SECC (NICHD ECCRN, 1996, 2000a) assesses process quality in all types of care using time-sampled behavioral counts of caregiver actions, peer interactions, and child activities as well as qualitative ratings of caregivers' behaviors. Age-appropriate versions are available for infants, toddlers, and preschoolers. Quality also is measured by structural/caregiver characteristics such as child-adult ratio and caregivers' training and education.

Motivated by the policy question of how to improve process quality, and the search for easy-to-monitor indicators, researchers have considered relations between structural/caregiver characteristics and process quality. Consistent findings have emerged from this work (Committee on Family and Work Policies, 2003; Vandell & Wolfe, 2000). In settings in which child-adult ratios are lower, caregivers spend less time managing children in their classrooms and children are less apathetic and distressed (Ruopp et al., 1979); caregivers are more stimulating, responsive, warm, and supportive (NICHD ECCRN, 1996, 2000a); and process quality scores are higher (NICHD ECCRN, 1996, 2000a; Phillips, Mekow, Scarr, McCartney, & Abbott-Shim, 2000).

The number of children in the group also is associated with process quality. In multivariate analyses that controlled for child-adult ratio, caregiver training, and caregiver education, the NICHD Early Child Care Research Network (1996, 2000a) found that caregivers were more responsive, socially stimulating, and less restrictive when fewer children were in the group. Process quality also is higher in child care homes that are in compliance with recommended age-weighted group sizes (Clarke-Stewart, Vandell, Burchinal, O'Brien, & McCartney, 2002).

Caregivers' education—both formal education and specialized training—also is related to process quality. Caregivers tend to be more stimulating, warm, and supportive; organize materials better; and provide more age-appropriate experiences when they have more formal education and more child-related training (Burchinal, Cryer, Clifford, & Howes, 2002; Clarke-Stewart et al., 2002; NICHD ECCRN, 1996, 2000a; Phillips, Mekow, et al., 2000). Two experimental studies—the National Child Care Study (Ruopp et al., 1979) and the Florida Child Care Improvement Project (Howes, 1997)—have provided evidence of causal relationships between structural/caregiver characteristics and process quality.

CHILD CARE QUALITY
AND CHILD DEVELOPMENTAL OUTCOMES

The development of measures of child care quality paved the way to examine the effects of quality on child developmental outcomes in a series of three logically related propositions (NICHD ECCRN,

2000a). The first proposition is that quality, measured by structural/caregiver characteristics and process quality, is related to child functioning in the child care setting. The second proposition is that child care quality is related to (influences) children's concurrent functioning in other settings such as home or lab. And the third proposition is that child care quality is related to (influences) children's long-term child developmental outcomes.

CHILD CARE QUALITY
AND CHILD BEHAVIOR IN CHILD CARE

A recent review by the National Academy of Sciences (Committee on Family and Work Policies, 2003) reported six studies as finding relations between process quality and children's behavior in the child care setting, and six studies as finding relations between structural/caregiver characteristics and child behavior in the child care setting. To summarize these findings, children appeared happier and more securely attached to caregivers in care settings in which process quality was higher and adult-child ratios were lower. Children appeared more prosocial and positively engaged with peers when caregivers were sensitive and positive to them and when child-adult ratios were lower. Children were rated as more cognitively competent during free play in child care settings that offered more opportunities for art, blocks, and dramatic play and in settings in which caregivers had college degrees and more early childhood training.

Recent research also has related child care quality to physiological measures (Dettling, Parker, Lane, Sebanc, & Gunnar, 2000). Children who attended child care homes that were higher in quality showed decreases in cortisol from morning to afternoon, whereas children who attended poorer quality child care homes showed increases in cortisol from morning to afternoon. This rise is the opposite of the typical pattern for circadian rhythm of cortisol, but it is similar to a rise across the workday that has been recorded in adult executives who were under high pressure at work.

Thus research suggests that children who attend higher-quality child care are exposed to different environments and hence engage in different behaviors and activities than children who attend poorer-quality child care. The next question is whether variations in quality are related to child functioning in other contexts.

Child care quality and concurrent cognitive and social development

Twenty-three studies were cited by the National Academy's Committee on Family and Work Policies (2003) as finding relations between process quality and children's cognitive and socioemotional development in other contexts, after controlling for family and child background factors. In particular, the committee noted that children whose care was higher in process quality scored higher on concurrently administered language and cognitive tests, had fewer behavior problems, and were more socially competent. Since the report was prepared, other investigators (Loeb, Fuller, Kagan, & Carrol, 2004; Love et al., 2003) also have found higher-quality care (measured by the ECERS and FDCRS) to be associated with better cognitive performance and fewer behavior problems.

The Committee on Family and Work Policies (2003) cited 14 studies in relation to structural/caregiver characteristics and child developmental outcomes. For example, the NICHD Early Child Care Research Network (1999b) found positive developmental outcomes, controlling for maternal education and parenting quality, when children attended centers that were in compliance with the American Public Health Association's recommended structural and caregiver guidelines. Children who attended centers that met child-adult ratio standards displayed fewer behavior problems and more positive social behaviors according to their mothers than children whose centers did not meet the standard recommended. When centers met the guidelines for specialized training and education for staff, children exhibited fewer behavior problems and obtained higher school readiness and language comprehension scores. In subsequent analyses at 4 1/2 years, larger group sizes were associated with lower academic achievement and lower cognitive development, and higher caregiver education was related to higher cognitive development and higher academic achievement, controlling for family factors and children's previous cognitive functioning (NICHD ECCRN & Duncan, 2003). Similar relations between structural/caregiver characteristics and child developmental outcomes have been found in child care homes (Clarke-Stewart et al., 2002).

Child developmental outcomes also have been examined in relation to aggregated structural/caregiver characteristics. Some programs, for example, trade off teacher training and group size by having teachers who have more training and education care for more children, whereas other programs have highly trained teachers assigned to fewer children. And in still other programs, centers fail to meet any recommended standards. In the SECC (NICHD ECCRN, 1999b), children who attended centers that met more standards had fewer behavior problems and higher school readiness and language comprehension scores. In these analyses, for example, 3-year-olds who attended centers that met none of the guidelines scored 14 points below the mean of the norming sample for the Bracken Basic Concept Scale, whereas 3-year-olds in centers that met all four standards scored 2 points above the mean of the norming sample, a 16-point difference.

The available experimental evidence indicates causal relations between child care quality and child developmental outcomes. In the National Day Care Study (Ruopp et al., 1979) preschoolers who were assigned to classrooms in which teachers had more education and training displayed greater gains in cooperative behavior, task persistence, and school readiness over a 9-month period relative to children assigned to classrooms in which teachers had less education and training.

Child care quality and longer-term outcomes

Eighteen studies cited by the Committee on Family and Work Policies (2003) examined relations between child care quality and children's subsequent development. Relations were more evident in studies that had assessed quality at several points in time (Burchinal, Roberts, et al., 2000; NICHD ECCRN, 2000b, 2002b) and less evident in studies that relied on a single assessment (Chin-Quee & Scarr, 1994; Deater-Deckard, Pinkerton, & Scarr, 1996). These discrepancies may be explained by the reliability of the child care scores. Because children often experience several care arrangements, longitudinal assessments of quality probably yielded more accurate indications of quality.

In the SECC (NICHD ECCRN, 2000b, 2002b, 2003b, 2005) cumulative measures of caregiver behavior as measured by the Observational Record of the Caregiving Environment predicted children's performance on standardized cognitive and language assessments through third grade (age 8 1/2 years), controlling for amount and type of care and an extensive list of family covariates. In the Cost, Quality, and Outcomes Study, a prospective longitudinal study of 579 children who attended 151 centers, process quality as measured by the Early Care Environment Rating Scale predicted cognitive, language, and social development during the early grade-school years (Peisner-Feinberg et al., 2001). Children who had closer relationships with their preschool teachers were more sociable in kindergarten, controlling for earlier child adjustment and family factors, and children who were enrolled in higher-quality child care displayed better math skills before they began school and during kindergarten and second grade. In other analyses from the Cost, Quality, and Outcome Study, children who had closer relationships with their caregivers at age 4 years were reported by their second-grade teachers to be more socially competent with peers, controlling for family factors and previous child functioning (Howes, 2000).

Relations between structural/caregiver characteristics and children's subsequent social and cognitive development also have been reported. Howes (1988), for example, found relations between structural/caregiver characteristics (teacher training, child-adult ratio, group size, a planned curriculum, and space) at age 3 years and children's functioning in first grade. Children whose early care met more structural/caregiver guidelines had fewer behavior problems and better work habits in comparison with children whose early care met fewer guidelines, controlling for family factors. In a different sample, children were rated as more difficult by preschool teachers and as more hostile by kindergarten teachers when they had a history of poor-quality care, as measured by a composite score of structural/caregiver characteristics (child-adult ratio, caregiver training, caregiver stability) at 18, 24, 30, and 36 months (Howes, 1990).

Thus the available evidence indicates that child care quality is related to child developmental outcomes during the elementary school years. We do not know whether these relations are maintained after this period, disappear, or are magnified over time.

How Large Are the Effects of Quality?

In addition to considering statistical significance, it is informative to consider the practical significance of effects (McCartney & Rosenthal, 2000). One way of evaluating practical significance is to compare the size of an obtained effect to other effects, such as parenting and poverty, that are believed to be important. In the case of cognitive functioning, effect sizes (d) associated with child care quality in the SECC were 0.39 for school readiness and 0.44 for expressive language at 36 months, whereas effect sizes for parenting and home quality were roughly twice as large, 0.83 and 1.01, respectively (NICHD ECCRN, 1999c). For children's preacademic skills at 54 months, the effect size (d) of child care quality was 0.39, and the effect size of poverty was 0.83. Thus the child care effects were roughly half the size of parenting and poverty. Against these benchmarks one can conclude that effects associated with child care quality are meaningful.

ARE QUALITY EFFECTS MODERATED BY CHILD AND FAMILY CHARACTERISTICS?

In addition to the main effects that I have already described, investigators have identified some instances of moderated effects. In some domains poor-quality care appears to function as a risk factor. For example, in the SECC low-quality care, coupled with low maternal sensitivity, was associated with insecure infant-mother attachment relationships (NICHD ECCRN, 1997b). In other cases, high-quality child care served as a protective factor for children who were otherwise at risk. In the SECC children of depressed mothers appeared to be more positively engaged with their mothers at age 4 1/2 years and first grade when they attended higher-quality child care (NICHD ECCRN, 2003c). In analyses of school readiness, receptive language, and expressive language, higher-quality child care was found to buffer young children from the negative effects of family poverty (McCartney, Dearing, & Taylor, 2003).

NEXT STEPS

The recent findings pertaining to the effects of child care quality are consistent with the summary conclusions of Lamb and Ahnert in the 2006 *Handbook of Child Psychology* that high-quality child care is linked to positive intellectual, verbal, and cognitive development, and that children receiving high-quality care have superior relationship skills, whereas children receiving poor-quality care have deficient skills. Furthermore, evidence from multiple studies of relations between structural/caregiver characteristics and process quality provide guidance for ways to support or improve quality.

At the same time a number of unknowns with regard to child care quality warrant further study. First, researchers have examined effects of quality only through the primary grades (third grade). We do not know whether the effects associated with quality are maintained through middle childhood and adolescence. Second, we do not know how many children attend poor-quality child care in the United States or elsewhere because only convenience samples have been studied. Quality estimates derived from the NICHD SECC, however, suggest that child care quality is not high. Positive caregiving was rated as "not characteristic" in fully 60% of the settings that were observed, and only 10% of the settings were rated as excellent (NICHD ECCRN, 2000a). Representative surveys of child care quality, conducted at regular intervals to assess quality trends over time, are clearly needed.

In addition, we have not studied the effects of child care quality beyond its effect on individual children. Studies of the aggregated effects of child care quality on public school classrooms are needed to ascertain whether high-quality care serves as a springboard for classrooms to function well or whether poor-quality child care places classrooms at risk. It seems likely that classrooms containing more children who had attended high-quality child care will differ from classrooms containing a preponderance of children who had attended poor-quality child care. Finally, we do not know which sets of policies are the best to adopt if we want to improve child care quality or to support high-quality child care. A number of proposals (Blau, 2001; Helburn & Bergmann, 2002; Lombardi, 2003; Vandell & Wolfe, 2000) have been put forward, but these proposals have not been tested. Experimental studies are needed to test the effectiveness of different approaches for improving child care quality (both process quality and structural/caregiver characteristics) and to relate these strategies to child developmental outcomes. Evaluations of these alternative models will be strengthened by further collaboration of scholars in psychology, education, economics, and public policy.

Do Amount and Timing of Early Child Care Matter?

Questions about the effects of amount and timing are also central to child care research. Jay Belsky (1986, 1988, 2001) has played a central role in framing these questions. Citing evidence of relations between amount of early child care and children's noncompliance and aggression in the initial research (Baydar & Brooks-Gunn, 1991; Bates et al., 1994; Schwarz, Strickland, & Krolick, 1974; Vandell & Corasaniti, 1990), Belsky argued that early and extensive hours place young children at risk for socioemotional problems. Others, however, countered that these relations could be explained by the quality of the child care (Phillips, McCartney, Scarr, & Howes, 1987), differences in family background (Richters & Zahn-Waxler, 1990), or a failure to distinguish between avoidance and independence in assessments of infant attachment relationships and between child assertiveness and aggressiveness in assessments of older children (Clarke-Stewart, 1989). Because the initial research investigating amount and timing of care did not include measures of child care quality, assertion, or independence and controlled for few family factors, testing these different possibilities was not feasible. In recent years, however, researchers have adopted more comprehensive study designs that have enabled them to evaluate these alternative explanations.

Although researchers and policy makers are interested in understanding both the effects of amount of care and the effects of when care was initiated, the reality of child care participation, at least in the Unites States, makes it difficult to disentangle these effects. For example, 84% of the children in the SECC experienced nonmaternal care on a routine basis by 12 months (NICHD ECCRN, 1997a). Of this group, 72% entered care by 4 months. At first entry infants were in care for 29 hours a week, on average. Furthermore, once care was initiated, the amount of time spent in care on a weekly basis remained more or less stable throughout early childhood. Thus timing and amount of care are highly correlated.

Investigators who have studied the effects of these naturally occurring variations in amount and timing have approached the problem of colinearity in two ways: by focusing on either the amount or timing in their analyses but recognizing that some (most?) of the variance may be shared with the omitted variable, and by including both amount and timing in their analyses and recognizing that focusing only on unique variance may result in substantial underestimations of both effects. Much of the evidence reflects the combined effects of amount and timing.

ATTACHMENT SECURITY

A central question motivating child care research in the 1980s and 1990s was whether early and extensive child care increased the likelihood of children's developing insecure attachment relationships with their mothers. In the initial studies (see Barglow, Vaughn, & Molitor, 1987; Belsky & Rovine, 1988) elevated rates of insecure attachment were reported in children who experienced extensive child care during the first year. None of these studies, however, controlled for child care quality, and most did not control for potential family differences.

More recently the SECC (NICHD ECCRN, 1997b) examined relations between early and extensive child care and child attachment at 15 months, controlling for quality and type of child care and for family background, in a large sample of children ($n = 1,153$). The strongest predictors of attachment security were mother's observed sensitivity with the child at 6 and 15 months, and the mother's psychological adjustment. Amount of early child care was significant only in conjunction with maternal sensitivity: the likelihood of an insecure attachment increased only if children were in child care for more than 10 hours a week *and* mothers were highly insensitive. If mothers were sensitive, being in care for more than 10 hours a week was not related to attachment quality. A similar interaction was observed at 36 months ($n = 1,140$) (NICHD ECCRN, 2001b): high hours were associated with an ambivalent attachment only when mothers were insensitive.

QUALITY OF MOTHER-CHILD INTERACTION

Researchers also have considered associations between the amount of early child care and the quality of mother-child interaction. Related studies considered the effects of early maternal employment. Some of these studies reported amount of early care to be related to more negative mother-infant interactions (S. B. Campbell, Cohn, & Meyers, 1995; Owen & Cox, 1988). Others have found positive effects of amount of care on mother-child interaction (Crockenberg & Litman, 1991; Vandell, 1979), and still others found no effects (Burchinal, Bryant, Lee, & Ramey, 1992). Much of the initial research in this area, like other research of the time, was limited because of small sample sizes, few controls for family background, and a reliance on a single time of measurement.

Recent reports have sought to address these limitations. In the SECC mother-child interactions were observed at 6, 15, 24, and 36 months for more than 1,000 families. More hours in child care were associated with less maternal sensitivity and less child positive engagement with the mother, controlling for quality and type of child care, family income, maternal education, marital/partner status, maternal depressive symptoms, maternal separation anxiety, child gender, child temperament, and ethnicity. The effect size of child care hours (0.15) was similar to that of maternal depression and difficult child temperament but considerably smaller than the effect associated with maternal education (0.70).

In a follow-up report (NICHD ECCRN, 2003c) the study of relations between amount of child care and mother-child interaction was extended to age 4 1/2 years and first grade. At these later ages relations between hours and mother-child interaction were evident only for particular subsamples. Higher hours were associated with less maternal sensitivity and less positive engagement in white children but greater maternal sensitivity and more positive engagement in African American and Hispanic children.

The Wisconsin Maternity Leave and Health Project (Clark, Hyde, Essex, & Klein, 1997) contrasted the quality of mother-infant interaction at 4 months in 198 families in which mothers had 6 weeks versus 12 weeks of parental leave. Shorter leaves were associated with mothers' expressing more negative affect and negative behavior toward their infants. In addition, mothers were less likely to express positive affect to their infants when short leaves were combined with maternal depressive symptoms and difficult child temperament.

BEHAVIOR PROBLEMS

Amount of child care also has been considered in relation to children's socioemotional adjustment (behavior problems and social competence) in a series of reports in which child care quality and type as well as family factors were controlled. At age 2 years children who had spent more hours in child care were observed to have more negative interactions with peers (NICHD ECCRN, 2001a) and were reported by their caregivers to have more behavior problems and by their mothers to be less socially competent than children who had fewer hours in child care (NICHD ECCRN, 1998). At age 4 1/2 years children who had been in child care for more hours were observed to have more negative play with a friend, were reported by caregivers to be less socially competent, and were reported to have more externalizing behavior problems and more conflicts with caregivers (NICHD ECCRN, 2003a). In kindergarten, children with more hours in early child care were reported by mothers and teachers to have more externalizing behavior problems, and teachers reported more teacher-child conflict. In follow-up analyses that were conducted when children were in third grade, the relations between hours and behavior problems were no longer statistically significant (NICHD ECCRN, 2005).

Several alternative explanations for the findings in regard to child care hours have been examined (NICHD ECCRN, 2003a). One possibility is that the relations were the result of other aspects of child care. Another possibility is that the hours effects were mediated by differences in mother-child interaction. These possibilities were tested in analyses that included controls for other aspects of child care (quality, type, instability, exposure to peers) and maternal sensitivity. The addition of these controls resulted in modest reductions in the hours coefficients, but the coefficients continued to be statistically significant, indicating that the hours findings were not explained by quality of child care or quality of parenting, at least as they were measured in this study.

Studies by Gunnar and colleagues (Dettling, Gunnar, & Donzella, 1999; Tout, de Haan, Campbell, & Gunnar, 1998; Watamura, Donzella, Alwin, & Gunnar, 2003) suggest a potentially fruitful avenue for understanding the relations between hours in care and adjustment. These investigators examined children's cortisol levels and patterns at child care and at home. Salivary cortisol was observed to increase from midmorning to midafternoon on those days when children were in centers but not on days when these same children were at home (Watamura et al., 2003). In other reports the largest increases in cortisol across the day were observed in children who had the most difficulty regulating negative emotions and behavior (Dettling, Gunnar, & Donzella, 1999), were more fearful (Watamura et al., 2003), less involved in peer play (Watamura et al., 2003), and less socially competent (Tout et al., 1998). Rises also were more evident in toddlers and preschoolers than in infants and schoolage children (Dettling, Gunnar, & Donzella, 1999; Watamura et al., 2003). These findings suggest that toddlers and preschoolers who are learning to negotiate with peers may experience group settings as socially demanding and stressful. What is not known is whether changes in the organization of child care programs or in caregivers' efforts might result in less stressful and more supportive social environments for children (Maccoby & Lewis, 2003).

HOW LARGE ARE THE QUANTITY EFFECTS ON CHILD BEHAVIOR PROBLEMS?

The practical significance of the quantity findings can be evaluated in several ways. In terms of effect sizes the effect sizes associated with amount of early care and behavior problems ranged from 0.08 to 0.20 in the SECC. Effect sizes for parenting quality were similar, ranging from 0.09 to 0.16. This comparison suggests that the quantity effects are meaningful.

A second way of evaluating the significance of the behavior problems findings is to compare the scores in the SECC to those of the sample used to norm the Child Behavior Checklist (CBCL). In the SECC, children who were in care for less than 30 hours a week received scores, on average, that were less than the norming sample mean of 50: children who were in child care for 0 to 9 hours a week scored, on average, 47.8, and children in care for 10 to 29 hours a week scored 49.0. Children who averaged more than 30 hours a week of child care from 3 to 54 months scored higher, on average, than the norming sample mean of 50. Children who averaged 30 to 45 hours a week received scores of 51.3 on average. Children in child care more than 45 hours a week from 3 to 54 months had the highest externalizing scores (53.1 at 54 months and 52.1 at kindergarten), a difference of about one-third of a standard deviation above the norm.

A third way of assessing the size of the quantity effect is to consider the proportion of children evincing "high" behavior problems, defined as 1 standard deviation above the mean for the CBCL norming sample. With this criterion one would, by definition, expect 17% of the children to score 60 or higher. In the SECC only the group of children who averaged more than 45 hours per week in child care from 3 to 54 months exceeded this expectation—24% were reported by teachers, and 26% were reported by mothers, to display high levels of behavior problems at 54 months. These analyses suggest that only children who spent substantial hours in child care (45 hours a week) over an extended period (3–54 months) displayed more externalizing behavior problems than might be expected within the population as a whole.

Cognitive and Language Development

Findings are mixed with respect to amount (and timing) of child care and children's cognitive, language, and academic performance. Analyses conducted by the NICHD Early Child Care Research Network (2000b, 2002b, NICHD ECCRN & Duncan, 2003) found no relations between amount/timing and cognitive and language measures at 15, 24, 36, or 54 months, controlling for other aspects of care and family factors. Others (Baydar & Brooks-Gunn, 1991; Brooks-Gunn, Han, & Waldfogel, 2002; Waldfogel, Han, & Brooks-Gunn, 2002), however, have detected amount/timing effects under some conditions. In analyses of the European American children in the SECC, Brooks-Gunn, Han, and Waldfogel (2002) reported that 3-year-olds whose mothers had worked 30 or more hours a week during the first nine months of their children's life had poorer preacademic skills than children whose mothers worked less than 30 hours a week during those first nine months. These effects were not evident in the cognitive performance of European American children younger than 36 months nor in the cognitive performance of ethnic minority children at 15, 24, or 36 months. These researchers also have found extensive maternal employment in the first year to be related to lower cognitive performance of European American (but not African American and Hispanic) participants in the National Longitudinal Survey of Youth (Baydar & Brooks-Gunn, 1991; Waldfogel et al., 2002). Vandell and Ramanan (1992), in contrast, found early maternal employment to be positively associated with academic performance in grade 2 for the subsample of low-income children in the National Longitudinal Survey of Youth.

NEXT STEPS

Additional research is needed to identify the processes that mediate relations between quantity of care and child developmental outcomes. By and large, in the work to date from the SECC, effects were not attenuated when maternal sensitivity and child care quality were included as controls, suggesting that the quantity effects were not mediated by the quality of caregiving provided by child care providers or mothers, at least as measured by the study investigators.

An important next step is to consider other aspects of child care quality. The quality of the peer environment is particularly important to consider (Fabes, Hanish, & Martin, 2003; Watamura et al., 2003). The specific strategies that caregivers use to promote children's social skills and to handle children's noncompliance and aggression also may help to explain the effects associated with quantity of care. The extensive child care observations conducted in the SECC, which are available in the public release data set, include peer-related items as well as observations of caregivers' socialization strategies. These observations could be useful in testing these mediation hypotheses.

Further research also is needed to disentangle the effects of amount and of timing. One possibility, if sufficient families are interested, is to mount an experimental study of paid parental leave in which children (and families) are assigned to varying amounts of child care (0–40 hours) and to different entry ages (2–24 months). Recent large-scale experimental studies of early education and work-based antipoverty programs indicate that such projects are feasible and compelling (Administration for Children and Families, 2002; Gennetian & Miller, 2002; Huston et al., 2001).

Does Type of Child Care Matter?

A third question central to child care research is whether child developmental outcomes are affected by different types of child care. In some cases correlational designs have related attendance at centers, child care homes, and relative care to child developmental outcomes. Others have used experimental and quasi-experimental designs to study the effects of participation in high-quality early education programs.

In an early study of 80 preschool-aged children in Chicago, Clarke-Stewart (1987) found child care centers, child care homes, and in-home care (nannies and relatives) to differ in a myriad of ways. Child care centers typically had more highly educated caregivers, larger group sizes, more time spent in "lessons," more structured activities, and more child-oriented materials, activities, and toys. Caregivers in centers had more professional orientations and were less likely to provide care as a favor to the family. In contrast, child care homes typically devoted more time to free exploration, casual learning, and watching television than did centers. Consistent with their more educational focus, children who attended centers scored higher on standardized cognitive assessments, controlling for family demographic characteristics and observed parenting. Children in center-based care also were more competent with strangers and independent of mothers in a laboratory playroom. Least advanced were children with caregivers in their own homes.

Similar findings were obtained in the SECC (NICHD ECCRN 1996, 2000a). Centers had the largest group sizes, the highest child-adult ratios, the most stimulating physical environments, and caregivers with the most training and education. Child care homes (sometimes called family day care) were intermediate between centers and the care provided by grandparents and nannies. Child developmental outcomes were related to type of care. Children who had more experience in center-based care (defined as the proportion of 3-month epochs that they had attended centers) obtained higher cognitive and language scores at ages 2 years, 3 years, and 4 1/2 years, controlling for family background characteristics and the quality and amount of child care (NICHD ECCRN, 2002b). Effect sizes in these analyses ranged from 0.21 to 0.43. Other analyses considered changes in cognitive functioning associated with center care: children who attended centers between the ages of 27 and 54 months (but not earlier) scored 4.1 points higher on cognitive tests relative to children who never attended centers during this period, controlling for family characteristics (effect size = 0.27) (NICHD ECCRN & Duncan, 2003).

Loeb and colleagues (2004) also determined center-type care to be related to cognitive benefits. In that study children in three sites (n = 451) were observed in centers, kith and kin, and child care homes after their parents began working in connection with TANF (Temporary Assistance to Needy Families). Children were 2 1/2 years on average at Wave 1 and 4 years on average at Wave 2. Children who attended centers during both waves and children who moved to centers by Wave 2 obtained higher cognitive and school readiness scores (effect sizes 0.6 and 0.4), controlling for family background and previous child performance. Participation in centers was not related to child behavior problems.

The available experimental and quasi-experimental evidence indicates that high-quality center-based care confers cognitive and academic benefits for children who are at risk for school failure. In the Carolina Abecedarian Project the treatment group attended a high-quality full-day program from shortly after birth through age 5 years, while the control group received family support social services, pediatric care, and child nutritional services. At 8 and 12 years the treatment group obtained higher IQ scores (F. A. Campbell & Ramey, 1994). At age 15 they had higher reading and mathematics achievement scores, were less likely to have been retained a grade, and were less likely to have been placed in special education (Ramey, Campbell, & Blair, 1998). At age 21 they were more likely to have attended a 4-year college (F. A. Campbell, Ramey, Pungello, Sparling, & Miller-Johnson, 2002). Not all the effects reported from this program were positive, however. In grade 1, children in the treatment group were reported by teachers to be more aggressive (Haskins, 1985).

A second experimental study, the Perry Preschool Project, also found long-term effects of participation in a high-quality center-based program, in this case a half-day program that began at age 3 years. This sample of 123 children has been followed to 27 years, at which time members of the experimental group had higher incomes and fewer arrests, and they were less likely to be receiving public assistance, than members of the control group (Schweinhart, Barnes, & Weikart, 1993).

A third experimental study, the Infant Health and Development Project, was a multisite randomized treatment study that included high-quality center-based care as a component of a comprehensive intervention that targeted low-birthweight premature infants. The treatment group received home visits from the 1st through the 3rd year and high-quality, full-day center-based programming during their 2nd and 3rd years. Children's cognitive and behavioral functioning was assessed at ages 5 and 8 years (Brooks-Gunn, McCarton, et al., 1994). The initial analyses contrasting the intention-to-treat group versus the control group found cognitive benefits at ages 5 and 8 years only for the heavier low-birthweight infants. A recent paper (Hill, Brooks-Gunn, & Waldfogel, 2003) has extended this study to consider dosage. The dosage analyses indicated considerably larger cognitive effects through age 8 years for both lighter and heavier low-birthweight infants who had attended the program for more days.

Results from quasi-experimental studies also support the proposition that high-quality center-based programs can have long-term beneficial effects for low-income children. In a series of papers (Reynolds, 1994; Reynolds & Robertson, 2003; Reynolds & Temple, 1998; Reynolds, Temple, Robertson, & Mann, 2001) Reynolds and colleagues have followed the educational and social development of African American and Hispanic children who lived in central-city Chicago. The treatment group consisted of children who participated in government-funded Title I early childhood programs in 1985–1986 (n = 989); the comparison group consisted of other children in the same neighborhoods who did not attend these programs and received the "treatment as usual" in the community (n = 550). The Chicago Parent-Child Center curriculum emphasized basic skills in language and math through fairly structured activities that were taught by teachers with college degrees; parent involvement was an integral part of the program.

Program effects have been found through age 20. Children who participated in the early childhood program obtained significantly higher math and reading achievement test scores at 5, 8, and 14 years, controlling for family risk status, child gender, and program participation during the primary grades (Reynolds & Temple, 1998). At age 20, participants were more likely to have completed high school and to have low rates of juvenile crime (Reynolds et al., 2001). Program participation also was associated with reductions in child abuse and child neglect, with the largest effects seen when children were 10 to 17 years old (Reynolds & Robertson, 2003).

The last 25 years have been marked by substantial progress in answering questions about the effects of child care quality, amount and timing, and type. This progress has occurred, in part, because of the study of large and diverse samples, the development of a common set of reliable and valid measures that facilitated cross-study comparisons, the use of sophisticated analytic strategies that minimized the likelihood of biased findings, longitudinal designs in which child care and the family were assessed at regular intervals, and the consideration of a broad array of social and cognitive outcomes evaluated by multiple methods.

With respect to child care quality, both process quality (the experiences that children have with caregivers, peers, and materials) and structural/caregiver features have been consistently found to predict children's cognitive, language, and social development, even when extensive covariates are included in analyses. Much of this research has reported main effects of quality, but there is some evidence that the effects of child care quality are larger in children who are at risk because of poverty, maternal depression, or poor parenting. Effects associated with child care quality are "small" or "moderate" by Cohen's 1988 standard, but they may still be judged as meaningful when compared to the effects of poverty and parenting.

With respect to amount and timing of child care, the research evidence suggests that substantial hours in care beginning in infancy are associated with less sensitive mother-child interactions and with more behavior problems in children in early childhood. In the NICHD SECC, children in child care for less than 30 hours a week from 3 to 54 months had externalizing scores that were, on average, below the norming sample mean of 50, whereas children in child care for substantial hours (i.e, more than 45 hours a week from 3 to 54 months) had externalizing scores that were, on average, 2 to 3 points above the norming sample mean. Children with substantial early hours also evinced a higher than expected rate of "high" levels of behavior problems, while children with less extensive hours did not. Further research is needed to identify the processes that mediate and moderate relations between amount of care and behavior problems.

Finally, with respect to the effects of different types of care, experimental studies of high-quality programs serving at-risk children have found positive short-term and long-term effects on children's academic, cognitive, and social outcomes. Correlational studies also indicate that attending child care centers is associated with higher cognitive and language scores.

Although much progress has been made in understanding the effects of early child care, further research is clearly needed because there is much we still do not know. Our unanswered questions include whether effects of child care quality, amount, and type continue to be evident during late childhood and adolescence. That is, are the effects of early experience maintained or do they dissipate? Also, what is the quality of child care in the United States? How much of the available care is of poor quality? Do measures of quality need to be expanded to reflect the peer context? Can effective policies be implemented to improve child care quality? Can the effects of amount and timing of early child care be disentangled? Finally, what are the effects of different parental leave policies on the well-being and development of children and families? As progress is made on these questions, child care research should help to advance developmental theory and application.

References

Administration for Children and Families (2002). *Making a difference in the lives of infants and toddlers and their families: The impact of early Head Start.* Washington, DC: U.S. Department of Health and Human Services.

Barglow, P., Vaughn, B. E., & Molitor, N. (1987). Effects of maternal absence due to employment on the quality of infant-mother attachment in a low-risk sample. *Child Development, 58,* 945–954.

Bates, J., Marvinney, D., Kelly, T., Dodge, K., Bennett, R., & Pettit, G. (1994). Child care history and kindergarten adjustment. *Developmental Psychology, 30,* 690–700.

Baydar, N., & Brooks-Gunn, J. (1991). Effects of maternal employment and child care arrangements on preschoolers' cognitive and behavioral outcomes: Evidence from the National Longitudinal Survey of Youth. *Developmental Psychology, 27,* 932–945.

Belsky, J. (1986). Infant day care: A cause for concern? *Zero to Three, 6,* 1–9.

Belsky, J. (1988). The effects of infant day care reconsidered. *Early Childhood Research Quarterly, 3,* 235–272.

Belsky, J. (2001). Developmental risks (still) associated with early child care. *Journal of Child Psychology and Psychiatry, 42,* 845–859.

Belsky, J., & Rovine, M. (1988). Nonmaternal care in the first year of life and the security of infant-parent attachment. *Child Development, 59,* 157–167.

Belsky, J., & Steinberg, L. D. (1978). The effects of day care: A critical review. *Child Development, 49,* 929–949.

Blau, D. (2001). *The child care problem: An economic analysis.* New York: Russell Sage.

Brooks-Gunn, J., Han, W.-J., & Waldfogel, J. (2002). Maternal employment and child cognitive outcomes in the first year of life: The NICHD Study of Early Child Care. *Child Development, 73,* 1052–1072.

Brooks-Gunn, J., McCarton, C. M., Casey, P. H., McCormick, M. C., Bauer, C. R., Bernbaum, J. C., Tyson, J. J., Swanson, M., Bennett, F. C., & Scott, D. T. (1994). Early intervention in low-birth-weight premature infants: Results through age 5 years from the Infant Health and Development Program. *Journal of the American Medical Association, 272,* 1257–1262.

Burchinal, M. R., Bryant, D. M., Lee, M. W., & Ramey, C. T. (1992). Early day care, infant-mother attachment, and maternal responsiveness in the infant's first year of life. *Early Childhood Research Quarterly, 7,* 383–396.

Burchinal, M. R., Cryer, D., Clifford, R. M., & Howes, C. (2002). Caregiver training and classroom quality in child care centers. *Applied Developmental Science, 6,* 2–11.

Burchinal, M. R., Roberts, J. E., Riggins, R., Zeisel, S.A., Neebe, E., & Bryant,

D. (2000). Relating quality of center-based child care to early cognitive and language development longitudinally. *Child Development, 71,* 339–357.

Campbell, F. A., & Ramey, C. T. (1994). Effects of early intervention on intellectual and academic achievement: A follow-up of children from low-income families. *Child Development, 65,* 684–698.

Campbell, F. A., Ramey, C. T., Pungello, E. P., Sparling, J., & Miller-Johnson, S. (2002). Early childhood education: Young adult outcomes from the Abecedarian Project. *Applied Developmental Science, 6,* 42–57.

Campbell, S. B., Cohn, J. F., & Meyers, T. (1995). Depression in first-time mothers: Mother-infant interaction and depression chronicity. *Developmental Psychology, 31,* 349–357.

Chin-Quee, D. S., & Scarr, S. (1994). Lack of early child care effects on school-age children's social competence and academic achievement. *Early Development and Parenting, 3,* 103–112.

Clark, R., Hyde, J. S., Essex, M. J., & Klein, M. H. (1997). Length of maternity leave and quality of mother-infant interaction. *Child Development, 68,* 364–383.

Clarke-Stewart, K. A. (1987). Predicting child development from child care forms and features: The Chicago Study. In D. A. Phillips (Ed.), *Quality in child care: What does research tell us?* Washington, DC: National Association for the Education of Young Children.

Clarke-Stewart, K. A. (1989). Infant day care: Maligned or malignant. *American Psychologist, 44,* 266–273.

Clarke-Stewart, K. A., Vandell, D. L., Burchinal, M., O'Brien, M., & McCartney, K. (2002). Do regulable features of child care homes affect children's development? *Early Childhood Research Quarterly, 17,* 52–86.

Cohen, J. (1988). *Statistical power analysis for the behavioral sciences.* Hillsdale NJ: Erlbaum.

Committee on Family and Work Policies (2003). *Working families and growing kids: Caring for children and adolescents.* Washington, DC: National Academies Press.

Crockenberg, S., & Litman, C. (1991). Effects of maternal employment on maternal and two-year-old child behavior. *Child Development, 62,* 930–953.

Deater-Deckard, K., Pinkerton, R., & Scarr, S. (1996). Child care quality and children's behavioral adjustment: A four-year longitudinal study. *Journal of Child Psychology and Psychiatry, 37,* 937–948.

Dettling, A. C., Gunnar, M. R., & Donzella, B. (1999). Cortisol levels of young children in full-day child care centers: Relations with age and temperament. *Psychoneuroendocrinology, 24,* 519–536.

Dettling, A. C., Parker, S. W., Lane, S. K., Sebanc, A. M., & Gunnar, M. R. (2000). Quality of care and temperament determine whether cortisol levels rise over the day for children in full-day child care. *Psychoneuroendocrinology, 25,* 819–836.

Fabes, R. A., Hanish, L. D., & Martin, C. L. (2003). Children at play: The role

of peers in understanding the effects of child care. *Child Development,*
74, 1039–1043.

Gennetian, L. A., & Miller, C. (2002). Children and welfare reform: A view
from an experimental welfare program in Minnesota. *Child Develop-*
ment, 73, 601–620.

Harms, T., & Clifford, R. M. (1980). *Early Childhood Environment Rating Scale.*
New York: Teachers College Press.

Harms, T., & Clifford, R. M. (1989). *Family Day Care Rating Scale.* New York:
Teachers College Press.

Harms, T., Cryer, D., & Clifford, R. M. (1990). *Infant/Toddler Environment Rat-*
ing Scale. New York: Teachers College Press.

Haskins, R. (1985). Public school aggression among children with varying
day-care experiences. *Child Development, 56,* 689–703.

Helburn, S. W., & Bergmann, B. R. (2002). *America's child care problem: The*
way out. New York: Basic Books.

Hill, J. L., Brooks-Gunn, J., & Waldfogel, J. (2003). Sustained effects of high
participation in an early intervention for low-birth-weight premature
infants. *Developmental Psychology, 39,* 730–744.

Howes, C. (1983). Caregiver behavior in center and family day care. *Journal*
of Applied Developmental Psychology, 4, 99–107.

Howes, C. (1988). Relations between early child care and schooling. *Devel-*
opmental Psychology, 24, 53–57.

Howes, C. (1990). Can the age of entry into child care and the quality of
child care predict adjustment in kindergarten? *Developmental Psychol-*
ogy, 26, 292–303.

Howes, C. (1997). Children's experiences in center-based child care as a
function of teacher background and adult:child ratio. *Merrill-Palmer*
Quarterly, 43, 404–425.

Howes, C. (2000). Social-emotional classroom climate in child care, child-
teacher relationships, and children's second grade peer relations. *Social*
Development, 9, 191–204.

Howes, C., Phillips, D. A., & Whitebook, M. (1992). Thresholds of quality:
Implications for the social development of children in center-based
child care. *Child Development, 63,* 449–460.

Huston, A. C., Duncan, G. J., Granger, R., Bos, J., McLoyd, V., Mistry, R.,
Crosby, D., Gibson, C., Magnuson, K., Romich, J., & Ventura, A. (2001).
Work-based anti-poverty programs for parents can enhance the school
performance and social behavior of children. *Child Development, 72,*
318–336.

Kontos, S. C., Howes, C., Shinn, M., & Galinsky, E. (1995). *Quality in family*
child care and relative care. New York: Teachers College Press.

Lamb, M., & Ahnert, L. (2006). Nonparental child care: Context, concepts,
correlates, and consequences. In W. Damon & R. Lerner (Series Eds.),
K. A. Renninger & I. E. Sigel (Vol. Eds.), *Handbook of child psychology: Vol.*
4. Child psychology in practice (6th ed., pp. 950–1016). New York: Wiley.

Loeb, S., Fuller, B., Kagan, S. L., & Carrol, B. (2004). Child care in poor communities: Early learning effects of type, quality, and stability. *Child Development, 75,* 47–65.

Lombardi, J. (2003). *Time to care: Redesigning child care to promote education, support families, and build communities.* Philadelphia: Temple University Press.

Love, J. M., Harrison, L., Sagi-Schwartz, A., Van Ijzendoorn, M. H., Ross, C., Ungerer, J. A., Raikes, H., Brady-Smith, C., Boller, K., Brooks-Gunn, J., Constantine, J., Kiskar, E. E., Pausell, D., & Chazan-Cohen, R. (2003). Child care quality matters: How conclusions may vary with context. *Child Development, 74,* 1021–1033.

Maccoby, E. E., & Lewis, C. C. (2003). Less day care or different day care? *Child Development, 74,* 1069–1075.

McCartney, K., Dearing, E., & Taylor, B.A. (2003, April). Quality child care supports the achievement of low-income children: Direct and indirect effects via caregiving and the home environment. In K. McCartney (Chair), *Child care and maternal employment effects in the NICHD Study of Early Child Care and Youth Development.* Symposium conducted at the biennial meeting of the Society for Research in Child Development, Tampa, FL.

McCartney, K., & Rosenthal, R. (2000). Effect size, practical importance, and social policy for children. *Child Development, 71,* 173–180.

Newcomb, N. S. (2003). Some controls control too much. *Child Development, 74,* 1050–1052.

NICHD Early Child Care Research Network. (1996). Characteristics of infant child care: Factors contributing to positive caregiving. *Early Childhood Research Quarterly, 11,* 269–306.

NICHD Early Child Care Research Network. (1997a). Child care in the first year of life. *Merrill-Palmer Quarterly, 43,* 340–360.

NICHD Early Child Care Research Network. (1997b). The effects of infant child care on infant-mother attachment: Results from the NICHD Study of Early Child Care. *Child Development, 68,* 860–879.

NICHD Early Child Care Research Network. (1998). Early child care and self-control, compliance, and problem behavior at twenty-four and thirty-six months. *Child Development, 69,* 1145–1170.

NICHD Early Child Care Research Network. (1999a). Child care and mother-child interaction in the first 3 years of life. *Developmental Psychology, 35,* 1399–1413.

NICHD Early Child Care Research Network. (1999b). Child outcomes when child care center classes meet recommended standards for quality. *American Journal of Public Health, 89,* 1072–1077.

NICHD Early Child Care Research Network. (1999c, April). *Effect sizes from the NICHD Study of Early Child Care.* Paper presented at the biennial meeting of the Society for Research in Child Development, Albuquerque, NM.

NICHD Early Child Care Research Network. (2000a). Characteristics and quality of child care for toddlers and preschoolers. *Applied Developmen-*

tal Science, 4, 116–135.

NICHD Early Child Care Research Network. (2000b). The relation of child care to cognitive and language development. *Child Development, 71,* 960–980.

NICHD Early Child Care Research Network. (2001a). Child care and children's peer interaction at 24 and 36 months: The NICHD Study of Early Child Care. *Child Development, 72,* 1478–1500.

NICHD Early Child Care Research Network. (2001b). Child care and family predictors of preschool attachment and stability from infancy. *Developmental Psychology, 37,* 847–862.

NICHD Early Child Care Research Network. (2001c). Nonmaternal care and family factors in early development: An overview of the NICHD Study of Early Child Care. *Applied Developmental Psychology, 22,* 457–492.

NICHD Early Child Care Research Network. (2002a). Child care structure to process to outcome: Direct and indirect effects of child-care quality on young children's development. *Psychological Science, 13(3),* 199–206.

NICHD Early Child Care Research Network. (2002b). Early child care and children's development prior to school entry. *American Educational Research Journal, 39,* 133–164.

NICHD Early Child Care Research Network. (2003a). Does amount of time spent in child care predict socioemotional adjustment during the transition to kindergarten? *Child Development, 74,* 976–1005.

NICHD Early Child Care Research Network. (2003b). Does quality of child care affect child outcomes at age 4 1/2? *Developmental Psychology, 39,* 451–469.

NICHD Early Child Care Research Network. (2003c). Early child care and mother-child interaction from 36 months through first grade. *Infant Behavior and Development, 26,* 345–370.

NICHD Early Child Care Research Network & Duncan, G. J. (2003). Modeling the impacts of child care quality on children's preschool cognitive development. *Child Development, 74,* 1485–1506.

NICHD Early Child Care Research Network. (2005). Early child care and children's development in the primary grades: Follow-up results from the NICHD Study of Early Child Care. *American Educational Research Journal, 43,* 537–570.

Owen, M. T., & Cox, M. J. (1988). Maternal employment and the transition to parenthood. In A. E. Gottfried & A. W. Gottfried (Eds.), *Maternal employment and children's development: Longitudinal research* (pp. 85–119). New York: Plenum.

Peisner-Feinberg, E. S., Burchinal, M. R., Clifford, R. M., Culkin, M. L., Howes, C., Kagan, S. L., & Yasejian, N. (2001). The relation of child care quality to children's cognitive and social developmental trajectories through second grade. *Child Development, 72,* 1534–1553.

Phillips, D. A., McCartney, K., & Scarr, S. (1987). Child-care quality and children's social development. *Developmental Psychology, 23,* 537–544.

Phillips, D. A., McCartney, K., Scarr, S., & Howes, C. (1987). Selective review of infant day care research: A cause for concern. *Zero to Three, 7,* 18–21.

Phillips, D. A., Mekow, D., Scarr, S., McCartney, K., & Abbott-Shim, M. (2000). Within and beyond the classroom door: Assessing quality in child care centers. *Early Childhood Research Quarterly, 15,* 475–496.

Ramey, C. T., Campbell, F. A., & Blair, C. (1998). Enhancing the life-course for high-risk children: Results from the Abecedarian Project. In J. Crane (Ed.), *Social programs that really work.* New York: Russell Sage.

Reynolds, A. J. (1994). Effects of a preschool plus follow-on intervention for children at risk. *Developmental Psychology, 30,* 787–804.

Reynolds, A. J., & Robertson, D. L. (2003). School-based early intervention and later child maltreatment in the Chicago longitudinal study. *Child Development, 74,* 3–26.

Reynolds, A. J., & Temple, J. A. (1998). Extended early childhood intervention and school achievement: Age 13 findings from the Chicago Longitudinal Study. *Child Development, 69,* 231–246.

Reynolds, A. J., Temple, J. A., Robertson, D. L., & Mann, E. A. (2001). Long-term effects of an early childhood intervention on educational achievement and juvenile arrest: A 15-year follow-up of low-income children in public schools. *Journal of the American Medical Association, 285,* 2339–2346.

Richters, J., & Zahn-Waxler, C. (1990). The infant day care controversy: Current status and future directions. In N. Fox & G. Fein (Eds.), *Infant day care: The current debate* (pp. 87–106). Norwood, NJ: Ablex.

Ruopp, R., Travers, J., Glantz, F., & Coelen, G. (1979). *Children at the center.* Cambridge MA: Abt Associates.

Sagi, A., Koren-Karie, N., Gini, M., Ziv, Y., & Joels, T. (2002). Shedding further light on the effects of various types and quality of early child care on infant-mother attachment relationship: The Haifa Study of Early Child Care. *Child Development, 73,* 1166–1186.

Schwarz, J., Strickland, R., & Krolick, G. (1974). Infant day care: Behavioral effects at preschool age. *Developmental Psychology, 10,* 502–506.

Schweinhart, L. J., Barnes, H. V., & Weikart, D .P. (1993). *Significant benefits: The High/Scope Perry Preschool study through age 27.* Ypsilanti, MI: High/Scope Press.

Schweinhart, L. J., Weikart, D. P., & Larner, M. B. (1986). Consequences of three preschool curriculum models through age 15. *Early Childhood Research Quarterly, 1,* 15–45.

Tout, K., De Haan, M., Campbell, E. K., & Gunnar, M. R. (1998). Social behavior correlates of cortisol activity in child care: Gender differences and time-of-day effects. *Child Development, 69,* 1247–1262.

U.S. Census Bureau. (2003). *Who's minding the kids? Child care arrangements: Spring 1999 detailed tables (PPL—168).* Retrieved May 12, 2006, from http://www.census.gov/population/www/socdemo/child/ppl-168.html.

Vandell, D. L. (1979). Effects of a playgroup experience on mother-son and father-son interaction. *Developmental Psychology, 15,* 379–385.

Vandell, D. L., & Corasaniti, M. (1990). Child care and the family: Complex contributors to child development. *New Directions for Child Development, 49*, 23–37.

Vandell, D. L., & Powers, C. (1983). Daycare quality and children's free/play activities. *American Journal of Orthopsychiatry, 53*, 493–500.

Vandell, D. L., & Ramanan, J. (1992). Effects of early and recent maternal employment on children from low-income families. *Child Development, 63*, 938–949.

Vandell, D. L., & Wolfe, B. (2000). *Child care quality: Does it matter and does it need to be improved?* Report prepared for the U.S. Department of Health and Human Services, Office for Planning and Evaluation. Retrieved May 12, 2006, from http://aspe.hhs.gov/hsp/ccquality00/.

Waldfogel, J., Han, W.-J., & Brooks-Gunn, J. (2002). The effects of early maternal employment on child cognitive development. *Demography, 39*, 369–392.

Watamura, S. E., Donzella, B., Alwin, J., & Gunnar, M. R. (2003). Morning-to-afternoon increases in cortisol concentrations for infants and toddlers at child care: Age differences and behavioral correlates. *Child Development, 74*, 1006–1020.

21

Early Learning and School Readiness
Can Early Intervention Make a Difference?

Craig T. Ramey and Sharon L. Ramey

The United States continues to evolve into a society that requires all its adult members to be literate, proficient in basic math, and facile with means of acquiring and using new knowledge. As automation of routine jobs increases and as globalization of business results in the transfer of manufacturing and service jobs to less expensive foreign labor markets, the pressures increase to become an even more academically accomplished society. Thus the educational bar in K–12 and college education is constantly being raised.

As the educational expectations and the bar for minimal competence are raised, a basic problem becomes more and more apparent. The experiences of children from different social classes lead to marked differences in skills and knowledge as measured by standardized tests administered when children enter kindergarten. These social-class discrepancies are of no small magnitude and are strongly related to subsequent school performance, as indexed by standardized measures of academic achievement, as well as to disproportionate rates of grade retention and special education placement (Donovan & Cross, 2002). Although the issue of social class is frequently construed as a practical educational issue, it is also directly germane to more fundamental issues of human development, including the extent of human cognitive malleability and the relative importance of various causal factors that regulate that malleability.

An ominous omen for American society is that since the mid-1980s approximately one-third of children entering kindergarten are consistently judged by their kindergarten teachers as not ready for typical kindergarten-level work (Carnegie Task Force, 1994). Since the 1960s we have been involved, along with a large number of colleagues from many life-science disciplines, in trying various early intervention strategies to understand better the causes of developmental discrepancies related to social class, with the ultimate aim of improving the intellectual performance and basic social competence of young children from high-risk family backgrounds. This chapter is a brief summary of that work and its historical and scientific contexts.

School Readiness and School Achievement

School readiness and school achievement are at the forefront of our country's domestic social policy concerns. How can we help all America's children to truly succeed in school and in life? A well-educated citizenry is vital to our country's future as a democracy and as a productive and economically strong nation. Unprecedented numbers of children start public kindergarten with major delays in language and basic academic skills. Children with these significant delays attend schools in every state; they are not concentrated in only a few large urban school districts or in desperately poor rural districts.

Waiting until these children fail in school and then providing remedial, pull-out, or compensatory programs or requiring them to repeat grades typically does not help these children to catch up and then achieve at grade level. Instead, the scientific evidence affirms that children who do not have positive early transitions to school—that is, those children who have early failure experiences in school—are those most likely to become inattentive, disruptive, or withdrawn. Later, these same students are the most likely to drop out of school early; to engage in irresponsible, dangerous, and illegal behaviors; to become teen parents; and to depend on welfare and numerous public assistance programs for survival (Shonkoff & Phillips, 2000). What can be done to end this predictable decline?

We have compelling scientific evidence that this negative developmental cascade can be prevented, but preventing it and promoting children's cognitive and linguistic development cannot wait until kindergarten or until children show signs of developmental delay. Rather, the commitment to improving K–12 academic achievement must begin by providing children in the prekindergarten years with a rich array of effective learning opportunities.

Recent scientific advances in the fields of child development science, neurobiology, and early childhood education affirm that the early years are a time of rapid growth and development. Scientists are mapping, in increasingly greater detail, this remarkable period of life. Collectively, these scientific findings indicate that learning and brain development are truly interdependent and that what happens early in development has lasting and important consequences.

Essential Experiences in the Early Learning Years

What are the crucial experiences needed in the early years of life? Does early caretaking or experience really affect brain development? Are these effects important or lasting? In recent scientific articles (e.g., Ramey & Ramey, 1998a) and books for parents (e.g., Ramey & Ramey, 1999a, 1999b), we have summarized a vast body of scientific evidence in terms of seven types of experiences that are essential to ensure normal brain and behavioral development and school readiness. Children have these experiences when they are

1. Encouraged to explore
2. Mentored in basic skills
3. Celebrated for their developmental advances
4. Encouraged to rehearse and extend new skills
5. Protected from inappropriate disapproval, teasing, and punishment
6. Taught to communicate richly and responsively
7. Guided in how to behave appropriately (Ramey & Ramey, 1999b, p. 145)

Right from birth, babies are actively learning throughout the day. This learning occurs through the types, amounts, and predictability of visual, auditory, and social-emotional experiences that the baby has with parents and other caregivers. These seven essential types of experiences are backed by extensive scientific evidence and causally linked to many aspects of brain functioning and child development. These experiences primarily reflect transactions that parents and other caring individuals can provide for children in all cultures; they do not require money or any special toys or equipment, but they do involve time, skill, and active commitment.

There is a positive quantitative relationship between receiving more (or less) of these seven essentials and children's development. Figure 1, from the work of Huttenlocher, Harght, Bruk, Seltzer, and Lyons (1991), illustrates one aspect of this quantitative relationship: during the first 24 months of life children's acquisition of language is highly associated with their mothers' speech to them. By 2 years of age children whose mothers speak to them frequently and responsively have vocabularies that are 8 times greater than those of children whose mothers speak less frequently. This strong relationship between the amount of parental language stimulation—as well as active parental teaching—and children's language and cognitive development has been documented in scores of studies, including the extensive naturalistic observation work by Hart and Risley (1995). But the most compelling findings are those experimentally produced results that demonstrate the significant benefits of providing enriched learning opportunities to those children who do not receive these on a regular basis in their homes (Ramey, Yeates, & Short, 1984). When given the right types and amounts of language and cognitive experiences, particularly within a warm and responsive social context, high-risk children show gains in their intellectual and linguistic competence.

Learning to read is vital for school success and relates strongly to children's early language development. Children who are in a rich and highly interactive language environment acquire strong oral language skills—the ability to understand increasingly complex spoken language and to express themselves through the use of increasingly specific words in conversational discourse. Phonological awareness is also important. In the preschool years children can learn much about the world of reading: that words are made up of a set of distinct sounds and that the printed word corresponds to the spoken word in orderly ways; that letters and combinations of letters relate to sounds and meaning, which in turn help readers to decipher words on a page; that words combine into sentences and have sequences that are important to telling a story or conveying useful information. Even very young children can acquire letter name knowledge and many other basic concepts about print. The children who have this set of diverse language and preliteracy skills are among those who are best prepared to receive and benefit from the right types of formal reading instruction in elementary school.

The Cumulative Toll of Limited Learning Opportunities

Limited learning opportunities and low expectations for children from high-risk home environments take an undeniable cumulative toll. Figure 2 shows the prototypical comparative course of development for children who do and those who do not receive positive learning experiences in the first 5 years of life. This figure, which includes data extrapolated from several studies that we and our colleagues have conducted, shows that high-risk children without a solid prekindergarten educational foundation (illustrated by the

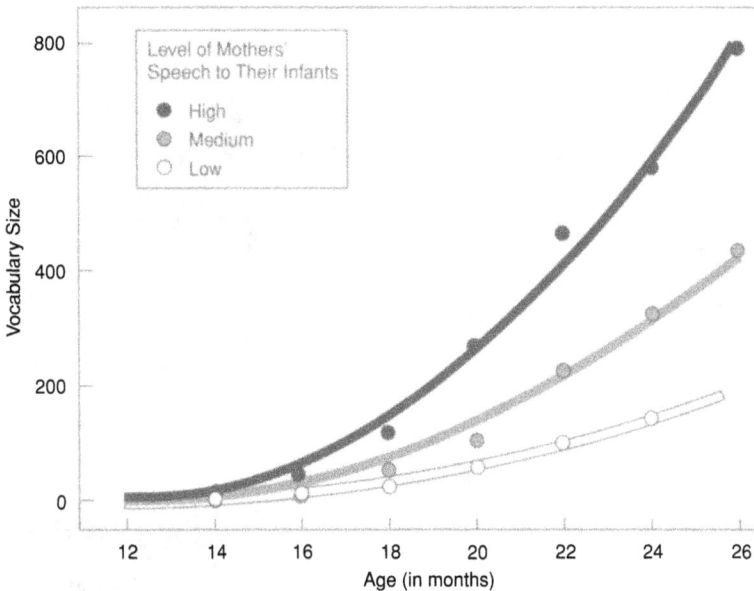

Figure 1. Effects of Mothers' Speech on Infant Vocabulary
Source: From "Early Vocabulary Growth: Relation to Language Input and Gender," by J. Huttenlocher, W. Harght, A. Bruk, M. Seltzer, and T. Lyons, 1991, *Developmental Psychology, 27,* 241. Reprinted with permission.

gray line) are likely to start kindergarten approximately 2 (or more) years behind their age-mates who are reared in more typical environments. Typically, those children who show developmental delays by kindergarten had developed at normal rates during the first year of life but evidenced slower rates of development beginning in the second year. (Of course, the difference in terms of developmental age or developmental competence is even greater when children from high-risk environments are compared with children from learning-enriched environments.) Delays of this magnitude constitute a serious educational challenge for classroom teachers and school districts, as well as for the children themselves.

Studies have confirmed that when children who are developmentally delayed enter good schools, they do learn and benefit—at rates that indicate that their learning is not truly impaired. Figure 3 shows that in 9 months of school, the children advance about 9 months developmentally in their cognitive and language skills. Yet

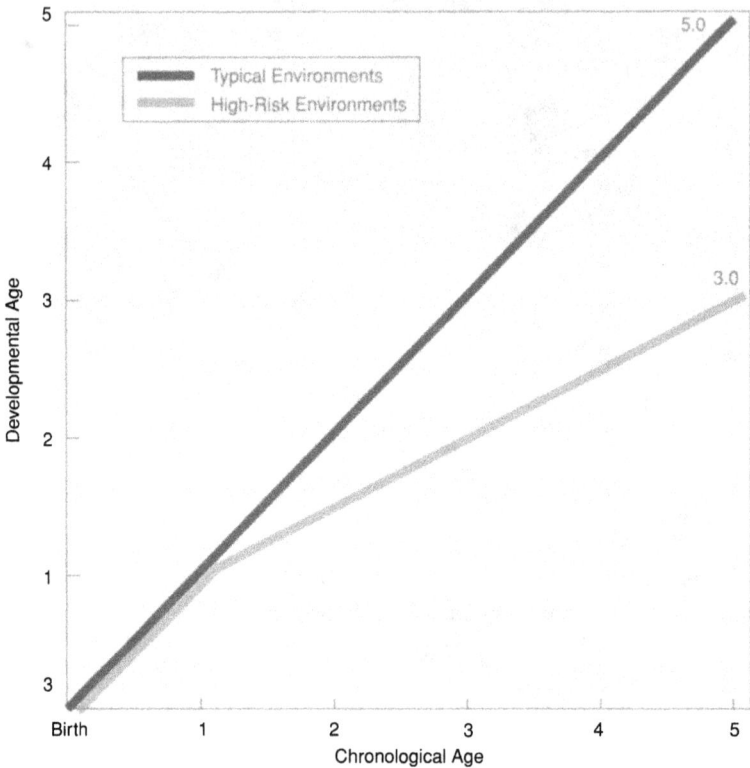

Figure 2. The Impact of Early Environments on Children's Developmental Competence

this rate of learning is not sufficient to compensate for their entry-level delays or to allow the children to fully catch up. That is, 5-year-old children whose cognitive and language skills are like those of a 3-year-old are ready to learn at their own level and show progress at a normal rate. A first-rate educational environment in kindergarten can definitely promote new learning. However, these delayed children are unlikely to be able to advance a full 33 developmental months in only 9 calendar months—that is, an amount sufficient to close the achievement gap. Just as important is that scientific studies have demonstrated that during the 3 summer months, children from homes that do not actively promote learning fail to show progress in their academic or language skills, whereas children from families that provide ongoing cognitive supports progress another 3

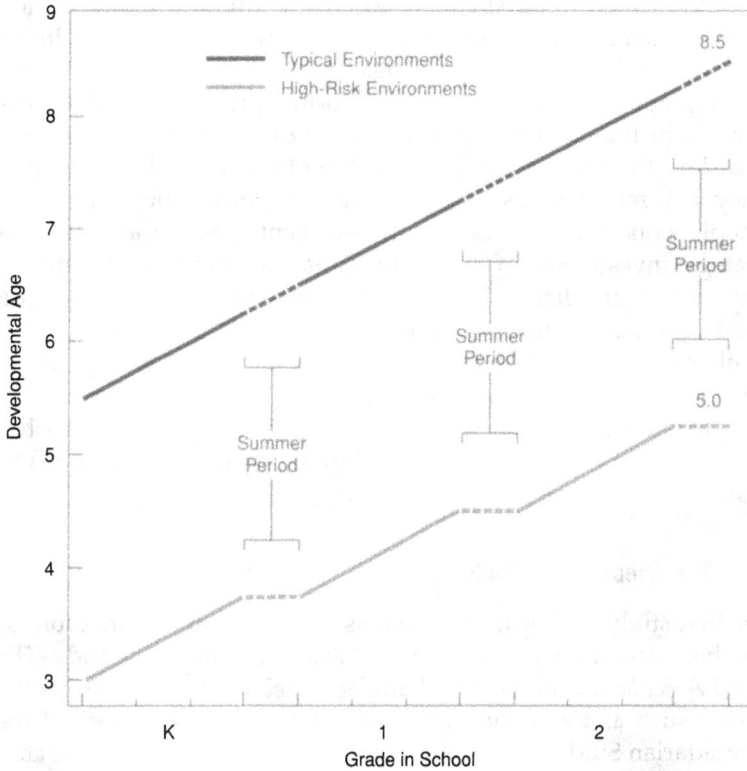

Figure 3. The Importance of Good Schools and Summer Programs

developmental months (Entwisle, 1995). This difference in children's learning during the summer months further increases the academic achievement gap between disadvantaged and advantaged children—even when the former are in highly supportive school programs during the academic year. As Figure 3 shows, by the end of second grade, children from high-risk environments who do not receive strong summer learning opportunities—despite their 3 years of a strong school-based program—will be even further behind their classmates from more advantaged homes. Similarly, there is increasing evidence that what happens in the extended day—that is, before and after school (and probably during the weekend days as well)—makes a difference in children's academic achievement.

As is readily apparent, children's learning is not restricted solely to their formal schooling hours. Children's achievement in the school years, just as in the first 5 years of life, is the result of all their learning opportunities—at home, in formal programs, on the playground, in the community. The totality of a child's experience is what lays the foundation for a lifetime of greater or lesser competency. This means that schools are vitally important, but our current schools alone cannot close the achievement gap. Rather, we need strategic investments in those programs and community supports that will ensure that children's developmental needs are met in a timely, consistent, and responsive way—so that they will have those "daily essentials" that undergird their becoming increasingly caring, cooperative, creative, and contributing young citizens.

In the next section we briefly describe our work, which has been aimed at preventing school failure by promoting school readiness.

The Abecedarian Study

The first study we began is known as the Abecedarian (pronounced "Ay-bee-see-der-ee-an," similar to ABCdarian) or ABC Study. The word *Abecedarian* comes from Latin and means "one who learns the basics, such as the alphabet." In the early 1970s we launched the Abecedarian Study of 111 children in North Carolina. All these children came from families that had extremely low income (below 50% of the federal poverty line), very low levels of maternal education (about 10 years of education), and low maternal intellectual attainment (with an average IQ near 80); most parents were single (about 75%) and unemployed. The children were healthy, full-term, normal birthweight infants. In this study we sought to answer the following question: Can the cumulative developmental toll experienced by socially defined high-risk children be prevented or reduced significantly by providing, from birth through kindergarten entry, systematic, high-quality early childhood education that emphasizes the seven essentials?

The Abecedarian Project is a randomized, controlled trial that tests the efficacy of early childhood education for high-risk children and their families. The design of the study, shown in Figure 4, focused on the added value of a high-quality, supportive educational program for young children. Accordingly, children in both the treatment group and the control group were given adequate nutrition in the form of free unlimited supplies of formula (no mother chose to breastfeed); were provided with social services for the family and referrals as needed (such as for housing, job training, and mental health and substance abuse problems); and were given free or reduced-cost medical care throughout the first 5 years of life (consistent with the highest levels of professionally recommended pediatric care). Thus the control-group children and their families were not "untreated," because their basic nutrition, health, and social service needs were addressed systematically for the first 5 years of life. As Figure 4 shows, the children in the treatment group were enrolled in a specially created early childhood center. All were enrolled before 6 months of age. This preschool program was a full-day program, 5 days per week and 50 weeks per year; children attended until they entered public kindergarten. The specially developed curriculum, known first as Learningames (Sparling & Lewis, 1979, 1984) and later as Partners for Learning (Sparling, Lewis, & Ramey, 1995), was informed by developmental theory and the burgeoning scientific evidence about how infants and toddlers learn. The Learningames curriculum had more than 500 specified activities for teachers to provide for children in the areas of cognition, fine motor development, social development and self-development, motor development, and language. The teachers were skilled in individualizing this program for each child, so that children were continuously challenged to progress to the next levels—that is, they were not placed in a rigid group curriculum that might have been too advanced or too simple for them. In addition, a special language curriculum was used that emphasized conversational skills and prereading activities (McGinness & Ramey, 1981; Ramey, McGinness, Cross, Collier, & Barrie-Blackley, 1981).

THE PRESCHOOL RESULTS

We measured many aspects of children's growth and development during the preschool years. In this chapter we will concentrate on the cognitive outcomes. To address ethical concerns about the developmental progress of children, we should note that referrals were made to development clinics if treatment-group or control-group children dropped below predetermined levels of performance on two successive measurement occasions. We believe that this feature, plus the other child and family services, render the treatment- versus control-group comparisons a more conservative test of the effects of the treatment program than otherwise would have been the case.

Treatment Group

- Adequate nutrition
- Supportive social services
- Free primary health care
- Preschool treatment;
  Intensive (full day, 5 days/week,
    50 weeks/year, 5 years)
  "Learningames" curriculum
    Cognitive / fine motor
    Social / self
    Motor
    Language
    Individualized pace

Control Group

- Adequate nutrition
- Supportive social services
- Low-cost or free primary
  health care

Figure 4. Abecedarian Preschool Program

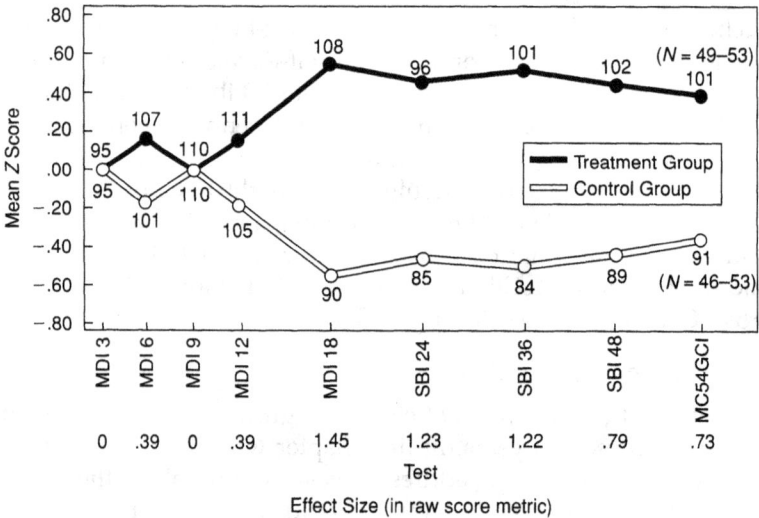

Figure 5. Z Scores and Mean Standardized Scores for High-Risk Preschool Treatment and Control Children in the Abecedarian Project at Nine Preschool Measurement Occasions
Source: From "Persistent Effects of Early Childhood Education on High-Risk Children and Their Mothers," by C. T. Ramey, F. A. Campbell, M. Burchinal, M. L. Skinner, D. M. Gardner, and S. L. Ramey, 2000, *Applied Developmental Science, 4,* p. 6. Reprinted with permission.

Figure 5 shows the results of individual cognitive assessments in which a score of 100 represents the national average. We standardized the scores by summing over both groups and have plotted the mean scores of each group at each age in Z-score metric. Above and below each age point we include the mean developmental quotient or IQ score for each group. The difference between the lines at each point represents the effect size of the treatment group relative to the control group on tests administered from 3 months of age through 54 months of age.

As Figure 5 shows, the two groups performed similarly during the first 9 months of life and performed above the national average. Thereafter, control-group children show a precipitous decline so that by 18 months they are performing at the low end of the normal range (a Bayley Developmental Quotient of 90), in contrast to the treatment-group children, who did not decline. Throughout the remainder of this preschool period, the treatment group averaged approximately 14 IQ points higher than the control group on two different types of developmental assessments (the Stanford-Binet IQ and the McCarthy General Cognitive Index). The effect sizes, shown on the x-axis, indicated the magnitude of the statistically significant differences. In the field of education an effect size of 0.25 or greater is widely accepted as worthy of changing practice and policy. The effect size from 18 months through 4.5 years ranged from 0.73 to 1.45 with a mean of 1.08—differences that are highly likely to be practically meaningful in children's everyday lives. This difference is also the typical reported difference between Caucasians and African Americans in population-based studies in the United States (Herrnstein & Murray, 1996). It is important to note that 98% of children participating in this study were African American. The implication of these experimentally produced differences is that experience clearly plays a major role in reported differences between blacks and whites. Further, this experience-driven disparity has a clear developmental course.

Figure 6 presents the results from a clinical perspective. It illustrates the percentage of children in each treatment group who score in the normal range of intelligence—earning scores of 85 or higher on tests that have a national average of 100. For children in the control group the cumulative toll is clear: more than 90% were in the normal range at 6 months of age, but this drops steadily to only 45% by age 4 years. In contrast, more than 95% of the children in the treatment group are in the normal range of cognitive abilities at all tested ages. This finding underscores the practical magnitude of the

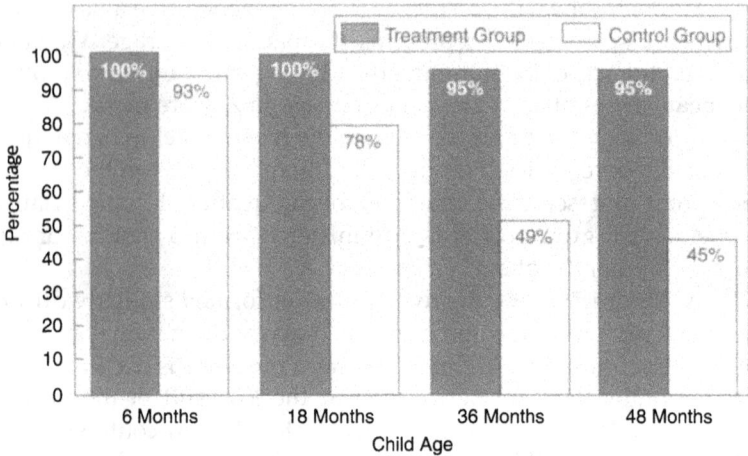

Figure 6. Percentage of Abecedarian Sample in Normal IQ Range (> 84) by Age (Longitudinal Analysis)
Source: From "The Prevention of Intellectual Impairment in Children of Impoverished Families: Findings of a Randomized Trial of Educational Day Care," by S. L. Martin, C. T. Ramey, and S. L. Ramey, 1990, *American Journal of Public Health, 80,* p. 845. Reprinted with permission.

treatment-group differences and illustrates the role of positive experiences in preventing intellectual disabilities.

REPLICATION OF ABECEDARIAN BENEFITS IN THE PRESCHOOL YEARS

The hallmark of science is replicability of procedures and findings. The ABC Project was replicated beginning in 1977 and 1978 in North Carolina in Project CARE (Ramey, Bryant, Sparling, & Wasik, 1985; Wasik, Ramey, Bryant, & Sparling, 1990) and later replicated in the Infant Health and Development Project, a randomized, controlled study of 985 low-birthweight, premature infants at eight different sites (Ramey, Bryant, Wasik, et al., 1992). For these nine replication studies significant benefits of the preschool educational treatment were documented in terms of children's higher performance on tests of intelligence, language, and social-emotional development at 3 years of age. The same developmental pattern that was observed in the Abecedarian Project also obtained in the Infant Health and Development Project (Ramey & Ramey, 1998b). Thus this pattern seems robust and generalizable.

One of the most pressing public policy issues is determining which young children need and can benefit from Abecedarian-style educational enrichment. For instance, do all premature and low birthweight infants need a special early educational intervention program, or are family resources an important contributing factor to degree of developmental risk? The findings from the Infant Health and Development Program are informative. In Figure 7 the 608 control-group children reveal the well-established effects of maternal education on children's intellectual and cognitive performance. That is, the children whose mothers have less than a high school diploma perform at the very lowest levels (with an average IQ about 85—the same average that appears in almost all inner-city schools throughout the United States), followed next by those whose mothers have a high school education, then by those with some college education, then a four-year college degree. This stepwise and orderly difference reflects what is termed the "achievement gap" when children enter school. The pattern is quite different for the 377 children who received the preschool education treatment. Essentially, the ABC preschool program leveled the playing field for these children by supporting their performance at slightly above the national average.

Notice, however, that the only children who did not display significant benefits of the preschool treatment were those whose parents had graduated from college: even though these babies were premature and low birthweight, they performed well above the national average whether they received the ABC treatment or the other types of natural stimulation and programs that their parents arranged for them. This confirms what a number of other studies have shown, namely, that not all children need additional systematic education or enrichment in the form of a planned preschool program. Rather, those children whose families have the least resources—best estimated by the parents' own educational and intellectual skills—are those who most need and most benefit from systematic provision of enriched learning opportunities. It is also important to note that there was no negative effect of the treatment on the intellectual performance of children from high-resource families. This is important because such families may seek high-quality care for their children for reasons other than educational enrichment—such as employment of the mothers.

Table 1 summarizes some of the major findings of the Infant Health and Development Project replication of the Abecedarian Project from 12 to 36 months of age (Gross, Spiker, & Haynes, 1997). Cognitive development shows a progression from no significant dif-

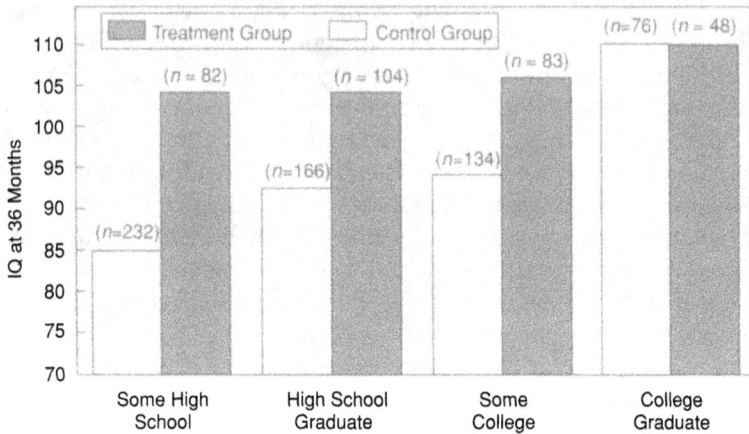

Figure 7. Infant Health and Development Program—Maternal Education ×
Treatment Group
Source: From "Prevention of Intellectual Disabilities: Early Interventions to Improve
Cognitive Development," by C. T. Ramey and S. L. Ramey, 1998, *Preventive Medi-
cine, 27*, p. 231. Reprinted with permission.

ference between the treatment and control groups at 12 months to
differences favoring the early education group at 24 and 36 months.
By 36 months the early education treatment group was superior to
children in the control group. Children in the treatment group were
more adaptive, prosocial, had fewer behavior problems, and had
better vocabularies, receptive language, and reasoning skills. Also,
by 36 months their homes were rated as developmentally more supportive and their mothers were observed as more positively interactive and better able to solve child-rearing problems. Thus, in addition to replicating the cognitive and linguistic findings of the
Abecedarian Project, the Infant Health and Development Project
provided evidence of a broad array of positive effects in the children's social and emotional functioning as well as of positive effects
on the home environment and maternal behavior. In times of limited
economic resources and many demands on states, it is important
that these findings be considered when deciding whether to provide
universal free preschool education or whether to selectively invest
in programs that reach those who truly are high risk and who will
likely demonstrate measurable gains. Our position is that universal
prekindergarten is highly desirable, but if that is not affordable, then
targeting is essential.

Table 1

Outcomes Affected Positively (*p <.01 by the Infant Health
and Development Program

	12 Months	24 Months	36 Months
Cognitive development	NS	+	+
Adaptive and prosocial behavior	–	–	+
Behavior problems	–	+	+
Vocabulary	–	+	+
Receptive language	–	+	+
Reasoning	–	–	+
Home environment	NS	–	+
Maternal interactive behavior	–	–	+
Maternal problem solving	–	–	+

NS = not significant
– = not measured
+ = significantly favoring the early intervention group over the control group

Note: Treatment children had fewer behavior problems than children in the control group.

SCHOOLAGE RESULTS OF THE ABECEDARIAN PROGRAM

In this section we briefly summarize the Abecedarian children's performance during their K–12 years in terms of key academic indicators. These data were presented in detail in articles by Ramey and Ramey (2000) and by Campbell, Pungello, and colleagues (2001).

Reading achievement (on the Woodcock-Johnson Tests) of the children who received the ABC preschool treatment was significantly higher at every age tested (Figure 8a). These assessments were individually administered by highly qualified assessors who did not know about the children's preschool treatment or their performance on earlier tests. Math achievement (Figure 8b) also was significantly higher at each age for children in the treatment group.

The children's real-world school performance is of paramount interest. Ramey and Ramey (2000) have reported two major practi-

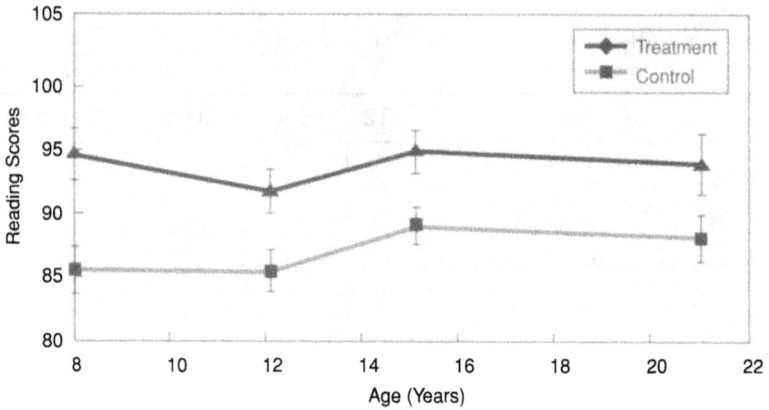

Figure 8a. Reading Achievement Over Time
Source: From "The Development of Cognitive and Academic Abilities: Growth Curves From an Early Childhood Educational Experiment," by F. A. Campbell, E. Pungello, S. Miller-Johnson, M. Burchinal, and C. T. Ramey, 2001, *Developmental Psychology, 37,* p. 237. Reprinted with permission.

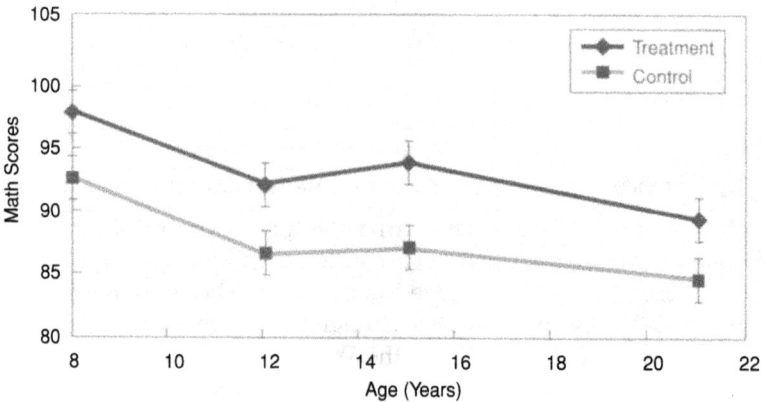

Figure 8b. Math Achievement Over Time
Source: From "The Development of Cognitive and Academic Abilities: Growth Curves From an Early Childhood Educational Experiment," by F. A. Campbell, E. Pungello, S. Miller-Johnson, M. Burchinal, and C. T. Ramey, 2001, *Developmental Psychology, 37,* p. 237. Reprinted with permission.

cal outcomes associated with children's receiving the ABC preschool treatment. The children's rate of retention in grade by age 15 (i.e., failing at least one grade) was 56% for the control group—a rate that was cut nearly by half for the children in the treated group (30%). Another important outcome, one with both fiscal implications for school districts and states and personal consequences for the children and their families, is placement in special education. Almost half the children in the control group (48%) were placed in special education by the age of 15 (often after repeated academic failures and social adjustment problems), compared to only 12% of those in the ABC preschool group. The national average for special education placement is about 11%. In general, special education costs are approximately 2.5 times the cost of regular education, and children in special education are entitled to free public education until the age of 22. The stigma associated with special education has been considerable for many children, particularly those from low-income and/or minority families who do not have medically diagnosed disabilities (see, e.g., Donovan & Cross, 2002). Thus the cost savings are substantial both in psychological and fiscal terms.

EARLY ADULTHOOD RESULTS

We have had the rare opportunity to be able to follow 99% of the living children into adulthood. Here are a few of the results when they were 21 years old (Campbell, Ramey, Pungello, Sparling, & Miller-Johnson, 2002). Not only were treated children still performing better on intelligence and reading and math assessments, but almost 70% of those who received the preschool treatment were also engaged in skilled jobs (above entry-level positions) or enrolled in higher education, in contrast to only 40% of those in the control group. What was particularly noteworthy was that children from the treatment group were three times more likely to attend a four-year college than were control-group children: 36% versus 12%. Another young-adult advantage was the delay of almost 2 years in their age of having a first child—waiting until after high school completion. These practical positive outcomes appear to be mediated by improved cognitive, linguistic, and social competence (Burchinal, Campbell, Bryant, Wasik, & Ramey, 1997).

SUMMARY OF ABECEDARIAN RESULTS

The key findings from the ABC/Abecedarian Project are consistent and encouraging. From 18 months through 21 years of age, the benefits include the children's higher IQ and higher reading and math scores; an improved understanding of their role in the educational process, reflected in improved "academic locus-of-control" scores (Walden & Ramey, 1983), where the children equate their effort and learning with their grades and achievement (rather than attributing them to factors such as teacher bias, chance, or luck), increased social competence, more years of education, and greater likelihood of full-time and higher-status employment. The rates of grade repetition, special education placement, teen pregnancy, and smoking and drug use were all significantly lower than in the control group. We believe that these findings and those from other early intervention research programs have established that early intervention can be a major positive factor in altering the developmental course of high-risk children. Not all early intervention programs have produced such positive results, however.

Why Do Some Preschool Programs Fail?

The field of preschool education and early intervention is not without controversy or mixed results. Some well-intentioned preschool programs implemented in community settings and funded with public or private dollars have not been able to demonstrate measurable benefits. Why? We have reviewed and analyzed these studies (e.g., Ramey & Ramey, 1998a, 2000), as have others (e.g., Haskins, 1989). Here are the most likely reasons that some programs have failed to close the achievement gap. First, many of those programs have not been able to provide the preservice and in-service training for teaching that ensures that the children receive a consistently high-quality learning and language environment. Second, many programs are not intensive—often they are provided after children are 4 years old, are offered for just 3 or 4 hours per day, or operate for only 7 to 9 months. Third, many failed programs have a remedial rather than a preventive focus, making it more difficult to overcome the cumulative toll of limited learning. Fourth, upon close analysis, many well-intended programs have primarily supported families and tried to help children only indirectly—and that indirect help did not include teaching important cognitive and language concepts to the children themselves. Although a family's total life situation is undeniably important, high-risk children themselves need to have firsthand experiences with mentoring and appropriate learning experiences in order to progress in their cognitive and linguistic skills. Unfortunately, there are many redundant and poorly coordinated family and early childhood programs that simply do not have adequate planning, professional expertise, or resources to deliver a preschool program that will result in major and sustainable cognitive and linguistic gains for children.

Recommendations for Public Policy

Based on the scientific evidence, we offer three major public policy recommendations. First, states and communities should develop strong leadership for a comprehensive early childhood educational initiative that is linked explicitly to K–12 learning and achievement within each state and community. In developing this initiative, it will be important to include the truly high-risk children (who are far fewer than all children in poverty), incorporate the scientific evidence about what really produces measurable benefits, and build upon the resources already available in states.

Our second recommendation is to combine funding streams and to promote innovative partnerships. This will help to strengthen existing programs that already are collaborative and can demonstrate positive outcomes; it will also be an opportunity to improve or eliminate those programs that are ineffective or poor in quality. In the future, continued support for preschool programs should be linked to ongoing performance measures of the program's quality and the demonstrated benefits to children in terms of their cognitive, linguistic, and social competence.

Our third recommendation concerns practical accountability. In the past most early childhood intervention programs did not have well-designed accountability systems that were useful in practice. Thus it has not been possible to characterize the quality of programs or to engage in comparative analysis. This situation cannot continue if we seek to maximize young children's outcomes at reasonable costs. Much controversy, anxiety, and frank politics surround proposed federal guidelines about measuring the development of young children. In fact, excellent procedures are available to observe and document the quality and amount of preschool education and child care. Child assessments should not be construed as high-stakes testing of children or a disguised effort to diminish public support for early childhood education; rather, child and program assessments should be seen as responsible (and long overdue) monitoring and evaluation procedures for public preschool services and supports targeted at our nation's most vulnerable young citizens. The cost of good accountability is relatively small and will not detract from the dollars and efforts available for direct services. To allow interventions and programs to be poorly monitored or not to hold them accountable for their educational quality or child developmental progress would not be in the best interest of our children or our country. Collectively, the well-being and the school readiness of our nation's children need to be major priorities so that all young children receive the essential transactions and the learning opportunities vital for their brain development and success in school. Since the mid-1960s we have witnessed remarkable and strong bipartisan support for efforts to serve high-risk young children. It is now time to act upon this knowledge and to provide high-quality preschool programs for all high-risk children. We believe that this is a civil right of all children in a high-resource and ethical society.

It is also time to rethink the research agenda concerning early experience and the modifiability of cognitive development and school readiness for high-risk children. For more than 40 years the predominant research question has been whether school readiness could be modified—the so-called efficacy question. We submit that the evidence that we have summarized and cited in this chapter adds up to a clear and consistent yes. We believe that the field of child development could make additional useful contributions by focusing on two major issues.

First, it would be helpful to know more about the epidemiology of lack of school readiness. Population-based samples, ideally at the state and community levels of analysis, should be examined on a recurring basis to document the geographical distribution and extent of the school readiness problem. Such research is likely to show systematic concentrations of individuals and their sociodemographic characteristics. Geographical Information System mapping can be a useful data display tool to better understand the resulting public policy issues and concerns, yielding information that would include where early intervention programs should be located and how large they need to be to adequately meet the need for service.

Second, comparative analyses of alternative curricular and program features can help to improve program effectiveness by identifying core essentials and control costs by eliminating weak or ineffectual program features and practices. This refocus would be a sign of the maturing science of human development that increasingly undergirds the provision of services to children and the institutions funded to support the development of individual children.

Yes, we now know that we can positively alter the development of young, disadvantaged children by systematically providing early childhood education. Now the question becomes: Can we do this better and more efficiently so that we can reach all children who need those services? We firmly believe that this new focus offers practical promise for children and society.

References

Burchinal, M. R., Campbell, F. A., Bryant, D. M., Wasik, B. H., & Ramey, C. T. (1997). Early intervention and mediating processes in cognitive performance of children of low-income African American families. *Child Development, 68*, 935–954.

Campbell, F. A., Pungello, E., Miller-Johnson, S., Burchinal, M., & Ramey, C. T. (2001). The development of cognitive and academic abilities: Growth curves from an early childhood educational experiment. *Developmental Psychology, 37*, 231–242.

Campbell, F. A., Ramey, C. T., Pungello, E., Sparling, J., & Miller-Johnson, S. (2002). Early childhood education: Young adult outcomes from the Abecedarian Project. *Applied Developmental Science, 6*, 42–57.

Carnegie Task Force on Meeting the Needs of Young Children. (1994). *Starting points: Meeting the needs of our youngest children.* New York: Carnegie Corporation.

Donovan, M. S., & Cross, C. T. (Eds.). (2002). *Minority students in special and gifted education.* Washington, DC: National Academy Press.

Entwisle, D. R. (1995). The role of schools in sustaining benefits of early childhood programs. *Future of Children, 5*, 133–144.

Gross, R. T., Spiker, D., & Haynes, C. W. (Eds.). (1997). *Helping low birth weight, premature babies: The Infant Health and Development Program.* Stanford, CA: Stanford University Press.

Hart, B., & Risley, T. R. (1995). *Meaningful differences in the everyday experience of young American children.* Baltimore: Paul H. Brookes.

Haskins, R. (1989). Beyond metaphor: The efficacy of early childhood education. *American Psychologist, 44*, 274–282.

Herrnstein, R. J., & Murray, C. (1996). *The bell curve: Intelligence and class structure in American life.* New York: Free Press.

Huttenlocher, J., Harght, W., Bruk, A., Seltzer, M., & Lyons, T. (1991). Early vocabulary growth: Relation to language input and gender. *Developmental Psychology, 27*, 236–248.

Martin, S. L., Ramey, C. T., & Ramey, S. L. (1990). The prevention of intellectual impairment in children of impoverished families: Findings of a randomized trial of educational day care. *American Journal of Public Health, 80*, 844–847.

McGinness, G., & Ramey, C. T. (1981). Developing sociolinguistic competence in children. *Canadian Journal of Early Childhood Education, 1*, 22–43.

Ramey, C. T., Bryant, D. M., Sparling, J. J., & Wasik, B. H. (1985). Project CARE: A comparison of two early intervention strategies to prevent retarded development. *Topics in Early Childhood Special Education, 5,* 12–25.

Ramey, C. T., Bryant, D. M., Wasik, B. H., Sparling, J. J., Fendt, K. H., & Lavange, L. M. (1992). Infant Health and Development Program for low birth weight, premature infants: Program elements, family participation, and child intelligence. *Pediatrics, 89,* 454–465.

Ramey, C. T., Campbell, F. A., Burchinal, M., Skinner, M. L., Gardner, D. M., & Ramey, S. L. (2000). Persistent effects of early childhood education on high-risk children and their mothers. *Applied Developmental Science, 4,* 2–14.

Ramey, C. T., McGinness, G., Cross, L., Collier, A., & Barrie-Blackley, S. (1981). The Abecedarian approach to social competence: Cognitive and linguistic intervention for disadvantaged preschoolers. In K. Borman (Ed.), *The social life of children in a changing society* (pp. 145–174). Hillsdale, NJ: Erlbaum.

Ramey, C. T., & Ramey, S. L. (1998a). Early intervention and early experience. *American Psychologist, 53,* 109–120.

Ramey, C. T., & Ramey, S. L. (1998b). Prevention of intellectual disabilities: Early interventions to improve cognitive development. *Preventive Medicine, 27,* 224–232.

Ramey, S. L., & Ramey, C. T. (1999a). *Going to school: How to help your child succeed.* New York: Goddard Press.

Ramey, C. T., & Ramey, S. L. (1999b). *Right from birth: Building your child's foundation for life.* New York: Goddard Press.

Ramey, S. L., & Ramey, C. T. (2000). Early childhood experiences and developmental competence. In J. Waldfogel & S. Danziger (Eds.), *Securing the future: Investing in children from birth to college* (pp. 122–150). New York: Sage.

Ramey, C. T., Yeates, K. O., & Short, E. J. (1984). The plasticity of intellectual development: Insights from preventive intervention. *Child Development, 55* (1913–1925).

Shonkoff, J. P., & Phillips, D. A. (Eds.), & Committee on Integrating the Science of Early Childhood Development. (2000). *From neurons to neighborhoods: The science of early childhood development.* Washington, DC: National Academy Press.

Sparling, J., & Lewis, I. (1979). *Learningames for the first three years: A guide to parent-child play.* New York: Walker.

Sparling, J., & Lewis, I. (1984). *Learningames for threes and fours: A guide to adult/child play.* New York: Walker.

Sparling, J., Lewis, I., & Ramey, C. (1995). *Partners for learning.* Lewisville, NC: Kaplan Press.

Walden, T., & Ramey, C. T. (1983). Locus of control and academic achievement: Results from a preschool intervention program. *Journal of Educational Psychology, 75,* 347–358.

Wasik, B. H., Ramey, C. T., Bryant, D. M., & Sparling, J. J. (1990). A longitudinal study of two early intervention strategies: Project CARE. *Child Development, 61,* 1682–1696.

22

Contextual Factors in Risk and Prevention Research

John E. Lochman

Efforts to understand the development of childhood psychopathology have placed growing emphasis on contextual factors that influence children's developmental trajectories and lead to antisocial outcomes. A child's developmental course is set within the child's social ecology, and an ecological framework is needed to understand these effects (Conduct Problems Prevention Research Group, 1992; Greenberg, Lengua, Coie, Pinderhughes, & Conduct Problems Prevention Research Group, 1999; Tolan, Gorman-Smith, Huesmann, & Zelli, 1997). Children have important interactions in their microsystems of growing social fields of child-family, child-peer, and teacher-student interactions, and these social fields relate to each other in important ways (e.g., the home-school exosystem; Bronfenbrenner, 1979). The influence of neighborhood context on the individuals, and on the other school and family contextual factors, can also be pivotal. In this chapter I briefly review the important role of contextual factors in developmental psychopathology and discuss four implications of contextual factors on the development, implementation, and evaluation of preventive interventions.

Contextual Effects Within Risk Models

The emphasis on ecological effects has led to the creation of comprehensive developmental models that indicate how contextual factors can have direct effects on children's outcomes (e.g., Conduct Problems Prevention Research Group, 1992). Neighborhood risk factors and family risk factors evident in maternal psychopathology, maternal life stress, and low socioeconomic status can directly influence young children's externalizing and internalizing behaviors and their academic achievement, although different contextual factors have been found to affect varying child outcomes (Greenberg et al., 1999).

In addition, the effects of growing up in a problematic neighborhood have still been found to be present even after controlling for other family and child risk factors (Greenberg et al., 1999).

A Contextual Social-Cognitive Model

This growing understanding of contextual effects can produce refined risk prediction models and lead to more comprehensive preventive interventions. Existing research suggests, for example, that a contextual social-cognitive model, as shown in Figure 1, can account for the development of aggressive behavior problems during the preadolescent and early adolescent years (Lochman & Wells, 2002). This model indicates that two relevant sets of potential mediators of adolescent substance abuse include (a) child-level factors (e.g., Tremblay & LeMarquand, 2001), including their poor social-cognitive and decision-making skills, poor self-regulation, negatively perceived peer context, and poor ability to resist peer pressure, and (b) contextual factors, including poor parental-caregiver involvement with, and discipline of, the child (e.g., Wasserman & Seracini, 2001). Broader contextual risk factors, such as the level of neighborhood violence (Luthar, 1999), presumably affect these mediational processes and children's subsequent behavior.

Child factors

The conceptualization of the child-level factors within this contextual social-cognitive model began as a model of anger arousal (Lochman, Nelson, & Sims, 1981) derived from Novaco's 1978 work with aggressive adults. In this conceptualization of anger arousal, which stressed sequential cognitive processing and concomitant physiological arousal, the child responded to problems such as interpersonal conflicts or frustrations with environmental obstacles (i.e., difficult schoolwork). However, it was not the stimulus event itself that provoked the child's response but rather the child's cognitive processing of and about that event.

This first stage of cognitive processing (appraisal) was similar to Lazarus's primary appraisal stage (Smith & Lazarus, 1990) and consisted of labeling, attributions, and perceptions of the problem event. The second stage of processing (problem solution), similar to Lazarus's secondary appraisal (Smith & Lazarus, 1990), consisted of the child's cognitive plan for his or her response to the perceived threat or provocation. The anger arousal model indicated that the child's cognitive processing of the problem event and of the child's planned response led to physiological arousal and to the child's ac-

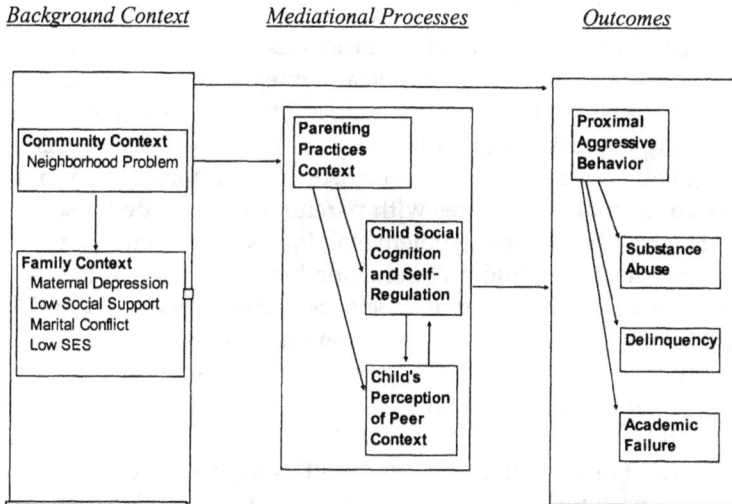

Figure 1. Contextual Social-Cognitive Model

tual behavioral response and its positive or negative consequences. In this model perceived provocation arouses children physiologically and causes attributional distortions in response (Williams, Lochman, Phillips, & Barry, 2003).

Because of research on children's social information processing (Crick & Dodge, 1994; Dodge, Laird, Lochman, Zelli, & Conduct Problems Prevention Research Group, 2002), the contextual social-cognitive model of children's aggression evolved, and the nature of the social-cognitive deficiencies and distortions and of the schemas that affect processing became more differentiated and refined (Lochman, Whidby, & FitzGerald, 2000; Lochman & Wells, 2002). Aggressive children have cognitive distortions at the appraisal stage of social-cognitive processing because of difficulties in encoding incoming social information and in accurately interpreting social events and others' intentions. They have cognitive deficiencies at the problem solution stage of social-cognitive processing by generating maladaptive solutions for perceived problems and having nonnormative expectations for the usefulness of aggressive and nonaggressive solutions to their social problems.

Parent and peer factors

These child-level social-cognitive processes are shaped by children's experience from the layers of social contexts that surround them. Most proximal, and most influential, are the effects of parents and the family context. As articulated by Patterson, Reid, and Dishion (1992), child aggressive behavior arises most fundamentally out of early contextual experiences with parents who provide harsh or irritable discipline, poor problem solving, vague commands, and poor monitoring of children's behavior. In an extensive review of the risk factors for adolescent antisocial behavior, Hawkins, Catalano, and Miller (1992) identified several parental risk factors that are also directly linked to childhood aggression, including deficient family management practices involving lack of maternal involvement and inconsistent parenting (e.g., Kandel & Andrews, 1987). Other, more family-level factors affect parents' abilities to provide consistent, effective expectations and consequences for their children, within a warmly involved relationship. These factors include parental psychopathology, the level of social support that parents receive, interparent conflict, and the socioeconomic status of the family.

Children's social-cognitive processes are also proximally affected by their peer group. Children's level of acceptance or rejection from their peers, their ability to form close friendships, and, in the adolescent age period, their involvement in deviant peer groups contribute to children's maintenance and escalation of problem behaviors (Conduct Problems Prevention Research Group, 2004). Just as bidirectional relations are evident in the degree of parents' positive involvement with their children and children's aggressive behavior over time (Bry, Catalano, Kumpfer, Lochman, & Szapocznik, 1999), children's aggressive behavior and their rejection by their peers affect each other reciprocally (Conduct Problems Prevention Research Group, 2004).

Neighborhood and classroom factors

Neighborhood problems, as perceived by children's caretakers, have a direct impact on the children's reactive aggressive behaviors (Lochman, Barry, Barth, & Wells, 2001) and on children's general levels of aggressive, antisocial behaviors (Greenberg et al., 1999; Schwab-Stone et al., 1995), above and beyond the effects of poor parenting practices. Neighborhood contextual factors appear to have heightened effects on the development of antisocial behavior during the middle childhood, preadolescent years (Ingoldsby & Shaw, 2002). Neighborhood factors have been found to contribute to children's risk for substance use (Dembo, Blount, Schmeidler, & Burgos, 1986; Luthar & Cushing, 1999; Schwab-Stone et al., 1995) and to have direct effects on parenting behaviors (Pinderhughes, Nix, Foster, Jones, & Conduct Problems Prevention Research Group, 2001). Neighborhoods can adversely influence children's development in part because of the deviant social influences that are apparent in problematic, crime-ridden neighborhoods.

Similar adverse effects from deviant social influences are also possible in other out-of-home contexts, such as the children's classrooms. Children's aggressive behaviors have been found to be enhanced when the children have been placed in a classroom with a high percentage of aggressive children, as children's aggressive behavior increases in those years, when they are in more toxic classrooms with a higher density of students with behavior problems (Barth, Dunlap, Dane, Lochman, & Wells, 2004). Thus neighborhood and school contexts influence children's behavioral and social development.

Contextual Effects as Moderators

Contextual factors also can moderate how other risk factors predict negative outcomes for children and adolescents. Although they possess identifiable risk factors, some children shift out of a developmental trajectory that would ordinarily be expected to lead to an antisocial outcome. Person-oriented research strategies can assist us in identifying important subtypes of children who may have these varying developmental paths. Thus children can display certain systematic patterns of fluctuation or desistance in problematic behavior over time, and contextual factors can contribute to these shifts.

Interactions between contextual factors and child-level risk factors can identify buffering or protective factors that can insulate a child from the effects of their natural level of risk (Masten, Best, & Garmezy, 1990) and indicate which children at risk will be most likely to experience a negative, antisocial outcome. Consistent with diathesis-stress models, contextual factors can be identified that are capable of triggering the underlying risk. Examples of these diathesis-stress models abound in the literature on child-level risk factors. Birth complications involving preeclampsia, umbilical cord collapse, forceps delivery, or fetal hypoxia increase the risk of later violence among children but only when the infants subsequently experience adverse family environments or maternal rejection (Arseneault, Tremblay, Boulerice, & Saucier, 2002; Raine, Brennan, & Mednick, 1997). Higher levels of testosterone among adolescents and higher cortisol reactivity to provocations are associated with more violent behavior but only when the children or adolescents live in families where they experience high levels of parental abuse or low socioeconomic status (Dabbs & Morris, 1990; Scarpa & Raine, 2000). Children who have a gene that expresses only low levels of the enzyme MAOA (monoamine oxidase A) have a higher rate of adolescent violent behavior but only when they have experienced high levels of parental maltreatment (Caspi et al., 2002). Similar patterns of findings have been obtained when children's temperament characteristics have been examined as child-level risk factors. Highly active children (Colder, Lochman, & Wells, 1997), children with levels of emotional reactivity (Scaramella & Conger, 2003), and infants with difficult temperament (Coon, Carey, Corley, & Fulker, 1992) are at risk for later aggressive and conduct problem behavior but only when they have parents who provide poor monitoring or harsh discipline. The children's family context can serve as a key moderator of children's underlying propensity for an antisocial outcome.

IMPLICATIONS OF CONTEXTUAL FACTORS FOR PREVENTIVE INTERVENTION

The field's increasing understanding of the role of contextual factors in the development of psychopathology has at least four key implications for intervention development and intervention research. Consideration of contextual factors can affect the construction of intervention components, an intervention may serve to moderate the effects between risk factors and later antisocial outcomes, contextual factors may predict who benefits from interventions, and contextual factors may predict how effectively interventions can be disseminated.

Intervention development

If contextual factors have clear direct effects on children's outcomes, those parental and peer contextual factors that are malleable and that are potentially able to be influenced by an intervention should be considered as intervention targets. An intervention model should reflect the developmental model that describes the emergence of the problem behavior (Conduct Problems Prevention Research Group, 1992). If certain parenting practices are key aspects of the model describing the development of conduct problems, logically the intervention should include a component addressing those parenting practices. Consistent with this premise, multicomponent interventions that include parent training directed at improving parenting skills and child training directed at their social problem-solving skills have been found to have stronger and more sustained effects on children's behavior than have single-component interventions (Kazdin, Siegel, & Bass, 1992; Webster-Stratton & Hammond, 1997). In research on the Coping Power program, which is based on the contextual social-cognitive model that I described earlier, the full program, with child and parent components, had more significant effects at a one-year follow-up on adolescents' delinquency and substance use than did the child component alone (Lochman & Wells, 2004).

Because children's peers and their classroom environment are contextual effects that influence children's behavioral problems, a broader universal intervention directed at whole classrooms can be appropriate. Classroomwide preventive interventions can lead to notable changes in children's interpersonal relations and behavior in the classroom as a whole (Conduct Problems Prevention Research Group, 1999), and they can reduce the likelihood of high-risk children's later substance use (Lochman & Wells, 2003). In conjunction with targeted interventions directed at high-risk children, classroomwide interventions can help these children improve their behavior at school, as follow-ups have shown (Lochman & Wells, 2003). The combination of targeted and universal interventions can be particularly powerful because (a) as the targeted intervention produces social and behavioral changes in the high-risk child, those changes can produce positive radiating effects on the surrounding children's behavior (Allen, Chinsky, Larcen, Lochman, & Selinger, 1976; Kelly, 1971); (b) the classroom intervention can affect the peer groups' social behaviors in positive ways, creating a less toxic, more accepting peer environment for the target high-risk child; and (c) the targeted and universal programs can have additive effects on the high-risk child's behavior through repeated exposure and practice on key intervention concepts.

Intervention as a moderator variable

One result of an intervention may be to alter the relation between a risk variable and the later behavioral outcome. If intervention status influences the relationships between predictor variables and outcomes, then predictor risk variables may relate to the outcome variables in different ways within the intervention and control conditions. Thus we could consider intervention to have an environmental effect on the risk-to-outcome relationship. In such analyses significant interaction effects would suggest that the intervention has altered children's distribution on an outcome variable and thus altered the relationship between predictor variables and outcome.

In analyses of Fast Track program effects, control parents who had little initial social support from friends were found likely to rate their children as having increasing problems with aggression three years later and to have children who were more likely to be involved in special education (Conduct Problems Prevention Research Group, 2002). In contrast, intervention parents who had similar low levels of social support from friends at the baseline were more likely to report lower rates of aggression by their target children after three years of intervention and to have lower rates of special education involvement by their children. Earlier research had suggested that low levels of social support from friends contribute to parental "insularity" and irritability, increasing parents' tendency to provoke aversive behavior from their children and reducing parents' responsivity to interventions (Wahler, 1980; Wahler & Graves, 1983). After three years of intervention the Fast Track intervention program appeared to have reversed some of the negative sequelae resulting from parents' having low initial social support and high parental insularity, perhaps because these parents were able to obtain the social support they needed from intervention staff and other intervention parents. Whatever the cause, this particular risk factor, low initial social support, no longer was an indicator of increasing problems for the intervention parents.

Contextual factors as predictors
of individual responsivity to interventions

Previously, intervention was discussed as a variable that might moderate the relation between a risk variable and an outcome. In an alternate approach that would involve prediction of outcomes, the intervention researcher is engaged in the relatively straightforward task of determining whether certain baseline risk characteristics predict which children will have better or worse outcomes on the defined outcome and therefore whether these variables predict intervention effects. The prediction literature on parental context risk factors is relatively mixed (Kazdin, 1995), as children of depressed mothers and single parents have been found to have poorer response to intervention in some studies (e.g., Dumas & Albin, 1986; McMahon, Forehand, Griest, & Wells, 1981; Webster-Stratton & Hammond, 1997) but not in others (Dumas & Wahler, 1983; Holden, Lavigne, & Cameron, 1990; Webster-Stratton, 1985). Similarly, children living in families with low socioeconomic status and with socioeconomic disadvantage have not benefited as much from intervention in some studies (Dumas & Albin, 1986; Holden, Lavigne, & Cameron, 1990; Webster-Stratton, 1985) as in others (Serketich & Dumas, 1996).

These results indicate that specific parental and family context risk factors are important to assess as potential predictors of intervention outcome but that the particular risk predictors may vary from one intervention program to another, depending on the format and characteristics of the intervention. The results also indicate that a certain risk predictor (such as maternal depression) can predict lack of intervention responsivity on certain outcomes (such as teacher ratings of school behavior) but not on other outcomes within the same intervention (such as parent ratings of children's aggression; Conduct Problems Prevention Research Group, 2002).

Contextual factors as predictors of adequacy of dissemination of interventions

Contextual factors can also affect the way in which interventions are disseminated to new service sites and can impair the likelihood of successful dissemination. A factor that increases the difficulty of detecting the effects of interventions in intervention research is that the interventions are typically implemented at a number of sites (Raudenbush & Willms, 1991). The degree to which the intervention is implemented fully, and the context in which the intervention is embedded, can vary markedly from site to site. With school interventions contextual factors such as the characteristics of the schools and the school climate can be markedly different across schools. As a result the effectiveness of an intervention could vary markedly from site to site. Raudenbush and Willms (1991) argue that this variation, rather than being a nuisance that must be controlled in analyses, can provide critical information and is more important than the overall average effectiveness of the intervention. Variations in the adoption, success, and maintenance of interventions across sites can have major implications for the effective dissemination of preventive interventions.

New interventions and programs need organizational support to be adequately disseminated and implemented (Forman, 1995). The characteristics of work environments—such as relationships to supervisors, openness of communication, and the supportiveness of the environment—can affect individuals' efforts to create change in the work setting (Moos & Moos, 1983), to be innovative in work settings (Anderson & West, 1998; Turnipseed, 1994), and potentially to influence the implementation of preventive interventions (Vincent & Trickett, 1983). School personnel who perceive that their school environment is negative have been found to think that innovations in their schools are burdens (McClure, 1980). In contrast, positive perceived school climate has been found to lead to successful implementation of reforms in schools (Bulach & Malone, 1994). Furthermore, collegiality, shared authority among colleagues, and positive leadership by principals have been linked to the ability to facilitate change in schools and to continue school improvements (Peterson, 1997). Thus factors such as organizational structure and organizational climate should be considered important contextual factors that can influence the delivery of new interventions in work settings such as schools, and these contextual factors should be central constructs in prevention dissemination research.

Summary of Role of Context in Risk and Preventive Research

When research on children's risk factors focuses on contextual factors, attention begins with the children's immediate social environment: their parents and peers. These early and ongoing experiences with parents and peers form children's developing social-cognitive processes and influence how children acquire enduring patterns of perceiving others and thinking about how to respond to social problems. The immediate parent and peer environmental effects on children's functioning are augmented by broader contextual factors evident in the children's neighborhoods and classrooms. The density of deviant peers and adults within the children's community can substantially increase their immediate risks for antisocial behavior. However, family and neighborhood risk factors may not only add directly to a child's risks for negative outcomes but may also moderate the effect of early child-level risk factors, such as difficult temperament, on these outcomes. Thus children's inherent risk factors may predict later negative outcomes but only for those at-risk children who have experienced certain forms of family disadvantage or harsh parenting. These contextual factors can be conceptualized as either triggering or buffering the underlying risk.

Contextual factors also have a clear role in the planning, evaluation, and dissemination of preventive interventions. First, when the growth of children's conduct problems is at least partially promoted by the family and peer contexts in which they reside, multicomponent interventions are necessary to address the malleable child, parent, and peer risk factors. To produce durable, generalizable effects on children's behavior, interventions should modify the immediate family and peer contexts surrounding the child. Second, as interventions are implemented and evaluated, we need to understand how the children's family, neighborhood, and school contexts may moderate the effects of intervention; this moderation makes it likely that some children will benefit more than others from the intervention and may in some cases actually reverse the direction of effect of the initial baseline risk factor (e.g., low social support for parents). Finally, as preventive interventions and prevention research moves seriously to the next level of widespread dissemination of empirically supported programs, understanding how contextual factors within school and work settings can enhance or impair the implementation of interventions will be increasingly necessary. Contextual factors impact not only the individuals in their settings but also how staff try to deploy preventive interventions. Ignoring contextual factors can substantially impair and undermine the effectiveness, durability, and sustainability of empirically supported preventive interventions designed to promote children's adaptive behavioral and emotional development.

References

Allen, G., Chinsky, J., Larcen, S., Lochman, J., & Selinger, H. (1976). *Community psychology and the schools: A behaviorally oriented multilevel preventive approach.* New York: Wiley.

Anderson, N., & West, M. (1998). Measuring climate for work group innovation: Development and validation of the team climate inventory. *Journal of Organizational Behavior, 19,* 234–258.

Arseneault, L., Tremblay, R. E., Boulerice, B., & Saucier, J. F. (2002). Obstetrical complications and violent delinquency: Testing two developmental pathways. *Child Development, 73,* 496–508.

Barth, J. M., Dunlap, S. T., Dane, H., Lochman, J. E., & Wells, K. C. (2004). Classroom environment influences on aggression, peer relations, and academic focus. *Journal of School Psychology, 42,* 115–133.

Bronfenbrenner, U. (1979). *The ecology of human development.* Cambridge, MA: Harvard University Press.

Bry, B. H., Catalano, R. F., Kumpfer, K., Lochman, J. E., & Szapocznik, J. (1999). Scientific findings from family prevention intervention research. In R. Ashery (Ed.), *Family-based prevention interventions* (pp. 103–129). Rockville, MD: National Institute of Drug Abuse.

Bulach, C., & Malone, B. (1994). The relationship of school climate to the implementation of school reform. *ERS Spectrum, 12,* 3–8.

Caspi, A., McClay, J., Moffitt, T. E., Mill, J., Martin, J., Craig, I. W., Taylor, A., & Poulton, R. (2002). Role of genotype in the cycle of violence in maltreated children. *Science, 297,* 851–854.

Colder, C. R., Lochman, J. E., & Wells, K. C. (1997). The moderating effects of children's fear and activity level on relations between parenting practices and childhood symptomatology. *Journal of Abnormal Child Psychology, 25,* 251–263.

Conduct Problems Prevention Research Group (1992). A developmental and clinical model for the prevention of conduct disorders: The Fast Track program. *Development and Psychopathology, 4,* 509–527.

Conduct Problems Prevention Research Group (1999). Initial impact of the Fast Track Prevention Trial for conduct problems: II. Classroom effects. *Journal of Consulting and Clinical Psychology, 67,* 648–657.

Conduct Problems Prevention Research Group (2002). Predictor variables associated with positive Fast Track outcomes at the end of third grade. *Journal of Abnormal Child Psychology, 30,* 37–52.

Conduct Problems Prevention Research Group (2004). The Fast Track experiment: Translating the developmental model into a prevention design. In K. A. Dodge & J. B. Kupersmidt (Eds.), *Children's peer relations: From development to intervention to policy* (pp. 181–208). Washington, DC: American Psychological Association.

Coon, H., Carey, G., Corley, R., & Fulker, D. W. (1992). Identifying children in the Colorado Adoption Project at risk for conduct disorder. *Journal of the American Academy of Child and Adolescent Psychiatry, 31,* 503–511.

Crick, N. R., & Dodge, K. A. (1994). A review and reformulation of social information-processing mechanisms in children's social adjustment. *Psychological Bulletin, 115,* 74–101.

Dabbs, J. M., & Morris, R. (1990). Testosterone, social class, and antisocial behavior in a sample of 4,462 men. *Psychological Science, 1,* 209–211.

Dembo, R., Blount, W. R., Schmeidler, J., & Burgos, W. (1986). Perceived environmental drug use risk and correlates of early drug use and nonuse among inner-city youths: The motivated actor. *International Journal of the Addictions, 21,* 977–1000.

Dodge, K. A., Laird, R., Lochman, J. E., Zelli, A., & Conduct Problems Prevention Research Group (2002). Multi-dimensional latent construct analysis of children's social information processing patterns: Correlations with aggressive behavior problems. *Psychological Assessment, 14,* 60–73.

Dumas, J. E., & Albin, J. B. (1986). Parent training outcome: Does active parental involvement matter? *Behaviour Research and Therapy, 24,* 227–230.

Dumas, J. E., & Wahler, R. G. (1983). Predictors of treatment outcome in parent training: Mother insularity and socioeconomic disadvantage. *Behavioral Assessment, 5,* 301–313.

Forman, S. G. (1995). Organizational factors and consultation outcome. *Educational and Psychological Consultation, 6,* 191–195.

Greenberg, M. T., Lengua, L. J., Coie, J. D., Pinderhughes, E. E., & Conduct Problems Prevention Research Group (1999). Predicting developmental outcomes at school entry using a multiple-risk model: Four American communities. *Developmental Psychology, 35,* 403–417.

Hawkins, J. D., Catalano, R. F., & Miller, J. Y. (1992). Risk and protective factors for alcohol and other drug problems in adolescence and early adulthood: Implications for substance abuse prevention. *Psychological Bulletin, 112,* 64–105.

Holden, G. W., Lavigne, V. V., & Cameron, A. M. (1990). Probing the continuum of effectiveness of parent training: Characteristics of parents and preschoolers. *Journal of Clinical Child Psychology, 19,* 2–8.

Ingoldsby, E. M., & Shaw, D. S. (2002). Neighborhood contextual factors and early-starting antisocial pathways. *Clinical Child and Family Psychology Review, 5,* 21–55.

Kandel, D. B., & Andrews, K. (1987). Processes of adolescent socialization by parents and peers. *International Journal of Addictions, 22,* 319–342.

Kazdin, A. E. (1995). Child, parent, and family dysfunction as predictors of outcome in cognitive-behavioral treatment of antisocial children. *Behaviour Research and Therapy, 33,* 271–281.

Kazdin, A. E., Siegal, T. C., & Bass, D. (1992). Cognitive problem-solving skills training and parent management training in the treatment of antisocial behavior in children. *Journal of Consulting and Clinical Psychology, 60,* 733–747.

Kelly, J. G. (1971). The quest for valid preventive interventions. In G. Rosenblum (Ed.), *Issues in community psychology and preventive mental health* (pp. 109–125). New York: Behavioral Publications.

Lochman, J. E., Barry, T. D., Barth, J., & Wells, K. C. (2001, May). *The influence of neighborhood context on children's aggressive and academic behaviors.* Paper presented at the Life History Research Society Meeting, St. Michaels, MD.

Lochman, J. E., Nelson, W. M., & Sims, J. P. (1981). A cognitive behavioral program for use with aggressive children. *Journal of Clinical Child Psychology 13,* 146–148.

Lochman, J. E., & Wells, K. C. (2002). Contextual social-cognitive mediators and child outcome: A test of the theoretical model in the Coping Power program. *Development and Psychopathology, 14,* 971–993.

Lochman, J. E., & Wells, K. C. (2003). Effectiveness study of Coping Power and classroom intervention with aggressive children: Outcomes at a one-year follow-up. *Behavior Therapy, 34,* 493–515.

Lochman, J. E., & Wells, K. C. (2004). The Coping Power program for preadolescent aggressive boys and their parents: Outcome effects at the one-year follow-up. *Journal of Consulting and Clinical Psychology, 72,* 571–578.

Lochman, J. E., Whidby, J. M., & Fitzgerald, D. P. (2000). Cognitive-behavioral assessment and treatment with aggressive children. In P. C. Kendall (Ed.), *Child and adolescent therapy: Cognitive-behavioral procedures* (2nd ed., pp. 31–87). New York: Guilford.

Luthar, S. S. (1999). *Poverty and children's adjustment.* New York: Sage.

Luthar, S. S., & Cushing, G. (1999). Neighborhood influences and child development: A prospective study of substance abusers' offspring. *Development and Psychopathology, 12,* 857–885.

Masten, A. S., Best, K. M., & Garmezy, N. (1990). Resilience and development: Contributions from the study of children who overcome adversity. *Development and Psychopathology, 2,* 425–444.

McClure, L. (1980). Community psychology concepts and research base: Promise and product. *American Psychologist, 35,* 1000–1011.

McMahon, R. J., Forehand, R., Griest, D. L., & Wells, K. C. (1981). Who drops out of therapy during parent training? *Behavior Counseling Quarterly, 1,* 79–85.

Moos, R. H., & Moos, B. S. (1983). Adaptation and the quality of life in work and family settings. *Journal of Community Psychology, 11,* 158–170.

Novaco, R. W. (1978). Anger and coping with stress: Cognitive behavioral interventions. In J. P. Foreyet & D. P. Rathjen (Eds.), *Cognitive behavioral therapy: Research and application* (pp.135–173). New York: Plenum.

Patterson, G. R., Reid, J. B., & Dishion, T. J. (1992). *Antisocial boys.* Eugene, OR: Castalia.

Peterson, A. M. (1997). Aspects of school climate: A review of the literature. *ERS Spectrum, 15,* 36–42.

Pinderhughes, E. E., Nix, R., Foster, E. M., Jones, D., & Conduct Problems Prevention Research Group (2001). Parenting in context: Impact of neighborhood poverty, residential stability, public services, social networks, and danger on parental behaviors. *Journal of Marriage and Family, 63,* 941–953.

Raine, A., Brennan, P., & Mednick, S. A. (1997). Interaction between birth complications and early maternal rejection in predisposing individuals to adult violence: Specificity to serious, early-onset violence. *American Journal of Psychiatry, 154,* 1265–1271.

Raudenbush, S. W., & Willms, J. D. (1991). The organization of schooling and its methodological implications. In S. W. Raudenbush & J. D. Willms (Eds.), *Schools, classrooms, and pupils: International studies of schooling from a multilevel perspective* (pp. 1–12). San Diego: Academic Press.

Scaramella, L. V., & Conger, R. D. (2003). Intergenerational continuity of hostile parenting and its consequences: The moderating influence of children's negative emotional reactivity. *Social Development, 12,* 420–439.

Scarpa, A., & Raine, A. (2000). Violence associated with anger and impulsivity. In J. C. Borod (Ed.), *The neuropsychology of emotion* (pp. 320–339). London: Oxford University Press.

Schwab-Stone, M. E., Ayers, T. S., Kasprow, W., Voyce, C., Barone, C., Shriver, T., Weissberg, R. P. (1995). No safe haven: A study of violence exposure in an urban community. *Journal of the American Academy of Child and Adolescent Psychiatry, 34,* 1343–1352.

Serketich, W. J., & Dumas, J. E. (1996). The effectiveness of behavioral parent training to modify antisocial behavior in children: A meta-analysis.

Behavior Therapy, 27, 171–186.

Smith, C. A., & Lazarus, R. W. (1990). Emotion and adaptation. In L. Previn (Ed.), *Handbook of personality: Theory and research* (pp. 609–637). New York: Guilford.

Tolan, P. H., Gorman-Smith, D., Huesmann, L. R., & Zelli, A. (1997). Assessment of family relationship characteristics: A measure to explain risk for antisocial behavior and depression among urban youth. *Psychological Assessment, 9,* 212–223.

Tremblay, R. E., & Lemarquand, D. (2001). Individual risk and protective factors. In R. Loeber & D. P. Farrington (Eds.), *Child delinquents: Development, intervention, and service needs* (pp. 137–164). Thousand Oaks, CA: Sage.

Turnipseed, D. (1994). The relationship between the social environment of organizations and the climate for innovation and creativity. *Journal of Applied Social Psychology, 24,* 782–800.

Vincent, T. A., & Trickett, E. J. (1983). Preventive interventions and the human context: Ecological approaches to environmental assessment and change. In R. D. Felner, L. A. Jason, J. N. Moritsugu, & S. S. Farber (Eds.), *Preventive psychology: Theory, research, and practice* (pp. 67–86). New York: Pergamon.

Wahler, R. G. (1980). The insular mother: Her problems in parent-child treatment. *Journal of Applied Behavior Analysis, 13,* 207–219.

Wahler, R. G., & Graves, M. G. (1983). Setting events in social networks: Ally or enemy in child behavior therapy? *Behavior Therapy, 14,* 19–36.

Wasserman, G. A., & Seracini, A. M. (2001). Family risk factors and interventions. In R. Loeber & D. P. Farrington (Eds.), *Child delinquents: Development, intervention, and service needs* (pp. 165–189). Thousand Oaks, CA: Sage.

Webster-Stratton, C. (1985). Predictors of treatment outcome in parent training for conduct disordered children. *Behavior Therapy, 16,* 223–243.

Webster-Stratton, C., & Hammond, M. (1997). Treating children with early-onset conduct problems: A comparison of child and parent training interventions. *Journal of Consulting and Clinical Psychology, 65,* 93–109.

Williams, S. C., Lochman, J.E., Phillips, N. C., & Barry, T. D. (2003). Aggressive and non-aggressive boys' physiological and cognitive processes in response to peer provocations. *Journal of Clinical Child and Adolescent Psychology, 32,* 568–576.

23

Integrating Developmental Scholarship and Society
From Dissemination and Accountability to Evidence-Based Programming and Policies

*Robert B. McCall, Christina J. Groark,
and Robert P. Nelkin*

Since the mid-1960s developmental scholarship has traveled an episodic and often bumpy road from isolation in the proverbial ivory tower to serious and meaningful attempts to integrate its knowledge with the needs of society and to contribute more directly to the welfare of children, youth, and families. While practitioners and policy makers have always demonstrated a certain receptivity to scholarly knowledge, today's policy and practice mantra is evidence-based programming, in which policy makers want to implement programs that research has previously documented to be effective.

As a result it would seem that applied developmental scholarship's policy time has come. While scholars should rejoice at this opportunity, we also should display humility, provide greater balance in methodology, recognize that others play crucial roles in the practice and policy process and that we must partner with those individuals, and broaden the academic value system to embrace and reward excellence in conducting applied scholarship and integrating it with social and policy needs.

Historical Legacies

While developmental scholarship is more accepting of and vigorously involved in practice and policy today, some of its historical roots still impede progress in applied work. A brief historical review, admittedly highly selective and personal in its perspectives, may help us to understand those legacies and prepare us to go beyond them (see also Rossi, Lipsey, & Freeman, 2004; Zigler, 1998).

Becoming a Science

The primary purpose of psychology during midcentury was to define itself as a science by focusing on the discovery of basic, generalizable, cause-and-effect laws of fundamental behavioral processes with respect to sensation, perception, learning, motivation, personality, and so forth. The set of such laws would presumably have the potential to explain a substantial amount of animal and human behavior.

Those in the discipline wanted psychology to be a science like chemistry and physics, so they focused on discovering basic laws using the experimental methodologies of the physical and biological sciences. As a result animal work, for example, was popular, because it permitted maximum experimenter control and the broadest possible range of experimental interventions, random assignment methodology, and precise measurement. Much research using human beings at the time was similar to that conducted on animals, representing experimental studies of the basic processes of learning and motivation (e.g., paired associate or nonsense syllable learning, eye blink conditioning).

The experimental methods honed during this era were well suited to their purpose. Because the primary goal was to discover cause-and-effect relations, the experimental method was vastly preferred to observational research that could not legitimately produce inferences of causality. It was tacitly assumed that context—stimuli, procedures, and environments—did not need to be varied systemically, because the processes under study were presumed to be so basic that they would operate essentially the same way across these circumstances. Individual differences were seen largely as nuisance factors and were often purged by studying homogeneous samples (e.g., only one gender, one age, under one set of stimuli and procedural circumstances), the members of which were randomly assigned to conditions to balance the remaining extraneous factors across groups.

The task was to build an integrated, coherent theory of learning, motivation, and personality, for example, so theory constituted the main rationale and justification for what was studied.

While the theoretical/experimental approach dominated, it was not appropriate for all questions under all circumstances even in its halcyon days. Some domains of study (e.g., personality, social, clinical, developmental, and educational psychology) did not lend themselves as easily as sensation, perception, learning, and motivation to experimental manipulation and had to be studied in large part by observational methods. Individual differences were of greater intrinsic interest in these fields, but in the dominant zeitgeist they were tangential to the purpose of describing general laws about basic processes, and scholars following these pursuits were regarded as being in a "separate discipline" of psychology (Cronbach, 1957, 1975).

Eventually, curiosity and research funding spread to processes more characteristic of naturalistic human behavior. The basic experimentalists followed the transition and brought their theoretical and experimental orientation with them, but they staked out new and decidedly separate claims in the hinterlands, calling their homesteads "experimental social psychology" and "experimental child psychology," apparently to distinguish them from the softer and less prestigious nonexperimental approaches. They even founded journals with such names that had editorial policies that excluded naturalistic observational research.

The experimental homesteaders lent both their methods and the prestige they enjoyed to these new disciplines, and developmental science benefited immensely as a result. While the field has changed and broadened dramatically since those times, legacies persist, especially a preference for experimental methodology and the requirement for a theoretical rationale as a basis for selecting and justifying research questions. These strategies have had and will continue to have their place in developmental science, but truly integrating developmental science with social programming and policies requires that we sometimes ask questions that society needs to have answered, not only those that theory might dictate (McCall & Groark, 2000). It also requires that we use and respect methods that emphasize external validity as complements to those that emphasize internal validity (McCall & Green, 2004), to ensure that principles and practices nurtured by basic research are also ecologically valid.

Two Early Attempts to Relate to Society

During the era in which psychology in general and developmental scholarship in particular were creating their identities as sciences, going public was definitely frowned upon (Zigler, 1998). Many felt that the discipline did not yet have enough information to be able to contribute in scientifically responsible ways to practitioners, policy makers, and the general public. Further, once information was injected into the public forum, scholars would lose control over it, and they feared it would be transformed in unanticipated and perhaps inaccurate ways to meet the nonscientific needs of practitioners, policy makers, and the public (McCall, 1987). Nevertheless, a few scholars, especially senior members of the profession, ventured forth in two ways, attempting to contribute directly to social policies and disseminating research-based information to the general public.

Social policy

Senior scholars, most notably Edward Zigler and Harold Stevenson, among others, felt that those in developmental scholarship needed to learn more about social policy. They invited political figures, including Walter Mondale (then a young senator from Minnesota who was a cosponsor of a comprehensive child development bill that ultimately was not implemented), to the Society for Research in Child Development (SRCD) conventions, albeit as nonprogrammic extra sessions, to talk about child development and social policy (Zigler, 1998). Then the Bush Centers were created at four universities, where students and faculty could study developmental scholarship and social policy. Some centers and some individuals (most notably Zigler) took much more active roles in the policy process per se.

Dissemination

At the same time scholars were recognizing that they could not remain isolated in colleges and universities—they had to "give psychology away" (Miller, 1969, p. 1071), that is, to communicate what those in the discipline had learned that might be relevant to practitioners, policy makers, and the general public (McCall, 1987). But most scholars felt that communicating their knowledge to practitioners and policy makers was someone else's job, typically academic practitioners', journalists', and teachers', and scholars perceived that these communicators often got the message wrong, which tainted the enterprise and perpetuated the cycle of scientific silence.

Again, senior scholars led the way, and for a period of time nearly every American Psychological Association (APA) president urged greater communication of research and best practice information to practitioners, policy makers, and the general public. The APA established a public information committee to facilitate its work in this regard, as did the Developmental Psychology Division of APA and the SRCD. The latter two sent out joint news releases to newspapers and magazines around the country.

Legacies

These were fractionated, if not bold, initiatives until the 1980s when President Ronald Reagan and David Stockman, director of the Office of Management and Budget, threatened to annihilate social and behavioral research from the federal budget and to dismantle the existing national databases. This external threat to the social and behavioral research jugular provided crucial motivation to those disciplines to convince the public and policy makers alike that their activities were worthy of support. This was best done by contributing knowledge that would be useful to society: altruism—in terms of giving psychology away—was deemed the most enlightened form of self-interest (Bevan, 1982). So one positive legacy of this era was recognition of the need to communicate and contribute to society, lest society decide we were expendable.

But the overtures to society in the early years were unidirectional—they often consisted of academics' telling policy makers and the public what research indicated they should do. While it was a valuable first step, some scholars were perceived as having arrogant attitudes, as if they thought, "I am the expert, you should do what I say." Further, although legislators seemed to want "one-armed" scholars who did not equivocate in their recommendations (e.g., "on the one hand research shows . . . and on the other hand"; Bronfenbrenner, 1977), policy makers rarely seemed to take even the one-armed academic's advice. As a result it became widely believed that social and behavioral science had little direct effect on social policy (C. Weiss, 1977, 1988, but see Chelimski, 1991; Leviton & Boruch, 1983). More likely, the problem was that scholars failed to understand that public policy must answer to many masters, scientific evidence being only one, and that the process of policy formation is highly interpersonal, often based on relationships that scholars rarely had.

The Rise, Fall, and Resurrection of Accountability

Accountability—demonstrating that publicly funded programs accomplish their goals—has long been desired, and sometimes required, by policy makers and funders, especially when large new initiatives are attempted. President Lyndon Johnson's Great Society was also the "experimenting society" (Campbell, 1969), because many of the national programs initiated at that time were rigorously evaluated, going so far as to use random assignment experimental or quasi-experimental designs. But such evaluation soon fell out of favor, partly because it constituted an expensive report card that delivered an effectiveness grade and little else (e.g., the program worked or it did not) and partly because that program effectiveness grade was often D or F.

Such accountability never permeated small and local programming, because it was too expensive and required expertise that was typically lacking at the local level. Instead, social services were valued for what appeared to be their inherent goodness and for providing what the community needed; "evaluation" consisted of data on the number of people of different races and genders living in specific areas of town who received different services. Little information was obtained on whether the participants benefited in the intended way from such services.

But as social and behavioral problems increased and resources declined in the 1990s, policy makers and funders grew dissatisfied with not knowing whether the millions, sometimes billions, of dollars they were putting into services were benefiting the participants. Consequently, accountability was resurrected at both the national and local levels. Nationally, for example, the government itself demanded accountability for its own actions in the Reinventing Government movement, and the national United Way urged its local affiliates to require evidence from their grant recipients that their services were effective for participants.

Toward Evidence-Based Programming and Policies

More recently, policy makers and funders have taken the next logical step beyond accountability. That is, instead of investing in unproven programs and waiting several years to find out whether they are effective, policy makers decided to invest initially in programs that have already been demonstrated to be effective. Thus the current era of evidence-based programming was born. Now funders and policy makers at the national and local levels essentially are insisting that they will fund new programs only if they replicate service programs that research has already demonstrated to be effective.

On the one hand, applied developmental scholars should rejoice—it would seem that not only is government paying attention to developmental science but it is insisting on it; indeed, developmental science has become the criterion for what services are funded for children and families. On the other hand, it is also an immense opportunity and responsibility that developmental scholars must cherish, respect, and participate in wisely. We should not forget that several decades ago, when program evaluators declared that many

Great Society programs were not very effective, it was the evaluator, not the program, who often was shot. An analogous murder could occur on an even broader scale if applied developmental science does not rise to the level of responsibility that policy makers and funders are now investing in it.

SOME ASSUMPTIONS OF EVIDENCE-BASED PROGRAMMING

In principle the rationale for the insistence on evidence-based programs is straightforward: identify programs that research says are effective and essentially replicate them elsewhere. But this approach makes several assumptions that both scholars and policy makers must carefully consider.

Need for evidence

The most obvious assumption is that programs that provide services have been created, implemented, and thoroughly evaluated. Unfortunately, problems in society usually precede the development and evaluation of treatment and prevention services, so the need for services is likely to occur before scholars have documented solutions. For some issues that have persisted over time, a vast literature on several model programs demonstrates which are effective and which are not for preventing or remediating certain problems or promoting desirable skills and behaviors. For example, preventing or remediating adolescent problem behaviors (e.g., substance abuse, risky sexual behavior, school failure, juvenile delinquency, and violence) has been the subject of extensive literatures, often involving hundreds of studies (see Weissburg & Kumpfer, 2003). But this is not true for every domain worthy of publicly supported services. Although we have four decades of research demonstrating the potential academic and social benefits of high-quality early childhood care and education, for example, we do not have a variety of curricula for promoting emerging literacy, numeracy, appropriate social-emotional development, and prosocial behavior with the same wealth of evidence behind them.

Other domains of public concern (e.g., child abuse, runaway and homeless youth) are costly to individuals and society but are low-frequency phenomena, making the effectiveness of prevention programs difficult or expensive to evaluate and leaving only a thin residue of research. Therefore, it is likely that developmental science will not have the "evidence" for evidence-based programming in every area that funders and policy makers desire it, and we can only hope that they will provide the funding now to generate the evidence for evidence-based programming later. Also, some provision should be made to fund creative programs, even in a well-researched area, based on compelling rationales and indirect evidence, to permit and promote innovation so that the field does not stagnate with only the tried and true.

What constitutes the evidence for an evidence-based program?

Scholars are well aware that programs are not simply proven or not proven but rather have evidence that supports their effectiveness to varying degrees of certitude. In short, not all evidence is equal; some evidence is more equal than others.

One attempt to characterize the strength or compellingness of the evidence for a program is to create a scale of levels of evidence. For example, Biglan, Mrazek, Carnine, and Flay (2003) propose a scheme of seven grades of evidence based in part on the Institute of Medicine's report on prevention (Mrazek & Haggerty, 1994) and others (Chambless & Hollon, 1998). The seven levels vary as a function of the availability of randomized trials and interrupted time series experiments and the number of independent replications.

We regard this scheme as a good first or second step, but it is narrowly defined at the upper levels by two research designs (randomized trials and interrupted time series) and therefore largely ignores evidence from other approaches (e.g., McCall & Green, 2004). Similarly, the scheme emphasizes internal validity but has no explicit criteria for external validity. Replication is desirable, but human services programs are rarely replicated with similar programs and methodologies (I'll return to this shortly); as a result replication is more like generalization and may be difficult to obtain. Also, the scheme does not provide for effect size, indexes of benefit used in other disciplines that communicate more clearly to policy makers the benefit of a program (Scott, Mason, & Chapman, 1999), and program cost effectiveness. Finally, the scheme does not distinguish between programs that have been evaluated but do not demonstrate effectiveness versus those programs that have not been evaluated at all. Clearly, levels of evidence are multifaceted, complicated, and compensatory, and it will be difficult to create a hierarchy of evidence that respects that complexity but is sufficiently specific and straightforward for policy use.

Programs packaging and availability

One of the great limitations of the intervention and service demonstration literatures is the infrequency with which the intervention is well described, packaged in an exportable format, and available for others to use. Even in the field of education, where curricula are often written in substantial detail, well-researched curricula are not widely available for the preschool years. Services in other areas may be even less likely to be well articulated, documented, and packaged. Thus the evidence may be strong that the program works, but often we are not sure precisely what "the program" is, and, whatever it is, it is not conveniently available for others to replicate.

Difficulty of replicating programs

Human services programs are widely regarded as not traveling well, meaning that they are not easily replicated by other providers in other locations for other groups of participants. All those nuisance factors we once tried to ignore in the search for general laws can make a big difference in the effectiveness of service programs. Programs may not replicate results for numerous reasons, including the possibilities that (a) the crucial successful elements of the program are program leadership, community support, supplemental resources, and the relationship between the providers and the participants; (b) programs are not specific enough to permit other providers to faithfully reproduce them; (c) providers need several cohorts to learn how to implement a program; (d) success may depend on providers' matching elements of the program to the particular characteristics of different participants rather than using a one-size-fits-all approach; and (e) effectiveness may depend on the match between the program and the cultural and other characteristics of the participants. The list goes on. These elements may not have been part of the program description available for replication and may not have been measured in the evaluations, and they are likely to be different from one incarnation of the program to the next.

We are pleased that funders and politicians have newfound respect for the methods and findings of developmental scholarship. But with every opportunity comes responsibilities, and the scholar's responsibility is to recognize the assumptions, complexities, and limitations of this endeavor on the one hand and yet provide policy makers with a relatively straightforward and useful set of guidelines on the other. This may require consensus panels that meet periodically and provide judgments of levels of evidence. Such panels may categorize and rate each study in a literature according to the type and level of evidence it provides, and these ratings might fit into a more complicated scheme that nevertheless produces a global assessment of level of evidence for each program, in addition to more specifics about the nature of that evidence.

But it may be more useful to identify the characteristics of successful programs, at least in addition to rating the level of evidence for each specific program. Characteristics of successful programs may form two levels, a set of generic characteristics that span specific programs and even specific domains (e.g., well-trained and well-supervised staff), plus characteristics particular to certain program domains (e.g., providing low-income adolescents with a perception of a chance for a self-fulfilling and independent future may be important to prevention programs for several adolescent problem behaviors).

Schorr (2003) operates such consensus groups, which consist of researchers plus service providers, policy makers, and other stakeholders. Their charge is broader than merely rating the evidence for a specific program—they are to review the evidence as well as their own experience and that of others to generate mental maps of characteristics of programs, both those documented by research and those widely believed to be effective. Such maps have the potential to be more stable across time and accumulation of evidence than the evidence level for individual programs, which could change with the publication of each study. Such characteristics would also permit greater flexibility in matching the details of a program to the specific local circumstances and participants, and it would encourage creativity within an evidence-based structure.

We would also urge funders and policy makers not to go to extremes in funding only evidence-based programming in any given area, lest creativity and innovation go unsupported. Funders and policy makers must also recognize that to have evidence for evidence-based programming, serious evaluations, which can initially cost as much or more than the program, need to be supported.

Finally, scholars should respect and be humbled by their new-found responsibilities in the human services and policy area. While there is a need to disseminate the conclusions of research to practitioners, funders, and policy makers, scholars need to avoid the arrogance they have frequently conveyed in the past. Instead, scholars have much to learn from practitioners, policy makers, and funders about the realities of funding and providing human services in community settings, the regulations that prescribe or limit what can be done, the characteristics of particular participant groups, the realities of the political power of certain groups in the population, and so forth. Thus scholars need to partner with, not prescribe to, their newfound colleagues in practice and policy making.

Toward Evidence-Based Policies

Since the mid-1960s human services have grown to be a large part of public policy but not the only part, and developmental scholars have a role to play in other aspects of social policy as well. Applied scholarship can identify a problem, its parameters, its cost to society, and its risk and protective factors. Such scholarship can determine needs for services in a community, and it can survey providers and participants to determine what both need, value, and are concerned about.

Generating policy in the past

Developmental scholars have given legislative testimony and produced briefing papers that identify problems and their scope, parameters, and potential solutions. While some policy issues have substantial lead times that permit scholars to review and gather information, many other legislative decisions are made on short notice. Jerome Kagan (McCall, 1993) characterized research as something like a fire station: most of the time you don't need it, but when there is a fire, policy makers need academic firefighters and scholars need to be ready. But scholars often are not ready on a moment's notice. Also, some policy makers make decisions based on their own personal experience or political principle (e.g., we will have parental choice, abstinence is the only pregnancy prevention alternative), whereas others are quite receptive to hearing what is known about a problem or issue, the alternatives that are available, and their relative effectiveness. But generally, policy makers rarely call the academic fire station. Therefore, for scholarship to contribute to policy, it needs to be constantly represented in the policy process, and at least some scholars and their representatives need to be able to drop everything and respond immediately to the information needs of policy makers.

For example, someone needs to be walking the policy beat to establish relationships with policy makers and to keep in constant touch with them so that scholars know what the current or impending issues are, can help make legislators aware that information exists on a topic when it looms on the public agenda, can help legislators access that information and select what is relevant to the policy question, can package that information in a way that can be used by policy makers, and can follow up with policy makers. It is likely that this someone is actually a team of individuals, perhaps including someone with political experience to maintain contact and develop personal relationships with policy makers; someone with scholarly knowledge to provide or arrange to obtain scholarly information; someone with communication skills to package the information in brief, clear, relevant fashion; and a bevy of academic and practice experts who can be called on to provide information in their respective areas of expertise, because the policy process jumps rapidly from topic to topic.

In addition to legislators, the administrative departments of government also have needs for scholarship, including program evaluation, lists of characteristics of successful programs with which to craft requests for proposals and evaluate grant applications, surveys of parents or children to establish needs and preferences, and consultants and members for advisory groups. This also requires personal relationships, especially between the academic contact person and key administrative department personnel, and immediate availability of information and skills when the need arises. Again, as for the legislature, a team is needed, and administrative departments often need immediate responses and demand unrealistic turnaround times for contracted research.

Most academics cannot or do not want to take major roles in such a process, partly because they are trained for different activities, they have other obligations, and the academic value system does not reward such activities (a topic to which we shall return). A variety of private and university units have emerged over the years to provide some or all of these services to the policy process. For example, some independent government agencies provide research and evaluation services (e.g., Government Accountability Office), while private think tanks and contract research centers (e.g., Brookings; RAND; Abt Associates; Mathematica Policy Research; Child Trends) stand ready to conduct policy-relevant research and program evaluations. Because they are outside universities, these organizations are not constrained by other duties or the academic value system. Conversely, university units typically take on projects with greater lead times and durations and those that have greater likelihood of contributing to scholarship and publications (e.g., conducting experimental trials of a given service intervention, issuing briefing papers on policy relevant topics, and performing certain types of program evaluation).

Each of these units has its specialty, but few conduct the entire range of policy-relevant scholarship. For example, a truly integrated center that contributes to the policy process would include a policy initiatives component staffed with one or more experienced policy makers who are the frontline contacts for legislators and administrative agencies and who become aware of policy issues and information and research needs. Not only would they have their ear to the policy ground, they would contribute to policy in a proactive way. For example, they would stimulate policies, serve on advisory groups, relate information to the specific policy process, and follow up with policy makers after information and research is delivered.

Such a center might also have the ability to implement innovative human services demonstration projects in collaboration with policy makers, funders, and community partners to test whether new services can be implemented in the community with community professionals. The center might also have a program evaluation unit that can work with community agencies and funders to monitor and evaluate the effectiveness of their programs. The center should also have professional communicators who can write and package information in formats that policy makers can use and someone who can contact those with expertise locally or nationally to help identify information sources and provide information for the policy process. This dissemination activity provides feedback for continuous policy improvement. These several functions must work together, providing feedback to each other in a learning systems approach (H. Weiss & Morrill, 1999).

Such a center must be responsive to policy makers' needs (although it may also be proactive; McCall & Groark, 2000), able to respond immediately and produce products and services rapidly and on deadline, and have flexible core support so that it can move quickly from one to another project and topic and tread water between projects.

One such center is the University of Pittsburgh Office of Child Development (McCall, Green, Groark, Strauss, & Farber, 1999; McCall, Groark, Strauss, & Johnson, 1995), but numerous other groups are performing some of these and other functions at universities across the country. Since most policy is set at the state and local level, local centers are valuable, but they could also benefit from a national consortium that could perform some functions that apply nationally (e.g., briefing papers that review national literature on various topics, consensus groups on levels of evidence or characteristics of successful programming, multiple sites for intervention trials or program evaluations, etc.). Such a coalition has been created but has yet to function in this way.

The academic value system

For faculty the kinds of activities that we have described are largely a tenured professor's privilege. While applied research, conducting intervention programs, and reviewing literature can generate credits toward tenure, the traditional value system does not reward publishing for nonscholarly audiences, conducting research on specific programs with limited apparent generality of results, or writing briefing papers for legislators. Although some colleges and universities have broader value systems, major research universities, which are in the best position to bring evidence to the policy process, tend to have more traditional and narrower criteria for reward and promotion—that is, single or lead author on articles in major refereed scholarly journals, research grant support, and various representations of review and approval by other academics (e.g., handbook chapters, editorial boards, invited presentations, etc.). But if scholarly activity is to achieve its full potential in contributing to the welfare of humankind, that value system needs to be broadened with respect to audience, type of communication, type of scholarship, and forms of implementing that scholarship in practice and policies (McCall, 1996).

Never before have policy makers been so receptive to scholarship, and this seems especially true in the area of children, youth, and families. Developmental scholars should seize this opportunity but with wisdom, responsibility, humility, and respect. They should also take the next step to partner with, rather than simply talk to, practitioners, policy makers, and funders to work collaboratively toward better practices and policies—and better research—for our citizens.

References

Bevan, W. (1982). A sermon of sorts in three plus parts. *American Psychologist, 37*, 1303–1322.

Biglan, A., Mrazek, P. J., Carnine, D., & Flay, B. R. (2003). The integration of research and practice in the prevention of youth problem behaviors. *American Psychologist, 58*, 433–440.

Bronfenbrenner, U. (1977). Toward an experimental ecology of human development. *American Psychologist, 32*, 513–531.

Campbell, D. T. (1969). Reform as experiments. *American Psychologist, 24*, 409–429.

Chambless, D. L., & Hollon, S. D. (1998). Defining empirically supported therapies. *Journal of Consulting and Clinical Psychology, 66*, 7–18.

Chelimski, E. (1991). On the social science contribution to governmental decision-making. *Science, 254,* 226–230.

Cronbach, L. J. (1957). The two disciplines of scientific psychology. *American Psychologist, 12,* 671–684.

Cronbach, L. J. (1975). Beyond the two disciplines of scientific psychology. *American Psychologist, 30,* 116–117.

Leviton, L. C., & Boruch, R. F. (1983). Contributions of evaluations to educational programs. *Evaluation Review, 7,* 563–599.

McCall, R. B. (1987). The media, society, and child development research. In J. D. Osofsky (Ed.), *Handbook of infant development* (2nd ed., pp. 1199–1255). New York: Wiley.

McCall, R. B. (1993). Jerome Kagan interview. In J. Rosenblith (Ed.), *Oral history of child development.* Ann Arbor, MI: Society for Research in Child Development.

McCall, R. B. (1996). The concept and practice of education, research, and public service in university psychology departments. *American Psychologist, 51,* 379–388.

McCall, R. B., & Green, B. L. (2004). Beyond the methodological gold standards of behavioral research: Considerations for practice and policy. *SRCD Social Policy Reports, 18,* 1–19.

McCall, R. B., Green, B. L., Groark, C. J., Strauss, M. S., & Farber, A. E. (1999). An interdisciplinary, university-community, applied developmental science partnership. *Journal of Applied Developmental Psychology, 20,* 207–226.

McCall, R. B., & Groark, C. J. (2000). The future of child development research and public policy. *Child Development, 71,* 187–204.

McCall, R. B., Groark, C. J., Strauss, M. S., & Johnson, C. N. (1995). An experiment promoting interdisciplinary applied human development: The University of Pittsburgh model. *Journal of Applied Developmental Psychology, 16,* 593–612.

Miller, G. A. (1969). Psychology as a means of promoting human welfare. *American Psychologist, 24,* 1063–1075.

Mrazek, P. J., & Haggerty, R. J. (Eds.). (1994). *Reducing risks for mental disorders: Frontiers for prevention intervention research.* Washington, DC: National Academy Press.

Rossi, P. H., Lipsey, M. W., & Freeman, H. E. (2004). *Evaluation: A systematic approach* (7th ed.). Thousand Oaks, CA: Sage.

Schorr, L. B. (2003). *Determining "what works" in social programs and social policies: Toward a more inclusive knowledge base.* Retrieved June 21, 2006, from http://www.brookings.edu/views/papers/sawhill/20030226.htm.

Scott, K. G., Mason, C. A., & Chapman, D. A. (1999). The use of epidemiological methodology as a means of influencing public policy. *Child Development, 70,* 1263–1272.

Weiss, C. H. (1977). Introduction. In C. H. Weiss (Ed.), *Using social research in public policy making* (pp. 1–22). Lexington, MA: Lexington Books.

Weiss, C. H. (1988). Evaluation for decisions: Is anybody there: Does anybody care? *Evaluation Practice, 9,* 5–19.

Weiss, H. B., & Morrill, W. A. (1999). *Useful learning for public action.* Cambridge, MA: Harvard Family Research Project.

Weissberg, R. P., & Kumpfer, K. L. (Eds.). (2003). Prevention that works for children and youth. Special issue, *American Psychologist, 58,* 425–490.

Zigler, E. (1998). A place of value for applied and policy studies. *Child Development, 69,* 532–542.

Contributors

NAZAN AKSAN, Department of Psychology, University of Iowa

THOMAS J. BERNDT, Department of Psychology, Purdue University

CLAIRE CHAMPION, Department of Psychology, Arizona State University

ROBERT J. COPLAN, Department of Psychology, Carleton University

KENNETH A. DODGE, Center for Child and Family Policy, Duke University

JUDY DUNN, Social Genetic and Developmental Psychiatry Centre, Institute of Psychiatry, Kings College London

CAROL S. DWECK, Department of Psychology, Stanford University

NANCY EISENBERG, Department of Psychology, Arizona State University

RICHARD A. FABES, School of Social and Family Dynamics, Arizona State University

JOHN H. FLAVELL, Department of Psychology, Stanford University

ELENA L. GRIGORENKO, Department of Psychology, Yale University

CHRISTINA J. GROARK, University of Pittsburgh Office of Child Development, School of Education, University of Pittsburgh

LAURA D. HANISH, School of Social and Family Dynamics, Arizona State University

JEROME KAGAN, Department of Psychology, Harvard University

ROBERT V. KAIL, Department of Psychology, Purdue University

GRAZYNA KOCHANSKA, Department of Psychology, University of Iowa

GARY W. LADD, School of Social and Family Dynamics and Department of Psychology, Arizona State University

JOHN E. LOCHMAN, Department of Psychology, University of Alabama

BONITA E. LONDON, Department of Psychology, Columbia University

YUE MA, Department of Psychology, Arizona State University

CAROL LYNN MARTIN, School of Social and Family Dynamics, Arizona State University

ROBERT B. McCALL, University of Pittsburgh Office of Child Development, School of Education, University of Pittsburgh

ROBERT P. NELKIN, University of Pittsburgh Office of Child Development, School of Education, University of Pittsburgh

Ross D. PARKE, Department of Psychology and Center for Family Studies, University of California, Riverside

ROBERT PLOMIN, Social Genetic and Developmental Psychiatry Centre, Institute of Psychiatry, Kings College London

CRAIG T. RAMEY, Georgetown University Center on Health and Education, Georgetown University

SHARON L. RAMEY, Georgetown University Center on Health and Education, Georgetown University

MARY K. ROTHBART, Department of Psychology, University of Oregon

KENNETH H. RUBIN, Department of Human Development, University of Maryland

ROBERT S. SIEGLER, Department of Psychology, Carnegie Mellon University

ROBERT J. STERNBERG, Department of Psychology, Yale University

ELLIOT TURIEL, Graduate School of Education, University of California, Berkeley

DEBORAH LOWE VANDELL, Department of Educational Psychology, University of Wisconsin, Madison

LAWRENCE J. WALKER, Department of Psychology, University of British Columbia

Index

Abecedarian Project, 319, 336–46; early adulthood results, 345; effects of preschool treatment on academic locus-of-control, 346; effects of preschool treatment on math achievement, 344; effects of preschool treatment on placement in special education, 345; effects of preschool treatment on reading achievement, 343, 344; percentage of sample in normal IQ range by age, 340; preschool program, 338; preschool results, 337–40; replication of benefits in preschool years, 340–42; schoolage results, 343–45; summary of results, 345–46; Z scores and mean standardized scores for high-risk preschool treatment and control children at nine preschool measurements, 338–39

abuse, shame and attributional style predict long-term adjustment following, 126

academic locus-of-control, effect of ABC preschool treatment on, 346

accountability: and developmental scholarship, 370–71; need for systems in early childhood educational interventions, 347–48

"achievement gap," 341

acontextual research, 270

active isolation, 165–66

Adaptive Strategy Choice Model, 63

adaptive strategy choices, 72–74

Adolph, K. E., 72, 73

adoption studies, 251, 255, 256

adult problem-solving strategies, 71

affective motivation, 230

affective neuroscience, and research on conscience, 245

Afghanistan, 297–98

age-related change, 76

aggression, 106–7, 160

Ainsworth's Strange Situation, 169

Aksan, Nazan, 7

Alessandri, S. M., 129

allele 4, 257

Allen, G. L., 60

Alpert, R., 239

Amato, P. R., 201, 202, 204, 207

American Psychological Association (APA) public information committee, 369

amygdala, 168

Anderson's ACT-R, 60

anger arousal model, 352

animal experiments, 367

antecedent emotion regulation, 106, 109

anterior cingulate cortex, 89

anterior cingulate gyrus, 91

antisocial behavior, contextual social-cognitive model of: child factors, 352–53; neighborhood and classroom factors, 354–55; parent and peer factors, 354

anxiety disorders, 160, 164

"anxious solitude," 166, 171

apolipoprotein E gene, 257, 258

appearance-reality (AR) distinction, 40, 46

approach, 84, 85

arithmetic word problems, role of global processes in solving, 59

Armer, M., 170

Hastings, P., 169
Hawkins, J. D., 354
head injuries, 256
Head Start, 262
Hecht, S. A., 59
Heisenberg, Werner, 31
helplessness, 128
Henderson, H., 167
Heterington, E. M., 200, 201, 202
Hoffman, Martin L., 18–20, 19–20, 23, 230, 234, 239, 241
Holland, J. H., 72
Hong, Y. Y., 47
Hook, L., 71
hormonal changes, effect on father-infant relationships, 212–13
Horowitz, Frances Degen, 22, 25
hostile attributions: found among aggressive children, 125; predicted by physical abuse, harsh discipline, or peer rejection, 127
Howes, C., 304, 309
Huang, J. T., 274
Hudley, C., 131
human brain, study of, 11
human genome, mapping of, 84, 88, 90, 92
Human Genome Project, 258
Huttenlocher, J., 331
Hymel, Shelley, 19, 22
hyperactivity, 160
hypothalamic-pituitary-adrenocortical axis, 168

individual differences, 83
Infant Health and Development Project, 319, 340, 341–42, 343
Infant/Toddler Environment Rating Scale, 304
infant vocabulary, effects of mothers' speech on, 333
information processing theories, contributed to the shift away from the study of learning, 68–69
inhibitory control, 84, 104
insecure ambivalent (C) attachment classification, and behavioral inhibition, 169

intellectual development: implicit lay theories of around the world, 273–76; Western emphasis on speed of mental processing, 273
intellectual self-assertion, 273
intellectual self-effacement, 273
intelligence: African concepts of, 275; American concepts of, 274; Asian concepts of, 275; Buddhist and Hindu philosophies of, 274; Confucian perspective on, 273; Eastern vs. Western concepts of, 273–76; fixed theory of, 125; as a form of developing expertise, 279; interpersonal, 273; intrapersonal, 273; Kenyan concepts of, 275–76; malleable theory of, 125, 131; practical aspects of, 281; social aspects of, 275; Taiwanese Chinese concepts of, 273; Taoist tradition of, 273; theoretical investigations of around the world, 276–83; views of different ethnic groups, 276
intelligence praise, and global negative self-attributions for difficulty, 129
intelligence tests: generalizeability of results, 284; measuring developing expertise, 279, 281; and patterns of schooling, 276–78
intensity, 85
intensity of reaction, 86
intergroup relations, 275
internalizing disorders, 104, 160; research on before the 1980s, 161–62
internal models, 123
interpersonal intelligence, 273
The Interpersonal Theory of Psychiatry (Sullivan), 139
interviews, 33
intimacy, 140, 141
intimate self-disclosure, in adolescent friendships, 143
intragroup relations, 275
intrapersonal intelligence, 273
intuition, role in moral functioning,

working memory, 58; and arithmetic word problems, 59; and elaboration of conceptual structures through childhood, 61
Wundt, Wilhelm, 290
Wynne-Edwards, D. E., 212

Yang, S., 273

Yoruba, 275
Yup'ik Eskimo children, importance of academic and practical intelligence, 278–79

Zahn-Waxler, C., 244
Zigler, Edward, 369
Zimbabwe, 275

www.ingramcontent.com/pod-product-compliance
Lightning Source LLC
Chambersburg PA
CBHW051947270326
41929CB00015B/2567